Lahore

A Framework for
Urban Conservation

The Aga Khan
Historic Cities Programme

Lahore

A Framework for Urban Conservation

Edited by Philip Jodidio

PRESTEL

Munich · London · New York

Contents

Preface

HIS HIGHNESS THE AGA KHAN

The Aga Khan Development Network (AKDN) has been providing a broad range of services in Pakistan for many years. AKDN has sought to create a critical mass of integrated development activities that offer people in a given area not only a potential increase in income, but also a broad, sustained improvement in the overall quality of life. It encourages self-reliance and a long-term view of development. In fact, many areas that received AKDN support in the past have well-educated communities that are now masters of their own development, building their own schools and health centres and taking other measures to care for themselves and those less fortunate. Component parts of AKDN – such as the Aga Khan University founded in Karachi more than thirty-five years ago, and the Aga Khan Trust for Culture (AKTC), long active in Gilgit-Baltistan and more recently in Lahore – have carried forward educational, architectural and urban renovation projects that have had a positive impact in the country.

The high mountain valleys of Gilgit-Baltistan, which were once a part of the Central Asian Silk Route, were inaccessible to vehicular traffic until the construction of the Karakoram Highway in 1978. Increased accessibility, coupled with the impact of tourism, introduced a rapid transformation of local customs and economic patterns, which called for new strategic development visions and adapted procedures capable of steering ongoing rapid change. The conservation of the 700-year-old Baltit Fort – the pre-eminent landmark monument in Gilgit-Baltistan – and the rehabilitation of the historic core of Karimabad in the Hunza Valley were the first major interventions of the Aga Khan Historic Cities Programme, completed in 1996.

Lahore, the capital of the province of Punjab and the second most populous city in Pakistan, is also known as the "City of Gardens" thanks to its Mughal heritage. A vital part of the Mughal Empire, this once fortified city has a concentration of monuments and buildings that reflect cultural diversity in architecture and, despite a dynamic and tumultuous past that spans several centuries, it has retained much of its historic urban form. The Walled City of Lahore is famous for several historic monuments, including Lahore Fort (a UNESCO World Heritage Site) and the Badshahi and Wazir Khan mosques.

Subsequent to the completion of the Shigar Fort project in 2005, the government of Pakistan requested that AKTC make technical contributions to the World Bank-funded area development pilot project along Shahi Guzargah, the Royal Trail, in the Walled City of Lahore. The work consequently carried out by AKTC through the Aga Khan Cultural Service-Pakistan was initiated under a 2007 'Public-Private Partnership Framework Agreement' with the government of Punjab. The first phase of this urban rehabilitation project, completed in 2014, included the design and improvement of infrastructure services and the documentation of major Mughal-period monuments. An important social and economic dimension aimed at poverty alleviation along with the creation of economic opportunities for local residents were facilitated through community participation. The technical engagement of AKTC continues today on the basis of a 'Memorandum of Understanding' with the Walled City of Lahore Authority.

There are many, today, across the Muslim world who know their history and deeply value their heritage, but who are also keenly sensitive to the radically altered conditions of the modern world. They realize, too, how erroneous and unreasonable it is to believe that there is an unbridgeable divide between their heritage and the modern world. There is clearly a need to mitigate not what is a 'clash of civilizations' but a 'clash of ignorance', where peoples of different faiths or cultural traditions are so ignorant of each other that they are unable to find a common language with which to communicate.

Working in the Walled City of Lahore, AKTC has engendered a significant transfer of competencies, demonstrating that the ancient heritage of the city is not something to be swept aside in favour of commercially driven modernity; it is, rather, a source of strength and a value for the future. By improving living conditions and beginning to heal the historic urban context and monumental heritage of this unique site, a step in the right direction has been taken. Pride born of an ancient civilization is progressively replacing substandard living conditions and deteriorating monuments, and, most importantly, this effort is now being led by local government and residents.

I wish to thank the governments of Pakistan and Punjab for their outstanding support and leadership, and the citizens of Lahore for their gracious participation. These projects could not have been carried forward without the active support of institutions and governmental authorities such as the World Bank, the Walled City of Lahore Authority, the Royal Norwegian Embassy, the US Ambassadors Fund for Cultural Preservation, AFD, and the government of the Federal Republic of Germany.

FOREWORD

KAMRAN LASHARI, DIRECTOR GENERAL,
WALLED CITY OF LAHORE AUTHORITY

I pen these words with great pleasure on the occasion of the publication of this new volume on Lahore and on the work the Aga Khan Trust for Culture (AKTC) has carried out in our city over the last twelve years. The Walled City of Lahore Authority, in partnership with AKTC, has meticulously and lovingly attempted to conserve and restore our heritage and past. It is not easy to undo the adverse effects of centuries of negligence, sporadic acts of malicious and deliberate damage and, of course, the inexorable decay of time, in addition to the presence of a vibrant and live city coexisting around and in this heritage.

In the public sector, I have served in positions such as deputy commissioner of Lahore, director general of the Parks and Horticulture Authority, and chief commissioner of Islamabad. My work, which has included creating Gawalmandi Food Street, restoring Mall Road buildings and Tollinton Market, and conserving Saidpur village near Islamabad, among others, reflects my passionate interest in cultural heritage, arts and beautification as a lifelong pursuit of excellence and perfection. I am cognizant of the impact of cultural heritage and art on civic life. Art is a repository of a society's collective memory. Sometimes art preserves historical records and heritage far better than factual historic records, simply because it enshrines the feel, vibe and colours of the moment. It captures the mood of the characters. It adds the vibrancy of a human soul and the depth of its emotion in a visual form that is far more expressive than words. It adds a dimension to history so that we can experience how it must have felt to live in that moment. Art is a bridge that allows people from different times to continue to communicate. It is a bridge that translates experiences and expressions across space and time. While working with AKTC, I have passionately sought to preserve these.

AKTC and its regional affiliate the Aga Khan Cultural Service-Pakistan (AKCS-P) have been working in the Walled City since 2007. In Pakistan, conservation was in its nascent stage and this work has enhanced understanding and appreciation of it. The Walled City of Lahore Authority (WCLA) is an autonomous body entrusted with the protection and management of historic Lahore. As Director General of the WCLA since 2012, partnership with AKTC/AKCS-P has been a priority. We are grateful to AKTC for having laid the foundations for a strong and long-lasting partnership premised on mutual respect.

The WCLA and AKTC/AKCS-P have achieved many milestones since 2012. In 2013 we initiated the conservation of the Shahi Hammam, the first monument conservation project executed in conformity with international standards, with co-funding from the

Opposite page, Badshahi Mosque. The courtyard seen from the prayer chamber.

Above, Shahdara, the Akbari Serai. Entrance to the Bagh-e-Dilkusha, containing Jahangir's Mausoleum.

Below, Lahore Fort. The Diwan-e-Khaas pavilion.

9

Left, a pavilion in the Shalimar Garden complex.

Right, Shalimar Garden. The Khwabgah, interior of the *dalaan* overlooking the first terrace.

Royal Norwegian Embassy. Its flawless execution and completion in 2015 were a significant accomplishment that received a UNESCO Award. The conservation of Wazir Khan Chowk was initiated in 2015 with assistance from the US Ambassadors Fund for Cultural Preservation. Both sites date from the seventeenth-century Mughal era. The Shahi Hammam and Wazir Khan Mosque, with its *chowk* or forecourt, are jewels in the Walled City, and their conservation has been a great source of personal pride and satisfaction. Conserving such buildings is a testament to the indomitable will of those who seek to conserve history and restore the ravages of time. These monuments salute the perseverance and endurance of humanity to eternalize the aesthetic ideal. They have also garnered recognition and awareness. Together with current efforts to complete the conservation of the seventeenth-century Wazir Khan Mosque itself, which has been in dire need of attention for decades, ongoing and future projects include several initiatives in Lahore Fort (a UNESCO World Heritage Site), which forms the most distinguished and significant area of historic Lahore, with interventions proposed in its surrounding Buffer Zone.

Any good, and sustainable, conservation effort cannot take place in isolation. Especially in developing country contexts where financial support and technical expertise for historic preservation is limited, preservation projects benefit greatly from joint efforts in the form of 'Public-Private Partnerships'. In the case of Lahore's historic Walled City, as this book will demonstrate, such partnerships have fostered capacity development, improved socio-economic conditions, resulted in the conservation and protection of several historic properties, generated tourism and promised new avenues for future initiatives.

Since 1991 AKTC/AKCS-P's experience in the area of conservation in Pakistan has made available a workforce comprising professional architects, engineers, technicians and social scientists capable of engaging a complex environment such as the Walled City of Lahore. Their partnership with the WCLA has provided a means to transfer some of these skills and expand the scale of the technical and social resources available. I strongly believe that capacity building – much more than the substantial financial resources brought in by AKTC and contributed by the government of Punjab – has been one of the most significant outcomes of the WCLA-AKTC/AKCS-P partnership, the benefits of which will be experienced for a long time to come. Among the gains we have made from this partnership is the knowledge that there is a profound relationship between the care, protection and enjoyment of our artistic and architectural heritage, on the one hand, and social and economic development, nation-building and the strengthening of collective identity, on the other. This relationship is visible in every instance of the work of AKTC in Lahore, and its work elsewhere in the country.

In Pakistan, where heritage conservation is often misconstrued as being limited to the protection and preservation of individual monuments, the work accomplished in the last few years offers a much-needed new perspective. The Mohalla demonstration project exemplified ways to rehabilitate historic quarters that are located in dense urban centres; the Shahi Guzargah project demonstrated the necessity and impact of urban conservation; the conservation of the Shahi Hammam entailed the adaptive reuse of the Mughal-period bathhouse into a museum; and the conservation of the Wazir Khan Chowk reclaimed a historic public space that had been encroached upon for decades.

For these initiatives in urban and monument conservation carried out in partnership with AKTC, I must express my gratitude to the government of Punjab for its consistent financial support, which has enabled compensating occupants removed from unauthorized buildings, the complete replacement of old infrastructure with modern water supply and sewerage, the introduction of storm-water drainage infrastructure, and, most of all, the removal of unsightly overhead wires and their placing underground. I must also acknowledge the untiring efforts of my colleagues in the Walled City of Lahore Authority for reaching out, working with and mobilizing the communities of the Walled City. In Lahore today we have introduced guided tours of a historic city for the first time in Pakistan. The rehabilitated sites of Delhi Gate and the Shahi Guzargah have become iconic for tourists to the city.

The work that AKTC and the WCLA have accomplished in the Walled City is only a starting point. It is my hope that this will inspire a much larger, more ambitious vision for heritage conservation – not just in the Walled City of Lahore, but all over Pakistan.

Above, the Walled City. Portion of Circular Garden on the southern perimeter (above) and the northern perimeter (below).

Left, Maryam Zamani (or Begum Shahi) Mosque, east of Lahore Fort, interior.

INTRODUCTION

INTRODUCTION

LUIS MONREAL

This book is the fifth published since 2011 in an ongoing series that concerns the projects of the Aga Khan Trust for Culture (AKTC) and its Historic Cities Programme.[1] The second volume in the series, *Heritage of the Mughal World* (2015), included a section about work in the Walled City of Lahore which has significantly advanced since that time and is now entering a new and final phase. The efforts of AKTC in Lahore have succeeded in generating a significant transfer of competencies to local organizations and craftsmen and done a great deal to improve living conditions in the Walled City, generating what has become a self-sustaining effort of conservation and renovation in one of the great historic sites of Pakistan. This project advanced along guidelines for economic sustainability previously established by AKTC in Cairo, Delhi and Kabul.

Although the origins of the city have not been clearly established by archaeologists, excavations carried out in Lahore Fort in 1959 revealed settlement strata dating back to the sixth century CE. In reality, little is known about the architectural history of the city until the first Mughal invasion of Babur in 1524. Although it is situated in the semi-arid flatlands of the Indus Valley, several *tibbas* or mounds inside the Walled City and elsewhere in Lahore suggest earlier occupation, albeit of uncertain origin. The city saw its greatest growth during the reigns of Akbar, Jahangir and Shah Jahan, from 1556 to 1658, when it was intermittently the capital of the empire. Of strategic and military importance, Lahore was known for its opulent palaces and gardens as well as its intellectual effervescence. Fortifications created under the reign of Akbar (r. 1556–1605) made it possible for larger numbers of residents to live within the city walls. And yet gardens such as that of Mirza Kamran, built between 1526 and 1529 across the river from the city, began to establish the reputation of Lahore as a "City of Gardens". The most famous of these is Shalimar Garden, built in 1641–42 under the reign of Shah Jahan and located seven kilometres to the east of the Fort. Shalimar Garden was inscribed as a UNESCO World Heritage Site together with Lahore Fort in 1981. By the mid-eighteenth century, the city had a population of about 500,000 people, the majority of them living in garden suburbs outside the walls.

Lahore Fort, in the north-western corner of the 252-hectare Walled City, was a seat of political power, but also the location of royal Mughal residences. The present Fort, in brick and solid masonry, was built during Akbar's reign between 1556 and 1605. The Fort itself is of similar inspiration to those of Agra and Delhi. It was during the reign of Jahangir (1605–27) that the northern and western walls were built. The

Preceding pages, Lahore, the Walled City. Urban fabric of the western half of the area.

Opposite page, Lahore Fort, Dalaan-e-Sang-e-Surkh. Part of the facade of the 19th-century palace of Rani Jindan.

Above, inside the Imperial Kitchens, after conservation.

so-called mosaic Picture Wall (1617–32) runs for a length of 461 metres and a height of 18 metres along the northern and western fortification walls.

The decline of the Mughal Empire after the reign of Aurangzeb, who died in 1707, resulted in greatly reduced political and cultural power for Lahore and the ruin of its garden suburbs. The former imperial capital was pillaged during the Persian and Afghan invasions that began in 1720 and lasted until 1769. But the city remained destabilized until 1799 when the first phase of Sikh rule ended. This was followed by the construction of new buildings and gardens under Ranjit Singh (1799–1839) that made use of marble and other elements removed from Mughal-era buildings and mausolea. Proclaimed maharaja of Punjab and emperor of the Sikh Empire at Lahore Fort on 12 April 1801, Ranjit notably added several pavilions on the upper ramparts. Lahore and Punjab were annexed by the East India Company in 1849 and came under direct rule of the British crown as of 1858.

During the colonial period, bricks were removed from Mughal and Sikh ruins for the new construction of military barracks, administrative headquarters and a large locomotive facility. The fortified city walls and gates dating from the time of Akbar were demolished after 1864, while the British rebuilt some of the gates in a mixture of Mughal and European styles. Although the British government did make urban improvement efforts, such as a piped-water system, on the whole the colonial period was characterized by an extensive degradation of the remaining Mughal heritage of the Walled City and Fort. British rule ended in 1947, and riots greeted the Indian Independence Act which separated India from Pakistan along religious lines. In the Walled City of Lahore, approximately ten per cent of the historic fabric was destroyed by acts of arson.

Commercial redevelopment beginning in the 1950s in a progressively less and less regulated environment led to aggressive speculation and demolition that further affected the historic areas of Lahore. The only saving grace of modern construction that filled in the scars of damage from 1947 near Delhi Gate was that it more or less respected the volumes of the old city. Although efforts were made in collaboration with the World Bank to upgrade infrastructure through the Lahore Urban Development and Traffic Study (1978–80) and the Lahore Urban Development Project (1980–89), many basic services were in a situation of near collapse at the beginning of the twenty-first century. It had been noted that the population of the Walled City had declined since the time of independence from 240,000 to about 150,000. Prior to the involvement of AKTC, properties of historic significance were being demolished or

Above, Lahore Fort, northern facade of the Picture Wall. Detail of glazed-tile mosaic panels.

Below, Wazir Khan Mosque, a view of the courtyard with people gathering for prayers.

Right, Shahi Hammam in the Walled City, the reception hall after conservation.

converted into warehouses for commercial reasons. Makeshift infrastructure, such as electricity cables and other utilities, had invaded the urban setting.

Wazir Khan Chowk, after conservation.

    In 2006 the governments of Pakistan and Punjab signed a loan agreement with the World Bank for the Punjab Municipal Services Improvement Project that was aimed at building technical and human resource capacity for urban management in a number of small municipalities in the province. Part of the sum was set aside for a pilot urban rehabilitation and infrastructure improvement project in the Walled City of Lahore. In 2007 AKTC signed a three-year 'Public-Private Partnership Framework Agreement' with the government of Punjab under which AKTC would provide technical assistance to the government for the conservation and development of the Walled City and for implementation of the pilot project. At the suggestion of AKTC, the pilot project became a more comprehensive undertaking addressing the main bazaar

Shahi Hammam, the reception hall, with the interpretation room in the background.

spines and secondary streets and their residential neighbourhoods as well as social and economic uplift for their mainly low-income population. AKTC developed a conceptual technical design and integrated development charter for utility infrastructure in the entire area of the Walled City, intended to be phased over twenty years. The 2008 'Preliminary Strategic Framework' plan for the Walled City emphasizes the importance of maintaining a large residential population in the Walled City by improving housing conditions and providing basic social services. A halt to the decay and demolition in the existing building stock would be necessary to lay the groundwork for future social and economic improvement. Further, the government made clear their desire to turn the Walled City into a destination for Pakistani and international visitors.

The area concerned by the pilot project was the Shahi Guzargah, the ceremonial route of Mughal dignitaries arriving at the Fort-Palace on the eastern side. The historic significance of the so-called Royal Trail can be discerned by the number of monuments built along the route. These include the Wazir Khan Hammam, the Wazir Khan Mosque, the eighteenth-century Sunehri Masjid of Nawab Bhikari Khan, and the Begum Shahi Masjid built by Queen Maryam Zamani, Jahangir's mother and the daughter of Raja Bihari Mal of Amber. Other Sikh and British monuments, such as

Delhi Gate, also mark the Shahi Guzargah. The World Bank initiative of 2006 and afterwards confirmed a greater recognition of the Walled City's heritage status and was markedly different from earlier approaches to the rehabilitation of the historic city. Social and economic improvement, seen as a desirable outcome of increased tourism, was an important objective with its related emphasis on the rehabilitation of heritage elements in the Walled City, on townscape improvement and, in a more general way, on the sensory and visual environment.

In the period between 2007 and 2009, AKTC carried out extensive topographic, physical and socio-economic surveys in the Walled City. Technical and financial assistance was also provided for a pilot neighbourhood rehabilitation project. The conservation of twelve historic homes in Gali Surjan Singh was carried out to demonstrate that the rehabilitation of old buildings could offer as much comfort as newly built residences while preserving the historic character of the area. The goal of AKTC in this process was to build the capacities of local workers and craftsmen, and thus to progressively transfer a sustainable ongoing project to committed local authorities, craftsmen and residents. The 'Preliminary Strategic Framework' devised in 2008 took these objectives into account in the context of a broader framework of integrated area conservation and development. A first phase of the Shahi Guzargah project was completed in 2014 and focused on urban fabric rehabilitation, improvement of infrastructure and documentation work on the most significant Mughal monuments in the Walled City. Simultaneously a programme intended to help create economic opportunities and alleviate poverty in the area was carried forward. Conservation work on the seventeenth-century Shahi Hammam at Delhi Gate was completed in 2015. This project received a UNESCO Asia-Pacific Award of Merit for Cultural Heritage Conservation in 2016. A panel of international experts stated: "Undertaken with a high degree of technical proficiency, the restoration of Shahi Hammam has safeguarded a unique example of the monumental seventeenth-century Mughal public bathhouse."

Examples of homes in the demonstration historic residence conservation project located in Gali Surjan Singh and Koocha Charkh Garan, part of the Shahi Guzargah pilot project.

Above, Lahore Fort, the Picture Wall. Inlaid terracotta 'filigree' friezes and panels.

Below, glazed-tile mosaic and fresco panels on the Picture Wall's north facade.

Opposite page, general view of the northern section of the Lahore Fort Picture Wall, conservation scheduled to be completed in 2021. Conservation of the western portion of the Picture Wall was completed in 2019.

The Wazir Khan Mosque saw its north facade conserved in 2016, while rehabilitation of the forecourt of the monument (Wazir Khan Chowk) was completed in 2017 with co-funding from the US Ambassadors Fund for Cultural Preservation. Further projects involving the Wazir Khan Mosque are underway at present. AKTC began documenting the Picture Wall in 2015. The Royal Norwegian and German embassies, who had earlier supported the hammam and Gali Surjan Singh projects respectively, now participated with grants that initiated the start of the complete digital documentation of the Fort and the conservation of the Picture Wall. Together with the Walled City of Lahore Authority (WCLA) and the Punjab government, AKTC is helping with the preparation of a master plan for the Fort. This 'Master Conservation and Redevelopment Plan' (MCRP) emphasizes not only conservation work but also the improvement of living conditions for the residents of the old city.

Over the past ten years in particular, AKTC has succeeded in encouraging a large-scale transfer of competencies on the basis of the original 'Public-Private Partnership'. As this was taking place, AKTC has been able to gradually decrease its own presence. AKTC became involved in an initiative concerning the Shahi Guzargah project at a time when it was in an embryonic phase. Because of the engagement and development of the Walled City of Lahore Authority, the overall project took on more and more importance. The visibility that the project gained allowed continual, long-term financing of the Authority to develop. Following the phased programme for infrastructure development prepared in 2010, a second even larger project, the Bhatti Gate project, is now being prepared by the WCLA. This means that the entire effort has become largely self-sustaining.

More than ten years after the initial involvement of AKTC in Lahore, a new phase of the project is beginning, with new partners. A significant part of the ongoing efforts will be devoted to the Lahore Fort Picture Wall. This unique, outdoor, decorated, mural composite includes glazed-tile panels, frescoes and a variety of sophisticated brick masonry patterns. Representing royal processions of the Mughal court, it is clearly one of the greatest treasures of the Mughal legacy in Pakistan. Conservation work by AKTC on the Picture Wall started in 2017 with an evaluation of the challenges to be faced to reverse the damage done to the decorated surfaces by harsh weather conditions over a long period of time. The general principle put forward is the need to preserve the historic decorations and make visually coherent their pictorial composition by minimal reintegration work. A prototype of this approach has been carried out over a 15-metre-high and 10-metre-wide panel on the western segment of the Picture Wall by AKTC and the WCLA. Work on this unique ensemble and adjoining structures is expected to continue for a period of five years and will require significant input from international experts to train a local team of conservators in up-to-date methods. Building local technical capacity in conservation is the ultimate guarantee of project sustainability, as AKTC projects have shown in Cairo, Kabul, Delhi and now Lahore.

1   These publications are: (a) *The Aga Khan Historic Cities Programme, Strategies for Urban Regeneration*, P. Jodidio (ed.), Aga Khan Trust for Culture, Prestel, Munich, 2011; (b) *Heritage of the Mughal World*, P. Jodidio (ed.), Aga Khan Trust for Culture, Prestel, Munich, 2015; (c) *Afghanistan, Preserving Historic Heritage*, P. Jodidio (ed.), Aga Khan Trust for Culture, Prestel, Munich, 2017; and (d) *Cairo, Renewing the Historic City*, P. Jodidio (ed.), Aga Khan Trust for Culture, Prestel, Munich, 2018.

THE WALLED CITY OF LAHORE PROJECT: A PARTNERSHIP APPROACH BETWEEN THE WCLA AND AKTC

CAMERON RASHTI

The Walled City of Lahore is fascinating for its historic integrity and form and remaining pertinence in the present "new urban age".[1] It is increasingly relevant regionally and internationally as a case study of the benefits of guided development as expounded in the UN's New Urban Agenda (Habitat III), adopted in 2016.[2]

The Aga Khan Historic Cities Programme's involvement with urban conservation planning and *in situ* urban and monument conservation initiatives in the Lahore Walled City dates back to 2007, following partnerships with the government of Punjab and the World Bank for the Shahi Guzargah Municipal Services Improvement Project. The main agreement anchoring this multi-year project was a 'Public-Private Partnership Agreement' (PPP) between the government of Punjab and AKTC, signed in 2007. A separate 'Memorandum of Understanding' was signed by AKTC and the World Bank to reflect their relative roles and responsibilities.

THE SHAHI GUZARGAH MUNICIPAL SERVICES IMPROVEMENT PROJECT

The Shahi Guzargah project packaged an ambitious programme of urban streetscape upgrade and conservation of buildings of historic value with a comprehensive improvement of urban infrastructure services along a principal and formerly royal route (the "Shahi Guzargah") of the historic town starting at Delhi Gate on its eastern end to Lahore Fort on its west. Designating the project boundaries thus required reflection on the organic character of the historic urban fabric along this path as well as the engineering network aspects of the infrastructure systems that relied partly on gravity flow and hence watersheds. The result was a multidisciplinary approach to urban conservation and redevelopment that was both vertical and horizontal in its integrated planning.

Strategically, the project was defined in broader planning terms as well, and the project from the start was considered as having relevance to many other interrelated aspects of the re-planning and redevelopment of the Walled City as a heritage and destination place. These included:

- urban planning;
- infrastructure development;
- socio-economic initiatives;
- conservation initiatives – heritage promotion and conservation of monuments;
- economic regeneration;
- tourism development;
- municipal services capacity building;
- conservation services capacity building;
- environmental improvement.

Opposite page, entrance to the Walled City through Delhi Gate.

Above, Koocha Charkh Garan after completion of the pilot neighbourhood rehabilitation project.

Preliminary proposals developed for Bazaar infill project

Wazir Khan Chowk: 17th c. urban square rehabilitated in April 2017

16th c. Begum Shahi/Maryam Zamani Mosque: preliminary proposals developed for conservation

Pilot urban rehabilitation project conducted in Gali Surjan Singh

Baoli Bagh: preliminary proposals developed

17th c. Wazir Khan Mosque: approved project, scheduled for commencement in 2019

18th c. Sunehri Mosque: proposed for rehabilitation

Pilot urban rehabilitation project conducted in Mohammadi Mohalla

17th c. Shahi Hammam restored in 2015

Proposed market with underground parking outside Delhi Gate

300 m

Extent of the Shahi Guzargah project along with other embedded conservation initiatives.

— Bazaar facade rehabilitation
░ Extent of Shahi Guzargah pilot project
▓ Neighbourhood rehabilitation
░ Conservation and urban design projects

The Shahi Guzargah project, in essence, involved the urban conservation and redevelopment of approximately nine per cent of the Walled City, and its initial phases were always meant to be succeeded by interventions that would capitalize on this pioneering project as 'add-ons', much as the original Walled City is the result of incremental development and evolution.

In prior decades, the Aga Khan Historic Cities Programme had tackled challenging urban redevelopment projects in historic cities as diverse as Cairo, the Stone Town of Zanzibar, Kabul and Aleppo, and these projects had revealed the need to adopt an approach that drew upon both a wide array of generalist and specialist planning, architecture and engineering services in the formulation of guidelines and solutions as well as the unswerving emphasis of entering all pre-existing and proposed elements of the emerging plan in a CAD and GIS (Geographic Information Systems) framework. These frameworks allowed for incremental surveying and problem proposals as well as for a hierarchy of spatial maps from the comprehensive to the local in scale. As the project was to be built in phases, the common denominator was these multi-layered and multidisciplinary digital plans.

OUTCOMES OF THE SHAHI GUZARGAH PROJECT

A summing up of the achievements of Phase I of the Shahi Guzargah project in mid-2010 already indicated major progress in the urban planning for this district:

- development of a comprehensive baseline of physical and socio-economic surveys linked to a robust GIS database;
- preparation of the high-level 'Preliminary Strategic Framework' (2008) for the overall Walled City, including definition of a proposed series of local area development framework plans, of which the Shahi Guzargah is a prime case;
- conceptual infrastructure improvement planning, involving a pilot mock-up of such services in narrow lanes on an off-site plot followed by an *in situ* demonstration project in two *galis*;
- based on the infrastructure pilot projects, the commissioning and coordination of an 'Integrated Infrastructure Concept Design' (2010) for the Walled City, followed by the development in coordination with the Sustainable Development of the Walled City of Lahore Project (SDWCLP) team of an upgrading package for the Mohammadi Mohalla Action Area;

In the foreground, Badshahi Mosque, with Lahore Fort and the northern edge of the Walled City in the background.

Existing elevation

5 m

Proposed elevation

Existing and proposed elevations of a section of the Shahi Guzargah trail.

‣ preparation of a detailed set of design guidelines for the urban architecture for the buildings facing onto the Shahi Guzargah street and urban architecture for the related streetscape;

‣ development of surveys and diagnostic reports on the Wazir Khan Mosque as a preliminary set of documentation to support a later stage of conservation;

‣ schematic design proposals for key Action Areas identified in the 2008 'Preliminary Strategic Framework', such as the North Circular Garden, Rim Market/Ali Park, and the larger Iqbal Park.

As the chapters in this publication detail, this initial but sizeable 'entry project' has been succeeded over time by closely related projects that focus on specific sites or clusters of historic buildings within its boundaries. This development was both expected and welcomed.

TENDING TO URBAN CLUSTERS

In 2013 intensive work focused on the two key monuments of the Shahi Hammam and the Wazir Khan Mosque. The former was completed in 2015 to high acclaim and opened under the management of the Walled City of Lahore Authority (WCLA); it received an Award of Merit in UNESCO's Asia-Pacific Awards for Cultural Heritage in 2016. It is said to have received 20,000 visits in the first five months after its opening and has become, as intended, a major node on the heritage route through Delhi Gate.

The external square or *chowk* of the Wazir Khan Mosque was completed in 2017 while the mosque continues to undergo a phased programme of conservation, reflecting the richness and complexity of its exterior facade and its internal spaces, both richly ornamented. Each phase that is completed reinforces not only the appreciation of this landmark building but also the importance of its large sphere of influence along the historic Shahi Guzargah route.

GROWING MOMENTUM: DEVELOPING A PLANNING FRAMEWORK
FOR THE ENTIRE WALLED CITY

In the interim, in 2012 the government of Punjab enacted the 'Walled City of Lahore Act', "Pakistan's first heritage-specific municipal-governance legislation aimed at the protection and development of an historic urban area".[3] The WCLA was given the responsibility of overseeing the development of a planning framework, including wide-ranging urban planning guidelines and building controls, for the Walled City. The WCLA and AKTC scoped out the elements of this framework in consultation with key municipal entities. In 2017 the WCLA and AKTC, together with its local affiliate the Aga Khan Cultural Service-Pakistan (AKCS-P), reached practical completion of a 'Master Conservation and Redevelopment Plan for the Walled City of Lahore' (MCRP).

Described in much greater detail in subsequent sections, the MCRP's strategy has been to define in concise spatial terms "Zones of Special (Heritage) Value" or ZSVs, whose intrinsic heritage values and functions (socio-economic, architectural and urban) are detailed and for which guidelines for protection and enhancement are laid out. Building owners, occupants and developers are given parameters for any permissible changes or modifications. This planning instrument is in the process of being officially ratified and, looking forward, should allow the Walled City to avoid the intense development pressures that it has been subjected to until now.

Restored historic homes located in Gali Surjan Singh and Koocha Charkh Garan, part of the pilot neighbourhood rehabilitation project: left, example of a restored courtyard; middle, view towards the street through the depth of a house; and right, a reception room in another house.

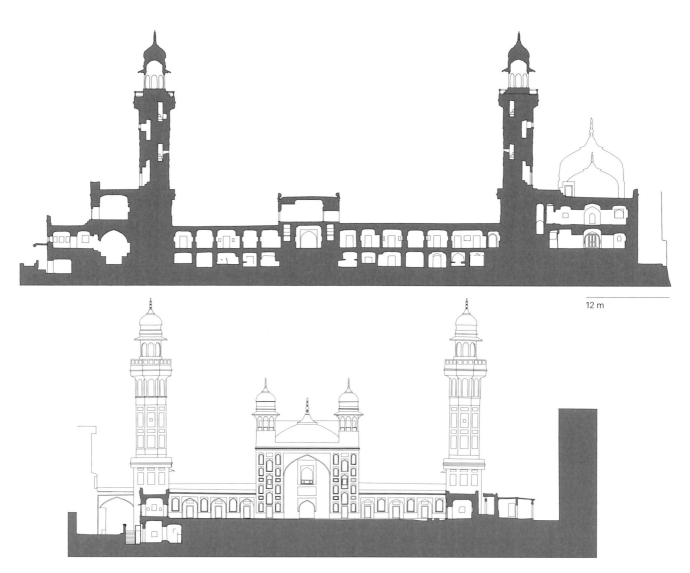

12 m

Above, sectional elevations of the Wazir Khan Mosque.

Opposite page, above, the interior courtyard of the Wazir Khan Mosque showing the prayer chamber at the rear. Below, plan of the Wazir Khan Mosque complex before the conservation of the *chowk*.

In pursuing these conservation and redevelopment projects, the WCLA and the government of Punjab have clearly opted for a cultural heritage agenda to lead and shape the further evolution of the Walled City and its areas of historic value. This implies the conservation rather than demolition of authentic historic fabric, its careful repurposing with more appropriate and less industrial uses, and the curating of the Walled City as an integral whole of outstanding value.

THE WORLD HERITAGE SITE OF LAHORE FORT
The investment in urban conservation and redevelopment over the decade of 2007–17 led inevitably to the question of Lahore Fort, the prime setting of Mughal architectural sophistication and expression during the period from Akbar to Shah Jahan. Inscribed in 1981 by UNESCO on its World Heritage List, in tandem with Shalimar Garden, some distance away, the Fort is almost overwhelming in scale and complexity. The work of several Mughal emperors, built on an imposing mound that pre-dates the Fort, and with pavilions, courtyards and gardens that interlock and adjoin, the site resembles a mini-city or campus. The Fort, the neighbouring Badshahi Mosque, commissioned by Emperor Aurangzeb, and various other pavilions, temples and enclosure walls erected

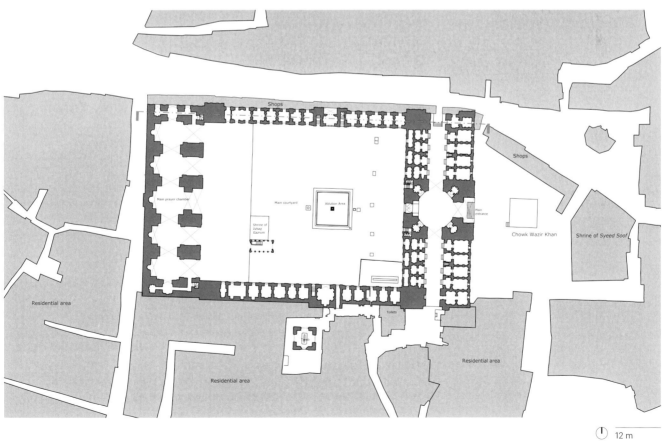

Shops

Shops

Main prayer chamber

Main courtyard

Ablution Area

Main entrance

Shrine of Ishaq Gazruni

Chowk Wazir Khan

Shrine of *Syeed Soof*

Residential area

Toilets

Residential area

Residential area

12 m

The primary Zone of Special Value in the Walled City, showing (i) the World Heritage Site of Lahore Fort, (ii) those elements proposed to be included in a future World Heritage Site, and (iii) the proposed Buffer Zone.

■ Zone of Special Value (Lahore Fort)
▨ Zones earmarked for inclusion into the future WHS
- - - Buffer Zone of the future WHS

during the Sikh period sit on the north-west of the Walled City with views overlooking Iqbal Park and the old bed of the Ravi River.

The Fort's prominence, visibility and massive enclosure walls seem to call for an ornamental statement to match. The Picture Wall, with an almost endless series of brick-framed ceramic mosaic and fresco-painted panels, depicts numerous mythological and royal scenes, the specific character of which are discussed in detail on pp. 294–323. The Picture Wall is cited as one of the key factors for the Fort's inclusion on the World Heritage List. The MCRP demarcates the Fort as Zone of Special Value 1 (ZSV 1) and AKTC/AKCS-P, together with the WCLA and the Department of Antiquities, since 2017 have initiated investigations and preliminary testing and conservation of a first series of projects within the Fort, including the western portion of the Picture Wall.

With a consortium of funding from the Government of Punjab, the Royal Norwegian Embassy, the German Foreign Office, the Agence Française de Développement and AKTC, this first phase of activity in Lahore Fort has been accompanied by the preparation of an updated conservation master plan for the Fort and its urban buffer zones: the 'Lahore Fort Precinct and Buffer Zone Master Plan' (2018). Planning and intervention are shown, once again, as essential counterweights in any significant conservation programme at this scale. Such was the case in the original Shahi Guzargah project, in the subsequent conservation of clusters of monuments along

that route, in the development of the 2017 'Master Conservation and Redevelopment Plan' (MCRP), and in this most recent case, in the planning of conservation initiatives for Lahore Fort within the framework of a 'Conservation Master Plan' that has been shared with UNESCO.

A group of girls on a school trip to the Badshahi Mosque.

CREATING AN ENABLING FRAMEWORK

Over the period 2013–17, AKTC and AKCS-P have entered into twelve 'Memoranda of Understanding' (including addenda and/or extensions to such memoranda) for technical assistance and conservation of specific sites. These agreements are offshoots, in many ways, of the original 2007 'Public-Private Partnership' agreement alluded to above. A key element of the Historic Cities Programme and the WCLA's strategy in repositioning the Walled City of Lahore has been based on comprehensive planning frameworks for urban conservation and redevelopment coupled with spatially interlocked and incremental interventions. The selection of key clusters of buildings with heritage value was built into the process from the start, in the 'Preliminary Strategic Framework' plan (2008), which allowed flexibility for periodic adjustments to its scope. Completion of coherent components – such as the Shahi Hamman – with high public appeal has helped gain broad governmental and popular support, in turn providing the enabling conditions for more complex undertakings, such as Lahore Fort, which are now well underway.

1   See Ricky Burdett and Philipp Rode, "Living in the Urban Age", in Ricky Burdett and Deyan Sudjic (eds.), *Living in the Endless City*, Phaidon, London, 2011, pp. 8–11, and the London School of Economics' wider "Urban Age Project" for signs of a renewal of focus on urbanism and all its dimensions. Further policy on the same has been agreed in the UN's New Urban Agenda, adopted at the United Nations Conference on Housing and Sustainable Urban Development (Habitat III) in Quito, Ecuador, in October 2016 and endorsed by the United Nations General Assembly in December 2016.

2   See above footnote. The New Urban Agenda represents a shared vision for a better and more sustainable future. If well planned and well managed, urbanization can be a powerful tool for sustainable development for both developing and developed countries.

3   AKTC/AKCS-P, "Lahore Fort Precinct and Buffer Zone Master Plan" (2018), p. 37.

GREATER LAHORE
AND THE WALLED CITY

LAHORE: THE CITY IN HISTORY

MASOOD KHAN

Lahore is Pakistan's second largest city, the capital of the province of Punjab, and the country's cultural heart. It has a known history over a period of more than 2,000 years. Before independence in 1947, Lahore was northern India's centre for thinkers and intellectuals, poets and writers, book publishing and journalism. It has retained much of that role today. The city has dozens of universities and institutions of higher learning and has produced many graduates of national and international acclaim. The exuberance and wit that Punjab and its people are famous for is focused in Lahore. Numerous traditional festivals deeply linked to the city's history are held annually, including festivals to honour Sufi poets and saints. The city provides an important base for the evolving civil society institutions of the country. The Human Rights Commission of Pakistan is based here, as well as numerous other governmental and non-governmental agencies.

By any measure, Lahore is an important city of the Islamic world, with a history that compares with that of Baghdad, Islamic Cairo and Isfahan. Lahore's metropolitan area measures 505 square kilometres, although a total area of 1,700 square kilometres is affected by urban Lahore in a variety of ways. By the latest count in 2017, the city's population was 11.3 million, ranking thirty-first among 1,047 cities in the world with a population of 500,000 or more.[1]

The citadel, Lahore Fort (قلعہ لاہور), is situated on the north-west corner of Lahore's historic core, its Walled City. The River Ravi, one of the tributaries of the Indus, flows at the north-western edge of the built-up area of the modern city, two kilometres from the Walled City. Although once the river clung to the edges of the Walled City flowing south-west around the Fort, it has progressively moved further to the west and, as a result of dykes built in the eighteenth century and thereafter, it now flows along a meandering plain at a safe distance. Historically the river was prone to late summer flooding, typical of the Indus River system as a whole.

Greater Lahore comprises four fairly distinct zones: firstly, a dense somewhat under-serviced older part, which includes the Walled City, and those colonial-period developments that were created for the traditional, non-Europeanized parts of the citizenry; secondly, a less dense colonial-period zone which contains older administrative, residential and commercial areas; thirdly, a colonial-period military zone – the Lahore Cantonment – established within a year of the formal British annexation of Punjab in 1849; and lastly, post-independence ongoing southward growth, characterized by residential communities with very low densities. Lahore's residential land distribution is inversely proportional to the income distribution of its citizenry.

Preceding pages, Shalimar Garden. A pavilion inside the garden on the middle terrace, with the central water tank in the background.

Opposite page, Shahdara, Jahangir's tomb, interior of the circumambulatory veranda.

Above, *Lahore City in the Punjab*, water-colour by Henry Ambrose Oldfield (1822–71), 1849. A boat bridge can be seen just behind the *baradari* of Kamran's garden, the building in the foreground.

5 km

**The Walled City in the context
of Metropolitan Lahore.**

- - - Lahore District Boundary
▬ The Walled City of Lahore
▬ Business District of Central Lahore
▬ Traditional / lower-income residential areas
▬ Colonial-period civil developments
      (including railway related)
≡ Colonial military establishment
▰ Post-independence upper-income residential
      areas
▬ Ring Road and M2 Motorway
'''' Railway tracks
■ Airports
▬ Bus and train rapid transit
▬ Canals

Upper-income and upper-middle-income households comprise a small fraction of the total urban population but use up the bulk of Lahore's area. On the other hand, the majority of the city's population consists of lower-income residents who occupy concentrated, poorly serviced and poorly built areas contained in a small proportion of the land. Roughly dividing these two residential types, and making distinct the new, better functioning parts of Lahore from the older ones, is the Lahore branch of the Upper Bari Doab Canal,[2] now an urban feature that for many Lahoris has become the identifying mark of the city. Upper-income areas of Lahore are more verdant, and in recent decades there has been a substantial effort at providing them with good roads, landscaping and a somewhat superior infrastructure system as compared with the older, dense, low-income districts.

Colonial-period Lahore continues to serve as the power base where many buildings and neighbourhoods act as the seat of the provincial administration. Some of these buildings, such as the Lahore High Court, the Lahore Museum and the Punjab Legislative Assembly, are noteworthy assets in the urban character of the city.

At some point in time Lahore acquired the epithet "City of Gardens". Lahore was famous for its gardens during the peak of Mughal rule when the countryside surrounding the fortified old city was dotted with large gardens of the nobility and the neighbourhoods that had sprung up around them. But except for magnificent Mughal gardens, such as Shalimar and the Shahdara complex, these traditional gardens have now disappeared. Colonial Lahore boasted several large new public gardens, the Anarkali Gardens (Gol Bagh), the Lawrence Gardens (Jinnah Gardens), the

Aerial view of the Walled City, with Lahore Fort and the Badshahi Mosque in the background.

Above, Lahore Fort, the Athdara pavilion. From *Recollections of India. Part 1. British India and the Punjab* by J. D. Harding.

Below, the *samadh* of Ranjit Singh photographed by John Edward Saché in the 1870s.

Government College Botanical Garden and the Lahore Zoological Gardens, as well as two large residential areas of the civil station that were laid out with lush green lawns and now have ageing trees. A 350-hectare central park was developed as part of the entirely residential Model Town established by local professionals in 1929. All these have survived. The Lahore Military Cantonment, nine kilometres from the historic core, started out in 1850 as a large, sparsely occupied development with many open landscaped areas, including a polo ground, cricket and soccer grounds, and parks. While these green areas have largely survived, most of its regimental training areas and field firing ranges are now upper-income residential developments, and a newer golf course.

A VENERABLE PAST

Lahore's beginnings are uncertain. Archaeological exploration in and around Lahore has been scant and much needs to be done to establish the facts of its early history. Whatever evidence there is[3] dates the Walled City's origins back several centuries prior to its associations with Muslim invasions and dynasties. The several historic mounds that comprise the Walled City point to the need for a great deal more archaeological work. Cultural layers ten metres deep are found whenever any soil investigations are carried out for construction work, even in the lowest parts of the city. Lahore Fort rises fourteen metres above the surrounding area, but, together with other equally prominent mounds in the Walled City, it is just one of many potential sources of knowledge hidden in the historical strata. The city's regional importance and much of its built form evolved during the period of the first six Mughal emperors (1526–1707), when it carried the title "Dar ul Saltanat".[4]

Lahore probably originated as one of the numerous towns that are said to have sprung up in the middle Vedic period in the inter-fluvial territories (*doabas*) of the Jhelum, the Chenab, the Ravi and the Sutlej rivers, all flowing into the Indus, and many more towns along the upper reaches of the Yamuna and the Ganges further east. These settlements are associated with the decline (*c.* 1500–1000 BCE) of the Indus Valley civilization in its late Harappan stage. Contributing to this change at about the same time was the arrival of Indo-Aryans from the Eurasian and Central Asian regions at various stages of social development. Recent archaeological and geomorphological[5] research in the larger geographic region has shown that this involved a process of slow change rather than a complete rupture from the Indus Valley culture. A new society evolved, characterized by the introduction of iron, and of the horse as a means of rapid mobility and warfare, accompanied by the fusion of religions and rituals. There was also a new impetus to trade across the trans-Indus region, along routes that led from Persia and the trans-Oxus to the Ganges Basin.[6] This was the historic setting in which the great epic Ramayana is supposed to have taken place, and ancient Vedic texts lend considerable strength to the tradition that Lahore and Kasur were two cities founded respectively by Lau and Kush, Rama Chandra's two sons.[7]

Lahore's location at a river crossing on a strategic trade route, and a route of attack, contributed to its being laid waste many times over, as well as to its persistence. The city appears to have evolved slowly. There has been confusion over its name, and for some it emerged at a much later date than the sources seem to suggest. Yet, despite large gaps in its history, Lahore seems in various ways to reappear again and again in epic sources and in the historical record.[8]

Many references to Lahore appear in the earlier Muslim sources. The Arab historian Baladhuri[9] refers in his *Futuh al-Buldan* to the early Umayyad-period mission of al-Muhallab ibn abu-Sufrah who "raided this frontier in the year AH 44 (664 CE)

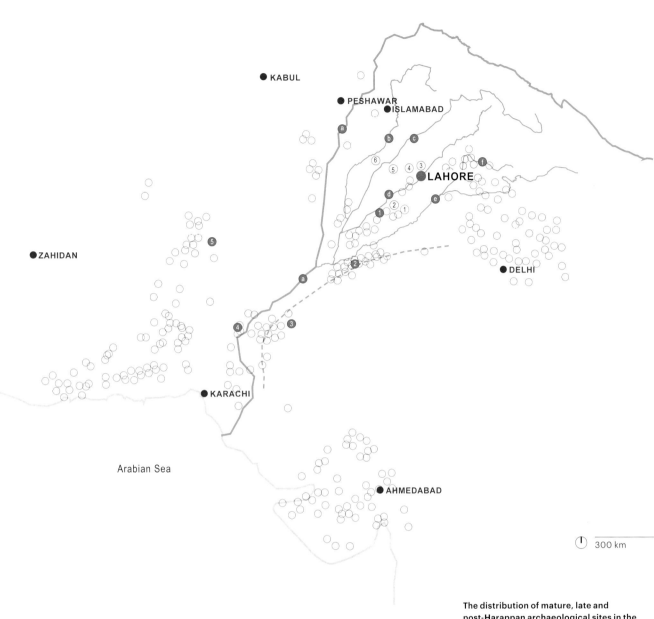

KABUL

PESHAWAR
ISLAMABAD

ZAHIDAN

LAHORE

DELHI

KARACHI

Arabian Sea

AHMEDABAD

300 km

The distribution of mature, late and
post-Harappan archaeological sites in the
Indus system (after L. Giosan et al.).

— Rivers
ⓐ Indus
ⓑ Jhelum
ⓒ Chenab
ⓓ Ravi
ⓔ Sutlej
ⓕ Beas

- - Ghaggar-Hakra (defunct river)

○ Distribution of archaeological sites

⬤ Principal known archaeological sites
❶ Harappa
❷ Ganveriwala
❸ Kot Diji
❹ Mohenjo Daro
❺ Mehr Garh

① Location of sampling sites
in the vicinity of Lahore
① Dipalpur
② Okara
③ Karan Shah
④ Kalokay
⑤ Doda
⑥ Jahanabad

and reached Bannah (Bannu) and Alahwar (Lahore) which lie between al-Multan and
Kabul". This expedition took place during the caliphate of Muawiya. It preceded that
of Muhammad bin Qasim's, which took place in 711 CE, and was probably followed
by others mentioned in the Rajput sources. Bin Qasim's conquests went as far up the
Indus as Multan and he does not appear to have encountered Lahore; Muslim incur-
sions impacting Lahore had to wait until the end of the tenth century.

In the first half of the tenth century, Lahore was the capital of a Rajput Hindu
kingdom that reigned over Punjab. The decay of the Samanid Empire in Transoxiana
had resulted in the rise in Afghanistan of the Muslim general Alaptagin. In an event
that marked that country's transition to Islam, Alaptagin took Ghazni and forced the
Brahman Shahi rulers of that province to relocate themselves across the Hindukush
in India. An alliance was then formed between the Brahman Shahis and Lahore's
rulers to defend their territory against the Muslim threat, which had intensified
under Alaptagin's son Subaktagin. The alliance fought and lost a major battle against

Subaktagin's forces near today's Jalalabad, and their political centre consequently shifted further east. During the next few decades Lahore became the capital of a Hindu regime stretching from the Hindukush across the trans-Indus region; at the end of the century, Lahore was ruled by the Hindu Shahi king Jaipal.

THE MUSLIM PERIOD

Lahore had therefore become an important regional capital by the time Subaktagin began his several military engagements with Jaipal II, grandson of Jaipal. Subaktagin's son Mahmud defeated the younger Jaipal in 1021[10] and established Ghaznavid hold on a major city in India. However, Lahore was decimated during this attack and was abandoned for several years until Mahmud appointed a new governor for the territory. This was Mahmud's friend, the freed slave Malik Ayaz, who is credited with repopulating the city and beginning a period of growth and development that lasted for the duration of the Ghaznavid Empire. With the loss of Ghazni to the Seljuks of Khwarizm, Lahore became the capital of a Ghaznavid Empire that had once encompassed all of Iran, the Caucuses and Khwarizmia, but which now comprised just the trans-Indus region.

During the rule of Mas'ud I, Mahmud's son, Lahore saw another arrival from Ghazni. In 1031 the Sufi, Ali bin Uthman al-Hajweri, arrived in Lahore and established his sanctuary outside the south-west corner of the Walled City. He served the people of Lahore until his death some time around 1072. As Data Ganj Bakhsh, he became Lahore's patron saint, and is today revered by people from all over South Asia. During Ghaznavid times, Lahore shared a brilliant intellectual climate with Ghazni, where the Persian epic the *Shahnameh* was completed by the poet Ferdowsi. Lahore too had an

Lahore Fort, the Diwan-e-Aam, or the hall of forty pillars, built by Shah Jahan to replace Akbar's tent structure. The building exists in a much-altered state due to British and later changes.

abundance of Ghaznavid culture and produced poets like Mas'ud Sa'd Salman, who wrote passionate verses yearning for the city of his birth, while in prison in Ghazni.

In 1186 the last Ghaznavid ruler was defeated and killed in Lahore by the Ghorids, a warring group from Afghanistan under Mu'iz ud-Din Muhammad bin Sam. This led to the establishment of the first Muslim kingdom based in India proper at Delhi, and to the beginning of the Sultanate period (1186–1526). The preoccupation of Muslim rulers with the Indian heartland began with Muhammad Ghori's successors, and lasted for hundreds of years. It was characterized by military engagements with native Rajput rulers, competing Muslim rulers and ruling families, and with rebellious provincial governors. Lahore continued as a strategic city located in a region vulnerable to attacks from the north.

Lahore Fort, Shah Jahan's Diwan-e-Aam seen from the south-west.

View of Greater Iqbal Park developed by the Punjab government north of Lahore Fort.

With the Mongol invasions in the early thirteenth century, Lahore was plundered and devastated several times, and the initial two invasions in 1221 (by the Mongol Turtai) and 1241 (under General Munggetu) were particularly destructive. The attacks continued for decades afterwards. A prolonged local resistance progressively weakened the attacks, which finally ended when the last Mongol army into India was defeated by a Lahore governor, Ghazi Khan, who immediately afterwards ascended the throne of Delhi (1321–25) as Ghiathuddin Muhammad Tughlaq. During this period remnants of the Mongol armies settled down some eight kilometres from Lahore at a locality still known as Moghalpura.

Amir Timur Gurgan (Tamerlane) spared Lahore on his advance eastward that ended with the sacking of Delhi in 1398. But he was angered when the Lahore ruler Shaikha Khokhar reneged on an agreement to stay neutral. A detachment of his army was sent back to Lahore under his sons, who plundered the city and imprisoned Shaikha and his family. The princes returned to Delhi with wealth collected in Lahore.[11] Timur left for his conquests in Western Asia and died within the following decade.

LAHORE AND THE MUGHAL EMPIRE
The Lodhis of Delhi were the last of the Delhi sultans, whose rule over India was decisively ended by Zahir-ud-Din Muhammad Babur, scion of a ruling family in Fergana, modern Uzbekistan. A descendant of Timur, Babur had succeeded his father when he

was very young and, after initial reverses, carved out a kingdom for himself in Afghan-istan with his seat at Kabul by the time he was twenty-one. He now set his sights firmly on India and made numerous exploratory excursions from Kabul. In the early 1520s Babur was approached with a deal by Lahore's governor, a rebellious relative of Sultan Ibrahim Lodhi. A combination of chance and broken words led Babur to turn upon the Lahore ruler in 1524, when he sacked the city and occupied it. In 1526, on his last march from Kabul, he finally defeated Ibrahim, the last of the Lodhi monarchs at Panipat, north of Delhi. Babur then declared himself the emperor of India, settled down at Delhi and Agra, strengthened his position militarily by subduing many Rajput principalities and provincial Muslim chieftains, and for four years indulged in a spree of building Timurid-style gardens and garden palaces in both these cities.

In 1530 Babur was succeeded by his oldest son Nasir-ud-din Muhammad Hum-ayun. His second son Mirza Kamran had been left in charge of Kabul. In the following years Kamran launched a claim to the throne, and with the Mughal troops under his

Shahdara, the Akbari Serai. The mosque separating the serai from the mausoleum garden of Asif Khan.

Preceding pages, view from the northern tower of Alamgiri Gate, looking west onto the Hazuri Bagh with the Badshahi Mosque behind.

Above, Lahore Railway Station, photograph by George Craddock, *c.* 1880.

Below, 19th-century lithograph by L. H. de Rudder depicting a street in Lahore with Sikh nobles on elephants passing onlookers on balconies.

command, annexed Lahore. Kamran built a large garden on the west bank of the Ravi. The nobility followed suit, and many Mughal gardens appeared over the next two decades on that side of the river.

A decade into his rule, Humayun was forced to flee, having suffered a series of crushing losses at the hands of Sher Shah Suri, an Afghan chieftain ruling the eastern province of Bihar, while all three of his brothers rebelled against him. In a last-ditch attempt to forge a compromise, Humayun and his brothers gathered at Lahore, but Kamran plotted with Sher Shah to drive Humayun out of India. After years of wandering, Humayun eventually found refuge in Iran at the court of the Safavid ruler, Shah Tahmasp I, and secured help at the cost of converting to Shia Islam.

In the mid-sixteenth century, while in Kabul, Humayun still struggled to put an end to his brother Kamran's attempts to oust him. Even though Kamran was made to flee Kabul, it was not until 1553 that he was captured and brought to Parhwar, near modern Islamabad. At the insistence of his nobles, Humayun had Kamran blinded. With his brilliant general Byram Khan, and with the armed assistance provided by Shah Tahmasp, Humayun was able to defeat the Suris in 1555. On his return to India after fourteen years, Humayun was welcomed by the people of Lahore, where he had himself proclaimed emperor once again. He re-established himself at Delhi, but died less than a year later.

Upon Humayun's death in 1556, his son Jalal-ud-din Muhammad Akbar ascended the throne of the empire at the age of fourteen. During the earlier years of his reign, Akbar visited Lahore at least three times. Beginning in 1586, Akbar stayed in Lahore for twelve years. He used Lahore as a strategic base to advance his control of the frontiers, and to annex Kashmir. During these years he expanded and fortified the city, strengthened Lahore Fort and built many palace buildings within it, encouraging his nobles to occupy the space outside Lahore's Walled City with palaces and gardens, a trend that was to last for a long period. During Akbar's reign (1556–1605), relative stability resulted from the status of Lahore as a second capital; the city expanded to accommodate a growing population and the historic settlement was expanded and fortified on all sides. As the built-up area spilled over its fortifications into the expanding garden suburbs, historic Lahore became better known as Androon Shehr, the "city within", or much later, the Walled City.

Akbar died in 1605. His half-a-century-long reign was packed with military assaults and sieges, conquests and annexations, rebellions and palace intrigues, and matrimonial arrangements with Hindu families. It was also a time for splendid buildings in an architectural style of rich cultural fusion. His rule ended with a vast Indian Empire and a brilliant administrative system that enabled his successors to rule for several centuries. His eldest son Nuruddin Muhammad Jahangir ascended the Mughal throne at Agra in 1605, and ruled for twenty-two years mainly on the strength of the administrative arrangements and vassalages that his father had created. Jahangir had many new structures added to his father's palace within Lahore Fort. His reign was marked by the rise to imperial power of his last spouse, the empress Nur Jahan, and her entire family. Both Nur Jahan and Jahangir are buried in the gardens that they built in Shahdara, Lahore's suburb across the Ravi, as is her brother Asif Khan, the father of the future queen Mumtaz Mahal.

Mumtaz Mahal's husband, Jahangir's son Shahabuddin Muhammad Khurram, was born in Lahore, and ascended the throne at Agra with the title "Shah Jahan" already bestowed on him by his father. The Mughal penchant for creating great architecture reached its apogee during Shah Jahan's reign, with spectacular palace architecture in Lahore Fort, created in the same decade as the Taj Mahal and the city

Above, the great court of the Badshahi Mosque, looking westwards towards the prayer chamber.

Left, detail of the carved red sandstone and marble inlay of Badshahi Mosque.

of Shahjahanabad. Lahore spread to its broadest expanse under the Mughals with scores of neighbourhoods with palaces and gardens at their centre spread across the immediate vicinity of the old city, including the magnificent Shalimar Garden.

Shah Jahan's son Muhammad Aurangzeb Alamgir ascended the Mughal throne, through a war of succession. Aurangzeb's time at the helm of affairs (1658–1707) began with tragic intrigue and fratricide. Lahore had already passed the peak of its Mughal-era fame, and new imperial priorities were focused more in the Deccan and the east, which meant that Lahore receded into the background. Still, the Badshahi Masjid (1673) was conceived and built, combining grand scale and an aptitude for urban composition.

The weakening Mughal rule led to the rise in Punjab of militant Sikhs, followers of a new syncretic religion founded in the late fifteenth century. The Sikhs became militarized against the Mughals during the seventeenth century, leading to a destabilization that would invite invasions from Persia and Afghanistan in the following one. These invasions were devastating for Lahore, and the city continued to be marauded during a brief Maratha invasion and through the rule of three competing Sikh clans, which lasted for thirty years. It was during this period of anarchy and spoilage that Lahore lost its glorious Mughal heritage outside the Walled City. With the Sukherchakia clan's Ranjit Singh, who took over from the Sikh Triumvirate in 1799, conditions returned to normal. New buildings were built, many of them using stone revetments of Mughal buildings. With the death of Ranjit in 1839 there was turmoil for succession within his family until the annexation of Punjab by the British East India Company in 1849.

The *samadh* of Ranjit Singh with the Badshahi Mosque in the background.

The British needed to build very quickly to create a functional colonial city.[12] For the decades following 1849, the ruined suburbs of Lahore and its historic fortifications provided a continuous supply of Mughal-period bricks, to the extent that even the foundation remains of Mughal buildings were excavated and reused. A new occupation was created with the supply of these building materials and, for those involved, fortunes soared.

The *samadh* of Ranjit Singh, detail.

49

THE WALLED CITY

There are two sites that could be the primordial points of the origin of Lahore[13]: the first of these is the Lange Mandi area, the highest in the Walled City, and its expansion to its west towards Tibbi Mohalla. The second site is the roughly triangular area near the southern limits of the present-day Walled City that comprises Mohalla Maulian. This observation is based mainly on the terrain elevations of the old city, and on its physical form and topographical features, including the annular rings formed by the street system of the city. The growth rings of the city seen in the pattern of development of the main streets in the Walled City lend support to ideas about the Ghaznavid city having grown rapidly, a theory supported by the sequence of locations of the burial places of notaries (such as the grave of Malik Ayaz, Mahmud's governor of Lahore, and the grave-shrine of the fourteenth-century Sufi Syed Muhammad Ishaq Gazruni, d. 1384) that were traditionally located outside the city walls that marked the city's perimeter. At least one ancient mosque marks the location from which an outward growth can be assumed. It would seem plausible that the Lange Mandi comprises a static pole whereas the annular rings represent a growing city. Would this not suggest respectively the site of the pre-Ghaznavid city sacked by Mahmud in 1021, and that of the Ghaznavid city in close juxtaposition?

Akbar's brick fortifications resulted in an expanded city; the new walls encircling many of these topo-historic markers with empty spaces were filled later. The Walled City, however, has remained in this form since it was first attained in the mid-sixteenth century.

With the Lahore railway station established in 1859 a kilometre away from the Walled City, in the decades following independence the condition of the Walled City was strongly affected by the nexus between the persistent location of inter-regional transportation activities and the regional markets that have arisen within the Walled City, as these contemporary modes of transportation foster inter-regional commercial linkages. The Walled City is now a part of the business hub of Central Lahore, which has a regional, national and in some respects even international reach. But, despite its miniscule size in Lahore's larger physical context, the Walled City continues to play a role as the wellspring of the cultural and economic energies that sustain the larger city.

Opposite page, part of the Shahi Guzargah project. The rehabilitated Delhi Gate Bazaar.

Above, dense urban fabric in the Walled City.

1   *Demographia World Urban Areas*, 2018, at http://demographia.com/db-worldua.pdf, accessed on 31.8.2019.

2   Built by the Mughals and upgraded by the British as part of their massive redevelopment of the irrigation canal system in Punjab.

3   "Excavation at Lahore Fort", in *Pakistan Archaeology*, no. 1 (1964).

4   Capital of the Sultanate.

5   Liviu Giosan, Peter D. Clift et al., "Fluvial Landscapes of the Harappan Civilization", *PNAS*, 2012, at https://www.pnas.org/content/109/26/E1688/1, accessed on 31.8.2019.

6   Romila Thapar, "Regional History: Punjab" and "The Archaeological Background to the Agni-cayana Ritual", in Id., *Cultural Pasts*, OUP, Delhi, 2000; also J. M. Kenoyer, *Ancient Cities of the Indus Valley Civilization*, OUP, Karachi, 1998.

7   Lahore probably started as Lau Kot (Lau's Fort), but it has been called/spelled/transcribed as Lau Pur, Lavokla, Lavapur, Lohawar, Al-Lahawar, Al-Ahwar, Lahanwar, Lahanur, Lahor and Lahore in various places, times and sources.

8   The second-century CE geography of Ptolemy lists Lahore as Labokla (Λαβωκλα) among many cities along the Ravi, while providing their geographical coordinates. Burnes, a nineteenth-century colonial explorer, associated Lahore with Sakala, the principal city of the leading Kathia tribe (the *Kathaioi*) sacked by Alexander the Great in 326 BCE. See Alexander Burnes, *Travels into Bokhara*, J. Murray, London, 1834. There appear to be few references to cities in the epigraphic sources of the Mauryan and the Kushan periods (320 BCE to the 4th century CE). But some useful links come down to us from sources such as the Puranas, and genealogical stories and chants from early medieval India. See Syad Muhammad Latif, *Lahore: Its History, Architectural Remains and Antiquities*, New Imperial Press, Lahore, 1892; J. Tod, *Annals and Antiquities of Rajasthan*, Calcutta, 1902; and T. H. Thornton,

"Lahore: A Historical and Descriptive Account (1860)", in H. R. Goulding, *Old Lahore: Reminiscences of a Resident*, Sang-e-Meel, Lahore, 1924.

9   Al-Baladhuri, *Kitab Futuh al-Buldan*, F. C. Murgotten (trans.; *The Origins of the Islamic State*), Columbia Press, New York, 1924, p. 210.

10   Jaipal II committed the *johar* (the Rajput honour-suicide).

11   Latif, *Lahore: Its History...* op cit., quoting *Malfuzat-i-Tymuri* and *Zafarnama*.

12   Lahore has no source of building stone in its immediate neighbourhood and burnt brick has been the chief building material for its construc-tions, excepting stone revetments for the most important.

13   These two sites were identified by the authors of this monograph: PEPAC (Pakistan Environmental Planning and Architectural Consult-ants), *The Walled City of Lahore*, Lahore Develop-ment Authority, Lahore, 1993.

LAHORE'S WALLED CITY

MASOOD KHAN

Today the Walled City of Lahore is a compact, clearly demarcated area of high-density urban fabric in the north-western part of Lahore. It is a part of Central Lahore, itself located in the north-western corner of the larger city. The historic city shares many characteristics with Central Lahore: a primarily low- to lower-middle-income residential population; businesses linked in dependence on entrenched freight transportation activity; poorly serviced neighbourhoods and commercial precincts; warehousing; and the tendency for established residential population to emigrate to upcoming lower-density neighbourhoods in the suburbs.

The footprint that the Walled City occupies on the map today continues to be small – it is half of one per cent of the size of Greater Lahore – and comprises a tight mass of some 22,000 individual land holdings (and an equal number of buildings) collected together in an area of approximately 252 hectares. After demolishing the city walls in the 1860s, the colonial government created a circular garden and a circular road surrounding the old city in the early twentieth century. Today, both Circular Road and Circular Garden are heavily encroached upon.

The Walled City is at the core of the cultural and economic energies of Lahore. However, over the last 175 years, as old Lahore's cultural presence has weakened, its economic strength has increased substantially. As part of the business hub of Central Lahore, the Walled City today has a strong share in the large national economic space which Lahore's central economic zone commands. But this economic ascendance largely takes the form of new informal wholesale commerce that is a massive externality, draining away all the value added that the Walled City's internal human and cultural resources contribute while putting at great jeopardy its very survival.

THE CITY AS HERITAGE

The cultural values of the historic core of Lahore are noteworthy. The events of 1947 and the scars they left on the Walled City notwithstanding, the complex structure of the urbanism and the history written into its very form and structure is significant. Exceptionally, it is one of those rare historic cities whose form and identity are markedly visible on city maps. This distinction from its surroundings is facilitated by Circular Garden and Circular Road and by the urban areas around it that arose mainly in the British period.

The city offers innumerable opportunities to represent the notion of 'a historic urban landscape' from the point of view of cultural authenticity, as well as its place-ment within a spatial and historical context. Spread all around the city are evidences

Opposite page, the Walled City. West facade of Delhi Gate, with a corner of the Shahi Hammam on the right.

Above, *Kashmiri Bazaar with the Sunehri Masjid at Its Terminal End*, watercolour by William Carpenter, 1855.

of Greater Lahore in the seventeenth century, the time of the city's historical zenith. These monuments and remains of gardens represent a continuum of change and transformation that has become Lahore's history. Within the perimeter of the Walled City are labyrinthine networks of streets and passageways that have changed little since Akbar's time. As one walks through many of these streets and bazaars, the atmospherics created by groups of late nineteenth- and early twentieth-century buildings are evocative and mesmerizing. As in many other historic cities, the names used for some of the retail bazaars and certain neighbourhoods and lanes often refer to merchandise, occupations or professional services that may not exist anymore. Still surviving are seven hundred individual historic buildings that complete the physical environment of those passageways. Many of these buildings strike one as architecturally and artistically valuable in their own right, but many are clustered together, and possess group value. There are thousands more that, once the crude plaster renders, modern repairs and concrete projections are removed, are highly likely to reappear in their historic authenticity as the urban rehabilitation continues.

Embedded in this historic fabric are many monumental artefacts, large and small – mosques, temples, squares, *havelis* and gates, described in the following chapter. On the Walled City's north-western corner is the World Heritage Site of Lahore Fort, the ancient citadel, described in detail on pp. 210–371. Their future, as well as the future of the ordinary historic urban fabric, depends as much on expert attention and care at appropriate standards of conservation as on serious political will, the proper enforcement of law and on municipal governance specially tailored to a historic city.

The Walled City. Sunehri Masjid (Golden Mosque), at the western end of Kashmiri Bazaar.

DEMOGRAPHICS

At the time of British occupation in 1849, the Walled City accommodated almost the entire population of Lahore. A grand Mughal city of 500,000 inhabitants had been reduced in a hundred years to just 50,000 people living behind the crumbling city walls. By 1947 a century of British rule had revived the Walled City with nearly 250,000 people living in it.

From 1947 onwards the Walled City steadily lost its resident population. Initially, refugees from India replaced the city's Hindu and Sikh population that had fled to India during partition. Following this, waves of migrant labour flocked to Lahore and found refuge in the Walled City. Each layer of immigrants moved out as their incomes rose. The 'Conservation Plan' prepared in 1988[1] estimated that the population in the Walled City had declined by twenty-nine per cent between 1972 and 1981. The 1998 and the 2017 census figures attest to the continuation of this process, with the Walled City's population at 160,734 and 148,000 respectively. The decline of population is a

The Walled City. The early 19th-century *haveli*, or palace, of Naunehal Singh, converted into the Victoria Girls High School in 1887 and still one of the city's premier institutions.

Restaurants along Fort Road, south-west of Lahore Fort.

measure of how non-residential land use has expanded and is attended by the loss of long-term and hereditary residents with a corresponding depletion of tangible and intangible heritage.

Many complex changes have pushed older residents out. In the decades following independence, some of these factors were the breakdown of municipal administration and services, infrastructure maintenance, regulatory processes, the condition of the building stock, health and education facilities, recreation, law-enforcement and so on. The process has not slowed despite attempts at improving infrastructure during the period 1978 to 1992 under a series of World Bank slum improvement projects.

ROADS, BRIDGES, TRAFFIC AND TRANSPORTATION

Even in the colonial period, with its emphasis on the development of railways, Lahore was connected to roads leading north with bridges at only one location, at a point which is today less than two kilometres to the north-west from the Walled City. A decade after the British annexation of Punjab in 1849, the centuries-old boat bridge was superseded by a new railway bridge and then a road bridge. This proximity of the bridge and the railway goods and passenger interchanges have resulted in a disproportionate presence of modern transportation functions around the historic core. A new bridge was added at the same location at the end of the 1960s. This remained the only river crossing for decades until newer bridges were built downstream.

The Walled City's nature as a compact historic urban area was endangered as soon as rail and road transportation links began to support a post-colonial industrial economy in the 1960s. This accompanied a breakdown of craft and small-scale manufacturing and commerce and the slow dismantling of the associated social and economic structures that were vital components of the urban ecology of old Lahore. The proximity to Lahore railway station (established in 1859) and to the national highway system, together with the perennial inadequacy of planning for land use/transportation at the scale of Greater Lahore, has strengthened the nexus between the transportation sector around the Walled City and the growth of wholesale and warehousing within the historic precinct. Retail, wholesale and the shoe trade are not only the most visible aspects of the economy of the Walled City, but are also the sectors on which most people depend either directly or indirectly for their livelihoods.

The disequilibrium in how Lahore houses its citizens was evoked on pp. 34–51. While Lahore's southward suburban development continues and increasingly caters to low-density gated residential communities, the Walled City has become hedged in within the business hub of Central Lahore. In recent years trucking activity has expanded to include all of the northern, eastern and southern perimeters of the Walled City, where lorries are parked throughout the night to facilitate the unloading and loading of goods.

The 1947 riots and accompanying arson left large gaping spaces in the dense urban fabric where the city had burnt. In the early 1950s the Shah Alami mixed-use district shopping area was created under the 'Punjab Development of Damaged Areas Act' of 1952. A major modern road now entered the Walled City, a dual carriageway with a green central reservation, and a traffic turn-around at its northern end where it connected up with the older bazaar system. There was arcaded shopping on both sides of this road, with residences on three upper floors. Other markets arose in adjacent burnt-out areas. These markets expanded rapidly thanks to lax land-use controls and the free operation of the informal sector. New commercial buildings were built, displacing age-old building types and the crafts, products and businesses the Walled City was known for. With little regulatory enforcement, 'commercialization' assumed an ideological colour. Officials in local government even decreed the 'commercialization' of the Walled City in its entirety, a move successfully challenged[2] by the citizenry in the superior courts. However, there has been enormous rise in property value amid aggressive purchases of residential properties for rebuilding.

Over the years Shah Alami became a hub of wholesale trading (with some specialized retail) and its impact has spread across the whole of the Walled City. With its now heavily congested dual carriageway, Shah Alami serves as the central access street for goods into the Walled City. Newer buildings are designed expressly for warehousing; some have their own roadside elevators. The southern end of Shah Alami offers an abundance of services, including food outlets. Close to Lohari Gate, there is also a

Above, shop encroachments obscuring Circular Garden along the south-eastern reaches of Circular Road.

Below, commercial activities in Rim Market, located east of Lahore Fort.

market in Circular Garden for opticians and lens makers. The area just outside Lohari Gate has also been the traditional venue of shops making and selling fresh flower garlands.

Apart from warehousing, manufacturing also dominates parts of the Walled City and generally tends to occupy basements and ground floors within older buildings. Various types of goods are produced – the most prevalent being leather and synthetic shoes. The term 'shoe market' in effect refers collectively to the wholesale market for raw material, 'cottage' scale manufacturing outlets that are dispersed across the commercial and residential localities in the Walled City, and warehouses and retail outlets.

In the nineteenth century the residential areas along Bhatti Gate Bazaar contained homes of the nobility of Ranjit Singh's court, and they seem to have continued to appeal to writers, intellectuals and other famous personalities into the twentieth century. Poet-philosopher Allama Muhammad Iqbal's student lodgings are located on the main bazaar just inside Bhatti Gate. But there are already intrusive signs of the expansion of shoe manufacturing in this predominantly residential locality.

Though changing, the south-eastern localities of the Walled City have a more residential character. Its main bazaar (between Mochi Gate and Akbari Gate) sells traditional items for celebrations. Commerce is still relatively small scale, and the pressure on older buildings is less intense. Mochi Gate Bazaar was also the centre of the making and selling of paper kites before the ban on kite-flying imposed in 2007. Residential mohallas also predominate in the eastern quarters of the Walled City, in the areas north and south of the Delhi Gate thoroughfare.

Other locations of commerce in the Walled City are historically significant and culturally important in character. These are Akbari Mandi, established along with the

Left, street food in the Walled City.

Right, inside Kasehra Bazaar. Stainless-steel and aluminium utensils have now replaced traditional copper and brassware.

Shops selling grains and spices in Akbari
Mandi.

city walls built by Akbar the Great, and Chowk Jhanda in the south-west of the Walled
City. Both of these locations are historically continuous traditional grain markets and
are characterized by culturally interesting business activities specializing in retail
grain, spices, dry fruit and so on.

ACCESS TO THE WALLED CITY AND VISIBILITY

Access to and arrival at the Walled City continues to be problematic. The practical difficulty of chaotic and heavy traffic, the time it takes to reach the Walled City and the
difficulty of finding adequate parking space limits the motivation to visit. Public transport has been nearly absent, except for rickshaws and the dangerous and polluting
qinqis. Road widths on Circular Road are adequate, except for severe constrictions
on some of the roads approaching it. But the modal mix and bad traffic behaviour
severely curtail road capacity. In addition, the Walled City is difficult to perceive even
when one arrives on Circular Road because of encroachments and the overall visual
clutter blocking sight corridors.

1   PEPAC (Pakistan Environmental Planning
and Architectural Consultants), *Conservation
Plan for the Walled City of Lahore,* Lahore, 1988.
2   See "Walled City 'Commercialisation'
Challenged", in *Pakistan Today,* 18 July 2011, at

https://www.pakistantoday.com.pk/2011/07/18/
walled-city-%E2%80%98commercialisation
%E2%80%99-challenged/, accessed on 31.8.2019.

THE ARCHITECTURAL HERITAGE OF LAHORE

MASOOD KHAN

In Lahore, architecture has been subject to rapid erasure through much of the city's history. There are two reasons for this. Until the late nineteenth century, Lahore had been vulnerable to pillage, perhaps much more so than other cities of the subcontinent. Kanhaiya Lal[1] recounts a total of thirteen major traumas, from the sacking of Lahore by Mahmud Ghaznavi in 1021 to the last invasion of Ahmad Shah Durrani, his seventh, in 1768. The building of the North Western Railway reflects the heedlessness of the British in wiping out vast tracts of heritage sites in Lahore for the construction of goods sidings, railway tracks, and locomotive and carriage repair establishments.[2] A second reason is the absence of structures built in stone. Brick, burnt or unburnt, has been the staple building material in this region for thousands of years. But the hot, partially humid climate creates harsh weathering conditions. Floods, too, were a regular annual event and played an equal role in the disappearance of architectural heritage.

After the British annexation of Lahore, three local historians began to make up for the absence of architectural historiography in earlier periods. Beginning with Nur Ahmad Chishti, who wrote his *Tehqiqat*[3] in 1864, Kanhaiya Lal[4] and Muhammad Latif[5] also described what they saw around them of Lahore's architectural past, which had lain in an advanced state of decay and had been progressively disappearing for a hundred years. These descriptions help fill in a picture of the missing past more thoroughly than the fleeting impressions of European visitors to Lahore from the sixteenth to the early nineteenth century.[6]

For the period before Islam, in 1882 Kanhaiya Lal identified at least two older temples that he claimed existed before the Ghaznavid conquest in 1021. The temple he called Shiwala Tibbi Wala, located in Tehsil Bazaar, is now submerged some two floors below the present street level. The second one, the *thakur dwara* of Bekhant Das, which had been repaired and renovated many times, stood at the end of Lohari Gate Bazaar.[7]

The still extant temple of Lau[8] in Lahore Fort seeks to support Lahore's ancestral link to its founder, Lau, the son of Rama Chandra. During the construction of Alamgiri Gate and the modification of the western apron wall in the early 1670s, this pre-existing edifice seems to have been thoughtfully pulled into a carefully created space to envelope and protect it. Buried remains indicate that the temple was a large and thriving affair that until then had existed outside the confines of the Fort's western wall.[9]

One of the first serious attempts at identifying extant remains of earlier Muslim-period buildings in Lahore was carried out by Muhammad Abdullah Chaghatai in the

Opposite page, terraces and pavilions in Shalimar Garden.

Above, Shahdara, the mausoleum of Asif Khan.

Below, the mausoleum of Asif Khan, *qalib-kari* (*muqarnas*) decorated with glazed-tile *kashikari*.

Shahdara, Jahangir's Mausoleum (c. 1630) is a single-storey square-plan structure displaying a perfectly symmetrical geometry derived from earlier forms in Delhi and Agra.

Left, marble inlay work in red sandstone.

Right, on all four sides, the mausoleum's arcaded facade consists of recessed inlaid marble panels.

late 1940s. He records the central *mihrab* and fragments of attached bilateral niches built into the wall of the enclosure of an ancient *'eidgah* or *musallah*[10] as an early relic. This was situated at Kot Khwaja Saeed, along the old grand trunk road to Delhi.[11] Chaghatai believes that these remains date from the early to mid-fifteenth century. The monument had impressive stucco ornament and calligraphy.

Lahore's other early monument is the grave of Sultan Qutbuddin Aibak, the first Muslim monarch in India after the death of Muhammad Ghori. Aibak, the builder of the Qutb Minar,[12] died in 1210 in Lahore in an accident. This grave existed until the early 1960s in an abandoned state, east of Anarkali Bazaar,[13] its domed mausoleum having disappeared in the Sikh period. In 1964 the government, responding to community pressure, bought surrounding properties and a new mausoleum was constructed by 1974, to designs prepared by the Department of Archaeology.

Another early Muslim-period monument is the Niwi Masjid,[14] located at the southern perimeter of the Walled City, near Chowk Matti. Although this is towards the lowest part of the Walled City, one must still climb down two metres to get to the floor of the courtyard of the mosque. If one accepts that under Malik Ayaz the Ghaznavid city was founded at this southern point and grew north-eastward (see pp. 52–59), then this mosque would be the Jami' mosque of that time. However, various sources ascribe it to the much later Lodhi period.

Almost the entire repertoire of Lahore's historic Muslim-period architecture thus belongs to the period of the first six Mughal emperors (1526 to 1707), which makes Lahore a pre-eminently Mughal city. The Sikh period contributed certain impressive structures, such as the *samadhs* of Guru Arjun and Ranjit Singh (1799–1839), along with those of Naunehal Singh and Sher Singh, and the small but impressively decorated *samadh* of Bhai Wasti Ram, which has recently been restored. But this was at the cost of some important Mughal buildings, from which large amounts of marble cladding are said to have been removed. Today's Lahore also owes much of its urban character to the colonial period and to the immense amount of construction that characterized the city after independence.

Unlike the majority of Sultanate-period rulers, the Mughals tended to retain their Central Asian ties. These links, strengthened by the memory of forebears such as Genghis Khan and Amir Timur, appear to have been as much cultural as political and military in character. Kabul and northern Afghanistan were never beyond the reach of the imagination, and physical distances were thus surmountable. Lahore was almost halfway to Kabul, and therefore, as a logistical base, of extreme importance.

The yearly travel of the emperors and their families to Kashmir was also often routed through Lahore. The month-long and arduous journey points to how much the summer-time weather of Transoxiana was missed. However, the imperial gardens in the plains also made up for this sense of loss and offered a welcome substitute. Airy pavilions, cool, thick-walled residences and invigorating baths set within the lush vegetation and water elements of these gardens created a residential garden-paradise in the oppressive climate of the Indian plains.[15] Such needs found abundant expression on the banks of the Ravi, around the historic Walled City of Lahore, and within the city itself in numerous *havelis* and palaces, some of which were large enough to host their own *chahar-baghs*. Pleasure gardens doubled as homes and homes doubled as gardens.

Zahir-ud-Din Babur's gardens in India date to 1527 and inspired Mirza Kamran, Babur's second son, to create an idyllic garden on the western banks of the Ravi.

Shahdara, Jahangir's Mausoleum, main entrance into the corridor leading to the cenotaph.

Kamran received his father in this garden in 1530, on Babur's last visit to Lahore. Other gardens on the right bank of the Ravi followed suit and were used in a similar fashion. These riverside gardens were also used as a place for the nobility to rest during the journey from Delhi or Agra to Kashmir or Kabul. The gardens served to launch game hunts in the several *qamargahs* (hunting grounds) in the area. And some gardens were built expressly for people to be buried in. In Shahdara we have three examples of these burial gardens, containing the tombs of Jahangir, his wife Nur Jahan and her brother Abul Hasan Asif Khan, each of which embodies one of the stylistic forms that prevailed at the time.

The river flowed close to the northern confines of the city during the sixteenth and seventeenth centuries and many gardens were also built on its left bank, of which the most significant is the famed Shalimar. Further south, as the river swung around the Walled City, gardens were built along the road to Multan, along the banks of the river. The following chapter (pp. 72–91) treats gardens as an integral and important part of Lahore in the sixteenth, seventeenth and early eighteenth centuries.

In Lahore there is little of the profusion of Sultanate-period architectural heritage that is found in and around Delhi. Ram Nath's view[16] that the Mughal tradition arose from an evolutionary fusion between the earlier Muslim tradition of the subcontinent and the pre-existing Hindu/Jain/Buddhist traditions finds good support in Delhi, but not in Lahore. Nevertheless, a few buildings erected in Lahore in the period of Akbar and Jahangir do indeed demonstrate the strength of this fusion. Akbar's move from Fatehpur Sikri to Lahore in 1586 transported living building expertise to the *dalaans* of the Jahangiri Quadrangle in Lahore Fort. There the red sandstone details in the Akbari/Jahangiri-period buildings reflect the vitality of the trabeated stone construction and stone carving, the use of animal forms and embellishment in stone of traditional Islamic ornamentation. Such architecture had evolved from the early

Sheikhupura, Hiran Minar garden complex. Jahangiri-period development of *c*. 1607. This octagonal pavilion was restyled during the reign of Shah Jahan.

monuments in Delhi built under Qutbuddin Aibak and its integration of Hindu traditions. Other buildings of the period in Lahore depict the continuation of some essential elements of Pathan-period architecture, itself with roots as far back as the Ilkhanid tradition of fourteenth-century Iran. The structural forms of the domes in buildings such as the mosque of Maryam Zamani (or Begum Shahi Mosque) and the mosque of Wazir Khan demonstrate a lingering continuity of that architecture. They have squat domes with low drums found hidden behind parapets, together with flatter four-centred arches, and the use of *naqqashi* as calligraphy as well as wall decoration, even on outdoor surfaces.

Sheikhupura, Hiran Minar garden complex. View from the tower erected in memory of a pet deer, overlooking a large water tank with the octagonal central pavilion (see opposite page) accessed via a causeway.

Left, the Walled City. The central entrance *iwan* of the Wazir Khan Mosque (1634) forms the outer facade of the Calligraphers' Bazaar.

Right, the interior of the Wazir Khan Mosque is extensively embellished with frescoes.

Opposite page, Wazir Khan Mosque (1634 CE / AH 1044). The east facade consists of a large *iwan* flanked by two projecting balconies. All architectural elements are profusely embellished with glazed-tile work.

In the region that stretches from Lahore to Delhi and Agra, in the early years of the seventeenth century this underlying continuity experienced a sudden superimposition of the architectural art of glazed-tile revetment. With a provenance that can be traced to Persia and Central Asia, architectural glazed tiles had long been in existence in the lower Punjab near the confluence of the Indus with its tributaries, and further down in Sindh. While variations of glazed/enamelled terracotta and stone are to be found in pre-Mughal buildings in central and northern India as well, these were rare and nominal. But in the early seventeenth century, a type of glazed-tile decoration called *kashikari* burst onto the scene between the Indus and the Jumna, only to die off within a hundred years having apparently lost its noble patronage, whose preferences had shifted to newer architectural forms.

But, before that happened, mosques, garden pavilions, gateways, serais, and tombs and domes with vividly coloured tile work proliferated. In Lahore, dozens of these buildings, including the famous Wazir Khan Mosque, were decorated with this unique form of embellishment, unprecedented in its exuberance, range of colour and artistic representation in cut glazed-tile mosaics forming geometrical, floral and calligraphic designs. This was a local interpretation of the art of glazed-tile decoration, one that combines tiles in colours ranging from green, yellow, mustard, rust, brown, blue, turquoise to white. In contrast, whether in Central Asia, Iran or southern Pakistan, the colours were predominantly blue and white. Of particular note is the very

Lahore Fort, Sheesh Mahal. Details of engaged column capitals (above) and *pietra dura* work on a column base (below).

Right, part of Shah Burj (completed 1632). The facade of the Sheesh Mahal consists of five multi-foliate cusped marble arches that are supported by paired columns.

large apron wall, the Picture Wall, of Lahore Fort decorated with the *kashi* work in panels with figurative animal and human representations, in some places evoking the symbolic and mythical sources of Mughal power, in combination with panels of fresco, while representing everyday courtly life in others (see pp. 294–309).

In the late Jahangiri and early Shahjahani period several new architectural elements emerged: the multi-cusped arch, "the multi-faceted column with a *muqarnas* capital and a cusped arch base," the co-option of the *bangla* pavilion, and many other features,[17] some of which distinguished the vernacular architecture in Lahore until the Sikh era. Some of these elements emerged in a tentative manner in late Jahangir-period buildings, such as the Moti Masjid. Many of Shahjahan's buildings in Lahore Fort were constructed at the expense of the integrity of Jahangir-period structures, as seen in the manner in which the quadrangle named after Shahjahan bears evidence of makeshift changes in the earlier buildings to make room for the exquisite Diwan-e-Aam. In Shah Jahan's time, the decorative idiom also shifted dramatically towards what some have claimed to be European influences. In Shah Burj, floral and vegetal motifs are used in exquisite *pietra dura* (*parchin kari*) on marble, both on columns of the Sheesh Mahal as well as, and more profusely, in the slightly later Naulakha Pavilion. Sheesh Mahal, the octagonal palace that forms the bulk of Shah Burj, was named after the newly introduced mosaic technique of using pieces of curved mirrors, mounted on a lime base on ceilings. In the Sikh period this technique was used to cover entire walls in the great rectangular hall, and the deep portico facing south.

Except in the reigns of Babur and Humayun, Lahore's nobility were active patrons of architectural excellence until the mid-nineteenth century and left numerous buildings as evidence of their love for aesthetic excellence. With Shalimar Garden setting the standards for elegance and beauty, the gardens that have not survived must surely have aimed to emulate its grandeur. Fortunately, many of the gateways and tombs built in these gardens have survived, though some of them are in the final stages of neglect. Nevertheless, many still portray an architectural maturity and grace worthy of the care and attention of the people of Lahore today.

Lahore Fort, Sheesh Mahal, interior of the south-facing veranda. The pavilion is adorned with mirror mosaic work, frescoes, *pietra dura* and carved marble.

Above, the tomb of Dai Angah, 1672. This is the tomb of a royal foster-mother. Located east of the Walled City, it is contained in the Gulabi Bagh, established in 1655.

Right, Lahore, Begumpura, the mausoleum of Sharf-un-nisa Begum, *c.* 1730. Known as Saruwala Maqbara (the Cypress Tomb), it is decorated with tile motifs depicting cypress trees and other floral motifs.

Far right, Dai Angah's tomb. Detail of surviving *kashikari* tile work on the dome.

Under Ranjit Singh, there was a spate of construction of Sikh and Hindu religious buildings. Kanhaiya Lal[18] records twenty-eight *mandirs, shiwalas, thakur dwaras* and *guru dwaras* that were built during this period while two were older buildings that underwent major repairs. Numerous *havelis* were built during this period too, such as the *haveli* of Naunehal Singh (used as a girls' school for almost a century now); many of these *havelis* were older, late Mughal-period buildings that were handed over to the Sikh nobility. A new neighbourhood of the residences of important Sikh and Muslim nobles also grew up, known as Bazaar-e-Hakeeman, near Lahore Fort.

The character of the city of Lahore today is no less informed by the developments of the early British period. This development began as early as the establishment of the Lahore railway station (1859), and continued until the completion in 1935 of the provincial legislative assembly building. And so this period saw the construction, among others, of the Lahore High Court building, the Museum and the Mayo School of Art (now the National College of Arts), Punjab University and the Punjab Secretariat. Along the principal Mall Road (now Shahrah-e-Quaid-e-Azam), newer mid-twentieth-century additions were also made, such as the WAPDA house.

The grand tradition exemplified by Lahore's Mughal architecture has now almost completely disappeared, although there have been quiet attempts at its revival. A popular form of this tradition existed as late as the 1980s in mosques and tombs built in the rural countryside of Punjab, before they were overwhelmed by a new 'Arabized' architecture, and popular kitsch. Yet there are buildings in the Walled City that have survived that still represent many forms of architectural expression originating in Lahore's Mughal architecture and its nineteenth-century derivatives in the Sikh period. In these buildings in the Walled City, other regional influences, specially from Kashmir, are also to be found. These buildings form the backbone of the architectural and urban values that reside in Lahore's historic urban core. Recent efforts to protect this heritage and to give it new value are described on pp. 152–175.

1   Rai Bahadur Kanhaiya Lal, *Tareekh-e-Lahore*, Victoria Press, Lahore, 1884.

2   A notable example is how the railway tracks to the north were driven through the burial garden of Empress Nur Jahan.

3   Nur Ahmad Chishti, *Tehqiqat-i-Chishti*, Matba' Koh-i-Noor, Lahore, 1867.

4   Kanhaiya Lal, *Tareekh-e-Lahore* op. cit.

5   Syad Muhammad Latif, *Lahore: Its History, Architectural Remains and Antiquities*, New Imperial Press, Lahore, 1892.

6   Anjum Rehmani, *Lahore: History and Architecture of Mughal Monuments*, OUP Pakistan, Karachi, 2016. This recent historical study provides a much-needed compilation of the available sources.

7   Then known as Chakla Bazaar.

8   The first available written record of the legendary association of the city with Lau is in Sujan Rai, *Khulasat-ut-Tawarikh*, (Persian) written in 1669, edited by M. Zafar Hasan, J & Sons Press, Delhi, 1918.

9   Alamgiri Gate is an essential compositional element in the development of the Badshahi Masjid and the Hazuri Bagh, when the Fort's fortified wall was angled out to conform to the Masjid's orientation towards the Kaaba.

10   An open-air enclosure for congregational prayers, which has all the other essentials of a mosque, including being oriented to the *qibla*, and a formal *mihrab*, centrally located in the *qibla* wall.

11   Muhammad Abdullah Chaghatai, "The Oldest Extant Muslim Architectural Relic at Lahore", in *Journal of the Pakistan Historical Society*, vol. XII, part I (1964).

12   Named after the Sufi saint Qutbuddin Bakhtiar Kaki (d. 1235 in Delhi).

13   Ihsan H. Nadiem, *Historic Landmarks of Lahore*, Sang-e-Meel, Lahore, 2006.

14   In Punjabi *niwi* refers to anything that is low, below.

15   Elizabeth Moynihan, "The Lotus Garden Palace of Zahir al-Din Muhammad Babur", in *Muqarnas Volume 5: An Annual on Islamic Art and Architecture*, E. J. Brill, Leiden, 1988.

16   Ram Nath, *History of Mughal Architecture*, Abhinav, Delhi, 1982.

17   For a description of these elements, see Ebba Koch, *Mughal Architecture*, Prestel, Munich, 1991, p. 93.

18   Kanhaiya Lal, *Tareekh-e-Lahore* op. cit.

MUGHAL GARDENS IN LAHORE: A HISTORICAL PERSPECTIVE

SAIFUR RAHMAN DAR

The history of gardens in Punjab can be traced back to the third century BCE.[1] But the history of gardens in Lahore goes back only to the period of the arrival of Muslims during the Ghaznavid era (977–1186). Fragmentary historical references and folk stories indicate the locations of at least five gardens in Lahore from the time of the death of Sultan Qutbuddin Aibak in 1210. All but one were funerary gardens. We have no notion how these gardens were laid out nor what kinds of buildings adorned them.[2] For all intents and purposes, the real history of gardens in Lahore starts with the arrival of the Mughals in the subcontinent during the first quarter of the sixteenth century.

The history of Mughal gardens in Lahore begins with Mirza Kamran. Although the first Mughal garden on the soil of the subcontinent was established by Babur in 1519 at Lake Kallar Kahar, midway between Lahore and Islamabad, he did not build a garden in the city of Lahore.[3] One of his sons, Mirza Kamran, governor of Kabul and Kandahar at the time of Babur's death in 1530, compensated for this fact and planted a spacious pleasure garden with royal buildings. Remains of this earliest garden have survived. It was laid out on the right bank of the Ravi, at a safe distance from the river, and was irrigated with a canal that tapped the river upstream. From the extant remains of its central pavilion (*baradari*), which stood in the middle of a large body of water and which was made accessible through a causeway, one can imagine the generous dimensions of the *chahar-bagh* that surrounded it. The garden was used as a halt by Mughal emperors during their journey to and from Kashmir and Kabul. From Prince Dara Shikoh in his book *Sakinatul Auliya*,[4] we learn that Mian Mir Jeo[5] – the much-revered seventeenth-century Sufi of Lahore – visited Bagh-e-Kamran with his disciples to meditate. It is unfortunate that during the reign of Muhammad Shah (1719–48) the river started shifting its course westward and began destroying this garden. The only surviving part of the garden is the central *baradari* with its high arches and beautiful fresco painting. As the river continued to shift westwards, the *baradari* virtually formed an island within the river. In more recent years, the central tank was cleared, the pavilion was rehabilitated and part of the Mughal garden around it was relaid, although not in the best of taste.

Kamran's intervention on the right bank of the Ravi falls within the period assigned to the reign of his older brother Humayun. On the other hand, according to some historians, during the troubled period of Humayun, another garden of the name of Naulakha Bagh[6] was also built on the right bank. There is reason to believe that this garden survived until as late as 1864.

Opposite page, Lahore Fort, the great court of the Diwan-e-Aam Quadrangle seen from the *chahl sutoon* (hall of forty pillars).

Above, Shahdara. The mausoleum of Nur Jahan is part of an ensemble of Mughal-period gardens across the River Ravi.

Below, Nur Jahan's Mausoleum. The reconstructed exterior of the tomb is decorated with red sandstone and marble inlay, and consists of an intricate marble parapet.

AKBAR-PERIOD GARDENS

This slow pace of garden-building was amply compensated for by Akbar the Great. Lahore became the capital of the empire for the period (1585–98) that Akbar remained away from Agra. During his stay in Lahore, a nine-metre-high burnt-brick wall was built to protect the city.[7] For his own residence, he expanded the old mud fort northwards, strengthened it with a burnt-brick wall and built his palace with Mughal-style gardens within. Nothing of these palace-gardens has survived except a vast grassy plot or *marghazar* (220 × 140 metres) in front of the Diwan-e-Aam or the Hall of Public Audience. The present-day treatment of this area, however, dates from 1929–30[8] during the British period.

Besides a palace-garden in the Fort, we know of the existence of at least eight other gardens that were laid out in different parts of the city during the reign of Akbar (1556–1605). Like Kamran's garden, four of these were on the right bank of the Ravi. They were Bagh-e-Andjan, Bagh-e-Dilafroze, Bagh-e-Mehdi Qasim Khan[9] and Bagh-e-Mirza Nizamuddin Ahmad. Bagh-e-Andjan was built by Qaleej Khan Andjani – a *subedar* of Akbar and Jahangir. It was situated on the south side of the canal that Mirza Kamran had built for his garden. This garden was frequently visited by the saint Mian Mir Jeo, although by that time, says Dara Shikoh, the buildings inside the garden were already in a dilapidated condition. The garden of Mirza Nizamuddin and his houses and *havelis* and so on were located in Lahore, where he is believed to have lived and died.

During the same period, four more gardens were developed on the city-side of the river – though still at a safe distance from its flood plain. These are Bagh-e-Khan-e-Azam, Raju Bagh, Bagh-e-Zain Khan Kokaltash and Bagh-e-Malik Ali Kotwal. Among

Left, Lahore, Shalimar Garden. View through the elaborate doorway of the eastern entrance to the upper terrace.

Right, Lahore Fort, the emperor's *jharoka*, or marble balcony for public audience, in the Diwan-e-Aam.

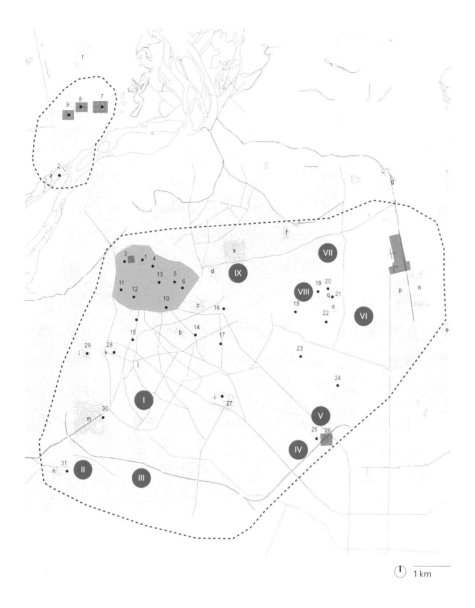

Mughal heritage in Greater Lahore

- - - Approximate Limits of Mughal Lahore
▢ The Walled City
▪ Extant Mughal-Period Gardens
● Mughal Neighbourhoods
 I Mozang
 II Nawankot
 III Ichhra
 IV Mianmir
 V Dharampura
 VI Mughalpura
 VII Baghbanpura
VIII Begumpura
 IX Chah Miran

Mughal-Period Monuments
 1 Lahore Fort
 2 Baradari of Kamran
 3 Badshahi Mosque
 4 Begum Shahi/Maryam Zamani Mosque
 5 Wazir Khan Mosque
 6 Wazir Khan Hammam
 7 Mausoleum of Jahangir, and Bagh-e-Dilkusha
 8 Mausoleum of Asif Khan, and garden
 9 Mausoleum of Nur Jahan, and garden
 10 Masjid Muhammad Saleh Kamboh
 11 Masjid Kharasian
 12 Unchi Masjid
 13 Sunehri Masjid
 14 Mausoleum of Sheikh Musa Ahangar
 15 Mausoleum of Sheikh Abdur Razaaq Maki
    (Neela Gumbad)
 16 Masjid Dai Angah
 17 Mausoleum of Muhammad Saleh Kamboh
 18 Buddhu ka Awa
 19 Mausoleum of Hazrat Khwaja Mahmud
 20 Mausoleum of Sharf-un-nisa Begum
 21 Gulabi Bagh Gateway and Dai Angah's Mausoleum
 22 Mausoleum of Ali Mardan Khan
 23 Mausoleum of Nusrat Khan
 24 Mausoleum of Zafar Jan Kokaltash
 25 Shrine-mausoleum of Mian Mir
 26 Mausoleum of Nadir Begum
 27 Tomb of Muhammad Qasim Khan
 28 Baradari of the garden of Wazir Khan
 29 Anarkali's Tomb
 30 Chowburji Gateway
 31 Nawankot Monument

▨ Known Mughal-period gardens which
   no longer exist:
 a Bagh-e-Mirza Kamran
 b Zain Khan's Garden
 c Naulakha Bagh
 d Bagh-e-Faiz Bakhsh
 e Bagh-e-Pervez
 f Bagh-e-Bilawal Shah
 g Mian Khan's Garden
 h Angoori Bagh
 i Bagh-e-Rauza-e-Muhammad Qasim Khan
 j Bagh-Rauza-e-Shah Chiragh
 k Bagh-e-Wazir Khan
 l Bagh-e-Anarkali
 m Bagh-e-Jahan Ara (Chowburji Garden)
 n Nawankot Bagh
 o Baghicha-e-Mahabat Khan
 p Bagh-e-Inayat Khan
 q Bagh-e-Sharf-un-nisa Begum
 r Bagh-e-Mehdi Qasim Khan
 s Dara Shikoh's Garden (approximate location)

① 1 km

these, Bagh-e-Zain Khan Kokaltash was probably also a palace-garden because it has been mentioned along with the grandiose *haveli* built in the locality called Mohalla Zain Khan, or still later as Maidan Zain Khan, outside Mochi Gate.[10] The remains of this palace were discovered some time after independence. It must have had a large garden as it is said to have had terraces, pavilions, corridors, arches, pathways and fountains. This is the first reference to a terraced garden in Lahore during the Mughal period. This garden had a *chini khana* (called the Sawan Bhadon) like the one in Shalimar Garden of the Shah Jahan period.[11] On the authority of Nur Ahmad Chishti, the author of *Tehqiqat-i-Chishti*,[12] it is known that this garden was intact as late as 1820.

Raju Bagh, on the other hand, was built during Akbar's period in the vicinity of Icchra and Daulatabad by one Raj Muhammad (d. 1606), a rich sayyid of Lahore and a *mansabdar* (a high-ranking official) responsible for raising 5,000 soldiers. Similarly, Bagh-e-Khan-e-Azam was built by another noble of Akbar's court, Shamsuddin Atga Khan-e-Azam. He was the foster father of Akbar and the father-in-law of two of his sons, princes Murad and Khusru. Murad is said to have had his palace in this garden. According to Dara Shikoh it was near the tomb-garden of Sheikh Johar,[13] which remains of uncertain identity and location. Dara Shikoh also refers to Bagh-e-Malik Ali Kotwal. But nothing more is known about this person or the location of his garden except that its existence before 1645 is confirmed by the author.[14]

JAHANGIR-PERIOD GARDENS

The momentum gained during Akbar's period continued during the reign of his son Nuruddin Jahangir (r. 1605–27). As compared with nine gardens built during the forty-nine years of Akbar's reign, in Jahangir's reign of twenty-two years a total of seven gardens were built. Both Jahangir and the empress Nur Jahan and her family had great love for Lahore. Nur Jahan's father, I'tmad ud-Daula, and her brother, Asif Khan, had built palatial *havelis* inside the Walled City.[15] The garden known as Bagh-e-Dilkusha is attributed to Nur Jahan. It is located in Shahdara on the right bank of the river at some distance north of Bagh-e-Kamran. Nur Jahan had a great fascination for this city. She appears to have spent her childhood in Lahore in the palace of her father and it was here that she opted to spend eighteen years of her widowhood (1627–45). In a Persian couplet she expressed the extent to which she liked the city:

لاہور را بہ جان بَرابَر خَریدہ ایم

جاں دادہ ایم، و جَنَّتِ دیگر خَریدہ ایم

"We purchased Lahore, life's equal in worth
We gave up our life, and bought a second paradise".

And this "paradise" she never abandoned – she was eventually buried in the mausoleum-garden she had constructed close to Bagh-e-Dilkusha, which, in 1627, in accordance with her late husband's wishes, was turned into his burial garden.

Shahdara. Jahangir's Mausoleum as seen from near the entrance pavilion in the western enclosure wall.

Fragmentary evidence suggests that out of seven gardens built during the twenty-two-year reign of Jahangir, four were built on the Shahdara side of the river and only three on the city-side, including the palace-garden inside the Fort.

The four gardens that existed on the Shahdara side of the river are: Bagh-e-Mirza Momin 'Ishq Baz, Bagh-e-Mehdi Qasim, Bagh-e-Dilamaiz[16] and Bagh-e-Dilkusha – probably all these were pleasure gardens, and at least one already existed during Akbar's reign. We have already mentioned Nur Jahan's Bagh-e-Dilkusha. This is by far the oldest site of a Mughal garden that has survived intact. Among the other three, Bagh-e-Mirza Momin 'Ishq Baz is claimed to have been a beautiful garden. It is

The gardens surrounding Jahangir's tomb are divided into four squares by paved walkways; each of these squares is in turn divided into four smaller squares.

Above, Shalimar Garden forms a rectangular, three-tiered complex consisting of numerous fountains and decorated pavilions.

Right and far right, the *baradari* of Wazir Khan's garden. This structure now serves as the reading room of the Punjab Public Library. Four towers on each corner of the *baradari* lead to the roof of the structure.

reported to have been quite close to a round hunting ground (*qamargah*) used by Emperor Jahangir, who spent a few days in this garden in 1621. Dara Shikoh writes that his mentor Mian Mir used to stay in this garden with his disciples, which shows that it was open to visitors.

On the city-side of the Ravi, only three gardens are on record: the palace-garden in the Fort, the garden of the mausoleum of Anarkali and Bagh-e-Shamsuddin (d. 1612), a saint of the period of Akbar and Jahangir. The last funerary garden was reportedly in the vicinity of Governor House. It was certainly flourishing during the reign of Muhammad Shah (1719–48) but vanished during the rule of the Sikhs.

In 1617–18 Jahangir commissioned the construction of his palace inside the Fort, modifying and adding to Akbar-period palaces, and in 1620 he visited the Lahore palaces. And here, in the Fort, the quadrangle in red sandstone (behind Akbar's Daulat Khana-e-Khaas-o-Aam) is attributed to his reign, and includes his sleeping chambers overlooking the Ravi. This was a Mughal *chahar-bagh* with a large square water tank with fountains, and with a marble throne (*mehtabi*) in the centre approached by a causeway. Obscured during British rule after 1849, the current layout belongs to the later British period after the Fort was handed over to the Department of Archaeology.[17]

Only three gardens or some garden elements of Jahangir's period have survived. These are the garden of Jahangir's Quadrangle in Lahore Fort, the garden formerly known as Dilkusha Bagh which now contains Jahangir's Mausoleum, and the so-called mausoleum of Anarkali inside the now-vanished Bagh-e-Anarkali.

The building called Anarkali's Tomb would have to be the earliest surviving Mughal mausoleum in Lahore, excluding Mehdi Qasim Khan's Mausoleum, around which Governor House was built. The two dates recorded on the sarcophagus in Anarkali's Tomb indicate that it was started in 1599 by Prince Salim and was finished by him as Emperor Jahangir in the year 1615. The exact identity of the person interred is not known, though it is usually agreed it was a lady.[18] The building is royal in its dimensions and style and was once surrounded by an equally sizeable garden. Although all vestiges of this garden have vanished, its existence is attested by Dara Shikoh writing in the time of Shah Jahan. Bagh-e-Anarkali was the earliest Mughal garden in Lahore that was named after a fruit tree (*anar*, Persian/Urdu for pomegranate) and probably had pomegranate trees as a landscaping theme.[19] The surviving building of this funerary garden is impressive in dimension and quite unique in its architectural features. It is currently being used as the Punjab Archives Museum.

Shahdara, the mausoleum of Asif Khan. The building is surrounded by a *chahar-bagh* garden with long pools and walkways in each of its four cardinal directions.

GARDENS OF THE SHAH JAHAN PERIOD (1628–58)

Garden-building in Lahore bloomed under the patronage of Emperor Shah Jahan, his family members and the nobility of the court. It is difficult to give an exact number of gardens in Lahore that came into existence during the reign of this Lahore-born builder-king.[20] This was the first time that members of the royal family built gardens outside the Fort. Three royal funerary gardens also came into existence. Today these are called Maqbara-e-Jahangir (d. 1627), Maqbara-e-Nur Jahan (d. 1645) and Maqbara-e-Asif Khan. Of these gardens, all built on the right bank or the Shahdara side of the Ravi, at least one was earlier, the Bagh-e-Dilkusha of Nur Jahan who later converted it into a mausoleum-garden. The other two gardens were created in the time of Shah Jahan. With no other pleasure garden built on the right bank of the Ravi after this, it seems that the Shahdara side of the river became a funerary zone restricted to royal burials. Garden-building activities of this period were concentrated only on the left bank of the Ravi – mostly to the north-east and east of the citadel and the Walled City and, with one exception, to the south of the Walled City near the left bank of the river,

Shalimar Garden. View north along the main axial parterre in the upper terrace, with the pavilion known as the "iwan" terminating the axis at the edge of the middle terrace. The multi-tiered Shalimar Garden has numerous water features on each of its terraces.

the so-called Chowburji Garden built by one Tabinda Begum, presumably Princess Jahan Ara Begum, daughter of Shah Jahan.[21] Most of the new gardens were developed by eminent persons of Shah Jahan's court, including one built by a royal lady. It is therefore not surprising that the majority of these new gardens clustered around the royal garden of Shalimar, and its general vicinity. These gardens are Inayat Bagh, Angoori Bagh, Bagh-e-Dara Shikoh, Mehtabi Bagh (also called Mewa Bagh), Bagh-e-Khwaja Ayyaz and two other gardens at Fatehgarh, Bagh Prince Pervez, Bagh-e-Ali Mardan Khan, Gulabi Bagh, Bagh-e-Nusrat Bahdur Jang and so on, to name only a few. Of these, gardens in the immediate vicinity of Shalimar were generally pleasure gardens, while funerary gardens were developed a little further away. These burial gardens include Gulabi Bagh, Bagh Maqbara Nusrat Jang Bahadur, Baghicha-e-Mahabat Khan and so on. Only one funerary garden, Maqbara Badruddin Shah, was inside the Walled City. It is unlikely that all Sufi saints were buried in gardens. We know that the tomb of Hazrat Eeshan (Zeeshan) had a garden around it, but this was not true of other saints, such as Hazrat Ali Hajveri or Hazrat Mian Mir.[22]

Mughal gardens in Lahore today are marked by their surviving principal elements. These may be central pavilions (Nakhla Wazir Khan behind Lahore Museum), a tomb (Maqbara Anarkali in the Lahore Secretariat), a monumental gateway (Chowburji

Gateway on Multan Road), or both a gateway and a mausoleum (Gulabi Bagh on the Grand Trunk Road and the mausoleum of Ali Mardan Khan inside the railway workshops). Only one garden at Fatehgarh[23] has its central pavilion, monumental gateway and enclosure wall intact, though all are in a very dilapidated state. Only Maqbara Jahangir in Shahdara still has all the essential components of a Mughal funeral garden,[24] as is the case, to a lesser degree, of the neighbouring sepulchral garden of Asif Khan.

SHALIMAR GARDEN

The essential elements of the pleasure garden of Shalimar, much altered during the Sikh period, still exist, although more could be expected of the upkeep of some of its important ancillary buildings, such as the hammam, the Queen's *Aranmgah* and so on. The adjoining structure called the "water reservoir" is already on the verge of extinction.

Among all the gardens of Lahore, Shalimar Garden is by far the most refined and complete Mughal garden that has survived. It has been considered as one of the best Mughal creations.[25] Inscribed by UNESCO on the World Heritage List, Shalimar is a walled garden, like most of its counterparts, and was built in 1641[26] under the

Shalimar Garden. Left, view of a red sandstone pavilion in the middle terrace.

Above, the pavilions are accessible via walkways piercing through the garden and its water features.

Below, the exterior wall of the garden consists of recessed panels finished in lime plaster.

Preceding pages, Shalimar Garden. An axial view of the Naqqarkhana entrance.

Above, Shahdara, Jahangir's Mausoleum. The wave-patterned stone revetment on the four corner *minars* invokes the movement of water.

Below, an interior view of the same mosque showing fresco work.

supervision of Ali Mardan Khan at a cost of eight lakh rupees. This figure included the cost of the *Shah Nahar* (the royal canal) that was directed to the site of the garden in 1633[27] from a distance of some 160 kilometres. Being a terraced garden, this was the first of its type in Punjab.[28] It is in the form of a perfect rectangle laid north-south and measures 502 metres by 222 metres. The rectangular enclosure is divided into three terraces of unequal size, each 4.5 metres below the other. The two larger terraces are square and are each further divided into sixteen parterres by means of running water channels, pathways and square water bodies at the intersections. The central terrace is the most beautiful. Unlike a typical Mughal *chahar-bagh*, it has an asymmetrical layout, with a raised central part containing a large pool of water with 152 fountains, a central platform and two causeways leading up to it. On the northern side of the raised water body, there are a pair of opposed pavilions, while, on the southern side, there is a marble throne placed under the shadow of an impressive marble cascade (*abshar* or *chadar*), the water from which flows under the throne and falls into the body of water. At the centre of the northern side of this pool, the retaining wall is modified to contain the two opposed pavilions and a central three-sided open chamber (the *chini khana*), the three walls containing recesses in which flower vases during the day or lighted oil lamps in the evening were placed, while sheets of water cascaded over them.

THE FUNERARY GARDEN CALLED MAQBARA-E-JAHANGIR

Despite the many vicissitudes this garden has passed through, Maqbara-e-Jahangir is still the best preserved and maintained funerary garden not only in Lahore but throughout Pakistan. Covering an area of about twenty-two hectares (471 × 471 metres), it is by far the largest surviving square Mughal garden.

Access to the garden is obtained by passing through an oblong forecourt, called the Akbari Sarai, which seems to pre-date the garden.[29] One enters this forecourt by means of gates in its northern and southern wall. From this forecourt, the entrance to the garden proper is from the west through a majestic 15-metre-high gate built in red sandstone, which marks the eastern end of the east-west axis of the forecourt. In the centre of each wall of the garden there is a gate; the main gate on the west and three smaller gate-pavilions. The garden proper is divided into sixteen equal-sized parterres by means of ornamental open-water channels, running within paved pathways. The water channels were fed by water from four large Persian wells. At each of the eight intersections, there were ornamental square basins. In the centre crossing, there is a large platform, where there was once a *baradari*, but which now hosts the flat-roofed building of the mausoleum proper. At each of its four corners, a tall minaret topped by a domed cupola stands. In the centre of this building is the square chamber with an exquisitely calligraphed cenotaph.

THE TOMB-GARDENS OF ASIF KHAN AND NUR JAHAN

Immediately on the west of Bagh Maqbara-e-Jahangir and contiguous to the western wall of the so-called Akbari Sarai is located the tomb of Mirza Abul Hasan Asif Khan, the father-in-law of Shah Jahan and the real brother of Nur Jahan. Asif Khan had a mammoth *haveli* inside the Walled City, where he died in 1641. His mausoleum and garden within enclosed walls were built within four years by the order of Shah Jahan, his son-in-law. The garden, measuring 239 by 238 metres, was entered through two gates, one each in the centre of the northern and southern walls. In the centre of the western wall a mosque was built, with its replica (*jawab*),[30] now in ruins, in the opposite wall. Both gate structures are decorated with panels of glazed mosaics. The

Above, Shahdara. The mausoleum of Nur Jahan consists of two marble cenotaphs – one commemorating Nur Jahan and the other her daughter Ladli Begum.

Left, Nur Jahan's Mausoleum, interior.

Lahore, the Hazuri Bagh. Ranjit Singh's *baradari* **(pavilion) is shown in the centre with the Badshahi Mosque in the background.**

garden itself is divided into four huge plots each divided from the other by a water channel running in a paved pathway. These channels converge on an octagonal podium with each side measuring 20 metres. On this platform stands the octagonal mausoleum with each side measuring nearly 11 metres. The double-dome above is pear-shaped and originally had white marble revetments, which were removed during the Sikh period. The grave-chamber is entered through four arched doorways each set in a cardinal direction. Traces of surviving, coloured, enamelled, mosaic tiles here indicate that these entry points were once profusely decorated with these mosaics, typical of Shah Jahan's period, with the characteristic yellow colour dominating others.

Apart from traces of a marble dado and elaborate stucco tracery (*ghalib kari*) on the ceiling, the only original piece that remains intact is the finely executed marble cenotaph with calligraphy and floral and geometric designs set in *pietra dura* and styled after the cenotaph of Jahangir in the adjoining garden. The octagonal podium, the octagonal mausoleum building, the pear-shaped double-dome, the bold stucco tracery and delicate glazed mosaics are all unique features of this garden and its structures and clearly reflect Shah Jahan's influence, rather than that of Nur Jahan, in its construction.

Contiguous to this building, but on its southern side, are what remains of the once beautiful funerary garden of the queen Nur Jahan (d. 1645). Here, in a subterranean chamber, the last remains of Nur Jahan and her daughter Ladli Begum were buried. Nur Jahan herself had this edifice and the garden built during her lifetime and hence it fully reflects her taste in its planning and decoration, as seen in the tomb of her husband's mausoleum nearby. The garden and the surrounding walls have totally disappeared as a result of Sikh vandalism of the nineteenth century,[31] followed by the tracks of the North Western Railway which were laid by the British a few decades afterwards.

The mausoleum proper is a square building (41 metres square and 6 metres high) which itself rests on a 48-metre-square and one-metre-high podium. The building has four corner turrets, or minarets, and a flat roof with no sign of a dome. With a core of brickwork, the entire building had red sandstone revetment further embellished with marble inlaid motifs, all removed in the Sikh period. The interior was finished with glazed plaster render with fresco painting, of which traces can still be seen.

The *baradari* in the centre of the Hazuri Bagh is faced with carved white marble.

GARDENS OF AURANGZEB'S PERIOD

With the beginning of the rule of Aurangzeb (1658–1707) there was a decline in garden-building activities in Lahore. But Aurangzeb gave to Lahore the gift of *Sadd-e-Alamgiri* – the 3.2-kilometre-long protective walls to save the city from recurring floods and the largest mosque in the world along with a walled forecourt enclosure, the *Sarai Alamgiri*, which was later on aptly turned into a Mughal-style *chahar-bagh* with a central *baradari*. Today this *chahar-bagh* is called the Hazuri Bagh.

However, a few enterprising individuals in the city did continue to build gardens. The names of at least four such gardens can be discerned. These are Baghicha-e-Mahabat Khan (d. 1687) near Shalimar Garden, Bagh-e-Shah Chiragh near Lahore High Court, and Bagh-e-Mullah Badakhshi and Bagh Maqbara Nadira Begum – both in the Mian Mir area. All are funerary gardens. Among these, Baghicha-e-Mahabat Khan is significant because it is the smallest of the Mughal funerary gardens built in Lahore. Its four walls are still intact. Among gardens of this period, the most impressive is the mausoleum-garden of Nadira Begum – the wife of Prince Dara Shikoh. She died when Dara Shikoh was in exile during the war of succession, which he ultimately lost. We do not know who built this graceful mausoleum-garden in the midst of a huge water tank next to the mausoleum complex of Mian Mir, the spiritual guide of Dara Shikoh. In all probability, this is the last grand Mughal funerary garden built in Lahore. Besides its scale, this complex has a few novel features never seen before in Lahore or elsewhere.[32] The tomb building is square in plan and of two storeys. Secondly, it was built in the middle of a large water tank beyond which extended the garden. The tomb

Two views of the tomb of Nadira Begum, wife of Prince Dara Shikoh. The mausoleum is surrounded by a garden, which was formerly a body of water. The tomb is accessed through arched gateways on the north and south by way of a bridge.

proper was reached through a causeway on one side. At the moment the garden is in partial disarray and ill maintained, and its original appearance is unknown.

THE LAST EMBERS

The last sixty-eight years of Mughal rule in Lahore resembled the last embers of a great dying star. There was no central authority and the weak provincial authorities were under pressure from all sides. The centre of all power was now Begumpura, a fortified new urban centre near Shalimar, and no longer Lahore Fort. In Begumpura, there was a garden called Bagh-e-Begum Jan, after the lady who built it. Elsewhere in the city, the names of only a few other gardens have been mentioned in the historical sources. These are: Badami Bagh (Almond Garden[33]), Bagh-e-Pir Muhammad Adalti near Governor House, Bagh-e-Mir Mannu (d. 1778), also called Bagh-e-Jani Beg, Bagh-e-Sayyid Abdullah Khan (d. 1721), the famous king-maker Sayyid brother of Lahore, the Pleasure Garden of Dai Lado in the mohalla named after her near the present-day Mayo Hospital, and lastly, Bagh-e-Sharf-un-nisa Begum. This is situated a little north of Gulabi Bagh Gateway. It was originally a pleasure garden built by Nawab Zakriya Khan (d. 1745), one of the last governors of Lahore, in honour of his sister Sharf-un-nisa Begum, a pious disciple of Shah Chiragh. The mausoleum is unique in size, plan and elevation. From a distance it looks like a solid tapering pillar only 6 metres by 6 metres at the base and 10 metres in height. The small grave-chamber is raised 4.75 metres and measures 4 metres square. The tapering pillar terminates with eaves (*chajja*) and is further surmounted with a low, four-sided dome and its pinnacle. The only element of decoration is the series of four cypress trees, 2.2 metres tall, green on each side against a ground of glittering white glazed tiles. Saruwala Maqbara, so-called after the cypresses, now stands in isolation. No vestige of the surrounding garden exists today.

Left, Lahore Fort. View of the Hazuri Bagh from inside the central *baradari* (pavilion).

Right, the central pavilion in the Hazuri Bagh is decorated with mirror mosaic work and white marble.

Above, the tomb of Dai Angah was constructed at the centre of a garden known as Gulabi Bagh. Over the centuries, much of the garden has been encroached upon and today only a narrow strip remains.

Right, the exterior of the tomb was once elaborately decorated with *kashikari* tile work.

The handful of remaining Mughal gardens in Lahore are poignant reminders of a brilliant era of building gardens with characteristics attributed to a single dynasty. Hailing from Central Asia, the Mughals and the nobility of their courts who built these gardens combined the Central Asian/Timurid, Iranian and Indian garden traditions in such an effective way that their gardens have become the hallmark of their heritage.

1   T. W. Rhys Davids (tr.), *The Questions of King Milinda*, Oxford, 1890. "…There is in the country of the Yonakas, a great centre of trade, a city that is called Sagala, situated in a delightful country … abounding in parks and gardens and groves and lakes and tanks, a paradise of rivers and mountains and woods." Yonakas in Pali refers to the Bactrian Greeks of the third/second century BCE.

2   Saifur Rahman Dar, "Whither the Historical Gardens of the Punjab", in M. Hussein, A. Rehman, J. L. Wescoat (eds.), *The Mughal Garden – Interpretation, Conservation and Implications*, Ferozsons, Lahore 1996, pp. 2–6; also Saifur Rahman Dar, *Some Ancient Gardens of Lahore*, Lahore, 1977.

3   Instead, Babur caused great damage to this city during his first invasion in 1524.

4   Dara Shikoh, *Sakinatul Auliya*. Urdu translation, published by Progressive Books, Lahore, 2000, pp. 113–114.

5   Sheikh Muhammad Mir, d. 1635, popularly known as Mian Mir Jeo, was a Sufi of the Qadiriya order.

6   This Naulakha Garden is different from the one of the same name that was later planted probably by Ali and that stretched between Delhi Gate and the Lahore railway station. For details see Saifur Rahman Dar, *Historical Gardens of Lahore*, Aziz, Lahore, 1982, pp. 10, 25.

7   [PEPAC (Pakistan Environmental Planning and Architectural Consultants)], *The Walled City of Lahore*, Lahore Development Authority, Lahore, 1993, second edition published by Sustainable Development of the Walled City of Lahore Project (SDWCLP), Lahore, 2009, pp. 54–55; Kanhaiya Lal, *Tareekh-e-Lahore*, Lahore, 1884, reprinted by Majlis-i-Taraqi-i-Adab, Lahore, 1967, p. 34; and Muhammad Saleh Kamboh, *Amli-i-Saleh*, 3 vols. Majlis-i-Taraqi-i-Adab, Lahore, 1967.

8   For different attempts to rediscover the garden layout within this vast enclosure and its results see: Masud-ul-Hassan Khokhar, "Conservation of Lahore Fort Gardens", in Hussain, Rehman, Wescoat (eds.), *The Mughal Garden…* op. cit., p. 130.

9   Some historians believe that Bagh-e-Mehdi Qasim Khan and Bagh-e-Dilafroze are only two names of one garden that was later known as Bagh-e-Dilkusha and today as Bagh Maqbara Jahangir. Bagh-e-Mehdi Qasim Khan is frequently mentioned during Akbar's period. His mausoleum is inside Governor House, Lahore.

10   This Akbar-period garden outside Mochi Gate is reported to have been a terraced garden. But we do not know details of this feature of a Mughal garden at this early stage (see Dar, *Historical Gardens of Lahore…* op. cit., pp. 13–14).

11   For *chini khana/savan bhadon* see also below under "Gardens of the Shah Jahan Period" on pp. 79–87.

12   Maulvi Nur Ahmad Chishti, *Tehqiqat-i-Chishti*, Punjabi Adabi Academy, Lahore, 1964, pp. 874ff. See also Lal, *Tareekh-i-Lahore* op. cit., p. 110.

13   Dara Shikoh, *Sakinatul Auliya* op. cit., p. 114.

14   Ibid.

15   The premises which house the Fatimah Jinnah College for Women used to belong to Jamadar Khush-hal Singh of Ranjit Singh's period. But, in the seventeenth century, Muhammad Saleh Kamboh discovered Asif Jah's *haveli* at this location (Kamboh, *Amli-i-Saleh* op. cit.).

16   Some say that Bagh-e-Dilamaiz was only another name for Bagh-e-Dilkusha. For Bagh-e-Dilamaiz, for example, see M. Baqir, *Lahore – Past and Present*, Punjabi Adabi Academy, Lahore, 1984, pp. 390–391.

17   For Jahangir's own description of this palace and another description by a nineteenth-century British traveller, Captain Leopold von Orlich, see Masud-ul-Hassan Khokhar, "Conservation of Lahore Fort Gardens", in Hussain, Rehman, Wescoat (eds.), *The Mughal Garden…* op. cit., pp. 130–131, fig. 3.

18   However, absence of a subterranean chamber for a female grave in a Mughal mausoleum, as in this case, may go contrary to this belief.

19   Later, several other gardens in Lahore were developed that were renowned for certain flowers or fruit trees, such as Gulabi Bagh, Angoori Bagh, Badami Bagh and so on. All such specialized gardens were planted on the left bank of the Ravi.

20   In *Historical Gardens of Lahore* (op. cit.) of 1982, I was able to list only sixteen gardens in Lahore belonging to the Shah Jahan period. But a fresh list prepared in December 2018 swelled this number to thirty-five newly built gardens during the same period. This number is in addition to nineteen earlier gardens that were still flourishing, as mentioned by Prince Dara Shikoh in his book *Sakinatul Auliya* (op. cit.).

21   Only the magnificent gateway with four minarets and beautiful glazed-tile work and inscriptions survive today.

22   The humble tomb of Mian Mir is surrounded by a walled enclosure but there are no vestiges of any garden layout between the four walls and the tomb.

23   Three Mughal gardens at Fatehgarh were first reported by Wali Ullah Khan ("Lahore's Vanishing Gardens", *Daily Pakistan Times*, Lahore, 15 February 1976), and were then thoroughly surveyed and reported by this author in 1995 (Saifur Rahman Dar, "Two Unrecorded Mughal Gardens of Lahore", *Journal of the Research Society of Pakistan*, Lahore, vol. 33, no. 2, April 1996, pp. 31–50, later reprinted in Musarrat Abid et al. [eds.], *Cultural Heritage of the Mughals*, Institute of Pakistan Studies, University of Punjab, 2000, pp. 155–175).

24   Parts of the enclosure wall on the east and south were washed away by floods and have been reconstructed in recent years.

25   Sylvia Crowe and Sheila Haywood, *The Gardens of Mughal India*, Thames and Hudson, London, 1972, pp. 148–153.

26   However, much confusion surrounds this date. Baqir has discussed this issue at great length and finally suggested this date (see Baqir, *Lahore – Past and Present* op. cit., pp. 395–398).

27   Crowe and Haywood, *The Gardens of Mughal India* op. cit., p. 148.

28   See footnotes 10 and 11 above regarding the garden of Zain Khan Kokaltash. But we do not know in detail how the *sawan bhadon* feature in a Mughal garden differed in the Akbar period (see Wali Ullah Khan, *Lahore and Its Important Monuments*, Anjuman Press, Karachi, 1966).

29   The architecture of the mosque in this space indicates that this forecourt belongs to an earlier period. Some even date it to the period of Sher Shah Suri. It seems to have been adopted as an entrance space for the funerary garden.

30   This is the only Mughal garden in Lahore that has a mosque and its replica.

31   The walls and garden are now being restored. Work is in progress on the four sides of the tomb building as well.

32   The only comparable complex is the mausoleum of Sher Shah Suri (1540–45) in Sasaram, who ruled India during the short interregnum when Humayun spent his life in exile.

33   No almond tree grows in Lahore today. But almond trees were mentioned by Hudud al-Alam – the earliest written source on Lahore: in Lahore there were: "…a great number of pine-trees (*chalgoza*), almond-trees (*badam*) and coconut trees (*joz-i-Hindi*)…" (see V. Minorsky, *Hudud al-Alam [The Regions of the World]*, Luzac, London, 1937, pp. 89–90, as quoted in Baqir, *Lahore – Past and Present* op. cit., p. 2).

THE AKTC INITIATIVE
IN LAHORE (2007–12)

CRAFTING A STRATEGIC PLAN FOR THE WALLED CITY

MASOOD KHAN, CAMERON RASHTI, FRANCESCO SIRAVO

When the Aga Khan Trust for Culture (AKTC) first began its collaboration with the government of Punjab in 2007, it could proceed in several directions. The promotion of a new 'Preliminary Strategic Framework' plan for the Walled City of Lahore could face the same risks and probable predicaments as previous planning documents for the historic core. Meticulously planned urban redevelopment proposals in the past had tried to reconcile two overriding objectives: preventing the loss of the area's economic vitality to severe environmental and socio-economic problems, and safeguarding the area's built heritage. Success on one front might spell failure on the other.

The 1988 'Conservation Plan' for the Walled City of Lahore[1] walked a careful line between these two pressures, while acknowledging the dependence of its success on the skilful resolution of higher-level urban issues that impact the Walled City and the outlying Central Area of Lahore,[2] as well as other areas located within Lahore's metropolitan territory. In 2007 the interdependency of these three levels of urban planning remained as critical as before, with the Walled City having lost more original fabric and experienced more intense economic pressure as a result of the expanding Central Area and Greater Lahore metropolitan system.

Two problems noted by the 1988 plan – the "lack of a socially responsible community" and administrative neglect – retained high strategic importance in any proposed method of response. While the first may still have remained worthy of action, the second was met through the creation of a project management unit called Sustainable Development of the Walled City of Lahore Project (SDWCLP) and later the establishment of the Walled City of Lahore Authority (WCLA)[3] by the government of Punjab. This was a major step towards addressing the serious urban dilemmas the Walled City faces. With the new institutional apparatus in place, and through a partnership framework[4] approach encouraging the participation of international development agencies, public stakeholders and the private sector, a balanced, consensual approach to the planning process for the Walled City was needed. This called for issues and opportunities to be outlined in a multi-stage process, allowing proposals to be prepared in increasingly local, detailed and spatially specific formats as the broader principles were gradually established.

For this reason, and due to an emphasis on a discrete group of project initiatives that could set the urban regeneration process in motion, a report titled "A Preliminary Strategic Framework" for the urban regeneration of the Walled City was completed in early 2008.[5] This report was a high-level strategic plan. It was not a conservation plan, a master plan, or a development plan – all of which are vital aspects of any

Preceding pages, entering the Walled City through Delhi Gate at night.

Opposite page, a spice shop in Akbari Mandi.

Above, selling freshly prepared *pakoras* at a traditional food outlet.

Key areas of interest in the Walled City of Lahore.

1. **Monumental Complex of Lahore Fort**
   Establish interpretative spaces and a visitor circuit in Lahore Fort

2. **Fort Road Priority Area**
   Remodel and landscape Fort Road and adjacent Ali Park

3. **Circular Garden and Circular Road**
   Reclaim Circular Garden

4. **Shahi Guzargah**
   Improve the Shahi Guzargah

5. **Priority Residential Area**
   Rehabilitate priority residential enclaves

300 m

Structural work in an older home taken up for rehabilitation.

urban rehabilitation agenda for historic centres, but none of which typically retains a general, or non-specialized, holistic vision of problems and opportunities. The 'Strategic Framework' redefined the relevant urban challenges and proposed benchmarks for necessary change with account taken of experience in other historic metropolitan areas, and shared findings from an analytical process, identifying hierarchies of issues. The analysis led to the formulation of a hierarchy of responses, some architectural, some engineering, some related to community redevelopment, some entrepreneurial and some institutional, all of which appeared necessary to launch the urban regeneration process on sound bearings.

This proposition implicitly endorsed the view that planning cannot be unitary and centralized in approach with all relevant data factored in from the start, but that it allowed for key planning principles and initiatives to be agreed upon, and for these initiatives to be further guided in their implementation by feedback from targeted sites, as well as further data and planning information received during the detailing phase of projects. Important initiatives would be implemented only after such results were received and final proposals drawn.

The objectives or meta-issues identified in the 2008 'Preliminary Strategic Framework' and the initial responses offered were:

1. *Preventing the further erosion of the Walled City's original building stock*
   It was ascertained that since the preparation of an inventory of 2,800 significant historic buildings in 1988, of which 1,400 were considered worthy of immediate protection, by 2008 a significant percentage of historic structures had been lost to further urban degradation. Loss of this remaining heritage could lead to the Walled City becoming a mere footprint in all but a few isolated spots, such as the Fort. The 'Strategic Framework' underlined that a 'tipping point' lurks not too far off on the horizon. The plan therefore retained a strong emphasis – as with past plans – on preventing such a catastrophic outcome. Proposed strategies would mitigate external metropolitan pressures, redefine land uses, contain/deflect vehicular traffic, reclaim public open space for enjoyment by residents and visitors, and reinforce the remaining residential use through building rehabilitation.

2. *Spatial reallocation of economic functions without impacting economic diversity*
   Already in 1988, wholesale market functions had exerted an unacceptable pressure on the historic structure of the Walled City. These functions had strengthened since then and gained additional economic power from their specialized activities, many of which are unsuitable for the area. This process still continues. The 2008 'Strategic Framework' looked at opportunities to resolve this problem through public and private remedial actions in specific sectors of activity. Proposed strategies included intervening in critical adjoining urban districts to create meaningful ensembles and promoting/introducing retail activities compatible with tourism. If the Walled City is to be a credible, attractive, cultural centre, a process of replacement and substitution of semi-industrial/intensive retail and wholesale activities with more service and tourist-oriented functions needed to be firmly established.

Significant facades in the Walled City.

View of Circular Garden.

3. *Tapping heritage as a catalyst for rehabilitation*

While the Walled City is by definition the end result to date of a series of development events spanning several centuries, with an extraordinary inventory of monuments and urban spaces, it could not be said in 2008 that that heritage had been a dominant factor in determining the course of the city's urban agenda. For half a century, the Walled City had been in a situation of relative 'disinvestment' with more objectionable uses supplanting earlier ones that had greater urban value. While item 1 (above) sought to prevent further urban-heritage loss, item 3 of the 'Strategic Framework' plan stressed the creative use of heritage assets as anchors of a more effective tourism and civil society strategy tied to the area's rich history. Of potential interest and benefit to the public and private sectors alike, the Walled City needed to highlight and present its heritage to its best advantage, as do other historic cities. Proposed strategies included preserving and enhancing the Walled City's cultural and built heritage assets and encouraging private investment in tourism infrastructure.

4. *Assisting the resident communities within the Walled City to participate in and benefit from the area's new development*

The urban revitalization of the Walled City must not leave residents behind as change takes place. The Walled City needs its communities to be the direct actors and beneficiaries of transformation so that they can, in turn, be its long-term custodians and guarantors. Historic cities without residents are akin to outdoor museums. In a short span of time, they become lifeless and consumed by their

Redefining prevailing land uses in the Walled City.

- Cultural Precincts
- Residential
- Commercial
- Institutional
- Religious
- Public Green Space

1. Restored monuments and well-managed cultural assests
2. Improved traditional housing
3. Higher quality commerce set in a pedestrian environment
4. Improved public services and facilities
5. Reclaimed and enhanced green spaces

Priority areas earmarked for detailed planning along Circular Garden.

- Circular Garden - Priority 1 Area
- Circular Garden - Priority 2 Area
- Circular Garden - Priority 3 Area
- Monumental Complex (Lahore Fort and Badshahi Mosque)
- Existing Green Spaces
- Encroachments (Public and Private)

Existing Gates
1. Kashmiri Gate
2. Sheranwala Gate
3. Delhi Gate
4. Lohari Gate
5. Bhatti Gate

Demolished Gates
1. Masti Gate
2. Yakki Gate
3. Akbari Gate
4. Mochi Gate
5. Shah Alami Gate
6. Mori Gate
7. Taxali Gate

Monumental Complex Gates
1. Roshnai Gate
2. Alamgiri Gate
3. Hathi Pol
4. Hazuri Bagh Gate
5. Akbari Gate

300 m

Proposed network of principal open spaces, pedestrian movement and visitor trails in the Walled City.

▓▓▓▓ Principal Public Spaces
—— Visitor Trails
···· Pedestrian Movement
① Connect the Iqbal (Minto) Park as a forecourt to LWC
② Reclaim the Circular Garden as a public ring park within easy access from the city mohallas
③ Create a pedestrian promenade around the south and east edge of the Fort
④ Establish four visitor routes connecting the principal monuments and commercial areas

Heritage buildings and sites in the Walled City.

▓▓▓▓ Architectural Heritage
▓▓▓▓ Streetscapes and other elements of interest
● Gates
① Lahore Fort: implement the UNESCO recommendations for the restoration, presentation and management of the monument
② Major City Monuments: apply international restoration standards and give priority to landmarks located in the Shahi Guzargah
③ Significant Buildings and Historic Houses: impose moratorium on demolition and implement rescue programme

◔ ——— 300 m

artificial sameness and uniformity. Ignored communities, alienated from meaningful
relations with their traditional neighbourhoods, become indifferent pawns in an
urban process fully propped up from external sources, only for urban squalor to
eventually re-emerge. The 'Strategic Framework' recognized that authenticity in
urban preservation requires more than adherence to the original construction
techniques; retaining a sense of the traditional cultural ethos in living communities
is essential to ensuring authenticity in a historic area, and to preserving its unique
attributes and significance. By providing roles for the community in the process of
urban rehabilitation, certain fundamental goals can be achieved, including meeting
human development needs, raising incomes and generating job opportunities.

5. *Advancing priority environmental upgrade proposals in coordination
   with the Central and Greater Lahore areas*
   In parallel with community participation, environmental standards must be raised/
   established (as the case may be) to make the area competitive with other cultural
   centres in Lahore. The strategic report focused on a discrete set of environmental
   upgrade packages, which dealt with urban infrastructure, transportation, public
   squares and parks, pedestrian systems, and better connections between monuments and their immediate surroundings. The Walled City's regeneration would
   depend, to a large extent, on its capacity to master the present environmental
   issues, thus attracting potential visitors from outside the Walled City. In this regard,
   the 'Strategic Framework' report recognized that, without the establishment of a
   stronger, voluntary interaction between visitors and residents of Greater Lahore
   with the Walled City, it was unlikely that Lahore's historic core will succeed in
   escaping the present downward spiral of urban decay. The Walled City's municipal

Aerial view of Lahore Fort.

Preceding pages, gathering for Friday prayers
in the Wazir Khan Mosque.

Right, location of the principal markets
and bazaars in the Walled City earmarked for
improvement.

—— Linear Bazaars and Key Markets
   Areas earmarked for improvement

▨ Other Market Areas
   Earmarked for improvement

Strategic Issues and Actions
• Reduce encroachment
• Lessen footprint of wholesale
and retail sectors
• Deepen engagement with
local community
• Increase variety of products
on offer
• Improve quality of products

Identification of potential heritage zones
adjacent to the Walled City.

▨ Monumental Complex of Lahore Fort
   and Badshahi Mosque

▨ Lahore Walled City Historic District
   and Greater Iqbal Park

▨ Potential Historic Area

Sites of importance:
① Christian Cemetery
② Data Darbar
③ Central Model School
④ District Courts
⑤ GC University
⑥ Delhi Muslim Hotel
⑦ Neela Gumbad
⑧ Anarkali Tomb
⑨ Anarkali Bazaar
⑩ Urdu Bazaar
⑪ Mayo Hospital and King
   Edward Medical College
⑫ Lakshmi Chowk
⑬ Islamia College Railway Road
⑭ Railway Station
⑮ Railway Road

300 m

infrastructure and services badly needed enhancements, with due consideration for its linkages with Greater Lahore.

While the 2008 'Strategic Framework' report did not provide ready plans to meet all the urban challenges and opportunities found in the Walled City, it envisioned a continuing advocacy role on the part of the new project development and administrative framework and potential members of a future 'Public-Private Partnership' endeavour. Some of the issues highlighted above required further deliberation, review of possible responses, and feasibility analyses of specific future actions and implementation programmes.

Aerial view from north of the Badshahi Mosque, part of Lahore Fort and the Walled City.

1   PEPAC (Pakistan Environmental Planning and Architectural Consultants), *Conservation Plan for the Walled City of Lahore,* Lahore, 1988, vols. 1 and 2.
2   Defined as the metropolitan zones immediately adjacent to the Walled City and having a historic developmental relationship to the latter.

3   Required to be established by the 'Walled City of Lahore Act' of 2012.
4   A 'Public-Private Partnership Framework Agreement' was put in place between the government of Punjab and AKTC in mid-2007, complementing already existing programmes for Municipal Services Improvement Projects in Punjab with the World Bank.

5   Aga Khan Trust for Culture/Aga Khan Cultural Service-Pakistan, *The Lahore Walled City, A Preliminary Strategic Framework,* Geneva/Lahore, 2008.

DOCUMENTATION OF THE WALLED CITY

MASOOD KHAN, FATIMAH KHAN

When the Aga Khan Trust for Culture (AKTC) and its local affiliate the Aga Khan Cultural Service-Pakistan (AKCS-P) began work in Lahore in 2007, a matter of immediate concern was the collection of cartographic data and surveys of the Walled City. A special assignment was tasked by the World Bank staff in Islamabad for the collection of all relevant data that existed on the Walled City. Maps, reports, planning documents from the past, documents pertaining to contracts awarded in the past for infrastructure development in the Walled City, and books were collected. A repository of this information was created in the project management unit and is today a part of the Walled City of Lahore Authority (WCLA) office. Subsequently, AKCS-P carried out their own research in the Punjab Public Library and in the Punjab Archives, unearthing certain interesting documents and facts.

There has been a significant absence of adequate cartographic material from the period after 1947. Except for the plane-table survey carried out by the Lahore Development Authority (LDA) in 1986, there has been no serious attempt to establish a cadastral database of land holdings in the Walled City. In 1986–88 PEPAC (Pakistan Environmental Planning and Architectural Consultants) had used paper *masawees* obtained from the Lahore municipal corporation which were tabloid-sized part-plans of the Walled City to a 1:240 scale (1 inch = 20 feet) prepared in 1945, but by 2007 these were lost, alleged to have been destroyed in a fire incident in the district registrar's office. However, the World Bank-sponsored collection of documentary data mentioned above did discover an extremely weathered and damaged cloth-bound survey of the Walled City prepared in 1907. This was to a 1:480 scale (1 inch = 40 feet), and was promptly photographed. It was particularly useful in synthesizing those parts of the Walled City that had been damaged in the 1947 riots.

PLOT AND BUILDING SURVEY

In the autumn of 2007 a plot and building survey was begun in the Walled City. The aim of this survey was to create a comprehensive baseline database of land parcels. Over a period of eighteen months, a team of young architects and engineers surveyed and photographed close to 22,000 land parcels. At the time, paper forms were used in the field to record several characteristics including existing land use, presumed original usage, approximate period of construction, architectural merit, building typology, structural condition, the number of storeys, and encroachments onto the public right of way. Property ownership and whether single or multiple families occupied buildings were also recorded. A separate data entry and data cleaning team

Opposite page, view through Chitta Gate, the axial entrance into the Wazir Khan Chowk. Shops currently occupy the gate.

Above, EDM topographic surveying of the Walled City.

Above, topographic survey of the Walled City.

Below, proposed pedestrian visitor routes seen in relation to principal monumental sites.

-- Proposed pedestrian tourist routes
■ Areas of historic importance
 1 Badshahi Mosque
 2 Lahore Fort
 3 Ali Park
 4 Pani Wala Talaab
 5 Begum Shahi/Maryam Zamani Mosque & Teja Singh Haveli
 6 Rung Mahal
 7 Baoli Bagh & Sunehri Mosque
 8 Wazir Khan Mosque
 9 Shahi Hammam
 10 Chohatta Mufti Baqar
 11 Chock Nawab Sb Haveli
 12 Masjid Saleh Kamboh
 13 Nevi Masjid
 14 Mohalla Maulian
 15 Chowk Sootar Mandi
 16 Lohari
 17 Unchi Masjid
 18 Chowk Jhanda & Naunehal Singh Haveli
 19 Allama Mohammad Iqbal's residence
 20 Bazaar-e-Hakeeman

complemented field data collection, along with on-site verification. Data entry took place simultaneously via a customized online data entry form. Data on each land parcel along with their photographs could be retrieved with a unique identification number based on the property numbering system created by the British-period municipality in Lahore, and which is still in use.

Delhi Gate Bazaar, part of the Shahi Guzargah after completion of the pilot project.

THE TOPOGRAPHIC SURVEY OF THE WALLED CITY
At the same time, to create an up-to-date record of the Walled City in its current condition, a topographic survey was initiated using state-of-the-art electronic distance measuring (EDM) instruments. This resulted in a survey of ± 3-millimetre accuracy providing data on land elevation profile, street rights of way and encroachments (mainly street-level and upper-floor projections into the right of way), length occupied by each property on the street, utility lines and appurtenances (manholes, poles,

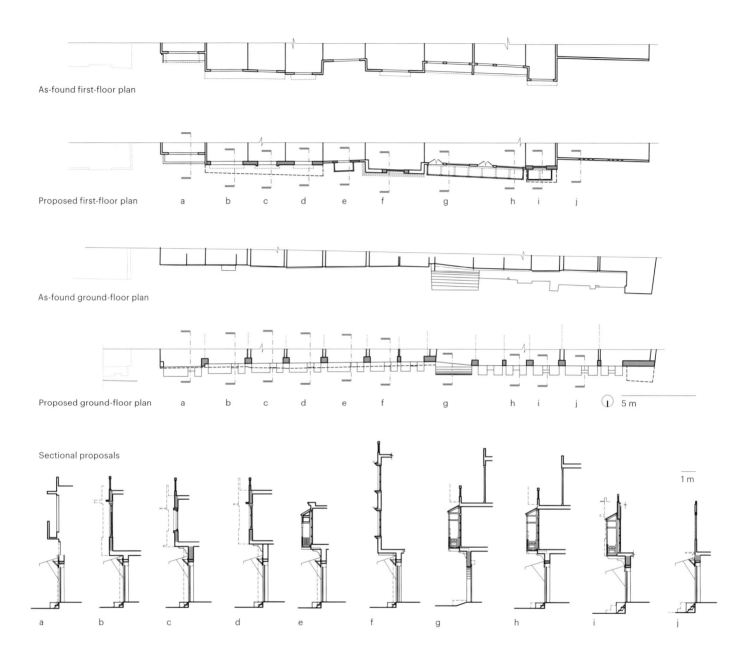

As-found first-floor plan

Proposed first-floor plan   a   b   c   d   e   f   g   h   i   j

As-found ground-floor plan

Proposed ground-floor plan   a   b   c   d   e   f   g   h   i   j   ① 5 m

Sectional proposals

1 m

a   b   c   d   e   f   g   h   i   j

Facade improvement in the Delhi Gate Bazaar, part of the Shahi Guzargah. As-found and proposed ground-floor and first-floor plans, and sectional proposals for specific buildings.

transformers) of electricity, water supply, sewerage and open drains, telecom and natural gas, as well as data on the toponymy of the Walled City. This topographic survey was completed in 2010 and is based on a CAD platform and scalable at different scales. Due to constraints of time and lack of necessary administrative arrangements, it was not possible to record the geometric properties of individual parcels of land. Data for these was obtained from the older plane-table survey carried out by the LDA, in 1986, and incorporated into the topographic survey.

In view of the high density of daytime traffic, the survey was carried out between the hours of 22:00 and 07:00. Security staff of the Sustainable Development of the Walled City of Lahore Project (SDWCLP; the predecessor of the WCLA) accompanied the joint surveyors' team, which averaged between six and ten people.

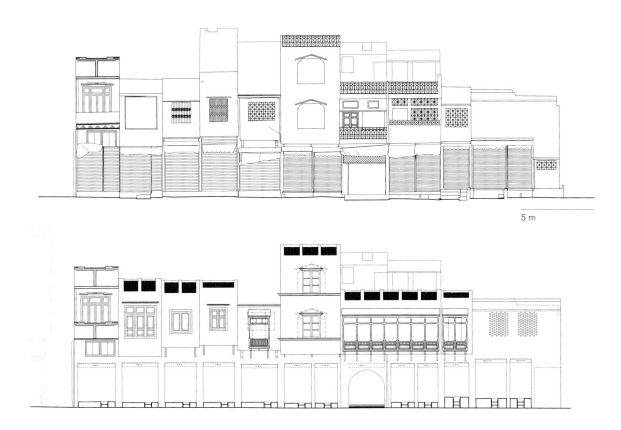

5 m

LAND USE AND OTHER ANALYTICAL MAPS

Data from the plot and building and topographic surveys were transferred to a GIS platform to produce a series of analytical maps describing the existing land-use conditions in the Walled City, as well as differential land use by type and scale of commerce or production. Other permutations of the conditions in the Walled City as recorded in the plot and building survey were also represented cartographically. These included the spatial distribution of the architectural merit of individual buildings, analysis of structural and infrastructure conditions and so on. The AKTC team was also able to use this database for the identification of twenty-four Zones of Special Value (ZSVs) in the Walled City as required by the 'Walled City of Lahore Act' of 2012. These twenty-four zones are divided into six main groups.

The GIS platform also allowed the database to be used for the integrated design of utility infrastructure carried out by AKTC consultants. This 'conceptual' design of infrastructure used the topographic survey as well as the plot and building database to generate several important methodological interpretations: for example, an elevation profile of the Walled City, the delineation of several watersheds in the Walled City which enable gravity-based disposal of rainwater and sewerage, the calculation of utility demand based on present and future land use and occupational densities, the distribution of high-, medium- and low-tension distribution network for electricity, the telecom network and the natural gas network, all of which were projected in an integrated framework of development in six different phases spread over a twenty-year time frame.

THE SHAHI GUZARGAH PILOT PROJECT AND THE DEMONSTRATION PROJECT

The Shahi Guzargah pilot project began mainly as an infrastructure project, but became an urban conservation and rehabilitation project. A principal component of this was the rehabilitation of the much-mutilated bazaar and street facades. To create

Delhi Gate Bazaar. Documentation of as-found condition of shops (above), as well as proposed improvements (below).

111

an in-depth understanding of the nature of historic urban fabric conservation, a demonstration project for the fine-grain conservation of the urban fabric was devised. The demonstration project was used to generate the necessary methodological and technical precedence for the main and much larger pilot rehabilitation project.

The demonstration project comprised two distinct pieces of the urban fabric located on opposite sides of Delhi Gate Bazaar. These included a relatively lower-income resident population where very few of the buildings that had not been already reconstructed were in a robust condition. The first one was on the northern side and consisted of Gali Surjan Singh and its cul-de-sac offshoot, Koocha Charkh Garan. This involved a total of twenty-six buildings accommodating thirty-two households. The second part of the demonstration project was Mohammadi Mohalla, which contained thirty-three buildings and some eighty families living in abject conditions in dilapidated structures. In both these streets the infrastructure was failing, a condition that was representative of the Walled City as a whole. Architects from SDWCLP and AKCS-P carried out house-to-house documentation of the two components of the demonstration project. Initially this was done with hand-measured triangulation. At this stage, young unemployed people from the neighbourhood were taught how to hand measure buildings and use a computer to transcribe the hand measurement to a CAD platform. In the process, the young residents of these mohallas became computer literate, and eventually became economically productive members of their households, some even joining the WCLA and AKCS-P as regular employees.

EDM instruments were added later to augment this documentation for creating cross sections of the buildings. For documenting the external facades, orthorectification photography and EDM measurement were used to create CAD drawings. However, the extreme distortions in the photographs due to the narrow width of the streets and lanes (at times just 1.2 metres wide) restricted this to a combination of methods, such as hand measurement of facade elements from scaffolding that had been erected.

Most aspects of the experience gained in documentation in the demonstration project were applied to the larger Shahi Guzargah pilot project. A particular challenge was the documentation of the bazaar facades. Here, as well as in the small lanes,

Above, work being carried out on the modest historic homes in Koocha Charkh Garan.

Right, the urban fabric of Gali Surjan Singh, Koocha Charkh Garan and Mohammadi Mohalla shown in the context of nearby streets and the Delhi Gate Bazaar.

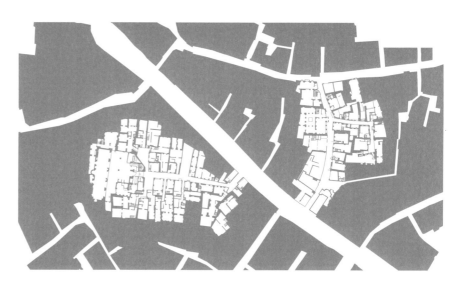

10 m

power lines were a major hazard. Scaffoldings were erected where hand measurement had to be carried out. The scaffolding pipes were fitted with rubber sleeves to protect the survey teams and the workers from possible electrocution. In the event, the detail at which the documentation was carried out also helped record the inadequate technical and visual qualities of the utility infrastructure.

The survey of bazaar facades was carried out in the early morning hours before the shops opened at about 10:00 by a team of eight architects using photographic recordings and electronic distance measuring (EDM) instruments. Facades on both sides of the bazaar measuring 1,544 linear metres were documented. The documentation not only covered the as-found state of buildings along the bazaar but also formed the basis for developing subsequent design proposals for the streetscape as a whole, which was carried out in collaboration with the property and business owners and other stakeholders. The survey and the documentation of homes, facades and suchlike created excellent opportunities for interacting with the communities who lived in and used the buildings and the public spaces, in particular as the exercise could be linked to an immediate objective – that of the larger project which was programmed to start at the end of the survey. This created confidence in the citizens and merchants of the Walled City and helped reduce the chronic scepticism that prevailed among them. This methodology of working with the stakeholders continues, as the

One of the large *havelis* in the Walled City which can profit by the expertise generated by work in Gali Surjan Singh and Koocha Charkh Garan.

Above, recording 3D documentation with an EDM total station.

Opposite page, the Wazir Khan Mosque. Above, documentation of the eastern facade (as-found condition). Below, monitoring and documentation of the tilt in the vertical alignment of the minarets.

experience of the pilot project documentation has been applied to the WCLA's new Bhatti to Taxali Gate project, which will cover a distinct second phase of infrastructure development and urban rehabilitation in the Walled City.

The GIS platform mentioned above was also used to identify and represent Zones of Special Value, required by the 'Walled City of Lahore Act', 2012. Intensive documentation was also undertaken for one of the twenty-one zones for inclusion in the 'Master Conservation and Redevelopment Plan' (MCRP) and is described further on in this volume (see pp. 152–175).

Expert documentation has also been carried out on monuments. A particular instance is the documentation produced for the Wazir Khan Mosque, published by AKCS-P in 2012, of which some illustrations are included in the chapter devoted to that monument (see pp. 190–209). Following this, intensive documentation was carried out for the Shahi Hammam, and at Lahore Fort as well, and became the basis for the new 2018 conservation master plan for Lahore Fort and its buffer zone.

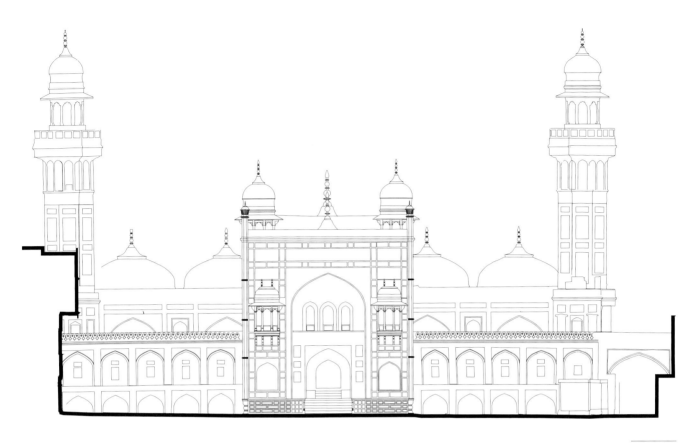

4 m

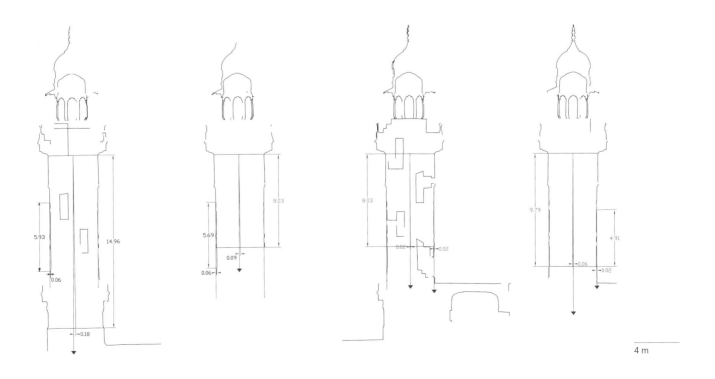

4 m

MAPPING A SOCIO-ECONOMIC BASELINE FOR THE WALLED CITY

JURJEN VAN DER TAS, FATIMAH KHAN

In spite of its declining population over the past few decades, the Walled City remains a densely populated area with up to 650 residents per hectare. There are nearly 25,000 households with an average household size of six people. The decline in population affects the Walled City at a time when the overall population in the metropolitan area continues to rise. Lahore's population stood at 6.3 million in 1998 whereas at present it is about 11.1 million, which indicates a growth of almost 76% over the past two decades or an average of 3.8% per year. The Walled City's population stood at 160,734 in 1998 and is currently 156,044. This indicates a decline of 3% over the past twenty years. Between the 1981 and 1998 censuses, the decline was much sharper at 15%. The influx of a transient population from the surrounding localities and rural areas, who come to the city in search of low-skilled employment, may partially explain the lower percentage of population decline in the past two decades.

Although Punjabi is the predominant language in the Walled City, the ethnic and social composition of the population is varied. Over the past decade the presence of Pashtuns has become increasingly more pronounced. The Pashtun population is mainly linked with specific trades. Notwithstanding the traditional identities associated with the Walled City, a relatively significant portion of the population lives below the poverty line. The population of the Walled City is relatively young, with close to half below the age of twenty-two. Primary school children constitute a significant proportion of those enrolled in educational institutions. Except for a few cases, schools in the Walled City tend to be in congested neighbourhoods and lack facilities such as playgrounds. In a number of cases, classrooms are significantly overcrowded. Occupations among residents are likely to be associated with self or daily wage employment in the commercial enterprises that are concentrated inside the Walled City. Most households are indebted to varying degrees and are at times in need of having to borrow money to meet daily or medical expenses. Women who are engaged in income-generating activities do so primarily from their home-base.

Many households do not have access to adequate sanitary facilities. A survey to ascertain the quality of potable water was carried out in 2008. Water samples were collected from public and private taps and from tube wells that supplied water to the Walled City. Over 95% of the samples showed alarmingly high levels of microbiological content. At the time, the average per capita consumption of water was thirteen litres per day. Water scarcity is further exacerbated by frequent or extended power cuts. As a result, residents have come to rely on private online water pumps that syphon off water from public mains – thus intensifying the overall shortage in the

Opposite page, the Naunehal Singh Haveli inside Mori Gate has housed the Victoria Girls High School since 1887.

Above, one of the *dalaans* of the *haveli* has been adapted into a classroom.

Concentration of residential buildings per quarter hectare in the Walled City.

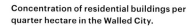

- 1-9
- 10-20
- 21-30
- 31-49

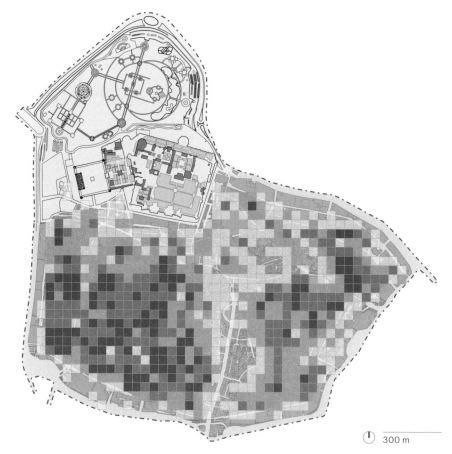

300 m

Commercial land use per quarter hectare in the Walled City.

- 1-8
- 9-23
- 24-50
- 51-98

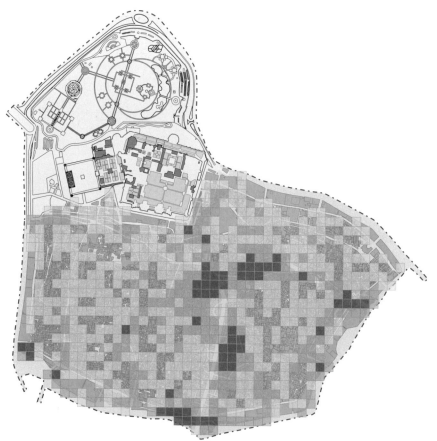

water supply network. Anecdotal evidence suggests that, as soon as financial means permit relocation, households tend to move out of the Walled City in search of better living conditions elsewhere in Lahore. Only in those areas of the Walled City that have undergone a radical overhaul of urban service provisions, such as the kind undertaken in the Delhi Gate Bazaar area and the residential mohallas around it as part of the Pilot Urban Rehabilitation and Infrastructure Improvement Project, have living conditions improved.

Socio-economic conditions in the historic core are better understood if seen in relation to the presence of commercial markets that are situated in or around the Walled City. These provide a flexible source of employment for the underprivileged population that does not have access to good-quality education or better-paid employment opportunities. Some examples include the wholesale shoe and cloth markets, all of which have regional or even national importance. Since shoes are primarily manufactured by hand, labour constitutes an important factor of production –

The Delhi Gate Bazaar at night.

Preceding pages, the Vaan Mandi in the Walled City. An artisan weaving the base of a *charpai*.

Above, an enterprise specializing in traditional men's shoes.

readily available in the Walled City from low-income populations. Training in this activity starts from a young age. For those not from Lahore, it is common for a group of people engaged in the same profession to share accommodation in the Walled City in order to be close to the workplace. Whereas raw materials for shoes are likely to be sold wholesale in Shah Alami, the assembly of different parts of a shoe takes place in the basements or ground floors of dwellings or within older houses or *havelis*. Low capital investments and a relatively high mark-up, as well as access to regional transportation networks, contribute to the widespread presence of shoe manufacturing in the Walled City.

The Azam and Pakistan cloth markets were established in the 1950s and 1960s in parts of the Walled City that were destroyed in 1947. Both markets are examples of state-induced commercialization of the Walled City. Both markets have grown significantly over time and have eaten into the historic residential fabric. Preliminary inferences from existing land use in the Walled City suggest a positive correlation between increasingly commercialized land parcels, through the expansion of specialized markets, and the loss of the residential population historically associated with the Walled City. Out-migration is likely to be higher in localities that are near Shah Alami or the Azam and Pakistan cloth markets as well as Moti Bazaar.

The presence of transportation services and facilities, such as goods-forwarding agencies and long-haul trucks, lorries, pick-up vans and so on, sustains a diverse range of activities that complement the predominant trades. The truck terminus stretches along the northern, eastern and southern fringe of Circular Garden and Circular Road, where lorries are parked all night for the unloading and loading of goods. Together, the commerce and transportation activities constitute a sizeable presence in terms of the land parcels occupied, thus obliterating the boundary between the historic core and its immediate vicinity. Transportation-related services and wholesale markets have driven an increase in the number of warehouses inside the Walled City. These vary in size from single rooms within residential buildings, usually the ground floor, to multi-storey buildings. In 1988 warehousing was identified as the most pervasive activity in the Walled City. Its sustained growth over time has affected the ability of residents to negotiate the use of both public and semi-private spaces daily. Owing to significant price differentials between residential and commercial land parcels, it is worthwhile for traders to acquire and amalgamate traditional residential structures with small footprints and convert these into higher-density buildings that accommodate wholesale activities and storage of goods. Plazas are further constructed in a manner that takes on entire sections of streets, thereby blocking passageways into residential cul-de-sacs.

The traders represent a dominant and well-organized interest group that dictates the nature of the land use in the Walled City where economic gains can be made. However, such gains do not necessarily contribute to the well-being of the residents. The concentration of specific activities in otherwise densely populated neighbourhoods negatively impacts the environment through the production of industrial effluent and other types of waste. In this context shoe manufacturing is a prime example of an urban hazard. The consequent disturbance of a relatively cohesive social network makes it difficult for residents to continue living in the historic core and the possibility to relocate in the lower-density suburbs of Lahore seems more appealing.

Above, artisans working on embroidered women's apparel.

Below, a metal workshop in the Walled City.

Left, homes in the Walled City are increasingly occupied by young, low-income families.

INTEGRATED CONSERVATION AND INFRASTRUCTURE DEVELOPMENT: SOLUTIONS AND DESIGN CRITERIA

DEON PRETORIUS

In November 2008 the Aga Khan Cultural Service-Pakistan (AKCS-P) commissioned Aurecon to carry out a city-wide conceptual design for infrastructure development in the Walled City of Lahore. A twenty-year development programme was developed in April 2010 in consultation with the public and private sector utility agencies in Lahore. This phased programme incorporated sector-wide and spatially integrated development of water supply, waste-water disposal, storm-water drainage, electricity, telecommunication and natural gas infrastructures, based on defined technical criteria and the topographic and historic characteristics of the ancient city. AKTC had already prepared a 'Preliminary Strategic Framework' plan in 2008 that stressed "the need to upgrade and enhance the Walled City of Lahore's municipal infrastructure services with due account of linkages to Greater Lahore." An inception visit to Lahore, further surveys, and a desk-top study of available data enabled an analysis of the existing situation and the identification of several critical conditions.

The city was found to be alive with existing utilities and population habits, making infrastructure solutions quite challenging. The water supply infrastructure was in poor condition. Strategies to address the shortfall, wastage and contamination of potable water were urgently required. Groundwater was the source of supply in Lahore, and of concern was the installation of new tube wells in areas where extensive effluent pollution was taking place. No dedicated sewage collection system existed in Greater Lahore, with the drainage network of open and partially covered surface channels, and piped networks only in certain locations, used for all effluent, storm water and industrial waste. This had resulted in extensive and profound impact on the natural environment, in particular in the severely contaminated Ravi River. The absence of any form of sewage treatment was alarming for a city the size of Lahore. In addition, the drainage channels in Lahore had become the dumping ground for solid waste. Given the high risk of disease under these conditions, it was essential to ensure that effluent is separated from the storm-water system at source and conveyed to a treatment facility in a dedicated sewerage network.

Electricity was supplied to the Walled City from three grid stations located in close proximity. High-tension cables (11kV cables and conductors) and 440V distribution cables were exposed. Sheathed cables hung on metal brackets fixed to poles, buildings and historic monuments. The low voltage and distribution network were symptomatic of the lack of good practice and indifference to engineering codes. The electrical infrastructure posed a serious safety risk.

Opposite page, open sewers running alongside houses still prevail in parts of the Walled City, but, as in the Shahi Guzargah project, they are to be replaced by closed sewers under the infrastructure improvement plan.

Above, solid-waste removal at the Bhatti Gate sewage pumping facility.

Infrastructure development: proposed phasing plan for the Walled City.

Phase 1
Phase 2
Phase 3
Phase 4
Phase 5
Phase 6
Pilot Project

Infrastructure planning zones.

- - - Major Watersheds
– – Demarcated Watershed Sub-zone
Pilot Project

Watershed Zones
Taxali Zone 1
Fort Zone North 2
Fort Zone South 3
Masti Zone 4
Kashmiri Zone 5
Sheranwala Zone 6
Delhi Zone West 7
Delhi Zone East 8
Bhatti Zone 9
Lohari Zone North 10
Lohari Zone South 11
Shah Alami Zone North 12
Shah Alami Zone West 13
Shah Alami Zone East 14
Akbari Zone West 15
Akbari Zone East 16
Mochi Zone 17

200 m

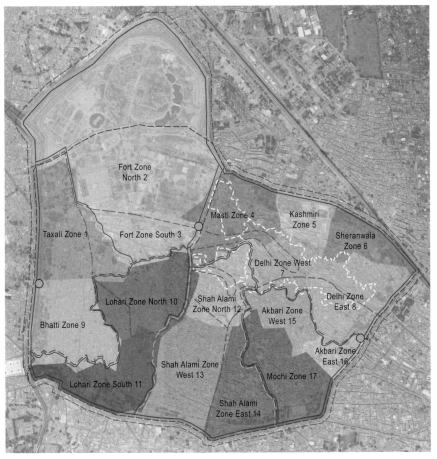

Pilot Project Boundary
Electric Grid Station
Electric Grid Station (to be inaugurated)
LWC Proposed Phasing
Waterways / Canals
Railway Line
Electricity Sub Station Zones
Water Reservoir Zones
Sewage and Storm-Water Zones

Taxali Zone 1
Fort Zone North 2
Fort Zone South 3
Masti Zone 4
Kashmiri Zone 5
Sheranwala Zone 6
Delhi Zone West 7
Delhi Zone East 8
Bhatti Zone 9
Lohari Zone North 10
Lohari Zone South 11
Shah Alami Zone North 12
Shah Alami Zone West 13
Shah Alami Zone East 14
Akbari Zone West 15
Akbari Zone East 16
Mochi Zone 17

200 m

The existing gas supply network was yet another layer of disorder and complexity. Gas distribution lines were underground with regulators and bunched consumer meters on building facades at the entrance to narrow alleyways or tenements, from where long runs of exposed metal pipes fed individual domestic connections. An integrated approach to the service corridors was required.

The solutions and conceptual design criteria proposed for each essential service sector – the result of discussions with stakeholders and authorities – are summarized below. These guidelines are intended to inform a sustainable solution for specific projects and to prompt the application of challenging and innovative solutions where appropriate. Importantly, for details and elaboration, the reader is referred to the Aurecon report,[1] which also highlights issues that are still in need of resolution going forward.

WATER
PER CAPITA CONSUMPTION
The agreed design criteria with respect to water supply pertain to several elements, one of which is per capita consumption. A common prevalent standard at the time was that the supply authority should endeavour to supply in the region of 360 litres per person per day. However, as this figure is at the high end of per capita water use compared to other countries, officials of the Water and Sanitation Authority (WASA) confirmed that water use of 230 litres per person per day was acceptable.

Proposed water supply reservoir zones in the Walled City.

—— Pilot Project Area
① Taxali Zone
② Fort Zone North
③ Fort Zone South
④ Masti Zone
⑤ Kashimiri Zone
⑥ Sheranwala Zone
⑦ Delhi Zone
⑧ Delhi Zone East
⑨ Bhatti Zone
⑩ Lohari Zone North
⑪ Lohari Zone South
⑫ Shah Alami Zone North
⑬ Shah Alami Zone West
⑭ Shah Alami Zone East
⑮ Akbari Zone West
⑯ Akbari Zone East
⑰ Mochi Zone

☐ LWC Water Zone 1
☐ LWC Water Zone 2
▨ LWC Water Zone 3
▨ LWC Water Zone 4

200 m

MEASUREMENT

Coupled to consumption rates is the practice of measurement, that is, whether or not to install water meters. It was understood that, contrary to WASA's policy, there were no water meters in the Walled City in 2009. Water meters installed for every consumer would mean that actual consumption could be paid for by the user which will contribute to reducing wastage running costs and the decline in the level of the groundwater source. The quantity of 'unaccounted for' water, the actual per capita water use and the various peak factors (maximum day and peak hour) can be established. The old adage of 'to measure is to know' is truly relevant in the Walled City. The WCLA has installed meters in the Shahi Guzargah project, and is likely to continue the practice in other projects.

DISINFECTION

Surveys of water quality indicated that the supplied water was polluted. At the time of investigations, the water from the tube wells was supposed to be disinfected by injecting sodium hypochlorite into the rising main. Getting the dose and contact time correct, and the shear logistics of supply to the dosing points at the twenty-one existing tube wells, seemed a daunting task. The plan recommended that water be treated with disinfectant at the point of collection, or entry point, at the reservoirs. As there would be fewer reservoirs than tube wells, disinfection will be easier, with better control established over the contact time of the disinfectant to ensure inactivation of bacteria. Regular sampling at the outlet of the reservoir would be possible and a history of readings would facilitate comparison with the World Health Guidelines.

RESERVOIR STORAGE

The British-period Pani Wala Talaab reservoir is neither the correct size nor has the correct elevation to provide the required pressure. Typically, a volume equal to two hours of the peak hour flow is recommended while current capacity is only equal to about thirty minutes. It was proposed that the Walled City be divided into four zones for water supply, each served by an underground reservoir and pump station. The average daily demand in each zone was between 10,606 cubic metres and 21,354 cubic metres per day. Using the WASA factors for maximum day and peak hour of 1.5 and 1.7 respectively, calculating the maximum daily demand and then applying WASA's storage rule of four to six hours of the maximum day requirement, the reservoir sizes ranged between 9,335 cubic metres and 18,242 cubic metres.

WATER SOURCE
The practice of abstracting water from tube wells sunk deep into the aquifer appears to be the only feasible option available for the Walled City. Other options for water sourcing would involve planning at a national or provincial level.

WATER PRESSURE
It was agreed with WASA that a terminal water pressure of 20 psi (1.4 Bar) be maintained outside each house connection at ground level. For the necessary system pressure, a system of underground bulk storage with booster pumps was recommended. Locating elevated reservoirs within the Walled City is not possible because of both the lack of space and the fact that they will detract from the Walled City's historic urban fabric.

WATER CONSERVATION
The initiatives required to reduce water wastage include replacing old (leaking) pipes, installing consumer meters, charging the consumer according to the amount of water used, installing meters at the tube wells, the reservoir intakes and the distribution pumps so that supply patterns can be established, and actively and methodically correlating the water drawn from the tube wells with the amount metered at the

Above, current practice of installing online centrifugal pumps to boost pressure. Water leakage is endemic in the Walled City.

Left, details of water supply air valve chambers.

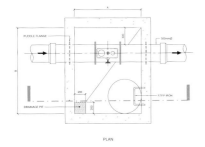

PLAN

PLAN

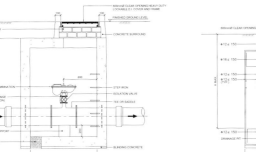

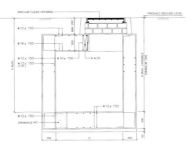

Above and photo on opposite page, sub-standard infrastructure 'upgrading' carried out in projects three decades ago.

Opposite page, above, design guidelines for drop manholes and other details.

consumer-end of the system. A system of reporting and fixing of all leaks in the public system was recommended with the aim of reducing the unpaid for water to about fifteen per cent of the water extracted from the tube wells. Public awareness regarding consumption and wastage will contribute to an informed community and ownership of the scarce resource.

WASTE WATER

DESIGN PRINCIPLES

A central feature of the infrastructure design proposal is the separation of the sewage and storm-water drainage systems. This has already been accomplished in the Shahi Guzargah project and will be applied in other projects in the Walled City.

Replacing the open drains with a modern self-scouring piped system will mitigate the issue of solid waste in the waste-water sewers. The new system drastically reduces the exposure to sewage with consequent health benefits.

DESIGN CRITERIA

WASA has comprehensive guidelines for the design of sanitary sewers. However, after discussions held in the technical workshop hosted by AKCS-P in November 2009, a general consensus was achieved for special design criteria relevant to the Walled City. These criteria involve the use of self-cleansing sewers without compromise and were used universally in the Shahi Guzargah project. In general, the sewage flows by

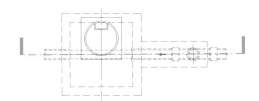
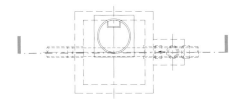

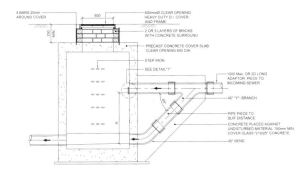

4 BARS 20mm
AROUND COVER

600

600mmØ CLEAR OPENING
HEAVY DUTY D.I. COVER
AND FRAME

250 MIN

2 OR 3 LAYERS OF BRICKS
WITH CONCRETE SURROUND

PRECAST CONCRETE COVER SLAB
CLEAR OPENING 600 DIA.

STEP IRON

SEE DETAIL"1"

1000 Max. OR 2D LONG
ADAPTOR PIECE TO
INCOMING SEWER

45" "Y"- BRANCH

PIPE PIECE TO
SUIT DISTANCE

CONCRETE PLACED AGAINST
UNDISTURBED MATERIAL 150mm MIN.
COVER CLASS "210/25" CONCRETE

45" BEND

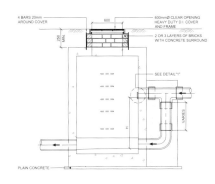

4 BARS 20mm
AROUND COVER

600

600mmØ CLEAR OPENING
HEAVY DUTY D.I. COVER
AND FRAME

250 MIN

2 OR 3 LAYERS OF BRICKS
WITH CONCRETE SURROUND

SEE DETAIL"1"

VARIES

PLAIN CONCRETE

25 75 D 75 25

75 D/2 25

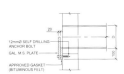

20

12mmØ SELF DRILLING
ANCHOR BOLT

GAL. M.S. PLATE

D

100

APPROVED GASKET
(BITUMINOUS FELT)

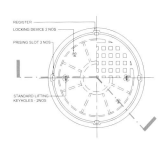

REGISTER

LOCKING DEVICE 2 NOS

PRISING SLOT 3 NOS

STANDARD LIFTING
KEYHOLES - 2NOS

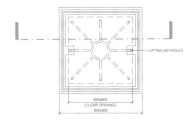

LIFTING KEYHOLES

600x600
(CLEAR OPENING)
800x800

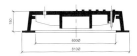

150

600Ø

810Ø

FINISH TO MATCH SURROUND

85

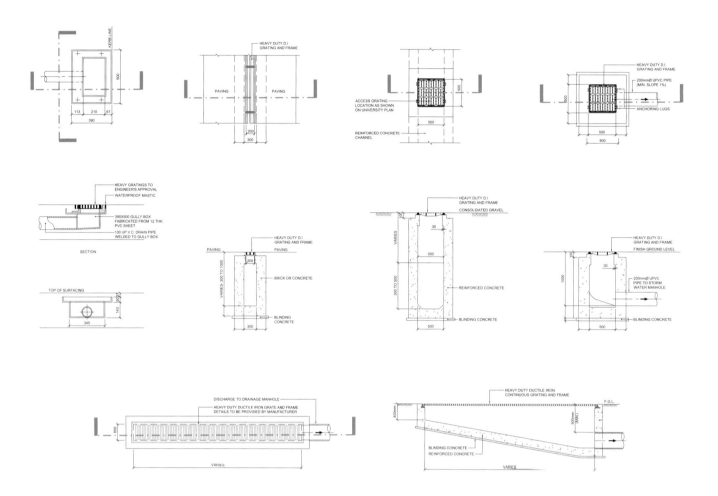

Storm-water gully sections and interceptor drain details.

gravity pipelines towards the perimeter of the Walled City and is collected in an open-to-air gravity sewer (*bad rao*) that runs around the perimeter of the Walled City just behind Circular Garden.

STORM WATER

DESIGN PRINCIPLES AND PROPOSALS

The separation of sewage and storm water as a principal issue has been discussed here. However, a nominal additional capacity in the waste-water sewers was recommended to cater for some storm-water run-off entering the system. Self-cleaning solid-waste grids, to keep solid waste out of the system, were proposed. To reduce blockages downstream, pre-treatment traps at storm-water egresses to capture sand and sediment before entry to open watercourses were provided.

To manage surface rainwater during storm events, an internal underground system was proposed that can cater for a two-year design storm connecting to an external outfall storm-water pipe culvert which can cater for a five-year storm, based on WASA drainage standards.

The Walled City was divided into several sub-catchment areas based on the topography of the site. The pipelines from these catchment areas were designed for a time of concentration of thirty minutes, a once-in-a-two-year return storm, and peak monsoon rainfall. At narrow road corridors, it was recommended that catchment

pipes be sized based on space available, with any excess allowed to remain as surface run-off, possibly entering the system downstream. The run-off collected in the piped system would be drained into the spacious perimeter Circular Garden, and be encouraged to infiltrate by means of large detention areas and soakage pits, the latter in line with the existing designs being utilized elsewhere in Lahore.

The water table is reported to be declining fast, and water 'mining' is taking place faster than aquifer replenishment. Lahore-wide shortage in groundwater is the result of significant extraction rates coupled with loss of infiltration as more and more previously pervious ground surface is developed. The purpose of these design criteria is to encourage recharge to replicate the original hydrologic cycle, thereby reducing overland flow and flooding and also to recharge groundwater levels in the depleted aquifers below. Percolation tests at infiltration basins should be carried out to ensure that design assumptions are appropriate while areas that present high potential-pollutant loads should be excluded.

ELECTRICITY
HIGH-VOLTAGE NETWORK
A major improvement needed in the high-voltage network was an increase in capacity. The upgrades of Transformer 1 at Bhatti Gate station and the placing of the 132kV cable from Fort grid station to Ravi substation underground will contribute to this end.

This circuit currently runs down a section of Fort Road, the iconic road that divides the city from the UNESCO World Heritage Site. As recommended, the Fort Road grid station has already undergone an upgrade. Also, the Sheranwala grid station planned by WAPDA/LESCO to gradually relieve the Fort grid station is now in an advanced state of completion.

MEDIUM-VOLTAGE/LOW-VOLTAGE NETWORK

The problems faced by this network are so numerous that the preferred solution to solving them and achieving a desirable and safe result would be a complete overhaul of the current installations. This would include a new 11kV network, with allowances made for future demands, buried underground within utility corridors, with new 11kV/400V transformers, either on the ground or in buildings, a new 400V distribution network, and new remotely read AMR electronic meters at consumer connections, all designed with an energization and changeover methodology to ensure minimal downtime of services. Some areas in the Walled City still contain many low-rated (40kVA) transformers, which together take up a considerable amount of space. In the redesigned network, already demonstrated in the Shahi Guzargah project, these transformers will be replaced by single higher-rated, enclosed, packaged transformer units (1000kVA or 630kVA), which contain the LV main switchboard for circuit protection of the outgoing circuits, provide suitable protection of all the systems and ensure no exposed live parts.

Consolidating the number of transformers reduces the number of 11kV cables and the area needed within the right of way for reticulation, while increasing the length of 400V feeders from the source transformer using higher capacity 200A cables. The recommended solution for power reticulation in the extremely narrow alleyways is aerial bundled cables, mounted onto building facades.

STREET LIGHTING

The majority of the streets within the Walled City are too narrow for vehicles and need only accommodate pedestrian/bicycle traffic. The requirements for pedestrian lighting are to provide a safe environment for residents. Fittings can be mounted to the side of buildings in small alleyways, to provide light to passing pedestrians, with concealed power supply cables. On larger roads and public spaces, pole lighting may be required, with larger luminaires, controlled by PE cells and time locks to ensure illumination during hours of darkness.

Above, telecommunication and cell-phone towers are usually placed in an ad hoc manner with negative impact on the historic environment.

Right and opposite page, newly installed gas meters as opposed to older gas meters installed with little consideration for order or safety.

TELECOMMUNICATIONS

To minimize a multitude of third-party providers installing above-ground network cables, a series of underground ducts should be installed and owned by the WCLA. These should be buried in the telecom corridors within utility cross-sections and rented out to service providers. Large trunk routes across the Walled City should carry twelve ducts; secondary routes should have six ducts, and two ducts in all other roads/alleyways. Due to the nature of data transmission along optical fibres, these can be laid within the same utility corridor as most other services, including power.

GAS

It was indicated that SNGPL does not reticulate gas pipelines through alleyways less than 1.5 metres in width. This gives rise to banks of gas meters in single locations, usually at the entrance to the alleyways.

The SNGPL restriction on alleyway reticulation also gives rise to gas pipelines (downstream from the meter) being reticulated at ground level next to water pipes, through narrow alleyways and in close proximity to electric cables. Limited comment can be made about the state or adequacy of the underground gas reticulation network due to access constraints.

The only improvement suggested for the gas network is the concealing of unsightly gas meters, removing electric cables to a safe distance and putting all pipelines underground, including unsightly house connections running above ground.

1   AureconGroup, Aga Khan Cultural Service-
Pakistan, *Lahore Walled City Project: Integrated
Infrastructure Concept Design*, 3 vols., 2010.

THE SHAHI GUZARGAH PILOT PROJECT AND AREA DEVELOPMENT PLAN

MASOOD KHAN, MARYAM RABI

In 2006 the World Bank signed a loan agreement with the governments of Pakistan and Punjab for the Punjab Municipal Services Improvement Project, which included a heritage component specifically intended for the Walled City. Subsequently, a project management unit, the predecessor to the present Walled City of Lahore Authority (WCLA), was established for the implementation of a pilot project.

The following year, 2007, the government of Punjab and the Aga Khan Trust for Culture (AKTC) signed a 'Public-Private Partnership' agreement to jointly pursue heritage-sensitive planning and development objectives, including a pilot urban conservation and infrastructure improvement project partially funded by the World Bank. Consequently, an office of AKTC and its local affiliate the Aga Khan Culture Service-Pakistan (AKCS-P) was established in Lahore. AKTC and the World Bank also signed a 'Memorandum of Understanding', which provided a framework for mutual collaboration on the pilot project, launched the same year.

The area of 23.5 hectares earmarked in the north-eastern quadrant of the Walled City for the pilot project had a bazaar spine known as the Shahi Guzargah, the purported ceremonial royal way from Delhi Gate in the east to the eastern gate of the royal palaces in Lahore Fort. Accordingly the project came to be known as the Shahi Guzargah project (see the maps on p. 389). The aim of the project was to develop methods for urban-heritage conservation and to demonstrate its benefits through the productive reuse of cultural assets. Lessons learned through this initiative were to serve as a reference for urban conservation in the Walled City at large. The area of the project comprised nine per cent of the Walled City's total area and was designed to include as many historic properties as possible along the route to Lahore Fort. The collaboration arrangements described here enabled AKTC to provide both technical and financial assistance for the project. As envisaged, today the project has been subsumed in a Walled City-wide framework of integrated area development.

At the larger scale, the objective of the pilot project was to transform and enhance the historic environment with the aim of achieving a healthy, economically improved and socially dynamic human context. Infrastructure development involved raising quantitative and qualitative performance to sustainable levels by adopting alternate and improved design standards. In preparation for the Shahi Guzargah project, AKTC carried out a Walled City-wide design for the integrated development of utility infrastructure. AKTC hired international consultants for this purpose and an 'Integrated Infrastructure Concept Design' as described on pp. 124–135 was carried out. This design and planning initiative produced a five-phase plan for the integrated

Opposite page, view of Gali Surjan Singh after completion of the Mohalla demonstration project in 2010.

Above, as-found condition of Gali Surjan Singh in 2008.

Looking in the direction of Delhi Gate from the bazaar along Shahi Guzargah.

development of primary and distribution infrastructure for waste-water disposal, separate storm-water disposal, electricity, telecom and natural gas, and the cross-sectional design of streets of various dimensions through which these services were to be delivered. Trunk infrastructure for water supply, upgraded a few decades earlier, was not included but water supply distribution infrastructure was to be replaced in all tertiary lanes and streets. The design framework developed was used as the basis for detailed design in the Shahi Guzargah project and has now been approved as the framework for infrastructure development in the rest of the Walled City.

COMPONENTS OF THE PILOT PROJECT

The Shahi Guzargah project broadly included community mobilization, establishing key baseline data, infrastructure design and improvement, the documentation and rehabilitation of street facades, removal of encroachments, street surface improvements, and provisions for fire hydrants, street lighting and street furniture. A number

The spatial limits of the World Bank-funded Pilot Urban Rehabilitation and Infrastructure Improvement Project (the Shahi Guzargah Project).

Commercial
Education
Health
Industrial
Heritage
Park
Public Service
Religious
Residential
Storage
Utility/Infrastructure
Vacant

100 m

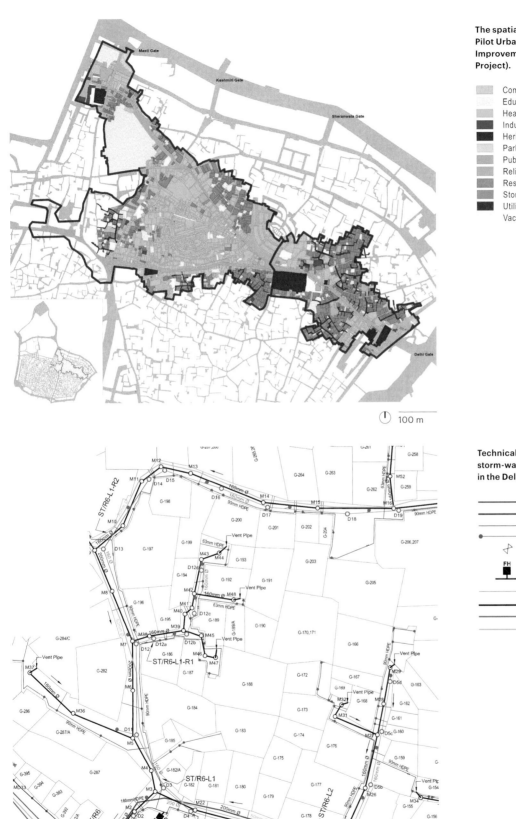

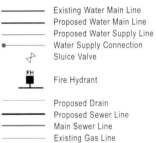

Technical design for water supply and the storm-water drainage system in several lanes in the Delhi Gate neighbourhood.

Existing Water Main Line
Proposed Water Main Line
Proposed Water Supply Line
Water Supply Connection
Sluice Valve

FH Fire Hydrant

Proposed Drain
Proposed Sewer Line
Main Sewer Line
Existing Gas Line

9 m

Above, topographical survey in progress.

Right, one of numerous meetings with stake-holders and members of the community.

of properties of significant architectural and historic value were conserved. Mohalla demonstration projects carried out in two residential neighbourhoods established the design standards and operational know-how for infrastructure distribution in the narrow lanes which constituted a large portion of the larger project.

Working in the bazaar and in the mohallas resulted *ipso facto* in working with the people who inhabit these urban areas. This inherent condition was thrown into sharp relief when certain decisions of the superior courts upon the initiation of the project threatened to enforce the sixty-one-metre zone of protection around listed monuments. These decisions posed imminent consequences to the interests of the trader communities, and protests broke out as a consequence. Drawing on the well-known community mobilization expertise of the AKDN network, the project management unit was able to bring the protesting trading communities on board, and such disturbances have not occurred again. In the residential neighbourhoods, the urban spaces and access system are so tightly controlled by the residents that it was impossible to even broach the project without interacting with the residents and community organizations. Such conditions created the need for an organized institutional presence for social advocacy and mobilization on the part of the Punjab government. The Social Mobilization Unit that was established in 2007 still exists in the WCLA.

Parallel to project preparation, AKTC/AKCS-P carried out a topographical survey of the entire Walled City and, as part of the planning activities, established other baseline data (see the two chapters on pp. 106–123).

The principal elements of the infrastructure design were based on design guidelines contained in the 2010 'Integrated Infrastructure Concept Design' mentioned above. Trunk infrastructure in the main spine street system as well as the distribution infrastructure network in the residential zones was implemented by contractors. The water supply system was integrated with the forward planning for water supply at the

Left, the historic home conservation project: finishing up with protective oil coatings.

Right, infrastructure upgrading in Gali Surjan Singh, part of the Mohalla demonstration project.

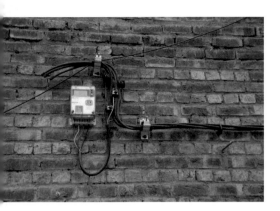

Mock-ups of the proposed infrastructure details were created and discussed with stakeholders – the utility companies and the community.

Above, aerial bundled cables as a viable solution for electricity distribution network.

Below, mock-ups of the new, sealed sewerage and storm-water drainage systems.

Opposite page, trunk infrastructure re-development being carried out in one of the principal thoroughfares. Installation of utilities along the Shahi Guzargah trail.

scale of the Walled City. The replacement of the existing water supply distribution network has resulted in a dramatic improvement in the water pressure, and contamination related to pressure losses and ageing pipes has been eliminated. Domestic electric centrifugal pumps installed on supply connections have disappeared as a result. A new separate storm-water drainage system was introduced to cater for peak flash discharges of storm water during monsoon rains. The electricity and telephone distribution networks were organized with aerial bundled cables attached to building facades in an ordered manner respecting the architectural features of the buildings. All street surfaces were repaved. The design of the pavement was carried out integrally with that of surface appurtenances (for example, manholes and manhole covers). A total of fifteen new fire hydrants were added to the project area. Street lighting was designed and implemented with lighting fixtures either attached to the facades or pole mounted.

AKTC/AKCS-P provided guidance to the infrastructure design consultants through the expertise of conservation architects, technicians and master building trades craftsmen. Currently, the capacity for providing such services has been replicated within the WCLA, and is expected to be augmented further.

In the project area, street facades were meticulously documented and designs prepared for their improvement. They were then rehabilitated according to a facade improvement programme carefully negotiated with building owners, occupants and tenants, shop owners, and other stakeholders. Facade improvement comprised removal of unsightly, recent, reinforced-concrete projections and structural components, and inappropriate interventions such as still joists inserted into the soft load-bearing brick walls. The removal of unsightly wiring after the new infrastructure was installed created a dramatically improved visual environment.

The project area did not contain sites for green landscaping. However, a programme for upgrading and rehabilitating urban open spaces was initiated and is being continued, along with the conservation of monuments in the pilot project area.

A significant component of the pilot project was the removal of establishments that were illegally located on the public right of way or shops that had been extended to occupy a portion of the street. The WCLA's Social Mobilization Unit carried out extended negotiations with the aid of a specialist resettlement and environmental impact consultant appointed by the World Bank, rates of compensation were negotiated and the affected shops were removed and owners compensated accordingly.

Before the appointment of the contractor for the larger pilot project, AKTC/AKCS-P designed and carried out a demonstration project for tertiary distribution networks of the infrastructure and urban fabric rehabilitation in Gali Surjan Singh (and its offshoot cul-de-sac Koocha Charkh Garan) and Mohammadi Mohalla, two small residential lanes off Delhi Gate Bazaar in the project area. This project was implemented by AKTC's own field supervisory staff and workmen. The demonstration project in turn set the standards for community mobilization and social extension services, the implementation of infrastructure in the residential neighbourhoods and their street systems, including street surfaces, and the standards to which historic residential buildings could be conserved. Of particular importance was the fact that the new standards were implemented after detailed review by the communities affected.

HISTORIC URBAN FABRIC CONSERVATION AND REHABILITATION
The conservation of the fine-grained residential urban fabric of the pilot project area became the single most important component of the project, addressing individual buildings and their street facades, the characteristic historic patterns of the streets

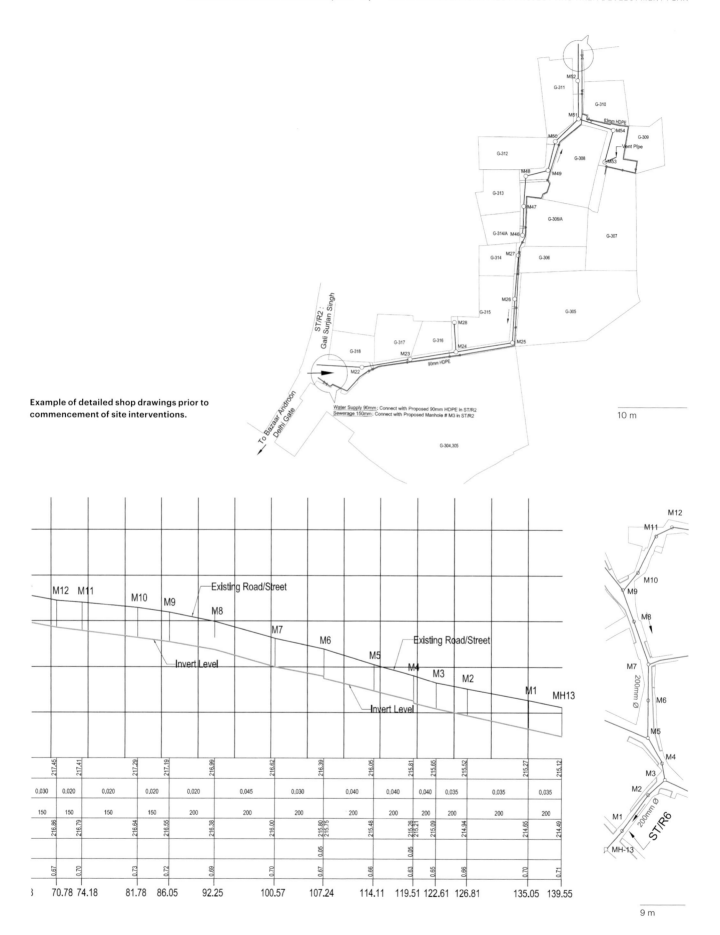

Example of detailed shop drawings prior to commencement of site interventions.

and paths, and the various infrastructure elements, including street lighting and other public facilities.

Residential buildings in the Walled City are subject to a common range of problems. Structural decay is endemic and caused by age as well as by water seeping into the superstructure due to the poor quality of plumbing, and by failing foundations as a result of poor drainage and water supply infrastructure. The improvement of private houses was paramount to the achievement of the basic objective of the pilot project.

The detailed design of infrastructure elements in the small lanes as well as in the main bazaar streets was carried out on a street-by-street and facade-by-facade basis. In the narrower lanes, the distribution lines for electricity and telecommunication as well as service connections to individual properties were surface-mounted on the facades and could only be installed once the facades were structurally consolidated in order to bear the stresses of the physical mounting of the infrastructure. In some cases, interventions could not be restricted to the house facade and entailed engaging with the way the interior spaces of a house were used and altering them. In other words, this involved working in the context of an eroded distinction between the upgrading of distribution infrastructure and house connections on the one hand, and intervention in private property on the other. Nevertheless, working on the facades made it possible for a close relationship to be developed between the owner-occupant and the implementing agency and elicited homeowners' desire to make their own investments in home repairs. The government of Punjab and the World Bank agreed to work under the principle that facade rehabilitation of individual properties and the mounting of infrastructure components on the facades was an investment in the public realm.

Urban fabric rehabilitation contributes in several ways to the improvement of the lives of the people who live in the Walled City. Given the widespread unemployment and underemployment prevalent here, working with the active participation of the

Koocha Charkh Garan – before and after the rehabilitation project.

Installation of a below-grade, multi-inlet sewer collector.

communities of the Walled City neighbourhoods provided opportunities for younger residents to be gainfully employed. The youth especially benefitted from exposure to new vocations in the building industry and the project demonstrated that given adequate training they can acquire skills that promise higher income levels.

MOHALLA DEMONSTRATION PROJECT – GALI SURJAN SINGH AND KOOCHA CHARKH GARAN

The Mohalla demonstration project constituted a part of the neighbourhood rehabilitation component of the Shahi Guzargah project. It was restricted to the residential locality comprising Gali Surjan Singh and Koocha Charkh Garan situated north of Delhi Gate Bazaar, and the neighbourhood known as Mohammadi Mohalla in the south of the bazaar. While funding for Gali Surjan Singh and Koocha Charkh Garan was provided entirely by AKTC/AKCS-P, Mohammadi Mohalla was a part of the larger World Bank-financed pilot project. The purpose of this initiative was to test the proposed urban rehabilitation and infrastructure improvement interventions as well as finalize the design concepts and construction methodologies prior to the launch of the larger Shahi Guzargah project. Additionally, these sub-projects demonstrated the social and environmental as well as visual impacts of urban rehabilitation in the context of the Walled City as a collectivity of heritage sites. They showed that the quality of life can be significantly improved by altering the built environment in a sensitive manner and in collaboration with the primary stakeholders – the residents.

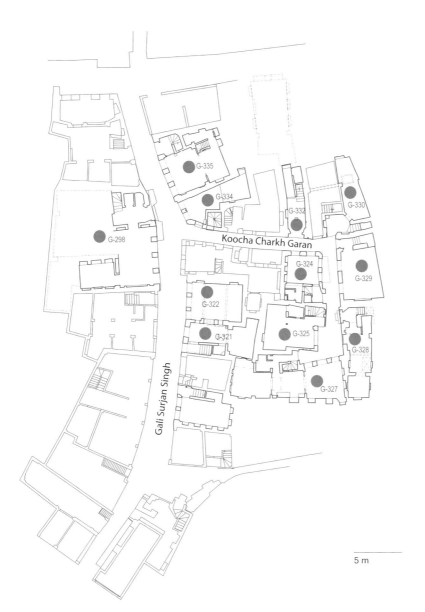

G-335
G-334
G-332
G-330
G-298
Koocha Charkh Garan
G-324
G-329
G-322
G-321
G-325
Gali Surjan Singh
G-328
G-327

Above, historic homes that were conserved and rehabilitated as part of the Mohalla demonstration project.

 Historic homes conserved and rehabilitated

5 m

Below, a new sewer being laid in one of the secondary bazaar lanes.

Existing elevation

Proposed elevation

8 m

**Existing and proposed elevation of buildings
in Koocha Charkh Garan.**

Detailed design guidelines were prepared and coordinated with utility agencies for both Gali Surjan Singh and Mohammadi Mohalla. Following a detailed assessment of the existing situation and the pilot conservation of a single historic house in 2008, physical work commenced in Gali Surjan Singh and Koocha Charkh Garan in December 2009. The project served close to 150 residents distributed across twenty-six households, most of whom were homeowners. The Mohalla demonstration project included twenty-three buildings, eighteen of which were over a hundred years old. Gali Surjan Singh consisted of an admixture of old and recently constructed houses and commercial outlets, while Koocha Charkh Garan (a cul-de-sac offshoot of Gali Surjan Singh) contained mostly old residential buildings that had been drastically altered over time. The total covered floor area of the buildings ranged from a minimum of 71 square metres to a maximum of 445 square metres. The project comprised infrastructure upgrading, building stock rehabilitation and home improvement.

The infrastructure upgrading included provisions for improved waste and storm-water disposal (a sealed sanitary network), improved solid-waste disposal and sub-surface layout of gas pipes, and infrastructure mounted on the facades of the building. The building stock rehabilitation and home improvement component addressed organizational and design issues within the internal spaces of houses and included, to varying degrees, structural repairs and consolidation, replacement of dilapidated and/or dysfunctional installations, and non-structural architectural intervention and finishes, for all of which negotiations were carried out directly with the homeowners and occupants. Intervening at the micro-level of the individual dwelling unit was essential to demonstrate to homeowners the ways in which their premises could be improved. It also demonstrated how tasks were to be prioritized according to degree of severity. The conservation of a single historic home completed by March 2009 generated substantial interest among the remaining homeowners and residents, who began requesting that similar work be done on their homes.

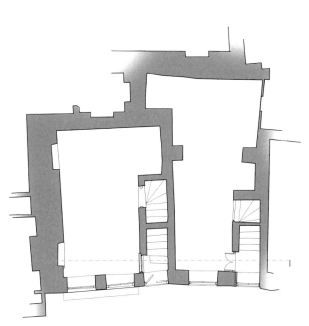

As-found ground-floor plan house G-321-22

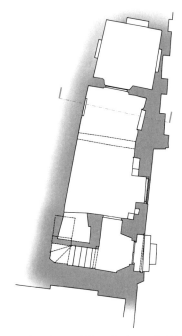

As-found ground-floor plan house G-328

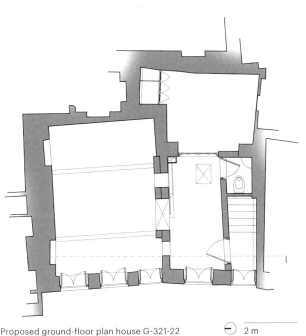

Proposed ground-floor plan house G-321-22   2 m

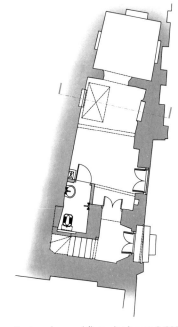

Proposed ground-floor plan house G-328   2 m

The German Ministry for Foreign Affairs provided the necessary financial support for the conservation of historic homes over a two-year period and complemented AKCS-P's efforts in infrastructure upgrading and facade consolidation at the scale of the mohalla. Since it was understood that the rehabilitation of private dwellings could not be sustained at a large scale or in the long run simply with external funds, the nature of the proposed physical work was discussed with the applicants at great length and owners' financial participation negotiated on a case-to-case basis. Agreements were finalized with sixteen families residing in thirteen historic homes. In order to be in a position to sustain the efforts of rehabilitating private buildings, homeowners' contribution was encouraged and, at the end of the project, owner equity ranged between five and fifteen per cent for specific houses. The demonstration project generated immense interest among owners of historic buildings in the Walled City.

As-found (above) and proposed (below) ground-floor plans of houses G-321-22 and G-328 in Gali Surjan Singh and Koocha Charkh Garan respectively.

INTEGRATED PLANNING AND
MONUMENT CONSERVATION (2013–17)

THE 'MASTER CONSERVATION AND REDEVELOPMENT PLAN FOR THE WALLED CITY OF LAHORE'

MASOOD KHAN

The Aga Khan Trust for Culture (AKTC) has been active in heritage conservation in Pakistan since the late 1980s.[1] In response to a request from the government of Pakistan in 2005, the Aga Khan Historic Cities Programme (HCP) offered to provide technical and financial assistance for heritage conservation in Lahore.

From 2007 onwards, the Walled City of Lahore – its urban heritage as well as its monuments – has been at the centre of HCP's contribution to conservation and development in Pakistan, demonstrating how the conservation and rehabilitation of an urban site such as the Walled City can be integrated with the conservation of individual monuments or groups of monuments in Lahore. One of the prominent issues has been the conflict between the spatial and topographic identity of the Walled City as a cultural artefact on the one hand, and, until new legislation was enacted in 2012, a diffuse local government system meant for Lahore as a whole on the other. The approach to conservation deriving from the British Victorian-era legislation that is still embodied in the principal Pakistani laws on monument conservation and archaeology[2] was another impinging issue.

THE INSTITUTIONAL CONTEXT

By the last decades of the twentieth century, increasing awareness had grown that the Walled City was a place of special historic and cultural significance. It was at the initiative of Lahore's planners in 1978 that a special project was created for the Walled City among the World Bank's infrastructure-oriented schemes of the 1975–90 period,[3] leading to the preparation of a conservation plan in 1988. But these plans could only be realized with World Bank financing, due to the limited capacity of poor communities in the Walled City to pay for improvements in the utility infrastructure. However, in 2006 a more holistic urban rehabilitation and conservation pilot project was co-financed by the World Bank with the Punjab government.[4]

In 2010 the Punjab government decided to enact new legislation specific to regulating the physical confines of the Walled City of Lahore. An earlier ordinance, by then obsolete,[5] was replaced in 2012 with the 'Walled City of Lahore Act' (WCL Act).[6]

The new legislation was adopted by consensus in the Punjab Assembly and promulgated in April 2012, as a result of which the Walled City of Lahore Authority (WCLA) came into existence in October 2012. The WCL Act is Pakistan's first specific urban-heritage municipal-governance legislation. To this end, the Act has invested the Authority with considerable planning and executive powers, while defining a broad planning framework to be prepared for the Walled City. It charges the WCLA with a

Preceding pages, the Wazir Khan Mosque in the Walled City. The eastern facade overlooking the *chowk*, restored to its 17th-century floor level, and the internal court behind.

Opposite page, non-enforcement of Walled City-specific building regulations creates a marked discord between the density, form and appearance of historic buildings and those constructed for new uses with contemporary materials and structural systems.

Above, satellite image of the Walled City of Lahore and the surrounding spaces that demarcate it.

wide array of responsibilities and invests powers in it to carry out many of the functions described here.

The salient features of the 2012 WCL Act are:

- the Act enjoins upon the Authority to prepare a *'Master Conservation and Redevelopment Plan'* (MCRP), "to include:
  - (i) a land use and zoning plan;
  - (ii) a plan for the conservation of heritage of the Walled City;
  - (iii) a plan for the development, improvement and maintenance of municipal services;
  - (iv) a plan for the development, improvement and maintenance of public passages, urban open spaces, public areas; and
  - (v) a plan for the development of enterprise and economic activities." The legislative mandate to prepare a particularly specified and structured plan is a first in the Pakistani context. Already the law has been used by the citizenry who have taken matters relating to some of these aspects to the superior courts' appellate jurisdiction;
- a Heritage Conservation Board was created with professional experts in the relevant fields. The Board's function is to assist in and authorize decisions relating to conservation policy;
- a Citizens Community Council, and a Trade and Business Council were established for consultative representation;
- listing, and the establishment of a Register of Heritage Properties and the identification, listing and conservation of Zones of Special Value in the Walled City;
- the WCLA is authorized to prepare and implement schemes relating to area conservation, conservation of a building or groups of buildings, rebuilding or rehabilitation of housing, tourism development, infrastructure development or improvement, promotion of cultural activities and festivals, promotion of the visual and temporal arts, promotion and revitalization of craft, traffic improvement and transportation, health or education sectors, resettlement and so on;
- among the corollaries of the new law are the several rules and regulations that have been created under its ambit.

Above, Lahore Fort. Akbari Gate provides access into the Fort complex from the east and is the terminal point of the Shahi Guzargah.

Below, traffic in the western zone of the Shahi Guzargah, with ongoing facade improvement.

Right, aerial photograph of the eastern side of Lahore Fort and its adjacent land use.

By mid 2014 the WCLA completed the first section of the Shahi Guzargah pilot project, and has proceeded to complete most of the remaining parts of the project with funding from the government of Punjab. With assistance from AKTC, it has contributed to several other conservation initiatives in the Walled City. These include monument conservation (the Shahi Hammam, the Wazir Khan Mosque, the Sunehri Masjid) and urban open-space rehabilitation in the Wazir Khan Chowk. The WCLA has also taken the first ever measures to establish various facilities for visitors to the Walled City, turning it into a relatively visitor-friendly city, and has raised its profile markedly. In addition, from 2014 the WCLA has also shouldered the task of managing the World Heritage Site of Lahore Fort, undertaking several large project initiatives (see the section on pp. 210–371 in this volume).

THE 'MASTER CONSERVATION AND REDEVELOPMENT PLAN' (MCRP)

The 2017 'Walled City of Lahore: Master Conservation and Redevelopment Plan' (MCRP) was prepared in response to the mandate of the WCL Act (Section 15). It is a joint in-house initiative of AKTC and the WCLA and responds to the requirements of the

Traffic conditions around and on Circular Road near Delhi Gate. On the right is the New Kotwali (police station), built *c*. 1860.

The Dina Nath Well in the Wazir Khan Chowk before (left) and after (right) its recently implemented conservation and rehabilitation work.

WCL Act by approaching these at two levels. The first translates into a higher-level strategic framework, while the second embraces the specific requirements of the Act.

STRATEGIES AND POLICIES

To provide a framework for the policies arising out of the MCRP, the plan proposes an array of strategic goals and corresponding policies. The overarching goal is that the Walled City's distinct character and identity must be cherished and preserved. To the world outside its perimeter, the Walled City must be visually presented as a clearly visible historic asset, which is well cared for and has a special place in the hearts and minds of Lahore's citizens. External pressures and the threats they impose on the Walled City must be mitigated, and negative developments should be identified and contained.

Historic precincts and monuments must be revalorized. The heritage of the Walled City must be protected in a sustainable manner and, to further this end, strong regulatory frameworks should be created and the means for enforcing them obtained and applied. Traffic conditions within the Walled City should be alleviated and disciplined, and related issues resolved. Suitable conditions must be created for tourism to play its role in the economic future of the Walled City.

Each of these goals call for strategic responses.

The Punjab government, at the highest levels of political and executive power, must support a conceptual understanding of urban conservation as an all-embracing, multidimensional process. The economic uplift of the resident population through tourism is to be prioritized. A continuous stream of adequate funding must be maintained from appropriate sources to fulfil these aims, as well as to support rapid recruitment and enlargement of in-house specialized skills and professional staff at the WCLA. Full participation of communities and individuals at the level of mohallas, *galis* and *kuchas* should be engendered, as in the Shahi Guzargah pilot project, through appropriate social extension and advocacy mechanisms.

Some strategic moves are necessary as high-priority initial actions in any urban conservation process, such as: inventorying and listing[7]; an accurate cadastral database of properties and property ownership information; and the launching of catalyst projects.

A major strategic move relates to issues of access and visibility of the Walled City from its peripheral access system. Policies need to be focused on improving the visibility of the Walled City, parking around and within the historic core, traffic management on Circular Road, and ensuring a sustainable future for Circular Garden. Strategies designed for improving traffic intersect with those for land use. The strategic goal of turning large parts of the Walled City into pedestrian areas is related to lessening the intensity of commerce, coupled with policies for parking and regulating delivery vehicles and services. Only a few critical roads in the vicinity require urgent widening, but a massive effort needs to be launched for the reorganization of public

As-found and proposed plans of one of the houses G-326-27 of the Mohalla demonstration project in Gali Surjan Singh.

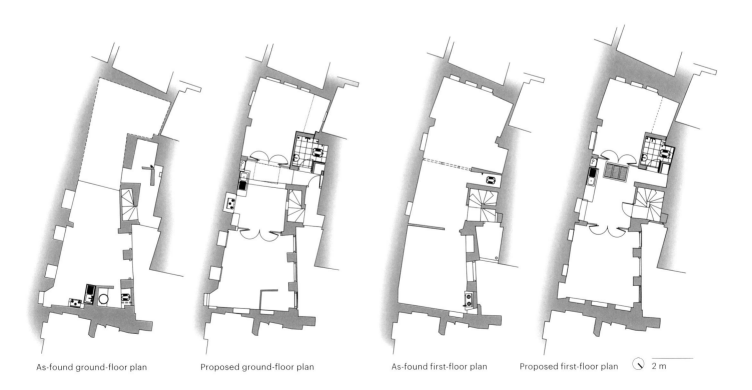

As-found ground-floor plan   Proposed ground-floor plan   As-found first-floor plan   Proposed first-floor plan   2 m

transport, creating an appropriate admixture of transport modes, training and disciplining of road users, control of use of roads as parking and loading/unloading space and so on.

Addressing external pressures will include the stakeholders coming to an adjustment in terms of long-term land use and transportation planning for Greater Lahore. The resultant weakening of the linkage between regional transportation and wholesale trade is expected to phase out the use of Circular Road as a trucking terminus. Other strategies spelled out in the MCRP include stopping forthwith the construction of commercial 'plazas' and other single-use buildings inside the Walled City, integrated with land-use and building control. Graded municipal taxes, licence fees and similar on all economic enterprises in the Walled City would be imposed.

Conservation in the Walled City

Goals and policies that are specific to heritage conservation would seek the conservation and rehabilitation of the entire Walled City, not just individual buildings and monuments, but townscapes and the historic urban landscape as well. The design and development of all new buildings would be in accord with the Walled City's historic and cultural values as embodied in its physical form, and as regulated under the building by-laws.

To attain these goals, the strategy for conservation in the Walled City in the MCRP would involve the maximum possible use of the powers vested in the WCLA by the Act. All owners (whether public-sector owners or private owners) must be bound to the provisions of the law.[8]

All historic residential properties should be proactively conserved, rehabilitated and modernized with the financial participation of the owners, in line with initiatives already demonstrated in the Shahi Guzargah pilot project. Social mobilization should be based on involving communities to set their own development priorities in consultation with design professionals. The Register of Heritage Properties and a notified list of Zones of Special Value should be implemented as planning overlays through which overlapping operational regimes can be coordinated, and attention and resources can be relatively more focused. The Heritage Conservation Board created under the

Historic buildings of architectural interest in the Walled City.

Act should play a strong, professional role. Eminent domain and the public interest should be the primary criteria for the protection of and interventions in sites of very high value, such as the World Heritage Site and its buffer zones.

Strategy for improving the quality of life in the Walled City
In the social sector particular attention is to be paid to spheres of culture, education, health (such as the integrated community health programme in parts of the Shahi Guzargah project), parks and recreation, and other aspects of a liveable city. A more balanced mix of resident income groups should be aimed for. Early childhood development, assistance to small schools being operated by local residents, and primary and secondary schools should be prioritized. Public-sector schools would be improved. Marketable technical skills would be increased among the unemployed and underemployed youth. Technical skills could also be imparted in participatory conservation projects. Cultural forums, institutions and festivals would be revived so that a vibrant intangible heritage would be revitalized. Residents, especially women and young children, would have access to green space and recreational facilities,

The entrance facade of the 19th-century *haveli*, or palace, of Naunehal Singh.

159

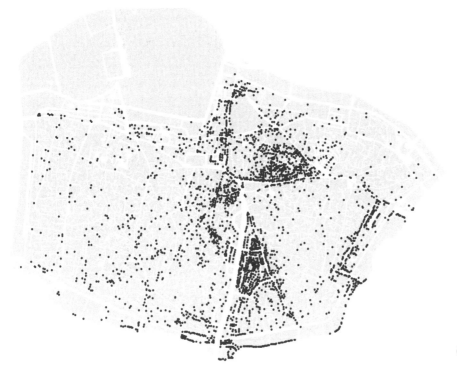

while home-based work for women would be facilitated. Reduction of the pressure on physical space caused by the expanding regional markets in the Walled City would be an important objective.

URBAN CONSERVATION

Under the MCRP, conservation in the Walled City will involve several planning and implementation overlays corresponding to:

- heritage protection, conservation and care;
- notifying/gazetting the Zones of Special Value and establishing special, more intense regulations and guidelines for land use, building construction, urban design and urban infill for them;
- urban and municipal management, enforcement of the Act and other related regulative instruments, such as the new 'Land Use Plan', the building regulations, and special regulatory provisions for heritage properties;
- undertaking phased urban upgrading, infrastructure development and conservation and rehabilitation of the urban fabric;
- mobilization of the communities within the Walled City, building heritage awareness, and creating social and economic development through tourism, skills development and raised income levels.

THE 'LAND USE PLAN'

One of the primary objectives of the 'Land Use Plan' is to protect the heritage of the Walled City. The heritage values in the Walled City and the urban structure they constitute are contained in a range of physical elements and the activities they make possible. These assets have been under a very real threat for decades, mainly for reasons of unregulated land use. The proposed 'Land Use Plan' is one of the instruments that can be used to mitigate these threats, and over the long term reverse them.

Opposite page, historic building stock of architectural value in the Walled City.

Above, warehouse / manufacturing as land use in the Walled City.

500 m

The Walled City, land use, 2009.

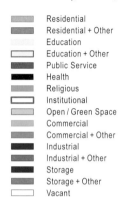

- Residential
- Residential + Other
- Education
- Education + Other
- Public Service
- Health
- Religious
- Institutional
- Open / Green Space
- Commercial
- Commercial + Other
- Industrial
- Industrial + Other
- Storage
- Storage + Other
- Vacant

Proposed land use.

- Residential A (primarily residential)
- Residential B (residential with low-intensity business)
- Main bazaar
- Secondary bazaar
- Cultural
- Public Facility / Institutional
- Religious
- Utility / Public Facility
- Parking
- Green space
- Shah Alami Overlay
- Areas to be redeveloped and / or non-conforming

500 m

Zones of Special Value – as identified in the 2017 'Master Conservation and Redevelopment Plan' (MCRP) for the Walled City.

▨ Zone Identifier
① Lahore Fort and its Buffer Zone
② The Circular Garden
③A Delhi Gate and Related Zone Extra Muros
③B Lohari Gate and Related Zone Extra Muros
③C Bhatti Gate
④A Delhi Gate Bazaar and its hinterland including the Shahi Hammam, Wazir Khan Mosque and Wazir Khan Chowk
④B Chowk Nawab Sahib to Chohatta Mufti Baqar
④C Mochi Gate to Chowk Nawab Sahib
④D Rang Mahal, Sunehri Masjid, Gurdwara Baoli Sahib
④E Chuna Mandi Haveli
⑤A Mohalla Sathaan
⑤B Pani Wala Talaab, Heera Mandi Bazaar
⑤C Haveli Raja Dhyan Singh and Tehsil Bazaar
⑤D Bazaar-e-Hakeeman, a part of Tehsil Bazaar and hinterland
⑤E Bhatti Gate Bazaar
⑤F Naunehal Singh Haveli and associate spaces
⑥A Lohari Gate Bazaar, Chowk Bukhari
⑥B Chowk Jhanda, Lohari Mandi Bazaar
⑥C Lohari Mandi Bazaar - 2
⑥D Lohari Mandi Bazaar - 3
⑥E Moti Bazaar
⑥F Wachho Wali
⑥G Sootar Mandi Chowk and Bazaar
⑥H Mohalla Maulian

The basic principles on which the 'Land Use Plan' is based are spelled out in Chapter IV, Section 15 (2) of the Act in which it is stated that the MCRP shall not be detrimental to (1) the territorial integrity of the Walled City; and (2) the heritage of the Walled City. While protecting to a reasonable extent the land-use rights of those who already benefit from a lawfully established land use, the 'Land Use Plan' describes the state of the land use as it is desired ten years after its promulgation, and after existing non-conforming uses have been phased out over a period of time.

The 'Land Use Plan' defers to traditional land-use patterns of the Walled City. It comprises a map indicating the areas of specific land use, and several schedules. The main schedule will contain a mention of the land use ascribed to each specific land parcel in the Walled City. In addition, there will be several subsidiary schedules, including:

▸ schedule of prohibited land uses and prohibited building types;
▸ schedule of non-residential use permitted in residential zones;
▸ schedule of non-residential use permitted in secondary bazaars;
▸ schedule of uses in main bazaars, including upper-storey uses.

THE 'CONSERVATION PLAN'
The 'Conservation Plan' responds to the requirements of Section 15 (3) (ii) and (iv) of the Act.

The 'Conservation Plan' endorses the principle that in all future deliberations and executive decision-making on the Walled City of Lahore's heritage, as defined by the Act, the guidelines in at least eight different international charters and conventions listed on page 82 of the MCRP document must be consulted and followed to the greatest extent possible.

Zone of Special Value 1.

—— Proposed World Heritage Site
- - - Buffer Zone

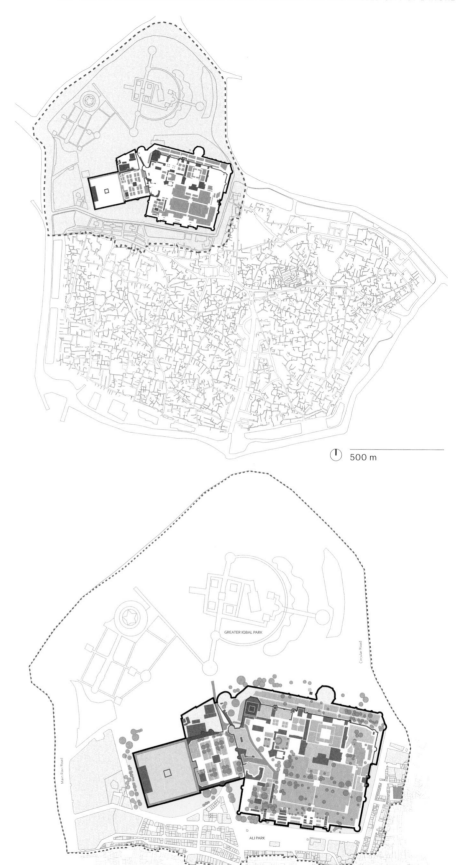

500 m

Lahore Fort, Badshahi Mosque and the neighbourhood context.

—— Proposed World Heritage Site Core
■ ■ ■ Zone of Special Value boundary
(same as boundary of proposed Buffer
Zone of the new World Heritage Site)

200 m

Existing and proposed World Heritage Site with points of access to the Zone.

Monument complex of Lahore Fort (existing World Heritage Site),

━━ Badshahi Mosque, the Hazuri Bagh and the Sikh monuments: to be proposed as a new World Heritage Site

-- Boundary of Zone of Special Value 1 as well as the Buffer Zone for the World Heritage Site

1 Access from North Circular Road
2 Fort Road East
3 Access from the Walled City via Begum Shahi/Maryam Zamani Mosque
4 Access from the Walled City via Pani Wala Talaab
5 Access from the south via Bhatti Gate/ Bazaar-e-Hakeeman
6 Access from the west via Taxali Gate/ Neewa Chait Ram
7 Fort Road intersecting Ravi Road
8 Access from Main Ravi Road

⊕ 200 m

Sections of the Walled City of Lahore's urban fabric included in this Zone of Special Value.

····· Boundary of the Zone of Special Value
━━ Peripheral boundary of the World Heritage Site

Existing urban fabric for rehabilitation

Area occupied by Rim Market proposed for redevelopment

Neewa Chait Ram residential buildings proposed for revalorization

Abandoned building

⊕ 200 m

Zone of Special Value 5D (Bazaar-e-Hakeeman),
existing condition: general context;
primary and secondary land use; structural
conditions; functionality; residential types;
and architectural merit.

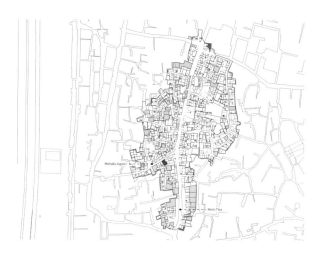

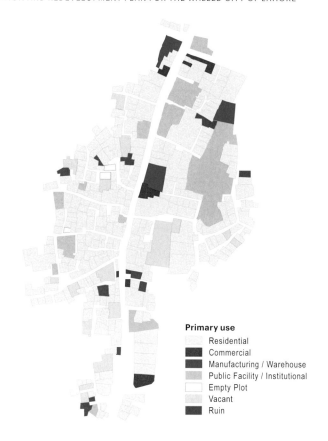

Primary use
- Residential
- Commercial
- Manufacturing / Warehouse
- Public Facility / Institutional
- Empty Plot
- Vacant
- Ruin

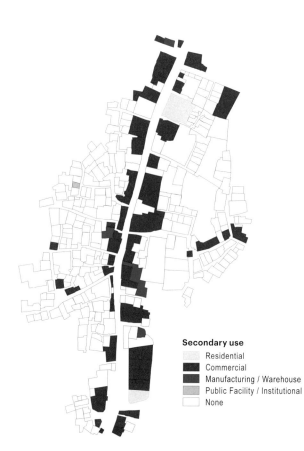

Secondary use
- Residential
- Commercial
- Manufacturing / Warehouse
- Public Facility / Institutional
- None

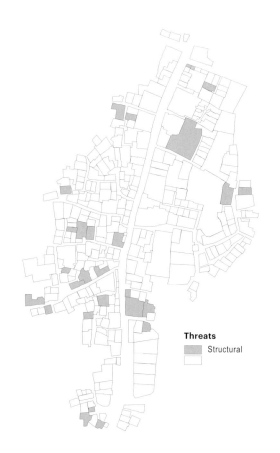

Threats
- Structural

Functionality

Functional
Undeveloped
Vacant
Ruin

Residential Type

Balakhana
Haveli
Makan with courtyard
Makan without courtyard
No information

Architectural Merit

High
Medium

The street in Mohalla Jogian
taken up for detailed study.

50 m

167

The objectives of the 'Conservation Plan' are (1) to identify, list, notify and bring the urban heritage under the protective arm of the law; (2) to initiate integrated conservation projects at all levels of the hierarchy of the elements of the urban heritage: urban open spaces, streets and bazaars, neighbourhoods and mohallas, groups of buildings, individual buildings and monuments; (3) to integrate conservation projects with infrastructure improvement and redevelopment; and (4) within the constraints of the historic environment, and in deference to it, to rehabilitate the urban context at high standards of urban design and landscaping.

Under the 'Conservation Plan' the actions to be taken are as follows:

‣ bringing the heritage under the protection of the law. Under Section 23 (Declaration of Heritage Properties), an inventory of all heritage properties is to be established immediately, and the procedure set out in the Act (Section 25) for the conservation of heritage properties is to be put into effect;

‣ Zones of Special Value are to be identified and listed under Section 24 of the Act; while identifying these zones, the 'Conservation Plan' defines their nature, lists the special procedures that are to be followed for them, and proposes test cases for two important Zones of Special Value in the Walled City;

‣ for the purpose of carrying out integrated projects for urban conservation and infrastructure development, the 'Conservation Plan' proposes a series of Area Conservation and Development Schemes and proposes the procedures to be used for documentation and preparation of technical dossiers for the Zones of Special Values, and conceiving, preparing and launching these schemes. In the preparation

Left, proposed case process flow for a single building project application.

Right, case process flow for applications for complex urban design, urban conservation and redevelopment projects.

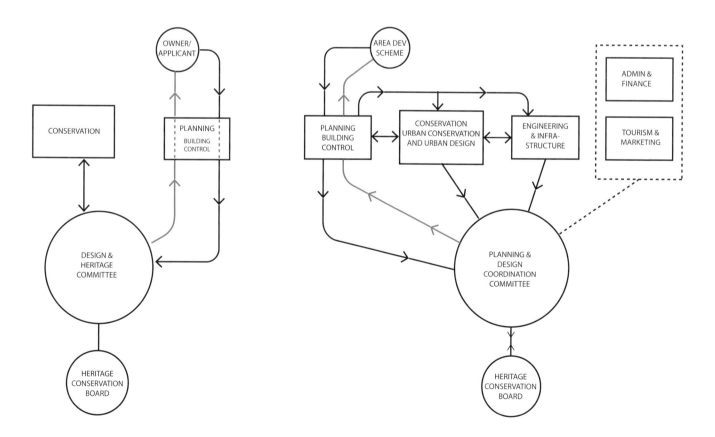

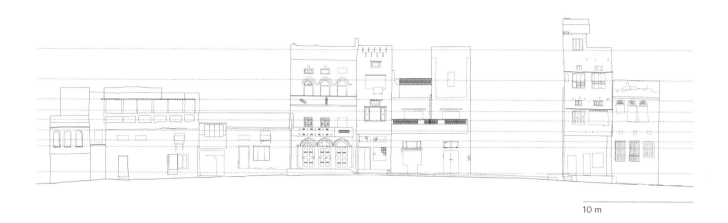

10 m

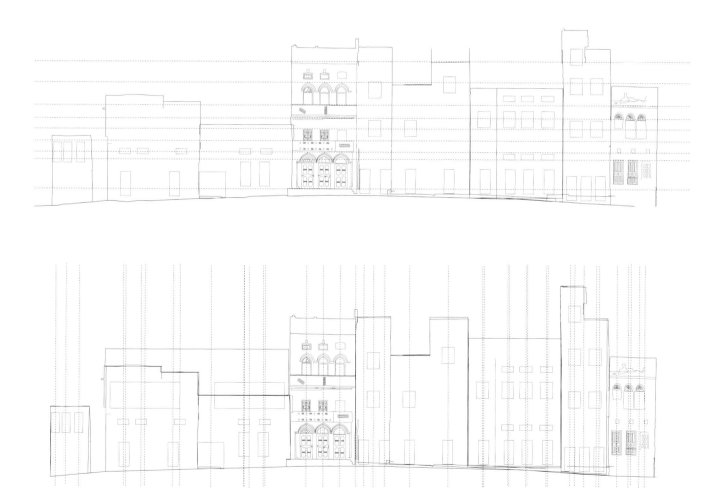

Street facade development and
control in Mohalla Jogian
(see plan on p. 167, bottom right).

Mohalla Jogian / Jogian Chowk:
documentation, analysis and reinterpretation
of the urban heritage.

Above, the as-found condition. Below,
proposals based on pattern analysis shown
on preceding page.

Southern side of street

10 m

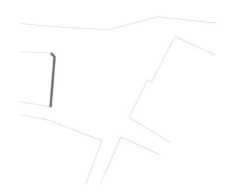

Mohalla Jogian Chowk:
street facade development. Above, the
as-found condition. Below, as proposed.

Western side
of chowk

Northern side
of chowk

Eastern side
of chowk

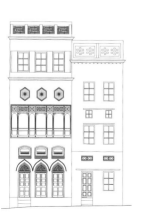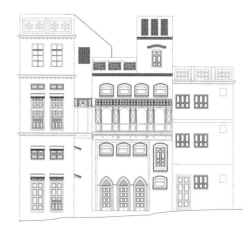

10 m

171

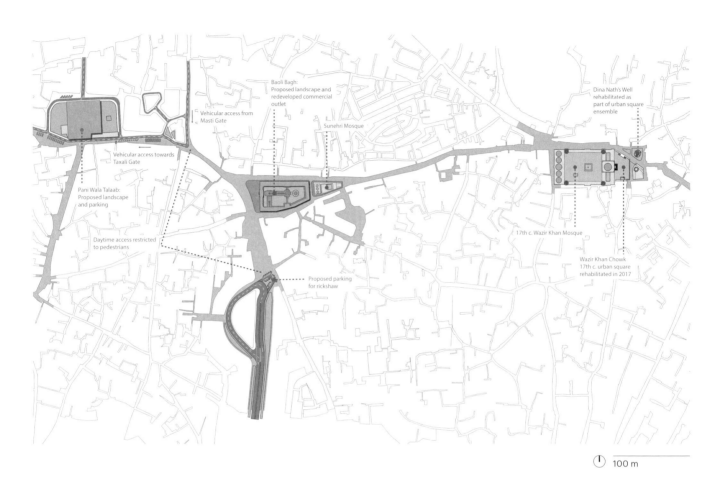

100 m

Masti Gate
Sheranwala Gate
Kashmiri Gate
① 1
④ 4
Circular Road
Yakki Gate
⑤ 5
Delhi Gate
② 2
Akbari Gate
⑥ 6
⑨ 9
⑦ 7
Brandreth Road
⑧ 8
⑩ 10
Mochi Gate
③ 3
Shah Alami Gate

① 300 m

Opposite page, above, proposed rehabilitation of certain public open spaces and streets.

Above, proposed urban redesign and traffic engineering on Circular Road (northern, eastern and south-eastern sections), showing areas of open and underground parking, and reclamation of green space.

1   Proposed parking along North Circular Road
2   Proposed parking along East Circular Road
3   Proposed parking along South Circular Road
4   Detailed drawing of parking spaces
5   Proposed market with underground parking
6   Proposed loading/unloading dock between Akbari Gate and Brandreth Road
7   Proposed intersection near Brandreth Road
8   Proposed rickshaw stand near Mochi Gate
9   Proposed redevelopment after removal of encroachments
10 Proposed rickshaw stand near Shah Alami Gate

Below, South Circular Road between Shah Alami and Mochi Gate: rendering of Circular Garden after proposed removal of roadside shops encroaching into the garden, and the green space shown visually connected to Circular Road.

173

1
Traffic engineering and redesign of North Circular Road, showing layout of parking zones and landscaping.

2
Detail of proposed service lane and parking along North Circular Road and along north periphery road near Sharif Hospital.

3
General plan of improvement outside Delhi Gate.

4
Traffic engineering and road improvement along the eastern Circular Road. Also shown is the new market with underground parking outside Delhi Gate.

5
General plan of improvements on South Circular Road between Shah Alami Chowk and Mochi Gate.

6
Detail of Masjid Bagh Wali intersection.

7
Detail of intersection of Brandreth Road and Circular Road.

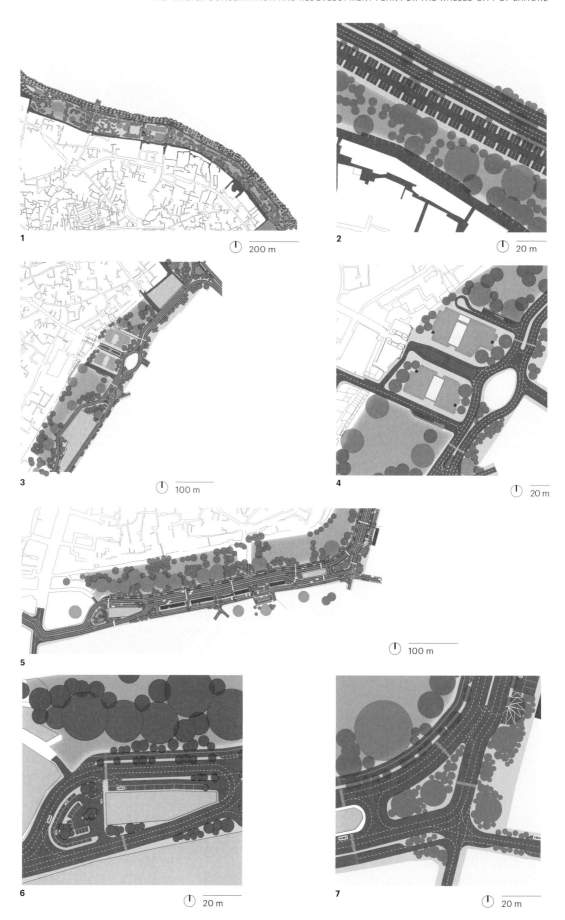

1   200 m

2   20 m

3   100 m

4   20 m

5   100 m

6   20 m

7   20 m

of such schemes or projects, the 'Conservation Plan' also contains proposals and guidelines in respect of the conservation, preservation and development of the circulation system (streets and pathways) of the Walled City, which fulfils the requirements of Section 15 (iv) of the WCL Act. The 'Conservation Plan' deals with several other aspects in which the modalities of integrating heritage conservation with infrastructure development are treated;

- the 'Conservation Plan' also provides guidelines for (1) the stabilization and conservation of endangered buildings; and (2) for the design and development of buildings that are inserted into the urban fabric;

- in addition, the 'Conservation Plan' proposes guidelines for the development of the necessary specialized skills required and to be created within the WCLA for carrying out the activities it identifies;

- lastly the 'Conservation Plan' also makes specific conceptual proposals for urban and traffic design on Circular Road, and for the rehabilitation of Circular Garden.

THE 'INFRASTRUCTURE AND MUNICIPAL SERVICES PLAN'

This requirement of the WCL Act was fulfilled by the 'Integrated Infrastructure Concept Design' prepared under the aegis of AKTC in 2010. This is described on pp. 124–135 of this volume, as the "plan for development, improvement and maintenance of municipal services" required under Section 15 (3) (iii) of the Act. The 'Integrated Infrastructure Concept Design' brings together the schematic design of seven utilities services in seven development phases covering the jurisdictional territory of the WCLA. These phases of development are the basis of the ongoing Area Conservation and Development Schemes, such as the Shahi Guzargah project and the forthcoming Bhatti Gate to Taxali Gate project.

1   After the conservation of Baltit Fort in 1996, AKTC went on to complete numerous other projects in the Gilgit-Baltistan region. These include Altit Fort, the historic village of Ganish, Shigar Fort Residence and Khaplu Palace.

2   Two pieces of legislation relating to heritage in Pakistan and in Punjab province must be mentioned. The first is the 'Antiquities Act' of 1975, a modification of the colonial-period 'Ancient Monuments Preservation Act' of 1904. The 1975 'Antiquities Act' was modified in 2012 to incorporate the changes made under the 18th amendment to the constitution of Pakistan devolving matters relating to culture to the provinces. This law operates under a restricted sense of the term "heritage" as meaning individual monuments, objects and artefacts, and concerns itself mainly with the functioning of the Department of Archaeology. In appreciation of the need to expand this definition, in 1985 the 'Punjab Special Premises (Preservation) Ordinance' had introduced the notion of "special premises" which, in addition to individual properties, was also interpreted to mean certain urban areas.

3   Lahore Development Authority and the World Bank, *Lahore Urban Development and Traffic Studies*, vol. 4, *Walled City Upgrading Study*, Lahore, 1980; PEPAC (Pakistan Environmental Planning and Architectural Consultants), *Conservation Plan for the Walled City of Lahore*, Lahore, 1988. See also *Case Study: Lahore, Pakistan – Conservation of the Walled City*, Donald Hankey (ed.), World Bank, South Asia Infrastructure Sector Unit, Washington DC, 1999.

4   The Shahi Guzargah pilot project (see pp. 136–149 in this volume).

5   The 'Punjab Historic Areas Planning, Development and Regulation Ordinance', 2007, became defunct mainly as the result of the 18th amendment to the constitution of Pakistan passed in 2010.

6   See the 'Walled City of Lahore Act', 2012, at http://punjablaws.gov.pk/laws/2500.html, accessed on 31.8.2019.

7   The Register of Heritage Properties mandated by the WCL Act, and identifying and establishing Zones of Special Value.

8   Under this policy, the regulatory functions and powers of the WCLA should apply to owners of all property, including properties owned by other government agencies, and agencies that act as trustees of certain properties, including properties protected under the 'Antiquities Act' of 1975 and the 'Punjab Special Premises (Preservation) Ordinance' of 1985. In all conservation-related matters the WCLA should receive possession of such properties for carrying out conservation operations, whether through administrative orders or changes/amendments to existing statutes. Such statutory changes/amendments should be made with the intention of rendering, without compromising rights of ownership or trusteeship, all overlapping realms of authority over properties in the Walled City subservient to the WCLA in so far as the conservation of these properties is concerned, and the later management of how these properties have been transformed and enhanced through conservation and rehabilitation.

CONSERVATION OF THE SHAHI HAMMAM

MARYAM RABI

HISTORICAL BACKGROUND

The Shahi Hammam is a seventeenth-century Mughal-period public bathhouse located just inside the Delhi Gate of the historic Walled City of Lahore. The monument was built in 1634 by Hakim 'Ilm ud Din Ansari, who bore the title Wazir Khan, and who was the governor of Lahore during the early years of the reign of Emperor Shah Jahan (r. 1628–58). The hammam was a fundamental part of an endowed urban complex centred on the Wazir Khan Mosque. The complex was commissioned to be built by the Hakim in 1634–35, and on its completion in 1641 he issued a *waqf* deed that endowed for the mosque's expenses, all the shops and houses on either side of the street from the mosque to Delhi Gate, a caravanserai that no longer exists, and a hammam that was designed to cater to the needs of both visiting travellers and inhabitants of the city. The endowment was intended for the proper upkeep of the mosque and to support the establishment connected with it.

The Shahi Hammam, as it came to be called, is a single-storey building covering an area of over 1,000 square metres. Built on the pattern of Turkish and Iranian bathing establishments, the hammam consisted of hot, warm and cool plunges, as well as sweat rooms and other related facilities. According to some historical accounts, the hammam was used extensively by the public during the Mughal era and was reserved for the exclusive use of women on a specific day of the week. The existing structure is a collection of twenty-one interconnected rooms and an additional room that is set at an angle facing Mecca, intended for offering prayers. Although private baths were popular during the Mughal and Sikh eras, the Shahi Hammam is one of only a handful of surviving monumental public bath sites from that period in the entire South Asian subcontinent, perhaps the only one of which the major part of the original buildings is still intact. For this reason, it was recognized as a cultural asset and declared a protected monument by the Department of Archaeology in 1955.

Following the decline of the Mughal Empire, Lahore experienced seventy years of strife during which the hammam was abandoned and fell into disrepair. When the British annexed Lahore in 1849, the bathhouse was found in ruins. The British demolished parts of the structure that were completely dilapidated and established the remainder of the building as their first magistrate's court and residence. After Pakistan was created in 1947, the hammam was taken over by the municipality and over the years used as a boys' primary school, a girls' vocational school, a dispensary, and as offices for functionaries. The north-western rooms of the monument were rented out as shops and additional shops were allowed to encroach along the length of the building's facades.

① 300 m

Opposite page, interior view of the Shahi Hammam post-conservation, showing the steel-and-glass walkway in the entrance hall looking towards the main door.

Above, the locational context of Shahi Hammam in the eastern half of the Walled City.

☐ Extent of Shahi Guzargah Pilot Project
═ Royal Trail
▬ 17th c. Shahi Hammam

In 1988 all schools and offices were moved out of the Shahi Hammam and, subsequently, it was handed over to the Tourism Development Corporation of Punjab (TDCP). In 1991 the Punjab government carried out restoration work in the hammam under the Punjab Urban Development Project, supported by the World Bank. This involved structural stabilization as well as refinishing of certain interior and exterior surfaces. Additionally, a new marble floor was installed over the existing British-period floors and walls were chased to make room for new plumbing and electrification. A vocational school for girls and a tourist information centre was then set up in the building. In 2005 the bathhouse was converted into a restaurant, and later, a TV set.

Despite being listed as a cultural asset and a protected monument by the Department of Archaeology in 1955, the Shahi Hammam underwent many alterations to adapt to its different uses over the years. These ill-conceived and materially insensitive modifications were detrimental to the building and resulted in considerable loss of the hammam's original fabric.

The project to conserve the Shahi Hammam was initiated in 2013, under a 'Public-Private Partnership Agreement' of collaboration between the Walled City of Lahore Authority (WCLA) and the Aga Khan Cultural Service-Pakistan (AKCS-P). The Royal Norwegian Embassy in Islamabad contributed generous financial assistance for the project and the government of Punjab granted additional funds and administrative support. The scope of the work substantially expanded over time as subterranean features of the building were uncovered. The ultimate financial outlay doubled during the conservation process, and the timeline increased from fifteen months to twenty-four months.

The Shahi Hammam's western facade after the removal of encroachments (left) and after conservation (right).

The Shahi Hammam after conservation
in its immediate surroundings.

CULTURAL SIGNIFICANCE AND HERITAGE VALUE

The significance of the Shahi Hammam is multifaceted, and stems from both the
characteristics of the monument alone as well as its place in an urban context that
has experienced a high degree of political, social and economic decay and fragmentation since it was built. The hammam has a history of nearly 400 years, and is one
of the few surviving Mughal-period public bathing establishments that form part of
a purpose-built urban complex, as evidenced in the *waqf* deed of Wazir Khan. The
hammam's architectural characteristics are significant indicators of society during
the height of the Mughal Empire. Its interconnected halls and communal spaces
are designed for social interaction. At an urban scale, its close proximity to a major
mosque and the once existing caravanserai on one of the main thoroughfares into the
Walled City provides a rare glimpse of everyday urban life during the Mughal period.
While the hammam had no direct religious significance, it played a major role in safeguarding the religious experience of the mosque complex.

The subterranean features of the hammam represent a record of how public
bathhouses were constructed from the time of the Romans through the adaptation
during the Umayyad caliphate of a system of mechanical elements necessary for the

179

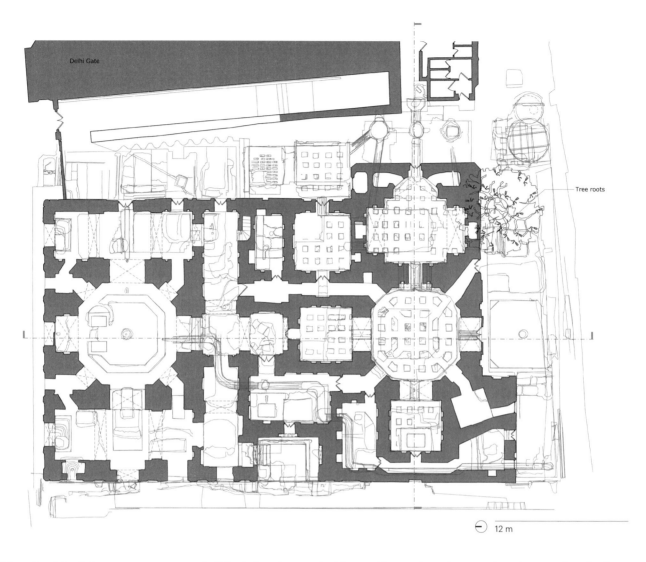

Delhi Gate

Tree roots

12 m

Ground-floor plan of the Shahi Hammam showing below-grade archaeological discoveries.

building's function as a bathhouse. These adaptations continued across the Islamic Middle East and characterize the hammams of Iran, Turkey, Afghanistan and Central Asia. It is natural that this long tradition found its way into the Indian subcontinent with the Muslim inroads from Central Asia and Persia, in particular with the Mughals. Apart from the characteristic form of the building, of special importance are the hammam's underground hypocaust system, the network of water supply channels built into the fabric of the building, and drains hidden in the floors for effective drainage of large volumes of water. Although no evidence has survived of the source of water, it is well established that animal-driven elevator water wheels (to elevate the water from wells) were the usual means of water supply where an elevated water source did not exist, as in Lahore.

Excavations carried out to lay infrastructure in adjacent streets revealed foundations, which indicated that there was a westward wing extending from the southern portion of the extant building at one time. Although it is now difficult to read the original configuration of this wing today, it is not beyond probability that the building complex was more elaborate than the rectangular block that today constitutes the building's form. The degree of degradation in some portions of the bathhouse, discovered during careful excavations, was such that at the time of the British takeover these ruined parts of the hammam were removed and it was left in the form in which it has remained since the early years of British occupation. In plan, this extant

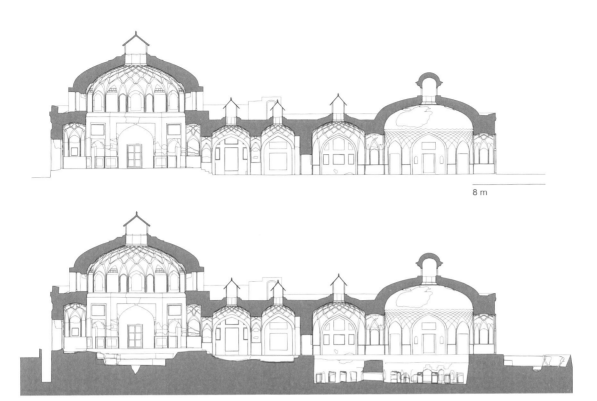

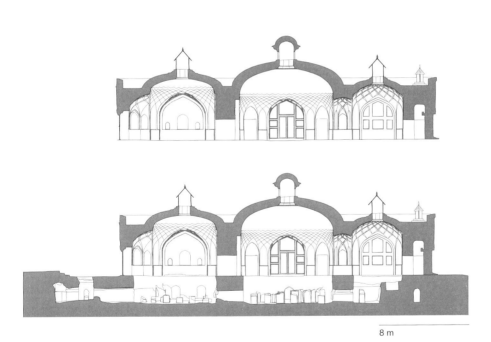

building has a rectangular form nearly 43 metres long and just over 24 metres wide. It has three major axes, one running lengthwise and two cross-axes that define major functional zones, allowing one to experience from within the entire length and width of the building.

The entrance *iwan* (archway) located on the western side of the hammam, the great hall of the building and several other rooms throughout the structure are decorated with frescoed panels of a distinctly provincial aesthetic, which is, nevertheless,

Upper two, longitudinal sections of the hammam building: above, as found and below, after explorations.

Lower two, transverse sections of the hammam: above, as found and below, after explorations, shown with the discovered hypocaust and heating furnaces on the left.

Above, Mughal-period *naqqashi* (wall painting on lime plaster) with angel iconography on the spandrels of arched openings around the main hall.

Below, the *naqqashi* panels depict angels, animals, birds, floral and geometric designs.

Right, decorated paintings found on the intrados of interior arches in the Shahi Hammam, seen after conservation.

related to the iconography of several instances of Mughal wall painting and glazed-tile murals in Lahore. The frescoes depict angels, animals, birds, floral and geometric designs. Additionally, the corbelled domes are vaulted with *qalib-kari, muqarnas* and skylights. It is rare for a Mughal monument of this scale to be adorned with frescoes as densely as those found in the hammam. The only other Mughal-period building of a similar aesthetic is the Wazir Khan Mosque.

PRELIMINARY ACTIVITIES

When the conservation of the Shahi Hammam began in 2013, the monument was in an extreme state of disrepair caused over time by neglect and mismanagement. Shops on three sides of the hammam had encroached directly onto the fabric of the building and had deeply invaded its interior, causing extensive interior and exterior damage. Additionally, the outer facades and part of the roof served as carriers of utility lines, which included telephone cables as well as distribution wires.

Preliminary activities pertaining to the project consisted in removing encroached shops, consolidating cables and placing them underground, and constructing a retaining wall around the Shahi Hammam. The purposes of the retaining wall were multiple. Firstly, it allowed the conservation team to clear accumulated debris and reveal the full facade going down to the original street level, making the facade accessible for consolidating its badly deteriorated brickwork; secondly, it created space between the building and the adjacent urban fabric, thereby protecting it from future encroachments; and thirdly, it re-established the boundary of the hammam site. Initial archaeological explorations carried out immediately outside the hammam structure led to the discovery of the original brick street surface, nearly 2.5 metres below the present street level. This was preserved with the objective of reinstating the monument's narrative, but a major amount of the original brick had to be replaced owing to its fragile condition. The second purpose of the retaining wall was to protect the monument from flooding in instances of extreme rainfall. This was especially important as archaeological evidence uncovered inside the hammam revealed severe damage brought about by a flood, and parts of the uncovered sub-floor structures, including the hypocaust, were found saturated with water seeping in from the inadequate drainage of rainwater from the streets surrounding the monument.

DOCUMENTATION AND ANALYSES

Documentation of the hammam and its immediate surroundings was carried out using electronic distance measuring (EDM) instruments. This resulted in scaled wire-frame models of the structure, which were then used to derive architectural drawings that included plans, elevations and cross sections. Simultaneously, photographic documentation and high-resolution photo-orthorectification was carried out, creating a photomosaic by stitching together numerous colour photographs overlaid on the EDM documentation, which captured the monument's existing details.

Archaeological excavations were carried out both inside the hammam and the area outside within its site boundaries. The objective was to remove contemporary floor structures that concealed the original subterranean features of the building. The discoveries that were made in the process helped understand the manner in which the bathhouse functioned. The Shahi Hammam drew water from an ox-driven Persian well and relied on gravity to circulate water throughout the building. It had two principal zones – a hot zone, which corresponded to the Latin caldarium, and a cold zone, the frigidarium. Cold water was routed along the exterior of the hammam and introduced into the building at various entry points. Hot water was channelled to various cisterns from a hot water tank located above three large furnaces that were situated in the south-east corner of the hammam. There were several small drains that collected waste water from various parts of the building and channelled into one large principal drain, which would then carry the water away from the hammam. The heating system below the floors (or the hypocaust) consisted of a network of underground tunnels through which hot air was circulated before it left the building through flu channels located in the corners of the hot rooms. Extensive amounts of extraneous fill below British-period floors, along with collapsed sections of the original floor system, were found. Certain archaeological finds indicated that some of the soil brought for the fill came from another historic site. Remains of British-period adaptations of the interior spaces in the great hall and its octagonal pool were also found.

Each archaeological discovery was documented, and any artefacts that were discovered during these explorations were carefully cleaned, catalogued and secured. Geotechnical investigations and structural analyses were conducted to determine subsoil conditions and features. These investigations helped identify key causes of structural and surface deterioration. Furthermore, an analysis of construction materials through laboratory testing allowed the examination of the physical and chemical properties of original materials. Additionally, a comparative study of other Mughal and Sikh-period hammams in the region was carried out.

Using the research and conclusions drawn from these investigations, a condition analysis of each surface was conducted. This included identifying and mapping layers of history and types of damage. The surfaces were then categorized according to

A squinch decorated with painted *muqarnas*. Domes and vaulted niches are adorned with *naqqashi* executed on *qalib-kari*. The main domes are topped with skylights.

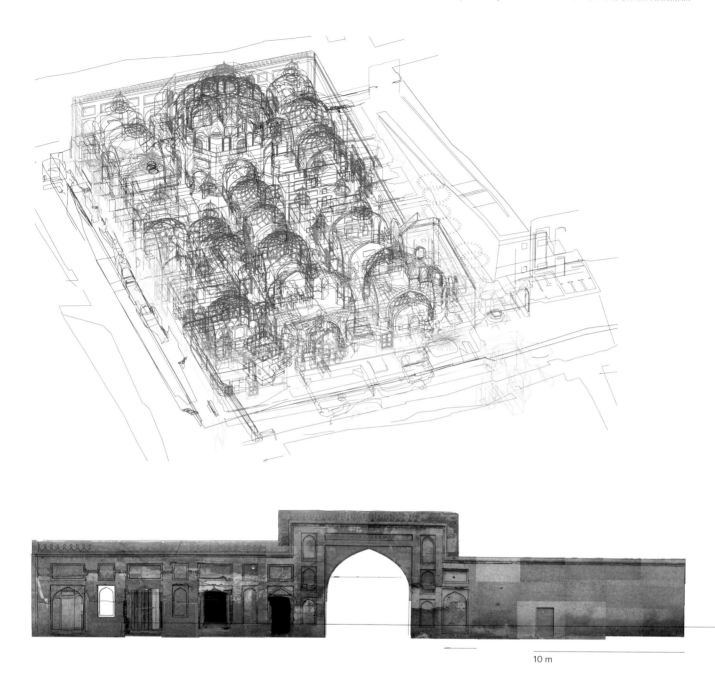

10 m

Above, documentation of the Shahi Hammam. A 3D CAD wireframe (top) and rectified photography mounted on a 3D CAD survey (bottom).

the period to which they belonged. Altogether, the documentation and analysis phase of the project provided a comprehensive understanding of the Shahi Hammam, especially with respect to identifying features that may have been lost over the years. Evidence was meagre, but enough for the conclusion that large parts of the hammam's floors were made of sandstone slabs. This, and the very elaborate surviving fresco decorations on the walls, led to the conclusions that at least the water pools that were at the centre of each large hall were probably faced with marble or sandstone, all removed most probably during the Sikh period, when the practice of removing stone revetment from Mughal buildings was common.

CONSERVATION AND ADAPTIVE REUSE

Prior to conservation proposals, restitution drawings were prepared to better understand the building's past configuration, based on, and to the extent of, the excavated

A steel shed was designed to protect elements on the east side of the Shahi Hammam uncovered during the conservation process.

remains. These drawings visually recreated the original form and function of the hammam, and included piecing together evidence relating to the building's hierarchy of spaces, air and water circulation, drainage system, and hypocaust network. Each of the features was then analysed in terms of significance and conservation decisions were made accordingly. Proposed interventions identified features that required stabilization and needed to be conserved in their as-found state. They also highlighted features that were to be partially restored using compatible materials, as well as those that needed to be reconstructed strictly based on historic evidence and prior investigations. The aim of the conservation project was not only to allow visitors to appreciate what remains of the original fabric of the building, but also to partially demonstrate in certain areas what it may have looked like at the time that it was a functioning bathhouse.

A similar course of action was adopted for the conservation of frescoes in the Shahi Hammam. The work involved a preliminary chemical analysis of the murals, a damage assessment and graphic documentation. The conservation of frescoes followed a programme of evaluation, and decisions were made as to the degree to which each identifiable part of the frescoes was to be treated. This was followed by the consolidation of damaged and detached plaster, removal of earlier fillings and insensitive interventions, cleaning and reattachment of the paint-bearing layers, and lastly the actual treatment of each panel of the fresco, depending on the level of damage, including detailed reintegration of the painting and treatment of lacunae using thin layers of removable and water-based paint. At a larger scale, the frescoes were

185

reintegrated into the fabric of the building based on their as-received condition, and their relevance to the presentation schema of the larger project.

Archaeological investigations revealed that a considerable amount of the original fabric of the hammam, especially its subterranean features, still existed. Since the cultural practice of using public bathhouses is now extinct in Lahore, it was decided to establish the Shahi Hammam as a museum site where the conservation and display of original features, reinforced with a sound interpretation of the history of the hammam as a cultural asset, would augment the public's understanding of how the seventeenth-century bathhouse functioned. The aim of the project was not to revert the hammam back to its original form, but, instead, to treat it as a historic artefact and to develop a narrative of its journey through history.

A steel-and-glass walkway was constructed over exposed historic subterranean features, surfaces and materials to protect them from wear and tear. The walkway first routes visitors from the original entrance on the western side of the hammam to its cold zone. One of the halls in this part of the building was converted into an

interpretation room equipped with audio-visual material pertaining to the history and conservation of the hammam. Also exposed in the frigidarium of the bathhouse is a large octagonal pool located in the great hall, with its surface finishes partially reconstructed. The walkway then leads visitors towards the caldarium of the bathhouse, where archaeological remains of the hypocaust system and other subterranean features are displayed. Throughout the route, illustrations demonstrating the original form and function of each of the spaces were intermittently installed onto the steel structure of the walkway.

The exterior archaeological remains of the bathhouse found east of the building included additional hot rooms, three large furnaces and a large water reservoir. Since these discoveries indicate that the hammam was originally a much larger establishment, it was imperative that they be displayed. For this reason, a protective shed was built over the exposed archaeological remains to shield them from the elements. Also discovered in the south-east section of the hammam was a principal city drain that most probably pre-dates the Mughal era, since its invert level is two metres below the

The main hall of the Shahi Hammam after conservation, showing how the reversible steel-and-glass walkway and light fixtures have been placed.

Above, partially reconstructed features in the tepidarium of the Shahi Hammam.

Opposite page, top, east-west section of the hammam after conservation, showing the steel-and-glass walkway installation, and the protective shed on the left.

Middle, longitudinal section of the hammam after conservation. Ancillary building is shown on the right.

Bottom, one of the interior spaces in the hammam has been converted into an interpretation / media room.

foundation-bearing strata of the hammam structure; adjacent to this an extant brick wall was exposed which stands on even earlier strata. An underground gallery was constructed to allow visitors, especially academics and researchers, access to view and examine these archaeological discoveries.

To support the Shahi Hammam's new function as a museum site, the conservation project also included the construction of an ancillary building. This building is located in the south-east section of the hammam site and consists of toilets, a restaurant kitchen, a souvenir shop and administrative offices. The open space south of the building includes outdoor seating for visitors, which also serves as outdoor space for the restaurant. These income-generating components ensure that the conservation of the Shahi Hammam, and its function as a museum site, will remain sustainable for the foreseeable future.

After the completion of the project, the hammam was entrusted to the WCLA which is now responsible for its daily operations and maintenance. The WCLA also has recourse to the skilled craftsmen, labourers and site and management staff from within the Walled City that were trained by AKCS-P during the conservation project.

In 2016 the conservation of the Shahi Hammam received an Award of Merit at the UNESCO Asia-Pacific Awards for Cultural Heritage Conservation. The project is the first of its kind and scale at both the local and national level. It has drawn considerable attention to a largely neglected historic centre, and has led to a significant increase in the number of tourists to the Walled City, who, in turn, contribute to the local economy.

8 m

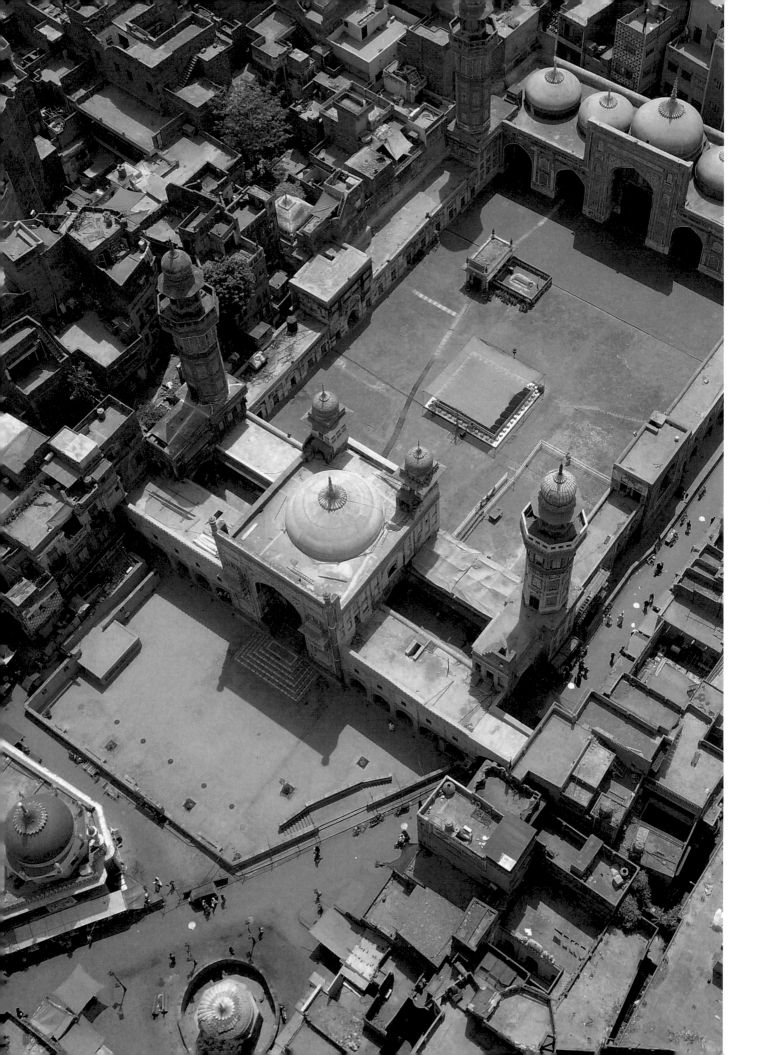

CONSERVATION OF THE WAZIR KHAN MOSQUE AND CHOWK

MASOOD KHAN, RASHID MAKHDUM, MARYAM RABI

HISTORICAL BACKGROUND

The congregational mosque of Wazir Khan was built in 1634–35 CE (AH 1044–45), by Hakim 'Ilm ud Din Ansari, Wazir Khan, a governor of Punjab during the reign of Mughal emperor Shah Jahan.[1] It consists of a complex of urban spaces and monuments that were built on the remains of an old Sufi complex and the grave sites associated with it.[2] The monument is protected under the 'Antiquities Act', and under the 'Punjab Special Premises (Preservation) Ordinance'. The mosque is a part of an endowment established in 1641 whose trusteeship is now the responsibility of the Punjab Auqaf Department.

The Wazir Khan Mosque is one of several monuments that were located along the route that the Mughal nobility traversed as they entered the city and made their way to the royal residence in Lahore Fort. According to the *waqf* document as reproduced in Syad Muhammad Latif's book on Lahore's history (1892),[3] the monumental ensemble contained a bazaar meant for calligraphers and bookbinders that was built as part of the entrance system of the mosque, in addition to the mosque itself. Additional shops were built into the body of the monument to sustain it; the *waqf* also included a serai, a hammam (presumably the Wazir Khan Hammam, today known as the Shahi Hammam), several wells and plots of open land. No specific mention has been made of the forecourt of the mosque, the Wazir Khan Chowk, but from a comparative review of other Mughal-period serais, the *chowk* (mosque forecourt) might pass as a small serai, indeed possibly the one mentioned in the *waqf* deed.

Today this urban ensemble includes the forecourt, and its entrance from the east – Chitta Gate – and other smaller monuments in the *chowk*, such as Dina Nath's Well and the shrine of Syed Suf, both of which owe their domes to nineteenth-century interventions, with a new 1990 intervention in the latter case.

The mosque itself includes a prayer chamber and a large courtyard. The latter is flanked on the northern and southern sides with twenty-eight *hujras* (series of small cells)[4] and two pavilions facing each other across the width of the courtyard. There are four *minars* (towers), marking the four corners of the courtyard. An important feature of the entrance system of the mosque is the Calligraphers' Bazaar that crosses the axis of entrance at a right angle, and is marked at this crossing with a large *dewhri* (entrance) topped by a dome, not unlike a Central Asian *charsu*.

The mosque complex, in its current form, still has profuse architectural ornamentation that embellishes exterior and interior surfaces, and qualifies it as one of the major historic monuments in the world. These decorations are of two kinds – exterior

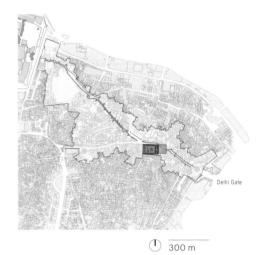

300 m

Opposite page, aerial view of the Wazir Khan Mosque. Its *chowk* (forecourt) seen after conservation.

Above, location of the Wazir Khan Mosque complex in the context of the Walled City.

☐ Extent of Shahi Guzargah Pilot Project
═ Royal Trail
▪ 17th c. Wazir Khan Mosque
▪ 17th c. Urban Square
● Other Monuments

surface decorations that are chiefly in the form of glazed-ceramic tile murals; and interior decoration in the form of *naqqashi* wall painting, a semi-dry form of fresco (painting on fine lime-plaster renders). Both these forms of embellishment have integral calligraphic components that draw on the Qur'an, the Hadith, components of ritual prayers and on verses, including chronograms. The exquisite tile work of the Wazir Khan Mosque is a specimen of unsurpassed beauty, skill and workmanship of Mughal-period architecture. The craft had reached its peak in Emperor Shah Jahan's rule when the mosque was built, a time characterized by richer and more elaborate tile work than that of other periods.

THREATS TO THE MONUMENT AND ITS PRESENT CONDITION

In 2009 Aga Khan Cultural Service-Pakistan (AKCS-P) carried out a comprehensive documentation and condition and risk assessment of the mosque, followed by a technical report[5] published in 2012. Architectural documentation was carried out using electronic distance measurement (EDM) and photo-orthorectification technologies coupled together, resulting in an accurate recording of the mosque's present conditions. The report presented an analysis of the structural condition of the building, and investigations into the geotechnical characteristics of the load-bearing soil.

While the mosque awaits conservation, its condition reflects decades of indifferent management, lack of technical and financial resources, the resulting inadequate conservation and upkeep, and the loss of municipal regulatory functions in the mosque's urban context. The need to reverse this situation was clear if the mosque was not to deteriorate to an extent that its conservation would become impossible.

The as-found condition of the complex in 2009–10 can be described under three general groups of information:

Some of the *hujras* (meditation cells) facing the courtyard of the mosque.

Above, the eastern facade of the Wazir Khan Mosque and its *chowk* after conservation.

Left, the interior is extensively decorated with *naqqashi* work.

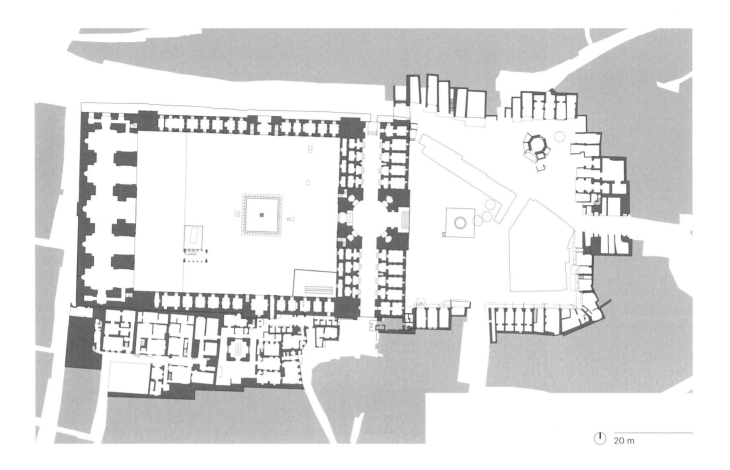

The as-found plan of the Wazir Khan Chowk, showing encroachments in the *chowk* and the residences that were allowed to be built in the open endowed land to its south.

1. The neighbourhood of the mosque includes the Wazir Khan Chowk, certain smaller protected buildings, and buildings not protected under any law but of a certain heritage value. Until the completion of the first phase of the Shahi Guzargah project, the neighbourhood context was one of generally unregulated land use, building activity and indifferent utility infrastructure. Some of these elements were deleterious to the mosque's fabric.

2. The mosque has suffered from several instances of structural failure, in addition to the effects of neglect and lack of maintenance and upkeep. These structural symptoms are manifested in the leaning outwards of the four *minars*, in the resultant structural cracks induced in the structure of the prayer chamber, in cracks caused by subsidence of south-eastern parts of the courtyard due to water ingress from inadequately sited and ill-maintained ablution and toilet facilities, and from the faulty egress of water from rooftops. These latter structural problems had also affected the buildings constituting the Calligraphers' Bazaar that run along the courtyard on its eastern flank.

3. The building fabric suffers from endemic failure of maintenance, from unfriendly use and from weathering decay. The decay is also reflected in poor understanding of historic materials used in the construction of the mosque.

CONSERVATION OF THE WAZIR KHAN CHOWK

Work on the rehabilitation of the seventeenth-century urban square began in October 2015. Financial assistance for the project was provided to the AKCS-P/WCLA partnership by the US Ambassadors Fund for Cultural Preservation and the Aga Khan Trust for Culture (AKTC).

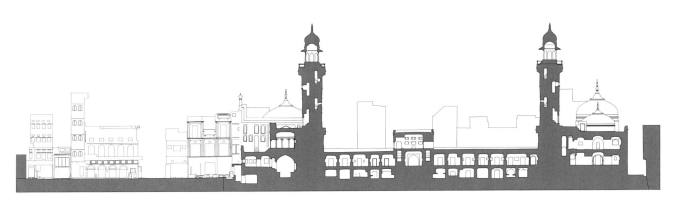

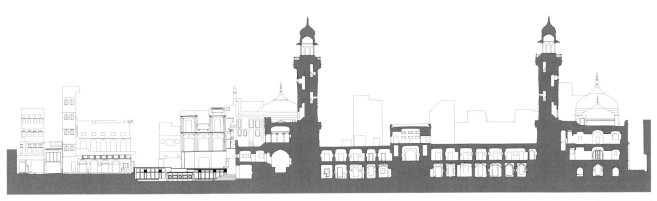

12 m

Above, two sections of the mosque showing the *chowk* in its as-found (top) and after-conservation (bottom) states.

Below, plan of the *chowk* after conservation.

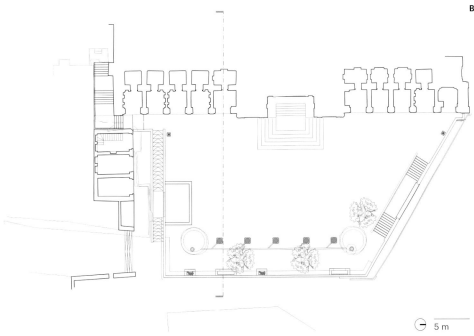

5 m

Shops dealing in metalwork occupied the *hujras* on the Wazir Khan Mosque's eastern facade prior to conservation.

A multitude of contemporary structures had encroached upon the space of the *chowk*, and there was little separating it from the untidy and unregulated condition of its immediate environment. These encroachments were removed and their owners compensated by the Walled City of Lahore Authority (WCLA),[6] allowing conservation work to be initiated. The work sought to restore the mosque's sense of place and history by creating a grade separation between the existing street level and the original ground level of the forecourt by lowering the floor of part of the *chowk* by about two metres.

The main components of the project, completed in September 2017, were:

‣ careful unearthing of the original Mughal-period floor with archaeological explorations and restoration of any discoveries made; excavations were conducted in a systematic manner and all material was filtered through a 10-millimetre sieve. Any archaeological finds were noted for location coordinates and depth of the stratum in which they were found. The floor was restored as were the main steps leading up to the entrance;

‣ construction of a 92-metre, reinforced cement-concrete retaining wall with seating alongside;

‣ construction of a stage in the *chowk* area and an equipment room beneath it;

- documentation, investigation and conservation of twenty-two *hujras*[7] in the Calligraphers' Bazaar, which also form the east facade of the mosque complex;
- provision of an electrification system and illumination of the *chowk* and the mosque's eastern facade;
- construction of two 22-metre-deep soakage wells and integration of rainwater collectors for an effective rainwater drainage system.

Part of the rehabilitation project of the Wazir Khan Chowk was the conservation of the Dina Nath Well – a Mughal-period, octagonal public well located in the north-east section of the *chowk*. Prior to the project, access to the Dina Nath Well was cleared by removing several adjacent shops and restaurants that had been built in proximity to the historic structure. Archaeological excavations inside and around the well structure resulted in the discovery of features belonging to the Mughal and Sikh eras.

The conservation of the Dina Nath Well has involved removal of inappropriate past intervention and the construction of a retaining wall around the octagonal structure. A study of the structure's features, especially its dome, was carried out, which led to the final conservation strategies. Only half of the lime renders over the well's dome were reapplied, with the remaining half conserved as found in the interest of authenticity and public information.

Negotiations have begun with the keepers of the shrine of Syed Suf – the dome over which was rebuilt to twice its nineteenth-century size in 1990 – to rebuild the shrine after removing the dome which obstructs the axial vista from Chitta Gate to the entrance of the mosque.

CONSERVATION OF THE WAZIR KHAN MOSQUE'S NORTH FACADE
The AKCS-P/WCLA partnership began the conservation of the Wazir Khan Mosque's north facade in September 2015. The project took place in two phases. The first phase focused on the conservation and structural consolidation of the building fabric and was completed in June 2016. The second phase of the project, which

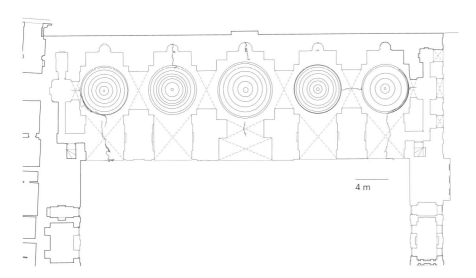

4 m

Above, a major crack in one of the arches of the prayer chamber.

Below, erosion of plaster and loss of frescoes due to high-pressure washing of the brick floor.

Left, documentation of structural cracks in the prayer hall of the Wazir Khan Mosque.

Following pages, a view of the Wazir Khan Chowk clearing showing encroachments and the Syed Suf Shrine, with a dome much enlarged in 1990.

commenced in July 2016 and was completed in August 2017, included the conservation and enhancement of the artistic features of the north facade that consists of glazed-tile-mosaic panels. Both phases were generously funded by the Royal Norwegian Embassy and AKTC.

Prior to its conservation, encroachments and accretions covered the entire north facade of the Wazir Khan Mosque at street level. Additionally, since the road level had increased over time by about 1.5 metres, water ingress resulting from poor rainwater drainage had damaged the foundations and the buried northern aspect of the mosque. Work on the 75-metre-long, 8-metre-high northern facade of the Wazir Khan Mosque included structural strengthening, repair of brickwork, installing new *katehras* (railings) and terracotta screens at courtyard-level openings, restoring the facade's decorative features, and upgrading the rainwater and drainage system. Due to time and financial constraints, the rehabilitation of minarets was not included.

Before conservation strategies were implemented, the AKTC team carried out a detailed as-found documentation of the northern facade using EDM and photo-orthorectification. An analysis of the facade's architectural embellishments, such as carved brick patterns, carved horizontal bands and terracotta screens, was carried out. Archaeological excavations revealed the buried section of the facade while the removal of 1.5 metres of centuries-old strata enabled the reclamation of the full height of the mosque's north facade. A reinforced-concrete wall was built to retain the weight of the higher-level road and traffic, while creating a space in front of the

Aerial views of the Wazir Khan Chowk after conservation.

excavated facade of the mosque. The retaining wall also protects the mosque's north facade from future encroachments. Subsequently, a condition analysis of the facade helped to identify priority areas and activities. Restitution drawings were prepared, based on information collected through this documentation and the analysis phase of the project, as well as historical evidence uncovered on site, which then led to the development of conservation proposals for the facade.

The first phase of the conservation of the Wazir Khan Mosque's north facade consisted of the following main components and activities:

▸ *Conservation and structural consolidation of* hujras

At its lowest level, the northern facade of the Wazir Khan Mosque consists of sixteen *hujras*, which are generally in the form of a single cell (2.5 × 2.2 metres) and an attached veranda (2.7 × 3.1 metres). Excavations carried out to expose the *hujras* revealed brick masonry walls which had deteriorated badly due to water ingress and excessive mutilation by encroachers. Additionally, the walls and dome surfaces had been plastered with a cement-sand mortar. The partition walls of the *hujras* were found damaged, with a considerable amount of masonry missing, caused by structural changes brought about by the removed occupants.

Image taken from the south-east corner of the Wazir Khan Mosque looking north towards encroachments within the *chowk* and on its perimeter.

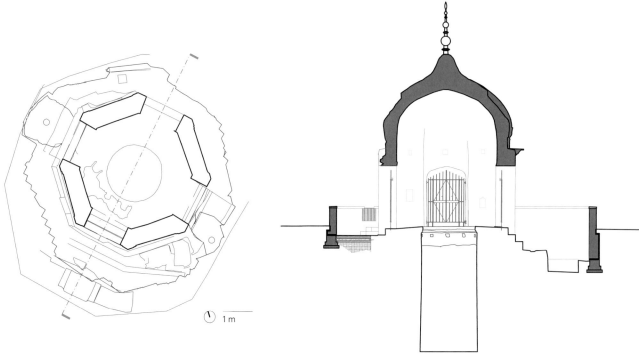

The conservation and structural consolidation strategies adopted for the *hujras* included careful removal of cement-sand plasters from brick surfaces; repair of damaged brick masonry using historic hand-moulded bricks and lime mortar; restoration of interior and exterior niches, brick masonry lintels and arches; installation of wooden doors; and cleaning of brick masonry surfaces.

▸ *Conservation and structural consolidation of the facade*

The ornamented features of the Wazir Khan Mosque's north facade include cut-and-dressed brickwork, carved brick patterns, horizontal masonry bands, brick medallions, brick-imitation work, terracotta screens, and wrought-iron railings. These were extensively damaged, especially at the lower, buried sections, by excessive dampness. The facade surface and decorative features had been inappropriately treated with cement-sand plaster, and most of the brick arches were deformed due to misuse of the *hujras* and lack of proper maintenance.

For the conservation of the north facade, a minimal intervention approach was adopted, consisting of: careful removal of inappropriate interventions; stabilization of damaged masonry sections with suitable brick tiles and lime mortar; repair of damaged arches, brick medallions and carved brick bands; restoration of all perforated terracotta screens; repair of wrought-iron grills, which were then repainted with epoxy corrosion protection; repair of wooden doors/windows; and installation of metal-clad wooden sunshades to protect openings from rainfall. Some of these items represented British-period interventions.

▸ *Restoration of brick-tile flooring*

After establishing the original floor levels of the previously buried *hujras* and the historic street, the base for a new brick-tile flooring was prepared by laying a 75-millimetre-thick layer of brick ballast followed by a layer of lime concrete. The street was laid with brick tiles arranged in a 90-degree herringbone pattern using lime mortar gauged with ten per cent cement. In the case of *hujras*, flooring was laid in a basket-weave pattern.

Opposite page, above, Dina Nath Well after conservation. Below, conservation plan and section of the well.

Below, left, an array of openings linking the outer porticos of the *hujras* located along the eastern facade of the Wazir Khan Mosque, after conservation.

Middle and right, details of the reconstructed elements of the dome of the Dina Nath Well.

4 m

▸ *Upgrading the rainwater disposal system*
The (approximate) 1.5-metre difference between the current road level and the historic street level prevented rainwater draining from the lower level into the elevated existing water drainage system. Traditional rainwater drains were rebuilt running along the length of the facade and finished in a lime render. Rainwater collectors were integrated into the historic streets' newly laid brick-tile flooring. The collected water was then piped to drain into the recently constructed soakage wells in the Wazir Khan Chowk.

▸ *Electrification and illumination system*
One of the *hujras* was used to house the electrification system of the north facade. This system controls the external lights installed to illuminate the facade, steps and niches. All outdoor wiring was concealed and buried underground, while indoor wiring was exposed and placed on the surface using safe conduits. The electrification system is designed to connect to an uninterrupted power source (UPS) in case of power outages, and for installing air-conditioning units if required. Additionally, the conservation project made it possible to install six surveillance cameras at three different locations on the wall retaining the existing road in front of the northern facade.

Opposite page, the Wazir Khan Mosque's northern facade before conservation, showing shop encroachments along the building.

Above, the Wazir Khan Mosque's north facade: partial photo-orthorectified documentation before encroachments were removed (top) and photo-orthorectified documentation after encroachments were removed and buried *hujras* were uncovered (bottom).

The second phase of the project began with a detailed documentation of the glazed-tile panels. The glazed-tile work is arranged in square and rectangular panels and, in the case of the Wazir Khan Mosque, they consist of geometric, calligraphic and floral patterns laid into a mosaic using cut glazed-tile pieces of different sizes and colours.

After the documentation, a condition analysis of the north facade's glazed-tile work was carried out. This included an analysis of traditional materials and tile-manufacturing techniques, and the following steps were taken for the conservation of the tile-work panels, as well as those found on the parapet of the mosque:

- all tile work was carefully cleaned, stabilized, consolidated and sealed against water penetration;
- in instances where tile work had been lost but there existed evidence of its pattern, the imagery was completed using appropriate methods and material;
- where tile work was missing and no evidence of the pattern could be found, the tile work was reconstructed based on symmetrical mirroring generally found in the facade, but using neutral coloured pieces;
- new, matching glazed-tile pieces were reintegrated into panels that were missing individual pieces or groups of glazed-tile pieces;
- in cases where the glaze was flaking off, the loose glaze was stabilized. Additionally, where there was loss of adhesion between the tile pieces and the mortar bed, these were grouted and consolidated accordingly;
- all open joints between existing tile pieces were pointed with fine lime mortar to seal the surface and protect the panels from water infiltration;
- in general, all glazed tiles that were produced to restore the ornamentation had a slightly matt finish, by adding tin or zinc in the glaze, so as to establish a distinction between the old and the new.

Wazir Khan Mosque's north facade showing shops extending out from it and concrete slabs inserted into the fabric of the building.

Artisans working on the conservation of *kashikari* (glazed-tile work) on the north facade of the mosque.

CONSERVATION OF THE REMAINING PARTS OF THE WAZIR KHAN MOSQUE

In 2017 the government of Punjab approved a project of PKR 555 (USD 5.33) million for the conservation of the Wazir Khan Mosque to commence in March 2018. The project, to be completed by June 2022 and implemented under a partnership agreement between the WCLA and AKCS-P, consists of two major dimensions: the rehabilitation of the neighbourhood context, and the conservation of the monument itself.

The rehabilitation of the neighbourhood involves the removal of intrusive structures, which include properties constructed on the southern side of the mosque abutting its southern wall, the rehabilitation of historic houses with some architectural or artistic merit built during the British period located on the southern perimeter of the Wazir Khan Chowk, rehabilitation of facades in the Wazir Khan Chowk, and conservation of Chitta Gate – the arched entrance way into the *chowk*, along with structures flanking the gate on its north and south. Also included are the acquisition, modification or reconstruction of several multi-storey structures on the northern perimeter; the construction of a structure containing public lavatories, ablution facilities and administrative offices; and the development of an open area on the southern side of the mosque, which would contain and frame the domed tomb of Imam Ghulam Muhammad (d. 1828), a *khateeb* (main prayer leader) of the mosque.

Above, *hujras* along the southern flank of the mosque's courtyard.

Right, shops in the Calligraphers' Bazaar.

The conservation of the mosque itself consists of several integrated components. They involve structural consolidation and strengthening of the mosque structure using compatible materials; rehabilitation of the building fabric, including making it weather resistant; conservation of the mosque's internal and external ornamented surfaces, detailed documentation and damage analysis, including laboratory testing of existing materials; identifying deteriorated areas, and developing the sequence of conservation activities; conservation of cut-and-dressed brick flooring; upgrading the mosque's electricity distribution system; installation of CCTV surveillance cameras and walk-through security gates at all major entrances to the mosque; upgrading the mosque's public address and sound amplification system; installation of a new HVAC system; and the integration of an improved drainage and rainwater disposal system.

Residential properties encroaching against the southern facade of the Wazir Khan Mosque. The tomb of Imam Ghulam Muhammad (d. 1828) can be seen in the foreground.

1   The name is also often transcribed as Hakim 'Aliuddin Ansari.

2   The Sufis who led this centre are buried in the vicinity: the grave of Syed Izhaq Gazruni (d. 1384) was incorporated in the mosque itself; Syed Suf is buried in the Wazir Khan Chowk and Syed Sarbuland in a neighbourhood to the north, just over 21 metres from the mosque.

3   Syad Muhammad Latif, *Lahore: Its History, Architectural Remains and Antiquities*, New Imperial Press, Lahore, 1892.

4   A *hujra* is one of a series of small cells, part of the sanctified space of a mosque.

5   Aga Khan Cultural Service-Pakistan, "Conservation of the Wazir Khan Mosque Lahore: Preliminary Report on Condition and Risk Assessment", Lahore, Pakistan. Aga Khan Historic Cities Programme, 2012.

6   The compensation was negotiated and paid, and the removals effected, as part of the joint Punjab Government-World Bank Shahi Guzargah Pilot Project, a part of the Punjab

Municipal Services Improvement Project. Similar settlements were made with other groups of businesses in that project.

7   In this specific case, a *hujra* is a cell used as a shop built into the body of the building.

THE MASTERPLAN FOR LAHORE FORT (2017–PRESENT)

LAHORE FORT: HISTORY, CONTEXT, THE MONUMENTAL AREA AND ITS BUFFER ZONE

MASOOD KHAN

EARLY DEVELOPMENTS

Lahore Fort had existed for centuries before Muslim invaders arrived from Central Asia at the end of the tenth century. Though scant, archaeological evidence corroborates its occupation from the sixth century. It is believed that the Ghaznavid invasion in 1021–22 laid Lahore to waste and that the city remained depopulated for several years. During the Sultanate period, local rulers were made responsible for the security of peripheral regions, while Delhi remained the locus of power. Lahore regained its political importance in the years following the first Mughal invasion of 1524 and then 1526 when Babur swept past it on his way to Delhi, defeating Ibrahim, the last Lodhi monarch, and establishing the Mughal Empire.

THE MUGHAL PERIOD

According to historical accounts, Akbar, the third Mughal emperor, was unhappy with the state of the Fort on his first visit to Lahore in 1557. This prompted an ambitious programme of repair and rehabilitation and the construction of buildings of befitting scale and grandeur. New walls to fortify both the city and the citadel were built. Akbar is credited with laying down the typology of the fortified Mughal palace-fort in Lahore and Agra, making large use of the Transoxianian and Timurid styles that the Mughals brought to India, while at the same time creating a rich and unique amalgam of influences by making use of Indian craftsmen, decorative patterns and architectural features. After Akbar moved to Lahore in 1586, Lahore Fort served as his strategic base for twelve years, almost until the end of his forty-nine-year rule. The Fort was successively added to, enriched and transformed by emperors Jahangir, Shah Jahan and Aurangzeb. These successive transformations have, in the past, been conveniently classified and attributed to discrete zones of the Fort as the legacy of one or the other of the four emperors. Their respective contributions are generally additive in nature, moving from the east to the west. However, careful consideration of the available evidence points to a complex layering of interventions made of demolitions, reconstruction, afterthoughts, adaptive transformations and additions to existing spaces and buildings, often turned into completely new and ostensibly independent entities.

THE AKBAR PHASE

Akbari developments occupy the central space of the Fort and came about as a consequence of Akbar moving his capital from Fatehpur Sikri to Lahore. Early European visitors to Akbar's court in Lahore describe a large enclosure with a southern sector

Preceding pages, a view over the Hazuri Bagh towards the Badshahi Mosque, with Ranjit Singh's *baradari* in the foreground.

Opposite page, the Sheesh Mahal, or Palace of Mirrors, is part of Shah Burj, built by Shah Jahan in Lahore Fort. The facade consists of five multi-cusped marble arches that are supported by coupled columns.

Above, Jahangiri-period glazed-tile work on the Picture Wall: courtiers bearing a fly-whisk and the royal sword.

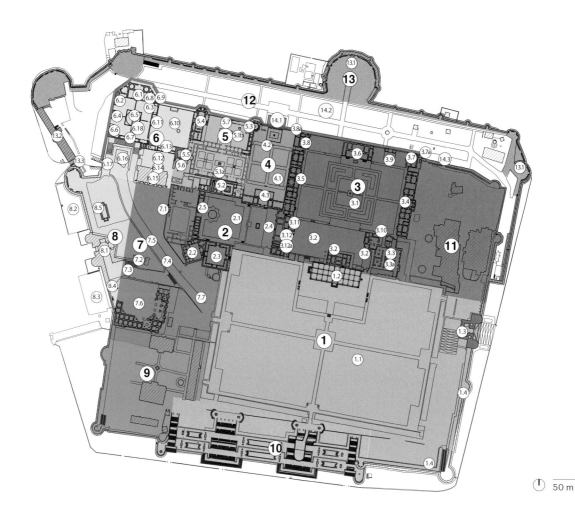

50 m

| 1. Diwan-e-Aam Quadrangle | 3.7 Mashriqui (Eastern) Suite | 6. Shah Burj Quadrangle | 7.3 Ramp of Alamgiri Darwaza | 13.2 Postern Gate Barracks |

1. Diwan-e-Aam Quadrangle
1.1 Maidan-e-Diwan-e-Aam
1.2 Diwan-e-Aam
1.3 Akbari Darwaza
1.4 East & South-East Fortification Wall

2. Moti Masjid Quadrangle
2.1 Moti Masjid Quadrangle
2.2 Moti Masjid
2.3 Makateeb Khana
2.4 Dalaan-e-Sang-e-Surkh & Open Terrace
2.5 Western Chambers

3. Jahangir's Quadrangle
3.1 Jahangir's Quadrangle
3.2 Daulat Khana-e-Khaas-o-Aam & its associate foundation remains
3.3 Eastern end of Akbar's Daulat Khana
3.3a Kharak Singh Haveli (upper floors of 3.3)
3.4 Mashriqui (Eastern) Iwans
3.5 Maghribi (Western) Iwans
3.6 Jahangir's Khwabgah

3.7 Mashriqui (Eastern) Suite
3.7a Mashriqui (Eastern) Burj
3.8 Maghribi (Western) Suite
3.8a Maghribi (Western) Burj
3.9 Sehdara Bangla Pavilion East
3.10 Junoobi (Southern) Iwan
3.11 Zenana Hammam
3.12 Western end of Akbar's Daulat Khana
3.12a Mai Jindan Haveli (upper floor of 3.12)

4. Shah Jahan's Quadrangle
4.1 Shah Jahan's Quadrangle
4.2 Diwan-e-Khaas
4.3 Khwabgah-e-Shah Jahani

5. Paeen Bagh Quadrangle
5.1a Paeen Bagh Quadrangle
5.1b Khilwat Khana Quadrangle
5.2 Hammam-e-Badshahi
5.3 Lal Burj
5.4 Kala Burj
5.5 Imperial Zenana Mosque
5.6 Sikh Temple
5.7 Khilwat Khana

6. Shah Burj Quadrangle
6.1 Sheesh Mahal
6.2 West Sehdara Pavilion North
6.3 East Sehdara
6.4 Naulakha Pavilion
6.5 Shah Burj Water Basin
6.6 West Sehdara Pavilion South
6.7 South Dalaans
6.8 Sikh Bath
6.9 Sikh Burj
6.10 Shah Burj Forecourt
6.11 Ath Dara
6.12 Hathi Reception Court
6.13 Gor Darwaza
6.14 South Dalaans
6.15 British Garages
6.16 Hathi Pol/Ghulam Gardish
6.17 Shah Burj Darwaza
6.18 Summer Palace

7. Western Remains and Imperial Kitchens
7.1 Western Ruins (adjacent to Moti Masjid Quadrangle)
7.2 Gateway to Western Palaces

7.3 Ramp of Alamgiri Darwaza
7.4 Vehicular Ramp
7.5 British Bridge
7.6 Imperial Kitchens
7.7 Car Park

8. Alamgiri Darwaza
8.1 Alamgiri Darwaza
8.2 Eastern Wall of Hazuri Bagh (N)
8.3 Eastern Wall of Hazuri Bagh (S)
8.4 Loh's Temple
8.5 Barood Khana (British Armoury)

9. PIATR and associated elements

10. Ceremonial Steps

11. Staff Quarters – Archaeological Zone

12. Picture Wall

13. Outer Fortication
13.1 Main Outer Fortification

13.2 Postern Gate Barracks
13.3 Postern Gate

14. Other
14.1 Arz Gah
14.2 Space between Picture Wall and Northern Fortification Wall (the moat)
14.3 Historic (arched) ruins discovered behind the recently collapsed retaining wall

for public and ceremonial audiences. On the northern side of this great court was a sprawling palace, the Daulat Khana-e-Khaas-o-Aam, which stretched 152 metres east to west from a point near the eastern gate, opening onto the city. Most probably, the palace also occupied the space currently used as staff quarters. On the southern face of this palace, overlooking the public enclosure, was the emperor's *jharoka*, the balcony where he would appear for public audience. On the north of the Daulat Khana was a somewhat smaller, private courtyard – a *chahar-bagh* – with a large body of water and palace structures overlooking the river to the north. Not many of these Akbari structures survive today, but some that do bear the unmistakable imprint of

Opposite page, inventory of the principal spatial entities and related structures in Lahore Fort.

Above, Akbar's Daulat Khana. Arched *dalaans* overlooking the northern (Jahangir's) quadrangle, showing interventions probably made during the Sikh period.

Above, the Moti Masjid, view from the south-east.

Right, the Makateeb Khana, the small square built by Jahangir in the north-west corner of the Diwan-e-Aam Quadrangle.

the architectural idiom of Fatehpur Sikri. *Dalaans* with red sandstone facades form the three remaining sides of this landscaped court. This courtyard is said to have been altered by Jahangir and is today called Jahangir's Quadrangle. It is plausible that, in this court, the northern, riverside row of buildings were radically altered during the Jahangir period; little is left, however, of the original state of buildings from this era on this side of the courtyard.

THE JAHANGIR PHASE

Jahangir's main contributions to the Fort are to be found further to the west and appear less cohesive and orderly than those of Akbar, as well as overlaid by Shah Jahan's later constructions. Two structures that were built during Jahangir's reign are the Moti Masjid[1] and the small square now called the Makateeb Khana, as attested by an epigram on its *iwan* entablature. The Moti Masjid and Makateeb Khana form the southern flank of the court called the Moti Masjid Quadrangle. The Makateeb Khana may, in fact, have been the entrance to the palace Jahangir mentions in his memoirs. It is plausible that the structures on the northern and western sides of this quadrangle also belong to the Jahangiri period, although on the northern side they were improved or rebuilt by Shah Jahan. The western facade of Akbar's Daulat Khana, known as the Dalaan-e-Sang-e-Surkh, is also attributed to Jahangir and forms the eastern side of this quadrangle. Two more structures fifty metres further to the north, Lal Burj and Kala Burj, punctuate the northern perimeter of this part of the Fort and are also to be attributed to Jahangir as attested by the European portraiture and iconography in Kala Burj. If so, the space occupied by Jahangir-period developments

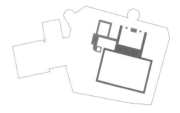

Above, buildings of the Jahangiri phase.

■ Akbar
■ Jahangir

Below, Lahore Fort. Aerial view looking north-west from the Diwan-e-Aam Quadrangle at the Moti Masjid Quadrangle, Shah Jahan's Quadrangle and the Paeen Bagh. Also seen on the left is the 1853 vehicle access road dug into the historical mound by the British military.

was actually much larger than Akbar's northern quadrangle and would have been framed by the Moti Masjid and the Makateeb Khana on the south, the structures of the Akbari Quadrangle to the east, the two Burjs to the north, and a series of structures that no longer exist except for a limited number of *hujras* to the west. Finally, Jahangir is also responsible for the beginnings of Shah Burj, but work on this was halted with his death in 1627.

THE SHAH JAHAN PHASE
It seems that the same quadrangle with Jahangir's various buildings mentioned above was altered with the addition of Shah Jahan's sleeping chambers (Khwabgah-e-Shah Jahani), the imperial hammam and the Diwan-e-Khaas, all built during the Shah Jahan period. Additional modifications occurred with the construction of the Paeen Bagh and its surrounding structures, which determined the consequent creation of Khilwat Khana Square.

The comprehensive redesign of Shah Burj and the overlays and replacements in most of the earlier constructions west of the Jahangir Quadrangle were carried out under Shah Jahan, and represent both size and architectural complexity. In Shah Burj, Shah Jahan was the first to defy the rectangular envelope of the earlier Fort and to introduce a new architectural idiom – a large rectangle with a half octagon at its north protruding from the confines of the old apron wall at the north-western corner of the Fort complex. There was, however, a clear overlap between the Jahangiri and the Shah Jahani palace developments. This is marked also by the Imperial Kitchens, which would have served the palace establishment during both successive reigns, although at present they are separated by a British-period road and partially ruined. In its advanced configuration, the Shah Jahani palace extended from the half octagon tower and adjacent forecourt all the way to the Imperial Kitchens.

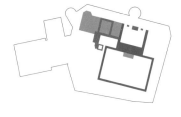

Above, building elements of the Shah Jahan phase.

■ Akbar
■ Jahangir
■ Shah Jahan

Below, interior of the great portico of the Sheesh Mahal, extensively decorated with mirror mosaics and wall paintings.

Above, Shah Burj. The Sheesh Mahal viewed axially from the southern side of the court. The marble columns and arches of the Sheesh Mahal portico are the focal point of the court.

Left, the Shah Jahan-period Diwan-e-Aam, described by contemporary writers as a *chahl sutoon* (hall of forty pillars), was much altered during the British army's occupation of the Fort. Photographed from Akbar's *jharoka* (the marble balcony for public audience) looking towards the great court of the Diwan-e-Aam.

Following pages, the Diwan-e-Aam seen on axis from the south.

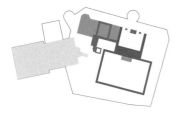

Above, building works of the Aurangzeb period.

- Akbar
- Jahangir
- Shah Jahan
- Aurangzeb

Below, left, detail of the facade of the Bad-shahi Mosque prayer chamber. The facade features red sandstone bas relief ornament on red stone, and white marble inlay and relief on sandstone. Right, the mosque's interior is decorated with stucco tracery, *naqqashi* fresco, semi-precious stone dados on the walls, intarsia stone inlaid prayer mats on the floor, and carved marble wall panel framing.

The Shah Burj palace was accessed through the elaborate Shah Burj Darwaza, one of the more exquisitely decorated gate entrances of the Mughal era, with a finely calligraphed inscription on the arch's transom frame. Mounted elephants carried royalty from the Hathi Pol, a courtyard behind the gate at ground level, by means of ceremonial 'elephant stairs' to an elephant dismounting court outside the palace confines some ten metres above. Before Aurangzeb's interventions, the Hathi Pol and the Darwaza would have been linked to the space *extra moenia* through the riverside Roshnai Gate and Taxali Gate further to the south-west. During the reign of Shah Jahan, the ornamented Picture Wall along the north and west side of the exterior apron wall of the citadel came to its completion. It marks a significant continuity of artistic expression that lasted three successive sovereignties from the time of Akbar to the closing of Shah Jahan's reign.

Shah Jahan also addressed a perennial need of the royal court in front of Akbar's Daulat Khana-e-Khaas-o-Aam, and had a large pavilion, the Diwan-e-Aam, built to protect the court assembly from the elements. Until then the court had had to make do with the large tent structure that Mughal courts were famous for. Having suffered severe damage from canon shots during Sikh-period warfare, this building still exists, albeit in a transmogrified form after its use by the British as a barrack-hospital and its restoration afterwards.

The sequence of developments during the respective reigns of Akbar, Jahangir and Shah Jahan can also be observed in the progressive variations in the iconography of the tile decorations on the Picture Wall – the name by which the apron wall of the Fort looking over the river and defining the northern and north-western limits of the Fort has come to be known. On this wall, the glazed-tile decorations from the late Akbari period are characterized largely by floral motifs. These change to include the depiction of human and animal figures during the period of Jahangir. Finally, during the reign of Shah Jahan, the scale and iconography of the Picture Wall become markedly enhanced and flamboyant both in narrative and decorative idiom.

THE AURANGZEB PHASE

Alamgiri Gate, to the south of the Shah Burj Darwaza and the Hathi Pol, is the principal addition of Aurangzeb's reign to the precinct of the Fort. This development was part of an ambitious new project – the construction of a new mosque for Lahore, the Badshahi Masjid, the largest congregational mosque built during the Mughal Empire. The mosque and Alamgiri Gate, and the serai that forms the intervening space[2] between the two call into play a new spatial organization based on the *qibla* direction This new development was connected to the inner precinct through the imposing new gate, built in the centre of the new external wall, angled to conform to the axial orientation of the new geometry. On the side of the Fort, the bent entrance of the gate led up via a ramp to the foot of the southern gate of the palaces that faced the Imperial Kitchens. Since the Shah Burj Darwaza built in the time of Shah Jahan already existed on the western side, it is unlikely that this new entrance to the Fort replaced an earlier entrance located at the same location.

THE SIKH PHASE

During the period that followed the death of Mughal emperor Aurangzeb in 1707 and the turbulent period of Sikh rise to power, the Fort fell into disuse as the seat of central power and was badly damaged. In the second half of the eighteenth century, the

Above, the entrance gateway of the Badshahi Mosque.

Below, interventions of the Sikh period.

- ■ Akbar
- ■ Jahangir
- ■ Shah Jahan
- ▨ Aurangzeb
- ■ Sikh Period

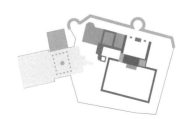

Sikhs achieved sporadic political and military dominance in Punjab. In 1799 Ranjit Singh assumed power over the province of Lahore. Styling himself Maharaja Ranjit Singh, he ruled for forty years over greater Punjab and the frontier areas all the way up to Kabul. Ranjit Singh and his immediate successors brought about many transformations in Lahore Fort. In Shah Burj, which was used as the private quarters of the maharaja, the prominent interventions made were in the Sheesh Mahal and its upper storey. A marked intervention was made in the eastern wall of its courtyard in the south-east corner, from where a *dalaan* pavilion was removed and a doorway introduced. The outer court of Shah Burj on its east was used for appearances by the maharaja in crowded court events associated with a new pavilion, the Athdara. A small temple was also built adjacent to the Zenana Mosque, possibly by sacrificing the formal entrance portal into the Paeen Bagh.

Additional structures were built on what remained of the Daulat Khana of the Akbari period. The western end became the new palace of Ranjit's queen, Maharani Jind Kaur. The *haveli* of Maharaja Kharak Singh was erected on top of the eastern end of the Daulat Khana. A small pavilion called the *baradari* of Khushhal Singh was built at the crossing of the maidan of the Diwan-e-Aam. Outside the citadel, Ranjit Singh converted the Badshahi Masjid's forecourt serai into the *chahar-bagh* garden named Hazuri Bagh. A two-storey marble *baradari* was erected in the middle of the

Interior and exterior views of Ranjit Singh's Hazuri Bagh Pavilion, which sits at the centre of the Hazuri Bagh Quadrangle. It consists of delicate cusped arches supported by coupled columns and has a mirrored ceiling and many delicate carved white marble details.

Hazuri Bagh on the crossing of this four-quartered garden. Quite significant and more momentous for the exterior appearance of the Fort was the construction of the outer fortifications of the city. These fortifications were demolished during the British period, except those contiguous to the Fort. Only the portion that lies north of the citadel and in front of the Picture Wall has survived.

THE BRITISH COLONIAL PERIOD

The British military occupation of the Fort began in 1849, the year Punjab was annexed by the East India Company. Evidence from this period demonstrates a marked disregard for anything of historic or cultural significance within the premises of the Fort. Following the occupation of the Fort, the two major Mughal-period gates, Akbar's eastern gate and Aurangzeb's Alamgiri Gate were bricked up and regular entrance to the Fort was established through the Hathi Pol. Subsequently, an outer wall was built to seal off the space in front of the Hathi Pol, which was then made accessible through a Postern Gate. This gate gave access to a new road cut into the mound of the citadel to allow vehicular access to the garages built on the southern flank of the Elephant Reception Square, as well as the rest of the Fort grounds. The road, which exists to this day, could be built only after the removal of the southern wall of the Hathi Pol courtyard. Making the various parts of the Fort accessible to vehicles was, in fact, an important consideration of the British army, which did not hesitate to demolish structures from the Mughal period where necessary for this purpose. In addition, several army barracks were built within the Fort, including three large military quarters in the Diwan-e-Aam maidan. The damaged Diwan-e-Aam was rebuilt and converted into a barracks, with a new veranda built along its front, later enclosed when the building became a military hospital. A significant modification was the removal of the original enclosure of the Diwan-e-Aam maidan, which consisted of arched cells that lined the eastern, southern and western sides, punctuated by central gates on the north-south and east-west axes. All British army buildings were gradually removed

Above, Lahore Fort. Aerial view looking south over the British Ceremonial Steps, which replaced the southern fortifications of the Fort.

Below, interventions of the British period.

- ▆ Akbar
- ▆ Jahangir
- ▆ Shah Jahan
- ▆ Aurangzeb
- ▆ Sikh Period
  British Colonial Period

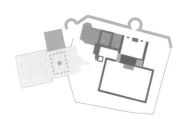

after the Fort was handed over to the civil authorities in 1924. Lastly, a significant transformation occurred along the south side of the Lahore Fort fortifications. These were largely demolished and replaced by a series of terraces connected by flights of steps in order to demilitarize the Fort.

LATER DEVELOPMENTS

Most of the transformations that followed the handing over to the civilian authorities focused on the adaptive reuse of existing buildings to serve as exhibition spaces and the construction of staff living quarters on the north-east angle of the Fort enclave. Office facilities for the staff of the Archaeology Department and the Pakistan Institute of Archaeological Training and Research (PIATR) were also built on the south-west sector of the Fort.

LAHORE FORT IN THE CONTEXT OF THE WALLED CITY AND CENTRAL LAHORE

Lahore Fort lies on the north-western corner of the Walled City by the old banks of the Ravi River. Lahore occupied an important strategic position, both militarily and commercially, along the way from Afghanistan to the northern Indian plains. These favourable conditions, however, proved to be double-edged. From the tenth century onwards, Lahore was vulnerable to attack in periodic invasions from the north that were the harbinger of Muslim rule in India, but which also laid it waste more than once.

For long periods of time Lahore remained part of the north Indian province centred on the city of Multan, some 375 kilometres to the south-west, and became the seat of the province bearing its own name during the reign of the first two Mughal emperors, Babur and Humayun.

Other geographic and urban development factors have contributed to and affected the way in which Lahore Fort and other core monuments relate to the rest of the urban fabric. Lahore Fort's relationship with the meandering course of the river changed over time along the western and northern edges of the city's fortifications, while in the city itself new neighbourhoods were created. The historic pathways that connected the city gates to the entrances of the Fort took on different meanings as they were altered during the Mughal, Sikh and British periods. The edges of the Walled City's urban fabric around the Fort and their relationship with the city's foremost landmark also evolved. These edges at first maintained a distance from the Fort to provide space for ceremonial events and military requirements but have progressively encroached upon the intervening space as a result of more recent commercial developments. The vicissitudes of time and the sheer dynamism of change have altered the context of the Fort and transformed the traditional relationship between the Walled City and its fortified citadel. The varied urban, visual and sensory relationships of Lahore Fort with the surrounding historic city have negatively affected the quality of the monumental complex and the important values it bears, especially in recent times.

THE BUFFER ZONE

The Buffer Zone comprises approximately fifty-seven hectares surrounding the Lahore Fort World Heritage Site and contains the following sub-areas and landmarks:

1. the North Sector including Greater Iqbal Park and the Minar-e-Pakistan, bounded by the newly established North Circular Road;
2. the East Sector aligned along the eastern portion of Fort Road, including the Akbari Gate access to Lahore Fort, Rim Market and the Maryam Zamani (or Begum Shahi) Mosque;

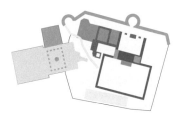

Above, developments after 1947.

■ Akbar
■ Jahangir
■ Shah Jahan
░ Aurangzeb
■ Sikh Period
░ British Colonial Period
Later Developments

Below, Rim Market, part of the eastern part of the Buffer Zone, seen from the ramparts of Lahore Fort.

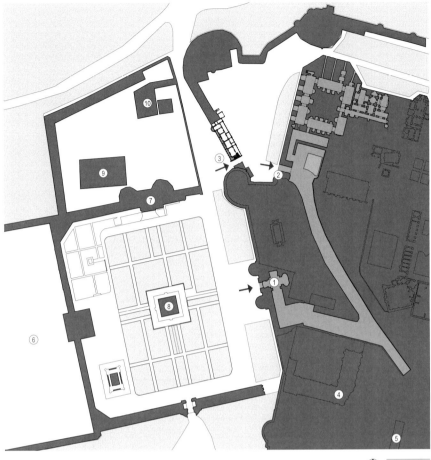

30 m

3. the South-East Sector defined by the southern portion of Fort Road below the Fort's Ceremonial Steps with the adjacent Ali Park and immediate surroundings;
4. the South-West Sector encompassing the so-called "Triangle", the principal south-western access to the Hazuri Bagh and the Badshahi Mosque and a portion of the historic fabric to the south;
5. the West Sector including the facilities and grounds of the Lady Willingdon Hospital flanking the limits of the Badshahi Mosque enclave.

THE NORTH SECTOR

A drive along the re-routed Circular Road shows that the only outer face of the old city that has maintained its skyline and historic features virtually intact, including the Sikh walls and Mughal fortifications, is the approximately one-kilometre-long stretch between the north-west tip of the town and Ravi Road. Today this space is occupied by the remodelled Greater Iqbal Park, which was inaugurated by the prime minister of Pakistan in 2016. The new park has joined together the former Minto and Iqbal parks, a combined fifty-two-hectare public green area.

Originally used as a parade ground, the area was converted into a racecourse at the beginning of the British period. It was subsequently transformed into the Minto and Iqbal parks when the resolution for the creation of a Muslim homeland was passed in 1940. The Minar-e-Pakistan, a 65-metre-tall memorial tower built in part of the former Minto Park, remains the symbol of the country's independence and is the new park's most prominent feature.

The heavy traffic and attendant polluting fumes that used to be concentrated along this former road have now been re-routed along the new artery in a curving

Above, the 1930s housing development in its present condition forming part of the southern flank of the Buffer Zone.

Opposite page, the Minar-e-Pakistan.

alignment around the new Greater Iqbal Park, which contains its own parking zones and pedestrian pathways. As a consequence, the old vehicular entrance into the Lahore Fort precinct, the Hazuri Bagh and the Sikh crematory sites no longer exists, except where and when vehicles are allowed to drive on the park's paved paths intended for pedestrians. This only happens when important guests are driven directly to the Hazuri Bagh, the Badshahi Mosque or the Fort through the Postern Gate.

Greater Iqbal Park remains an area of paramount importance for the safeguarding and presentation of Lahore Fort. Now that the old Circular Road has been relocated, the exterior appearance of the monument along the north prospect of the Walled City should remain protected and unaffected by visual clutter and pollution.

THE EAST SECTOR

The polluting Rim Market is the reason for the concentration of traffic along Fort Road, which affects both the southern edge of the Badshahi Mosque and the southern and eastern edges of Lahore Fort. The combination of traffic and market activities constitutes not only a strong impediment to pedestrian circulation, but also a visual eyesore, given the market's close proximity to the Mughal fortifications.

The problems and the potential of this area are cited in the World Bank feasibility study of 2005. Both the World Bank programme and subsequent 2008 schematic plans prepared by AKTC for the area recommend the removal of the highly polluting

Preceding pages, view of Greater Iqbal Park.

Right, the eastern, south-eastern and south-western sectors of the Buffer Zone.

■ ■ ■ Buffer Zone Boundary

▨ East-Sector (Rim Market Area)

▨ South-East Sector (Ali Park and its vicinity)

▨ South-West Sector (Triangle and neighbourhoods)

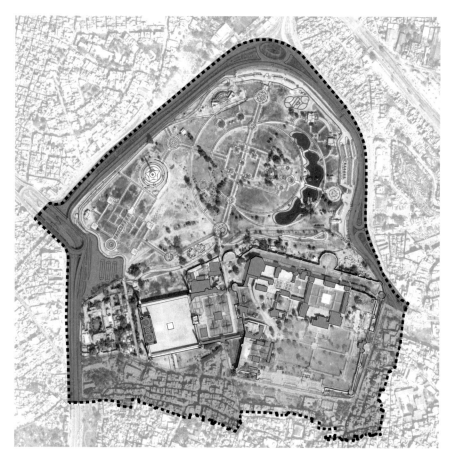

200 m

workshops of Rim Market, decontamination of the area and replacement of the current market with local craft workshops catering to visitors coming from the Fort through Akbari Gate. The scheme calls for the area in front of the gate to be organized and landscaped with a drop-off point for coaches and cars, as well as parking, while Akbari Gate itself is to be reopened to allow visitors to go into Lahore Fort from what was traditionally its most important entrance.

The AKTC plans are meant to dovetail with reopening the view of the Maryam Zamani Mosque, or Begum Shahi Mosque, which is currently encumbered by the shops of Masti Gate Bazaar that conceal the prayer hall's central portal. Built in 1611, the mosque is a classic example of Mughal architecture, with a paved rectangular court and a beautifully decorated prayer hall. The interventions proposed by AKTC in 2008 foresaw the removal of later additions and restoration of the mosque's paved rectangular court, as well as other original features that have been inappropriately altered.

THE SOUTH-EAST SECTOR

This area is centred on Ali Park, a public park that is located below the Fort's Ceremonial Steps. The area is characterized by:

▸ the properties situated south of Ali Park – originally in use as residential properties, these buildings are being substituted or modified for commercial purposes;

▸ the PTCL telecommunication building located in the middle of Ali Park is a potential candidate for adaptive reuse more in keeping with its setting in the park;

▸ on the eastern edge of the park lies the campus of the Government Special Education Centre, a school for special-needs children that necessitates rehabilitation and landscaping;

▸ beyond this, to the east, is the Lahore Fort grid station. It has been proposed in the past that this facility be put underground, as should the cables associated with it. This would allow for the removal of all pylons currently along the north-eastern, eastern and south-eastern sides of the World Heritage Site.

THE SOUTH-WEST SECTOR

This sector includes a portion of the historic fabric south of the so-called "Triangle" and the principal south-western access to the Hazuri Bagh and the Badshahi Mosque. The Triangle has gradually been converted into a 'food street' in recent years, something that has had an unfortunate visual impact on the nearby Badshahi Mosque. In future, the Triangle should be conserved and recycled with care, vision and architectural competence.

Further south of Heera Mandi are the Uncha Chait Ram and beyond that Sheikhupurian Bazaar. The latter is still the only place in the Walled City where traditional shoes crafted in rural Punjab are sold. As a bazaar with historical value this is a fitting place to be included in the zone. South of the Triangle, on the other side of Fort Road in the area known as Neewa Chait Ram, are a series of residential buildings organized around small squares. These buildings were constructed in the first half of the twentieth century in a local derivative of Art Deco and have considerable potential as candidates for rehabilitation to recover their period value.

On the south-east corner of the Triangle, a building purchased by an entrepreneur in 2005 to construct a new hotel lies abandoned and half in ruins due to failed sheet-piling operations. This site provides an excellent opportunity to resurrect the fabric of the area south of the Fort. At the eastern end of this block and east of the grid station are two other elements of note. The first is the shrine of Nathe Shah and Shabeh Shah, and the second is the historic Ikhara of Khalifa Boota (known these days as the Ikhara of Shahia Pahalwan). Both lie under a cluster of old trees and are surrounded on their eastern and southern sides by recent commercial and residential structures.

THE WEST SECTOR

The area is occupied to a large extent by the facilities and grounds of the Lady Willingdon Hospital, next to the Badshahi Mosque enclave. The hospital is a teaching institution active since 1930. It is named after the wife of the twenty-second British viceroy of India and is affiliated with Lahore's King Edward Medical College. It attracts nurses and students at the undergraduate, graduate and postgraduate levels specializing in gynaecology and obstetrics. The land belongs to the Punjab government and there has been unsubstantiated speculation in the past two or three years that it may be demolished. The College of Dentistry is located nearby on the other side of Fort Road.

The area is fairly densely built up with a series of brick structures separated by green spaces. Heights are low, however, and do not conflict visually or aesthetically with the massing and views of the mosque, which remains the dominant landmark when seen both from afar and from nearby locations.

Above, the new Food Street located on Fort Road and facing the Badshahi Mosque.

Below, Rim Market with Akbari Darwaza in the background.

1   Opinions differ as to whether this was constructed during the Shah Jahan period or not, and investigations are needed to ascertain this.
2   This space was to be become the Hazuri Bagh during the reign of Ranjit Sing.

THE 2018 MASTER PLAN FOR THE CONSERVATION OF LAHORE FORT

FRANCESCO SIRAVO

The 'Lahore Fort Precinct and Buffer Zone Master Plan' prepared in 2018 presents a new vision for the conservation and rehabilitation of the Lahore Fort World Heritage Site in the context of the significant financial investments to be made over the next several years. It anticipates a new institutional setting for the Lahore Fort World Heritage Site. This is in view of the proposed expansion of the World Heritage Site to include the Badshahi Masjid, the Hazuri Bagh and the Sikh funerary complex north of Roshnai Gate, and of the addition of a 'buffer zone' around the site – as per the current requirements of the UNESCO World Heritage Committee.

In preparing this new Master Plan, AKTC and the Walled City of Lahore Authority (WCLA) assessed the different components of Lahore Fort and established conservation priorities in light of the degree of their deterioration and their cultural, historical, architectural and archaeological significance. While presenting a prioritized programme of investment and interventions, the 2018 Master Plan aims to establish an acceptable system for the presentation of the World Heritage Site, together with new policies for its management in the framework of recent interventions and future programmes. This Master Plan recognizes the Zone of Special Value 1 (ZSV 1) as a protected sector created under the WCLA's 'Master Conservation and Redevelopment Plan for the Walled City of Lahore' (MCRP) of 2017. Its redevelopment is to be carried out after the clearance and infrastructure improvements planned by the government of Punjab. The 2018 Master Plan contains preliminary urban design proposals prepared in keeping with the requirements of the officially designated World Heritage Site.

Lahore Fort is a large complex with more than twenty-one monuments in need of urgent attention. The urban area surrounding the Fort contains additional significant monuments and relevant sectors of the Walled City's urban fabric. This area, designated in the 2018 'Lahore Fort Precinct and Buffer Zone Master Plan' as the "buffer zone", impacts directly on the upkeep and management of the Fort, and is equally in need of rehabilitation, appropriate development and improvement of municipal services.

In 2014 the Fort came under the direct management of the Walled City of Lahore Authority (WCLA), which today has civic jurisdiction over the Walled City and the Fort in accordance with the stipulations of its parent legislation. In February of 2017 the government of Punjab approved a project worth PKR 964 million (USD 6.893 million) for conservation works in Lahore Fort. These are to be carried out in the Fort by the WCLA, with technical assistance from the Aga Khan Cultural Service-Pakistan

Opposite page, the prayer chamber of the Maryam Zamani (or Begum Shahi) Mosque.

Above, the northern octagonal bastion of the Shah Burj with its decorated Picture Wall.

Below, interior view of one of the Summer Palace reception rooms.

General view of Lahore Fort looking west,
with the Badshahi Mosque in the background.

(AKCS-P). The Royal Norwegian Embassy in Islamabad, in addition to its previous grant to AKCS-P to document Lahore Fort, is also funding the conservation of Shah Burj (2017–19). This initiative is under implementation and includes the Picture Wall and the Summer Palace, tentatively earmarked as a future museum and interpretation centre.

While important, these initiatives will need to be complemented by additional efforts, including investments in urban design and rehabilitation, landscaping and

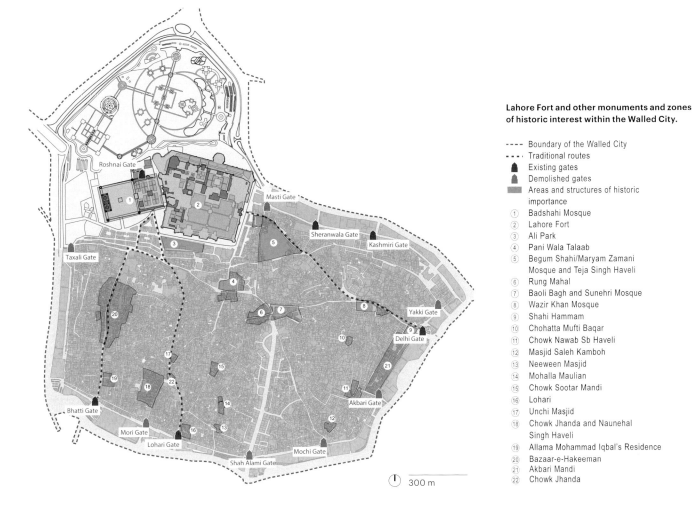

Lahore Fort and other monuments and zones
of historic interest within the Walled City.

---- Boundary of the Walled City
--·- Traditional routes
▲ Existing gates
▲ Demolished gates
▬ Areas and structures of historic
   importance
① Badshahi Mosque
② Lahore Fort
③ Ali Park
④ Pani Wala Talaab
⑤ Begum Shahi/Maryam Zamani
   Mosque and Teja Singh Haveli
⑥ Rung Mahal
⑦ Baoli Bagh and Sunehri Mosque
⑧ Wazir Khan Mosque
⑨ Shahi Hammam
⑩ Chohatta Mufti Baqar
⑪ Chowk Nawab Sb Haveli
⑫ Masjid Saleh Kamboh
⑬ Neeween Masjid
⑭ Mohalla Maulian
⑮ Chowk Sootar Mandi
⑯ Lohari
⑰ Unchi Masjid
⑱ Chowk Jhanda and Naunehal
   Singh Haveli
⑲ Allama Mohammad Iqbal's Residence
⑳ Bazaar-e-Hakeeman
㉑ Akbari Mandi
㉒ Chowk Jhanda

300 m

monument conservation. These efforts should aim at improving the state of conservation and upkeep of the Fort and surrounding Buffer Zone in order to reconnect Lahore Fort with the rest of the Walled City and make it a destination of choice for residents and visitors. To meet these ambitious objectives, as well as contribute to the ongoing conservation initiatives of the WCLA and AKTC/AKCS-P, additional contributions are being sought from the Agence Française de Développement (AFD), the French overseas development agency. As a result, it is expected that during the period 2018–22 investment will be made to support and expand activities under implementation within Lahore Fort, as well as urban conservation, landscaping and development work in the Lahore Fort Buffer Zone. Altogether, these actions will contribute to capacity and skill development within the WCLA and other local stakeholders engaged in the conservation and rehabilitation of the Walled City.

The 2018 Master Plan for Lahore Fort and the Buffer Zone was in fact partially funded by the French AFD agency. One of its principal objectives was the identification of the priority actions and projects to be advanced with the additional funding made available by AFD. To this effect, the Master Plan includes analyses and proposals for the UNESCO-designated World Heritage Site, as well as the southern and eastern sectors of the Buffer Zone. While it generally follows the UNESCO 'Lahore Fort Master Plan' of 2006, the new 2018 Master Plan is the first to consider the adjacent monumental zone to the west of the citadel, as well as part of the historic fabric of the Walled City included in the WLCA's designated Zone of Special Value 1. It also departs from the 2006 Master Plan in three important respects: firstly, it attempts a technical definition of the various conservation actions to be carried out in the different areas

The legal entities responsible for oversight and upkeep of Lahore Fort.

- - - Walled City of Lahore Authority
■ ■ ■ Zone of Special Value 1
(Buffer Zone)
/// Federal Department of Archaeology
- - - Punjab Archaeology Department
▢ Evacuee Trust Property Board
(Federal Government)
▨ Parks and Horticulture Authority
Auqaf and Religious Affairs
Department
- - - Punjab Rangers

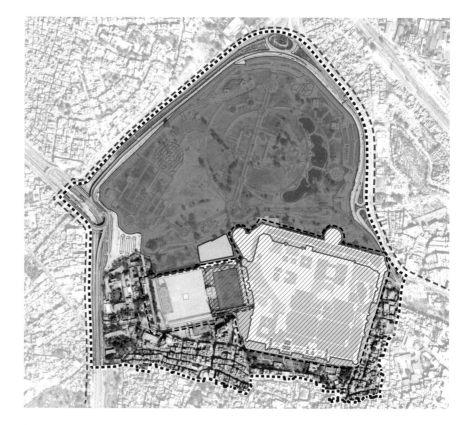

Site boundaries and components.

The Core Monuments
▨ The present WHS
▨ Zone proposed for designation as
part of the future UNESCO WHS
ⓐ Badshahi Mosque
ⓑ Hazuri Bagh
ⓒ Ranjit Singh's Samadhi

The Buffer Zone
■ ■ ■ Boundary of the Buffer Zone
ⓓ Minar-e-Pakistan
ⓔ Greater Iqbal Park

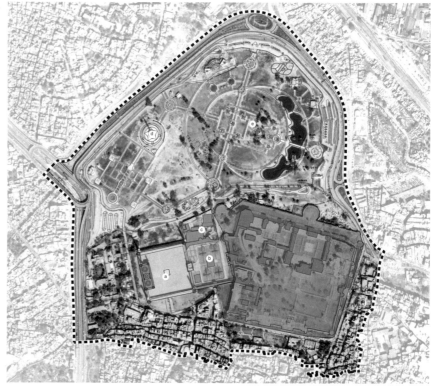

⊕ 200 m

of the Fort's monumental core; secondly, it proposes broad planning schemes for the various sectors of the Buffer Zone; and thirdly, it consolidates a programme for the visitation and management of the monument in light of the changes that have occurred since 2006 and those proposed by the 2006 UNESCO Plan itself.

Aerial view of Greater Iqbal Park.

LEGAL FRAMEWORK AND HERITAGE CONTROLS

As a UNESCO World Heritage Site, the Lahore Fort precinct[1] and its twenty-one listed monuments are subject to the provisions of the World Heritage Convention adopted by UNESCO in 1972 and ratified by Pakistan in 1976. At the international level, as a state party signatory to the Convention, Pakistan is bound by the stipulations of this global instrument that defines and regulates the natural and cultural sites inscribed on the World Heritage List. At the national level, the governing legislation is the 'Antiquities Act' of 1975 (Act VII of 1976). Following the constitutional amendment of April 2010, the 'Antiquities (Amendment) Act' of 2012 devolved control of all culture and heritage matters in the Punjab province to the government of Punjab. These legislative documents stipulate, *inter alia*, that the protected monuments must be on a roster of properties listed by the government through an executive order, and that no construction can take place within a perimeter distance of close on sixty-one metres without the permission of the director general of the Federal Department of Archaeology and Museums and, after the devolution of 2012, of the director general of the Punjab Archaeology Department.

SITE BOUNDARIES AND COMPONENTS

The study and planning area of the 2018 Master Plan for Lahore Fort and its Buffer Zone consists of a total surface of approximately 104 hectares. Located at the north-west corner of the Walled City of Lahore, it functioned in history as the monumental

Above, Ranjit Singh's *samadh*, as seen from inside the Fort. The *samadh* is juxtaposed with Aurangzeb's Roshnai Gate. On the right is the British arsenal building.

Below, the interior of Ranjit Singh's *baradari*, or pavilion, in the Hazuri Bagh.

core and bulwark of the Walled City's defences. This core, consisting of Lahore Fort and its adjoining monuments, is surrounded by a protective belt around the historic property. Following the demolition of the city walls by the British government in the nineteenth century, the area is today bound by a system of roads that includes Circular Road to the north, Data Darbar Road to the west, and Fort Road to the east and south. The entire area is articulated into a number of distinct zones defined as follows:

1. The Lahore Fort precinct, inscribed by UNESCO in 1981 as a World Heritage Site, surrounded by an inner fortification wall encircling approximately 19.5 hectares of royal structures and formal gardens. Occupied since the sixth century CE, this area was largely built and developed in its present configuration by four Mughal emperors (Akbar, Jahangir, Shah Jahan and Aurangzeb) between 1556 and 1707.

2. Other monuments contiguous to the western side of the World Heritage Site, recommended for inclusion on the World Heritage List in a revised nomination, aimed at expanding the property to encompass the monumental structures adjoining the Fort precinct. Paramount among these is the Badshahi Mosque, the Hazuri Bagh and the adjoining cremation sites (*samadhs*) dedicated to prominent Sikh personalities. This zone also includes the open areas pertaining or adjacent to these monuments that have remained so far largely excluded from protection and comprehensive planning. Altogether, this area has a total surface of approximately 8.55 hectares.

3. All areas included in the Zone of Special Value 1 (ZSV 1) identified in the 2017 'Master Conservation and Redevelopment Plan' (MCRP) for the Walled City of Lahore. This area, which also includes a few minor monumental sites located along its boundaries, has a total surface of 76.5 hectares. It acts to all effects as a protective belt around the core monuments and could in fact be considered the 'buffer zone' of the renominated World Heritage Site, thus redressing an evident shortcoming of the original nomination; it should be noted in this respect that the 1981 inscription did not contain a buffer zone, which is today *de rigueur* for all UNESCO World Heritage Sites.

These three components, as a whole, represent not only the extent of the 2018 Master Plan's study and planning area, but also the prospective ambit of the renominated World Heritage Site, encompassing all core monuments and the associated Buffer Zone.

ZONE OF SPECIAL VALUE 1 AND COORDINATION OF THE WCLA WITH OTHER PUBLIC ENTITIES

As part of the 'Master Conservation and Redevelopment Plan' (MCRP) prepared by the WCLA in 2017, a number of Zones of Special Value (ZSVs) were identified in various sectors of the Walled City, including ZSV 1, which is centred on the Fort and its immediate vicinity. The zone, as defined by its geographic boundaries, includes the precinct of Lahore Fort, defined by the 1981 World Heritage Site nomination, as well as other monuments and some areas of the Walled City's historic fabric.

Although the WCLA has legally mandated municipal control over the entire ZSV 1, this mandate is carried out in coordination with other public entities. More directly, the WCLA responsibilities over the Lahore Fort World Heritage Site are shouldered in cooperation with the Directorate General of Archaeology of the government of Punjab. In addition, various other public entities are involved in the monumental area located to the west of the Lahore Fort precinct, potentially eligible for inclusion in a revised World Heritage Site nomination. These include the Parks and Horticulture

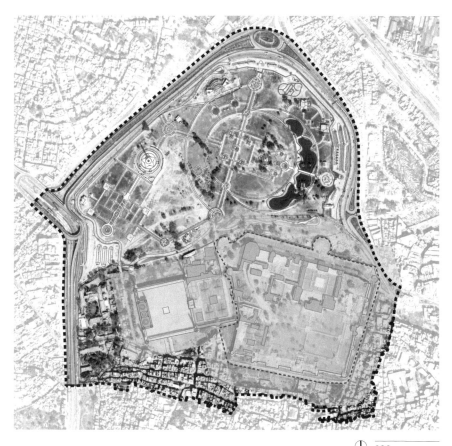

The boundaries of the 1981 World Heritage inscription and the 61-metre 'no development zone' mandated by the 'Antiquities Act' of 1975.

■■■ Proposed Buffer Zone
---- UNESCO World Heritage Site (1981)
···· 200-feet/61-metre Control Zone mandated by the Antiquities Act (1975)

⊕ 200 m

Zone of Special Value 1 and its principal landmarks.

▬ UNESCO WHS 1981
▨ Zones earmarked for inclusion into the future WHS
-·-· Buffer Zone of the future WHS

　Significant ZSV 1 Components
- - - Picture Wall
① Diwan-e-Aam Quadrangle
② Moti Masjid
③ Jahangir's Quadrangle
④ Shah Jahan's Quadrangle
⑤ Kala Burj
⑥ Hathi Pol
⑦ Shah Burj
⑧ Shah Burj Darwaza
⑨ Imperial Kitchens
⑩ Hazuri Bagh Pavilion/Ranjit Singh's Baradari
⑪ Badshahi Mosque
⑫ Gurdwara Dera Sahib
⑬ Samadh of Ranjit Singh
⑭ Roshnai Gate
⑮ Postern Gate
⑯ Akbari Gate
⑰ Begum Shahi/Maryam Zamani Mosque
⑱ Rim Market
⑲ Ali Park
⑳ Greater Iqbal Park
㉑ Mid-1930s residential development on the land of the Sikh-period Heera Mandi
㉒ Sheikhupurian Bazaar

⊕ 300 m

Buildings and structures included in the proposed new World Heritage Site nomination.

- - - - Zone proposed for designation as
        part of the future UNESCO WHS
━ ━ Badshahi Mosque
━ ━ Hazuri Bagh
━ ━ Sikh Funerary Complex
▨ Residual or Interstitial Green Spaces
① Hazuri Bagh Pavilion / Ranjit Singh's Baradari
② Allama Iqbal Mausoleum
③ Grave of Sardar Shaukat Hayat Khan
④ Alamgiri Gate
⑤ Roshnai Gate
⑥ Samadh of Naunehal Singh
⑦ Samadh of Kharak Singh
⑧ Samadh of Ranjit Singh
⑨ Samadh of Guru Arjun
⑩ Hazrat Mian Mir Block

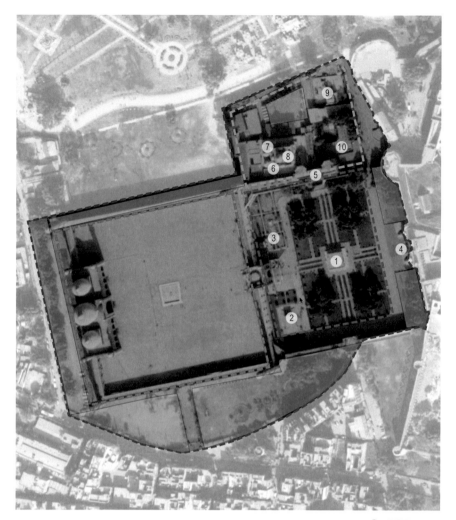

50 m

Authority (Hazuri Bagh and surrounding elements built along its north and south sides), the Auqaf Department (the Badshahi Masjid), and the Federal Evacuee Trust Properties Board (the Sikh crematory monuments of Guru Arjun and Ranjit Singh). In view of these multiple controls and jurisdictions, in the past the Punjab government has contemplated special administrative arrangements.

WORLD HERITAGE INSCRIPTION

Lahore Fort and its twenty-one surviving monuments were inscribed on the World Heritage List in 1981 at the fifth session of the World Heritage Committee (WHC). Initially proposed on its own, the nomination was eventually extended to Shalimar Garden, seven kilometres away. Both these sites comprise an extraordinary repertory of architectural forms and landscape design from the apogee of the Mughal period, displayed with continuity for a period of 151 years (1556–1707). According to the nomination, they constitute as a whole a masterpiece of human creative genius and present an important interchange of human values, which had a great impact on the development of artistic and aesthetic expressions of the Indian subcontinent. Together, Lahore Fort and Shalimar Garden embody a unique and exceptional testimony to the Mughal civilization at the height of its artistic manifestation and development.

The Statement of Significance accompanying the UNESCO 'Lahore Fort Master Plan' of 2006 underlined the importance of the Fort as the foremost Mughal

Above, front elevation of the Badshahi Mosque's prayer hall.

Left, the *baradari* of Ranjit Singh, or the Hazuri Bagh Pavilion.

monument in Pakistan for its continuity of cultural and artistic expressions from the earliest centuries to the present. It also identified in the *chahar-bagh* quadrangle arrangement the hallmark of Mughal design. Its formal composition integrates architecture and landscape elements into a coherent ensemble that provides a physical and symbolic transition between public and increasingly private spaces. In addition, the 2006 Master Plan emphasized the relevance of the monument as a repository of community and cultural values, and as a remarkable didactic experience for Pakistan's present and future generations.

RECOMMENDATIONS OF THE PERIODIC REVIEW AND MONITORING MISSIONS
In 2000 the property was included in the List of World Heritage in Danger. This was done largely on account of the destruction of the external hydraulic works of Shalimar Garden, which occurred as a result of road works carried out in the vicinity of the site. At that time, concerns were also expressed about Lahore Fort, with particular reference to the severe water infiltration in the mirrored ceiling of the Sheesh Mahal. Repairs to the hydraulic works in Shalimar Garden have now been carried out, together with the elimination of water infiltrations in the Sheesh Mahal ceiling and other actions aimed at the restoration of significant structures within the Fort complex.

Additional concerns about the two sites included the loss of authenticity in function and setting, noting how the original uses have been replaced by public visitation

The gate leading from Shahi Mohalla Street into the Hazuri Bagh.

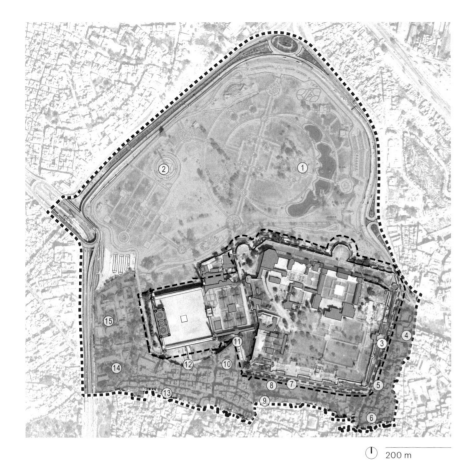

⏻ 200 m

and tourism, and how the sites have been adversely affected by the growing impact of traffic and contemporary urban developments in close proximity of the monuments. Eventually, during the thirty-sixth session of the World Heritage Committee (WHC), it was recommended by the joint UNESCO-ICOMOS Reactive Monitoring Mission that the two sites be removed from the List of World Heritage in Danger. The mission's report noted "the significant efforts invested by the authorities in Punjab to address the threats that led the property to be inscribed on the List of World Heritage in Danger and the overall progress made with the implementation of the corrective measures, as identified by the WHC at its thirty-first session (Christchurch, 2007)." It therefore expressed "the opinion that the State Party has fulfilled the requirements for achieving the Desired State of Conservation for the removal of the property from the List of World Heritage in Danger." The Committee ratified the Recommendation on 1 July 2012.

UNESCO REACTIVE MONITORING MISSION, 2018

Subsequently, between 2015 and 2018, the development of the Orange Line Metro project impacted Shalimar Garden, as well as numerous monuments across Lahore, very negatively, resulting in the courts responding to civil society petitions and halting the half-completed works with stay orders. A UNESCO Reactive Monitoring Mission was delayed until April 2018, and could take place only after the Supreme Court of Pakistan took the decision to allow the Orange Line project to proceed. The extensive recommendations of the UNESCO mission focused mainly on Shalimar Garden. While the mission made extensive general recommendations regarding the two properties (enlarge the buffer zones, reinforce stakeholder participation, improve landscaping and the environment, protect intangible heritage and mitigate the impact of visitors on the monuments), it also made the following recommendations that apply specifically to Lahore Fort:

View of Rim Market along the east wall of Lahore Fort.

- advance the ongoing projects and rehabilitation activities;
- pay greater attention to the preservation of interior spaces and to the effects of water infiltration into the fabric of the monuments;
- consider the inclusion of the Badshahi Mosque and the Sikh cremation sites into the boundary of the World Heritage Site;
- expand the protective areas surrounding the property.

Most emphatically, and mainly in view of what has happened in Shalimar Garden, the mission recommended that the World Heritage Committee once again place the "Fort and Shalamar Gardens in Lahore" on the List of World Heritage in Danger.

PROPOSED REVISION OF THE WORLD HERITAGE SITE BOUNDARIES

The issue of the boundary of the Lahore Fort World Heritage Site and the merits of revising the original limits of the site, reiterated by numerous UNESCO monitoring missions, has been a subject of discussion since 2003. It was noted how the Badshahi Mosque and the monumental cremation sites of Maharaja Ranjit Singh and Guru Arjun, even though located outside the inner walls of the Fort, constitute an integral part of the complex. It was therefore recommended that they be included in a revised inscription to truly reflect the full integrity of the property. It was also proposed that, on the occasion of the revised inscription, Lahore Fort and Shalimar Garden be nominated as two distinct World Heritage Sites.

Additional discussions took place on the official limits of a 'no development zone,' which, at present, is legally set by the 'Antiquities Act' of 1975 (amended in 1992 and 2012) to include a radius of sixty-one metres from the "protected immovable antiquity" (Art. 22). This limit is considered by UNESCO insufficient to prevent the negative effects of urban developments on the two sites. In particular for Lahore Fort, the south and west sectors around the fortification appear greatly affected by traffic and uncontrolled urban transformations.

View of Ali Park and the Ceremonial Steps.

Detail of Rim Market.

Subsequent to its appointment in 2012 as the principal custodian and manager of the Walled City, the Walled City of Lahore Authority (WCLA) took on the responsibility in 2014 of managing the conservation and development of the entire Lahore Fort World Heritage Site. As a result, as part of the 2017 'Master Conservation and Redevelopment Plan' (MCRP) prepared by the WCLA, the Fort was identified as a Zone of Special Value (ZSV 1) and the boundaries of the Buffer Zone expanded from the original sixty-one metres to the new limits set by the ZSV 1. These include a much larger area outside the fortifications to encompass the sectors especially affected by adverse urban transformations.

The ratification of the 2017 MCRP by the Punjab government is still pending. As the state party indicated in its 2018 submission to the UNESCO World Heritage Committee, an ad hoc committee made up of members of national and provincial authorities has been set up to review and confirm the proposed new boundaries, and the issues related to the social and economic impact of this measure. Even though the matter is still pending, the 2018 'Lahore Fort Precinct and Buffer Zone Master Plan' assumes that the boundary of the World Heritage Site Buffer Zone will eventually coincide with the one identified by the WCLA for the protection of Lahore Fort's Zone of Special Value (ZSV 1).

OTHER PLANS FOR THE WORLD HERITAGE SITE AND THE MASTER PLAN FOR THE WALLED CITY

Apart from the UNESCO 'Lahore Fort Master Plan' of 2006, no other master-planning document has dealt in a holistic and comprehensive way with the precinct of the World Heritage Site and the related sixty-one-metre buffer around the property. Two other documents should, however, be mentioned as they focused and made various recommendations on the Walled City as a whole, and the immediate surroundings of the Fort in particular. The first one is the 2008 'Preliminary Strategic Framework' report presented to the government of Punjab by AKTC and its local affiliate AKCS-P. This document looked at opportunities for the improvement of traffic and access, and for a de-densification of certain contradictory and highly problematic land uses in the vicinity of the Lahore Fort precinct. Among these opportunities were the so-called "Triangle" (a group of buildings immediately to the south of Hazuri Bagh and the Badshahi Masjid), Ali Park to the south, and Rim Market and Maryam Zamani (or Begum Shahi) Mosque to the east. Many of these earlier proposals have now been absorbed in the programmes developed under the 2018 'Lahore Fort Precinct and Buffer Zone Master Plan'.

The second, more detailed document focuses on the Walled City. This is the 'Master Conservation and Redevelopment Plan' (MCRP) for the Walled City, prepared by AKTC and the WCLA in 2017 in partial fulfilment of the requirements of the 'Walled City of Lahore Act', 2012. The document identifies six Zones of Special Value (ZSVs) within the Walled City, many of them divided into sub-zones. The MCRP document makes recommendations about the formal revisions of the UNESCO World Heritage Site's boundary and other institutional arrangements necessary to give the WCLA a coordinating role in planning and administering the ZSV 1 in accordance with the 'Walled City of Lahore Act' of 2012. It also identifies the discrete components of the zone, which are to be planned in conjunction with those of the World Heritage Site and associated monuments to the west of the Fort, earmarked for inclusion in a revised World Heritage Site nomination.

More specifically, the 2017 document looks at access to the zone, the monuments included in it, the significant structures, parks and green spaces, and various portions

Residential fabric in the south-west sector of the Buffer Zone.

of urban fabric with particular attention given to Ali Park and environs, Rim Market, the Maryam Zamani (or Begum Shahi) Mosque and the reopening of Akbari Gate on the Fort's eastern flank. For each of these components, the document provides a brief and rationale for the types of interventions to be carried out. Furthermore, the plan to reopen an eastern entrance through Akbari Gate is linked to a revision and further elaboration of the internal visitor circuits presented in the 2008 'Preliminary Strategic Framework'. Two separate circuits or tiers are now proposed to achieve an improved management of visitors and diversified offers through graded admission fees that give access to discrete sectors of the monumental complex.

These proposals were the subject of further review and development in the 2018 'Lahore Fort Precinct and Buffer Zone Master Plan'. Overall, this new Master Plan provides the general framework for the identification of implementation strategies and detailed plans of action necessary to advance the UNESCO Master Plan of 2006, and sets the stage for many of the planning proposals presented in it.

1   The 1981 listing also included Shalimar Garden, which is located seven kilometres further to the east. All references to the World Heritage Site in the context of this chapter, refer solely to the Lahore Fort precinct.

REVIEW AND ANALYSES
OF CONDITIONS

DIDIER REPELLIN

FORMAL AND VISUAL ANALYSES: ACCESS, AXES AND VIEWS

The description of the components and structures of the Fort's monumental area on pp. 212–233 provides the basis for an analysis of the area's formal composition and design principles. These appear to be dictated by several consistent and fairly recurrent tenets. A review of a nineteenth-century plan of the site, supplemented by archaeological information and observations made in the field, were an intrinsic part of the analysis.

In observing the general composition of the Lahore Palace-Fort, it is difficult to differentiate the organization of the architectural elements from that of the gardens as both stem from a single, unifying principle of iterated axial geometry. It is, indeed, a highly structured geometry, based on the *chahar-bagh* principle of the quadripartite organization of space by means of axial lines that intersect at the centre, commonly interpreted as a metaphorical reference to the four gardens of Paradise mentioned in the Qur'an.

This principle, combined with the specular symmetry of the various design components, governs the disposition of covered structures, gates, walkways, plantings, water pools and canals throughout the complex. The axial pathways are never casually oriented, but invariably linked to focal points that take the form of pavilions, porches, raised platforms, textured water cascades, fountains and other decorative elements. Decoration itself, whether interlaced floral motifs or geometric patterns, in marble or *pietra dura*, stuccowork or wall frescoes, reflects the order and harmonious symmetry of a 'tamed' natural world. Water plays a fundamental role as a source of visual and sensual pleasure, and also reflects the changing hues of the sky in pools of still water and strengthens the allusion to Paradise.

This balance and perfection can best be attained and measured within the limits of perceptible, self-contained spaces, where the scale of the composition allows the observer to appreciate at the same time the whole and the details. A noticeable characteristic of the overall composition of Mughal complexes is that high walls separate the courtyards into self-contained spatial entities. The aesthetics of the individual spaces are thus combined with a wish for privacy. Direct views are impeded, and there is a clear distinction between more public areas, generally accessible to the public and the court at large, and private residential quarters reserved for the emperor and members of his inner circle, sheltered women's residences, religious places, bathing areas (hammams) and other secluded areas. The entire system is, in fact, modulated as a sequence of spaces arranged to achieve increasing levels of privacy.

Opposite page, Shalimar Garden, the water body in the middle terrace.

Above, "The Arrival of Emperor Humayun in Lahore". Folio from the *Third Akbarnama*, painted by Makra with portraits by Mukund (*c.* 1595–1600).

251

Formal and visual analyses: access, axes and views in Lahore Fort.

1. Shah Burj Quadrangle

2. Paeen Bagh Quadrangle

3. Moti Masjid Quadrangle

4. Shah Jahan's Quadrangle

5. Jahangir's Quadrangle

6. Neglected area with staff quarters; archaeology not yet explored

➤ principal fort entrances
→ other entrances
┈┈► composition axes

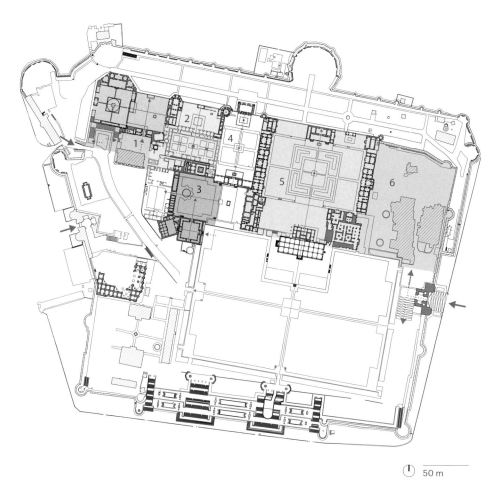

50 m

Today, some of the walls that separated the different courtyards are missing. This impedes a full understanding of the palace-fort's complex spatial relationships and the interior quadrangles have lost their definition and their perfect symmetries. Access to each of the secluded spaces occurs haphazardly in the absence of walls with carefully positioned entry points, and the original hierarchy of spaces and functions can no longer be perceived. We are now accustomed to the transformations wrought during the Sikh period and the British occupation, but the original layout can still be discerned in the nineteenth-century map referred to above (see p. 253, below).

UNDERSTANDING THE HYDRAULIC SYSTEMS

Such were the expectations of the Mughal emperors that the finesse of the designs and the technical abilities of artists and engineers rose to unimagined peaks of playfulness and beauty. The manipulation and presentation of water in patterns of three-dimensional geometry exceeded nature. Combinations of fourfold channels, tanks, ponds, fountains and sculpted water chutes turned simple hydraulics into an inspired pursuit of visual and audible effects. Sunlight and lamplight were made to flicker, flash and sparkle along carved water chutes (*chadars*), while blue skies and tall, dark cypresses were reflected in pools of water rendered absolutely still. Running water was made to splash, gush and gurgle by the simple power of gravity and the silent mechanics of a pipe.

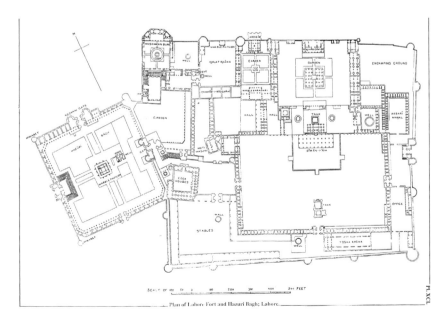

Above, aerial view of the Paeen Bagh
Quadrangle in Lahore Fort.

Left, plan of Lahore Fort drawn in 1894.

253

The spirit of the Mughal garden is to be found in its playful use and manipulation of waterworks and life-giving irrigation systems. Whether aimed at renewing the practical pursuits of horticulture or the historic water features for the pleasure of residents and visitors, restoration of the original waterworks in the Lahore Fort palace-gardens is a very promising and achievable possibility with minimal modern means.

WATER SUPPLY, DRAINAGE, SPECIAL WATER EFFECTS AND FEATURES

The prospect of renovating Lahore Fort's water features and hydraulic systems must begin with a full understanding of their inner workings. Water played a major and indispensable role in Mughal planning and architecture, a fact that is even more remarkable when one considers Lahore's relatively arid climate: little rainfall for nine months followed by two or more months of heavy rains during the monsoon period in July, August and September. Good water management was essential, and special ingenuity was required to obtain and regulate the water needed for the patron's satisfaction.

WATER SUPPLY

The highly contrasted seasons make rainwater storage during the long dry period difficult, as the stored water would inevitably deteriorate. In fact, there were few water reservoirs on site, and the ones visible today are of small capacity. Their purpose was not to stock rainwater, but to store the water coming from the many wells that existed within the Fort. Water was drawn from the water table by means of mechanical waterwheels (also known as Persian wheels) to fill rooftop reservoirs. Water was then channelled by gravity via wall-top channels and distributed throughout the complex for their various intended uses.

WATER DRAINAGE

The heavy rainfall during the monsoon season required an effective storm-water drainage system. Today, because of the changes that occurred over time, the majority of rainwater is drained via spouts and channels towards the Picture Wall in the northern end of the complex. This has been the cause of severe deterioration of both the structure and decoration of the Picture Wall. Additional surveys and testing are needed to identify the original features of the drainage system and fully understand how it worked and how best to redirect the water away from the northern wall, which is affected by the penetration of water coming from the spouts installed during the British period.

WATER FEATURES FOR COMFORT AND PLEASURE

Each courtyard of the Fort contained ornamental water features, including pools, fountains, channels, cascades and even water-misting systems to cool the air. Water played a central role in the Fort's architectural layout by emphasizing and punctuating the principal axes of symmetry in the quadrangles and other open spaces. Shalimar Garden is a good example of the variety and effect of Mughal waterworks at a larger scale. A similar richness was to be found at a smaller scale within the Fort. The quality of the hydraulic systems in Lahore Fort bears the hallmark of a sophisticated civilization capable of managing its limited water resources to achieve spectacular results through the experience and skills of gifted engineers, artists and builders. The full extent and exceptional quality of their original expression deserves to be rediscovered and presented.

Preceding pages, the shallow, square marble fountain and waterspout in Shah Jahan's Quadrangle.

Above, a water channel along the top of a wall in Agra Fort.

Below, a hypothetical hydraulic system near the well belonging to the Zenana Mosque.

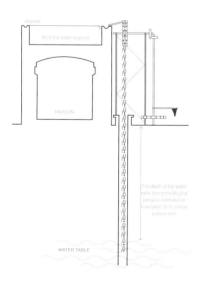

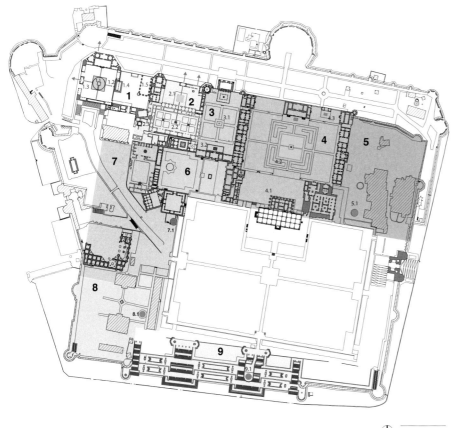

50 m

THE THREE SOURCES OF WATER

1. *Groundwater table.* The main source of water in the Fort was groundwater. Despite the fact that the current depth of the water table has dropped more than thirty metres compared to its much higher level during Mughal times, it should still be possible to obtain the water needed from the wells that exist on site. Persian wheels (*charkhs*) used to bring water up from the subsoil to raised storage tanks and small rooftop reservoirs. The water would then flow by gravity into a well-designed system of water channels and pools located at various levels throughout the complex.

2. *Rainwater.* The monsoon season is characterized by heavy rains concentrated during a short period of time. It is assumed that the same rooftop water reservoirs that were used to store groundwater would also have been used to collect and store rainwater during the wet season. The rainwater was then distributed using the external and internal channels that fed the various palaces and courtyards.

3. *Water from the Ravi River.* During Mughal times, a section of the Ravi River used to flow directly below Lahore Fort's north wall. Since the volume of water available from groundwater was insufficient to meet the water requirements of the fortified complex, we can assume that it was possible to make use of water from the river in more or less limited quantities depending on availability during the different periods of the year. This water source would have required a very efficient system to lift water up to the top of the fortification.

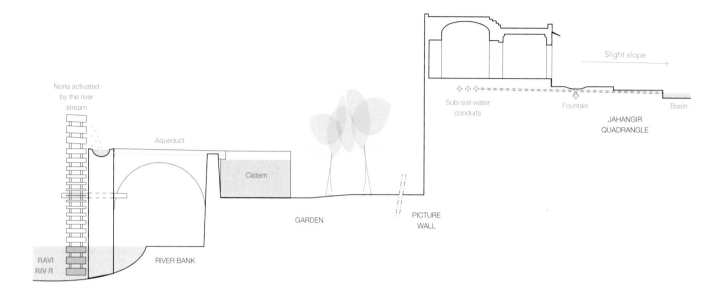

A hypothetical hydraulic system in the Khwabgah Pavilion.

THE WATER DRAINAGE SYSTEM

Today, Lahore Fort's storm-water drainage system no longer functions properly due to the successive transformations that have affected the drains. Improper flows of rainwater have contributed to the dilapidation of various structures and buildings in the complex. During the Mughal period, clean drainage water presumably passed into the pools and fountains before being drained away. But today the water drainage system is independent of the general hydraulic system. In the case of Shah Burj, for example, rainwater coming from the terraces is drained via channels running inside the building, just above the Sheesh Mahal's ceiling. This involves the risk of leakage, which in turn causes the deterioration of the wall's decorations. Rainwater draining from the courtyard is channelled for the most part towards the Picture Wall. In some cases, the flow passes through downpipes, but in others the rainwater seeps out directly onto the ornamented wall.

The Lal Burj tower contains a number of drainage outlets that discharged storm water at the foot of the Fort's apron wall into the moat. In all probability, a major part of the rainwater drainage system was directed towards this section of the exterior wall. A detailed endoscopic analysis of this location would lead to a much better understanding of the rainwater drainage system during historic times.

EVIDENCE OF THE MUGHAL GARDEN TRADITION IN LAHORE FORT

The configuration of the landscape of the palace-fort, its grounds and formal gardens reveals multiple layers of architectural and horticultural interventions and transformations. Such spatial and stylistic changes are to be expected over a long span of time, given the different actors that transformed the site down the centuries, from Mughal emperors to Sikh rulers, British colonials and contemporary administrators, not to mention international technical advisers. Buildings may leave a relatively clear footprint, but the form and plantings of gardens and waterways are less easily discovered, and provenance and authenticity are often difficult to capture.

The artistic and poetic record of great Mughal garden designers and their planting palettes inspire an appreciation of their principles for successful gardening in challenging climates and in an acutely codified tradition based on geometric principles.

The integration of architecture and garden design was in itself monumental. From the first to the last emperor who built and expanded the Lahore Fort complex, the art, science and architecture of Mughal gardens grew to unparalleled greatness. The very fact that many gardens from that era have survived at all is by itself quite surprising. The highly skilled manipulation of grand designs of external spaces, with levels and geometries that were then embellished with the finest decorative floral inlays, no doubt elicited universal appeal. The artwork is fine enough to identify plants, trees and palm species, as well as the beloved tulip, pomegranates and cypresses. Over time, these landscapes have become an expression of cultural heritage that belong to all mankind.

There is confusion in the public perception of what constitutes a Mughal garden created by the 'restorations' initiated by Lord Curzon under British rule. Expedient simplification of the landscape, visual sanitization and the glorification of dominant architecture became the order of the day. Lush gardens gave way to the mown lawns of order and over-pruned greenery. The exercise of control, even of plants, was the prerogative of the British Empire. This misconception persists today. The real and fulsome Mughal garden is yet to be rediscovered in its original form and glory.

The extensive pools for water in the Jahangir Quadrangle were restored based on an example in Shalimar Garden.

Jahangir's Quadrangle, looking south towards the northern facade of the Daulat Khana-e-Khaas-o-Aam.

PRINCIPAL FEATURES OF THE MUGHAL GARDENS

Mughal garden designs aspired to philosophically and practically assemble a codified selection of architectural and gardening elements in the pattern of paradise. It was a reference that had at the same time a religious, symbolic and cultural significance. Structures and landscape were arranged as holistic and compliant compositions. The garden paradigm began with massive enclosing walls, safeguarding and insulating the defined space from the outside world. In the spirit of the times, these walls captured a portion of the sky, by day and by night, as the roof of heaven. The internalized garden space was always organized on a square or rectangular plan, terraced where possible to facilitate practical irrigation requirements and playful waterworks. This was the basis for the *chahar-bagh*, the paradise garden made fourfold by the quartering of holy rivers with the world at its centre. Such four-way divisions in plan were emphasized by raised formal walkways, and shallow, running canals with water captured from natural water sources or by means of the ingenious Persian wheel, an animal-powered water-lifting device. Even at low pressure, cleverly designed fountains could dome and spurt, cascade, ripple and sparkle.

In early Mughal examples, a raised platform or tomb occupied the centre of the garden, though later examples show a grander mausoleum offset to the side to better enjoy the long garden view and the borrowed scenery of the countryside. Numerology was clearly evident as the base for geometrical garden subdivisions into orchard and flower-filled components and the strong axial and cross-axial plantings of closely spaced columnar trees and hedges, literally distorting perspective for advantage. The water supply circulated through the garden by segmented, terracotta pipe layouts, or open channels perched or inset on top of the boundary or internal walls. In plan, the quadratic divisions were realized by running water channels provided with fountain tanks and platforms at regular intervals. Grand axial alignments and long garden vistas focusing on kiosks and pavilions manipulated space and views for the joy of the visitor. Respite from the sun was found on vivid carpets offered in gloriously patterned tents for shade, made livelier by entertainment and social interaction. The living components of the garden were equally joyful. Collective Mughal plantings were as spectacular and lush as their marvellously ornate and decorated buildings. These were a sensory delight: the taste of fresh fruits and nuts from the trees; the scent of fresh flowers, sweet grasses, aromatic herbs and the beloved roses; the touch of velvet foliage and rose petals; and the awe produced by the stature of iconic trees, such as plane trees, columnar cypresses and clipped pomegranates, contrasted against the exotic date palms and other magnificent subtropical flowering trees.

WHAT SURVIVES TODAY
The most compelling evidence of the Mughal landscaping tradition lies in the surviving patterns of its garden-framing walls, often reduced today to rows of foundations. The geometric placement of visible axial and focal garden structures, pavilions, kiosks, fountains and platforms, read in conjunction with the systematic layout of waterworks, canals and irrigation channels, reveals a spiritual spatial intent imbued with religious

Jahangir's Quadrangle from the south-east corner.

symbolism. This is evident in the observation of old plans and 'ground-truth' data from modern satellite and drone photography.

Taken together, these remaining elements portray a physical, spatial arrangement in orientation, scale and pattern pointing to the existence of a past garden, or gardens. In some instances, their genealogy may be obvious; in others, supporting evidence from other sources is required for certainty. Determining exactly the provenance of a particular garden requires supporting archaeological evidence. This is to be obtained through measured excavations and inventorying, supplemented by investigation of the pollen in the sediments, for clues on historic species. Non-invasive ground-penetrating radar (GPR) may also be helpful. It can be assumed that gardens covered a very large area of the Fort mound.

ASSESSMENT OF SIGNIFICANCE AND MATRICES OF VALUE

The range of significance that can be assigned to Lahore Fort's individual elements and components has been assessed on the basis of many different aspects. Evaluations may fail to encapsulate in full the multiple levels of significance that can be attributed to a site, but an attempt can be made to identify a consistent set of criteria and ratings that can facilitate the future identification of options for the use, presentation and management of a monument, as well as help ensure that future transformations contribute rather than detract from the tangible and intangible values and authenticity of the site.

THEMATIC CHARACTERIZATION AND ATTRIBUTES

The historical and archaeological significance of Lahore Fort is unquestionable. Each of the historic periods has left a mark on the Fort, by itself the most significant embodiment of the political, economic and military fortunes of the old city, and arguably the main repository of its heritage and history. It also constitutes the tangible evidence left by the many political, military and commercial events and contacts that, thanks to Lahore's strategic position, linked the city to the rest of the subcontinent and to Western and Central Asia in the pre-Islamic, medieval and post-medieval periods. Evidence of the past is not only embodied in the monument's visible structures, but also related to the site's potential to offer rich and potentially rewarding new insights on past events, human activities, transformations and uses.

▸ *The architectural and aesthetic significance* of Lahore Fort is contained in its outstanding repertory of Mughal architectural forms and aesthetic achievements, both as a distinct typological form and as an individual work of art that has evolved over more than a century and a half on the basis of consistent planning principles and a highly characteristic architectural vocabulary. These qualities are, in fact, the basis of the UNESCO nomination of 1981, further confirmed by the many evaluation missions carried out by international organizations and by the UNESCO 'Lahore Fort Master Plan' of 2006. In spite of various modifications, the integrity of the original plan of Lahore Fort and its principal architectural features can still be fully appreciated and make it an exemplary structure from an aesthetic standpoint.

▸ *The Fort's landscaping and contextual significance* are closely associated with its architectural and aesthetic values. This association is especially abundant in the case of Lahore Fort and can be understood only in relation to the total organization of the buildings, and the open spaces and gardens around them. The highest contextual values are, in fact, concentrated in the better-preserved quadrangles, where architecture continues to act as a counterpoint to the surrounding elements, and becomes the focal point of a larger landscaped composition. In many respects,

Pietra dura work (*parchin kari*) inside the Sheesh Mahal.

Mughal planning achieves its highest and most accomplished results in this integration between solids and voids, and, within voids, between the different elements of the landscape. These configurations are, in turn, formed by the axial subdivision of space, through arrangements of plantings, raised pathways and platforms, decorative patterns and diverse water features.

▸ *The site's technological significance* stems from its dual purpose, as a residence for the emperor and as an imperial court, but also as a defensive fortification during turbulent times. The archaeological record shows evidence of destructions that occurred sometime in the early eleventh century, when Lahore is believed to have been sacked by Sultan Mahmud of Ghazni. Further destructions took place during the eighteenth century after the virtual demise of Mughal power, a period marked by the Durrani invasions from Afghanistan and the internecine wars of the Sikhs. Defensive techniques changed in relation to the evolution of weaponry and its use. The outer fortifications, built during Ranjit Singh's time, show decisive construction and technological improvements influenced by new defensive techniques involving projected and rounded bastions. But the greater technological achievement documented in Lahore Fort goes back to Mughal times and is best observed in the complex system of procurement, storage, distribution and display of water.

▸ In addition to its physical attributes, Lahore Fort presents aspects of *intangible significance* based on cultural and communal values, as well as benefits that can be

The Sheesh Mahal is considered a monument of "outstanding significance".

Above, visibly rotten beams are proof of the damaged roof and poor drainage above the Sheesh Mahal.

Below, a close-up of its deteriorated cornice and exposed masonry.

associated with direct economic returns and the potential for cultural tourism. The cultural and social values of Lahore Fort reside in the realm of the intangible, but are nevertheless indispensable for a full understanding of the place. They pertain to meanings and experiences that relate to past and present uses, traditions and symbolic values that go back generations and are still perceived by today's inhabitants as important to their identity and collective memories.

▸ *The economic relevance of Lahore Fort* resides in its considerable potential as a generator of tourism and economic opportunity at the national and provincial levels. Recent figures indicate a robust trend towards more visitations by domestic visitors, in part linked to the recent redevelopment of nearby Iqbal Park. The number of international tourists continues to be fairly modest, but, as security conditions improve, there is no doubt that the Fort, together with Shalimar Garden, will be at the top of the list for foreign visitors as well. As evidenced around the world, there is clearly an appetite for genuine cultural and heritage experiences, where visitors can absorb the history of a place, and explore its artistic and material culture. A fully restored and functioning Fort will attract a greater share of both national and international cultural tourists. It is at present the most significant dormant asset within the Walled City of Lahore, capable of creating financial returns that can be reinvested in the site's maintenance and improvements. No doubt Lahore's palace-fort has the potential to stimulate higher-end economic activities in the tourism sector. This will require appropriate physical restoration, upgraded interpretative materials and exhibition spaces, a bookstore and gift shop, better merchandizing and a general reconfiguration of visitor circuits within the complex to provide a fuller understanding of how the Fort was used and experienced in historic times. In addition, there are a number of potential economic spin-offs in the nearby area and wider heritage zone through the Fort's long-established links with the Walled City area, particularly along the eastern flank of the citadel, directly accessible through Akbari Gate. This is in turn linked to the Delhi Gate of the historic city, located along the city's eastern perimeter via the Shahi Guzargah, the imperial trail used by the emperors to enter Lahore and reach their palaces.

Altogether, the combination of the above 'aspects of significance' explains why the structure has been listed as a national monument and provides a number of compelling reasons to ensure that it is not only protected as a physical ensemble, but also considered an investment of the highest priority towards the enhancement of Lahore's tangible and intangible heritage.

A close-up of the deteriorated parts of the Picture Wall.

MATRICES OF SIGNIFICANCE AND GRADING CRITERIA

The various aspects of relevance outlined above have been applied to particular tangible elements, as well as intangible aspects, associations and issues that have a bearing on the overall significance of the site. This is fully consistent with the Burra Charter guidelines, which provide the following general definition: "Cultural significance means aesthetic, historic, scientific, social or spiritual value for past, present or future generations. Cultural significance is embodied in the place itself, its fabric, setting, use, associations, meanings, records, related places and related objects."

Each of the elements of the site has thus been evaluated and a level of importance assigned based on the impact that it has on the monument and its context. Not all elements necessarily make a positive contribution. In other instances, they may even intrude, detract or adversely impact the monument and its surroundings, thus becoming prime candidates for mitigating interventions or removal.

The evaluation matrices used for the assessment of significance through ratings and comments were based on the above criteria, and were the result of analyses and discussions held by members of the team and various AKTC consultants leading to eventual consultations with the management and staff of the Walled City of Lahore Authority, as well as other relevant stakeholders, particularly the Department of Archaeology. The matrices express, for each component of the site, a relative level of significance for the different thematic characterizations identified. Often, more than one attribution has been applied to a single item, indicating the simultaneous presence of different types and levels of significance. Ratings that have been applied to determine the various degrees of significance are: (1) outstanding significance; (2) considerable significance; (3) moderate or low significance; (4) neutral element(s); and (5) negative value.

AN ASSESSMENT OF THE PRINCIPAL CAUSES OF DETERIORATION AND DAMAGE

This section provides a preliminary description of the main cases and causes of dilapidation found in the monumental area. The review of deterioration observed in each building was performed by using a common set of criteria and assigning a ranking of high, medium or low to the level of dilapidation observed on individual structures. In particular, the damage assessment noted the following recurrent dilapidation issues:

- water seepage from roof parapets and faulty cornices;
- defective or missing waterproofing on roof;
- faulty drainage caused by the inverted water flow;
- rising damp at the base of walls;
- structural failures on columns, floors and walls;
- eroded masonry caused by the action of birds;
- loss of facing or lacunae in masonry walls;
- vandalism.

The most common and widely observed type of deterioration is caused by rainwater ingress in building structures. Exposure of poorly insulated structures to heavy rainfall is aggravated by faulty rainwater drainage. This problem can be observed on all roofs, wall tops and open courtyards throughout the complex. In addition, localized structural issues were noted. Their resolution calls for a programme of structural consolidation and repairs that will have to be carried out case by case. Other forms of deterioration are due to environmental and social factors and include birds (pigeons), humans (vandalism), and the erosion of sensitive stone and marble elements by an atmosphere carrying acidic pollutants. Security arrangements are simply insufficient,

Above, biofilm deposits and vegetation growth on the Picture Wall east of the Shah Burj.

Below, an example of vandalism in the Fort.

and the problem is likely to continue until monitoring is improved and stronger forms of public education and awareness implemented.

The following review lists the main causes of deterioration organized by type and listed in order of importance:

1. defective waterproofing on flat roofs resulting in rainwater penetration into masonry structures;
2. broken or missing cornices combined with inappropriate parapet details;
3. faulty drainage brought about by inverted flows unable to dispose of the rainwater;
4. rising damp caused by inadequate drainage at the foot of walls;
5. growth of vegetation and microflora due to the presence of trapped moisture;
6. mechanical and structural hazards;
7. other types of dilapidation and abuse.

DEFECTIVE WATERPROOFING AND RAINWATER PENETRATION INTO MASONRY STRUCTURES

Waterproofing layers are in critical condition and no longer perform their function on the flat roofs of most historic structures. This results in severe water infiltrations and penetration into the masonry and decoration below. Additionally, during the monsoon season, the overflow from roofs due to poor drainage allows water to percolate down the walls, resulting in moisture involving biological growth on exterior surfaces, a condition observed throughout the site. Additional infiltrations result from wall and roof installation of fixtures, metal plates and clamps. Over time, protracted water infiltration can cause: (a) general weakening of bearing structures; (b) deterioration of wooden ceilings; and (c) detachment and severe damage of ornamental wooden panels and painted decoration.

Left, defective roofing and poor drainage are major causes of deterioration.

Right, the broken Kala Burj cornice no longer protects its exposed masonry below against rainwater infiltration.

Altered ground slopes prevent water from draining away, causing water to stagnate in the Shah Jahan Quadrangle.

MISSING OR DETERIORATED *CHAJJAS* (EAVES)

Often the projecting eaves and cornices meant to protect wall tops are either missing or much deteriorated. They no longer fulfil their protective role on wall tops and facades. Faulty rainwater disposal along the upper portions of walls results in: (a) leakage, stains and fungi on wall surfaces; (b) dislocation and loss of material properties of glazed tiles; (c) deterioration of lime-plaster surfaces; and (d) spalling of bricks and brick mosaics as a result of moisture penetration.

FAULTY DRAINAGE CAUSED BY THE INVERTED RAINWATER FLOW

The rainwater disposal system was originally oriented towards the centre of the quadrangles with connections to an underground network, whose extension and routing is yet to be fully assessed and understood. Today, as a result of modifications carried out during the British period, the entire drainage system was reoriented towards the north of the complex and discharges directly onto the Picture Wall. This results in serious water penetration along its decorated surfaces.

RISING DAMP

The absence of subsurface drains creates rising damp conditions at the foot of the walls, an additional general cause of deterioration. In the case of the citadel's north wall, the presence of humidity is aggravated by the earth fill that has accumulated at the base of the structure. The ponding of rainwater during the monsoon season exacerbates rising damp conditions and results in: (a) deterioration and spalling of lime-plaster surfaces; (b) cracking and erosion of historic brick paving; and (c) severe water infiltration at various locations.

GROWTH OF VEGETATION AND MICROFLORA DUE TO TRAPPED MOISTURE

The ingress of rainwater from wall tops washes out the mortar in the masonry joints and creates cavities that encourage the growth of vegetation. These hardy weeds find ideal conditions for growth in persistently damp walls. The risk posed by their uncontrolled growth contributes to: (a) disaggregation of wall masonry and loss of material; and (b) propagation of seeds and vegetative growth throughout the Lahore Fort complex.

MECHANICAL AND STRUCTURAL HAZARDS

Several cases of structural instability have been observed within the complex, mostly localized and easy to detect, where conditions of structural instability are not systemic but intrinsic to individual structures. Two examples are the columns of the Diwan-e-Khaas, encircled by metal collars to facilitate an appropriate load transfer, and the rotten beams throughout the Mai Jindan *haveli*. Structural instability can also be noted in the case of the unstable cantilevered elements over the Picture Wall.

PIGEONS

Pigeons are a serious nuisance for all buildings. The birds' behaviour causes loss of cohesion of brick masonry by their pecking away at lime mortar, reduction in the walls' load-bearing surface and a gradual destruction of the decorative surfaces with severe loss of visual integrity on facades. Bird droppings are a source of deterioration in the affected areas of the buildings, especially cornices, windowsills and wall tops. Droppings are high in nitrogen and acid content, encouraging the growth of fungi on building surfaces.

VANDALISM

Intentional damage, defacement and destruction of decorations, surfaces and fixtures can be observed in many locations, including, most unfortunately, the areas of the Lahore Fort complex that are of the highest value and most sensitive from an architectural and artistic point of view. Vandalism should be considered a clear and present threat in the monumental area, which may be on the rise, even though precise statistics are not available. The result is damage and loss of precious details and decoration throughout the site. Mitigating the damage is difficult and expensive. At times the damage is irreparable, thus jeopardizing the future restoration of valued buildings and structures.

Above, nailed brickwork deteriorating in the Maghribi Tower.

Left, pigeons resting on bands and cornices along the Picture Wall.

CONSERVATION ACTIONS: APPROACH, PRINCIPLES AND PRIORITIES

CHRISTOPHE BOULEAU

The profile of Lahore Fort's values and the description of the decay and dilapidation issues described on pp. 250–269 provide the framework for the conservation of Lahore Fort's monumental area and establish the main priorities of intervention. The aim is to offer a methodological blueprint for future action, rather than ready-made solutions or final recipes for specific interventions on individual structures or components of the site. The following pages briefly discuss the international norms that apply to UNESCO World Heritage Sites and examine the conservation principles to be followed before, during and after interventions on monuments and historic structures. This overview is followed by an indication of the conservation techniques that will probably be applied widely in Lahore Fort in relation to its principal dilapidation issues. These are further distinguished into immediate, medium-term and long-term actions.

INTERNATIONAL CONSERVATION CHARTERS AND REGULATIONS

The recommendations for the conservation of Lahore Fort's monumental precinct presented in the 2018 'Lahore Fort Precinct and Buffer Zone Master Plan' follow international norms and principles. These standards developed incrementally during the course of the twentieth century starting with the Athens Conference on the Restoration of Historic Buildings of 1931. The Athens conference represented a major step forward in the evolution of conservation ideas as it reflected a growing consciousness of the concept of universal heritage, shared by all and protected by international conventions. In 1964 the Second Congress of Architects and Specialists of Historic Buildings held in Venice produced the International Charter for the Conservation and Restoration of Monuments and Sites, better known as the "Venice Charter", and created the International Council on Monuments and Sites (ICOMOS).

The Venice Charter expanded the concept of monument to include more modest forms of tangible heritage that have acquired cultural relevance and continues to provide the fundamental principles of modern conservation. The Venice Charter also established important distinctions between various forms of intervention. The latter were elaborated in the Burra Charter, prepared in Australia in 1979, which further defined basic principles and procedures to be followed in conserving heritage places, and brought forward the notion of "cultural significance" to reflect the values associated with aesthetic, historical and scientific meanings, as well as the life of groups and communities, thus introducing a social dimension to the preservation of monuments and sites.

Opposite page, exchange and training opportunities with international experts are part of the ongoing programme at Lahore Fort.

Above, conservation tools and materials in use at the Picture Wall.

The Burra Charter also identified three levels of repair to be applied to heritage structures:

1. Preservation: maintaining a place in its existing state and preventing its further deterioration.
2. Restoration: returning a place to a known earlier state by removing accretions or by reassembling existing elements without the introduction of new forms and materials.
3. Reconstruction: returning a place to a known earlier state; it is distinguished from restoration by the introduction of new material.

In 1987 the Washington Charter defined principles, objectives and methods necessary for the conservation of historic towns and urban areas, and supplemented the existing corpus of normative principles with reference to living heritage settings. The Nara Document on Authenticity, prepared in 1994, recognized authenticity as a central concern in the conservation of cultural heritage, while addressing the need for a broader understanding of cultural diversity and cultural heritage.

In 2005 UNESCO's World Heritage Centre issued the Vienna Memorandum, later expanded into the UNESCO Recommendation on the Historic Urban Landscape (2011), with the aim of furthering an integrated urban approach linking forms of sustainable city development with the existing historic fabric in all its contextual and architectural complexity. The Recommendation adds new reasons and dimensions to the effort to preserve the urban historic heritage for future generations, such as the:

▸ consideration of the emotional connection between people and their historic environment;
▸ recognition that the cultural and heritage dimension of a city is fundamental to its social and economic success and to the attainment of a better quality of life for its residents;

View of Lahore Fort on a national holiday.

Aerial view of Lahore Fort.

▸ acknowledgement that urban transformations should not jeopardize or compromise community values derived from the character and significance of the historic urban environment;

▸ recognition that short-term economic gains and interests should not supersede the long-term preservation of heritage assets.

These principles were confirmed by the New Urban Agenda issued by UN-Habitat in 2017 after a process of wide-ranging international consultations. This document explicitly recognizes the role of culture in urban regeneration for the first time in an international document dealing with the planning of cities, and reaffirms heritage-oriented planning instruments as important tools towards ensuring sustainability and quality of life in the more general process of urban development.

Areas of archaeological sensitivity in the Fort.

- Picture Wall
- Mughal chambers underneath the Sheesh Mahal
- Mughal chambers in the Kala Burj area
- Passageway cut into the site's topography in the 1670s
- Road carved into the historical mound in 1853
- Putative area of expanse of Akbar's Palace
- Perimeter structures defining the Diwan-e-Aam Quadrangle during Mughal & Sikh times
- Approximate location of the 1959 archaeological dig
- Other chambers behind Picture Wall facade
- Archaeological potential (UNESCO 2006 Master Plan)

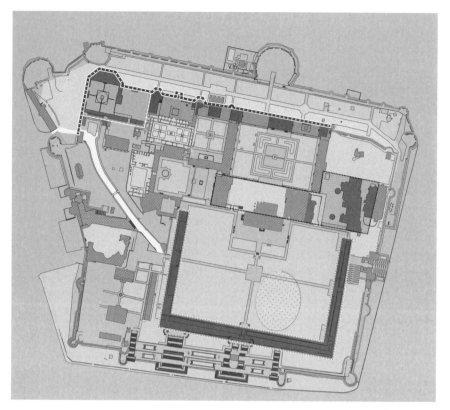

50 m

CONSERVATION PRINCIPLES

Conservation practice involves procedures that are necessary to understand the complexity of a structure and assess its level of dilapidation in order to adjust the proposed solution to the specific requirements on a case-by-case basis. While each case is different due to its nature, immediate context and general environmental conditions, there are universally accepted principles, procedures and methods that regulate the implementation of conservation projects, whether focused on individual heritage structures or larger sites. These principles cover the full range of pre-construction surveys and studies, principles of good practice during implementation, as well as post-construction archiving, and form the methodological framework applicable to all present and future conservation interventions in Lahore Fort:

- preliminary documentation, studies and surveys;
- historical research of archives and evidence of authenticity;
- use of traditional construction methods and introduction of modern conservation techniques if proven more efficient or effective;
- minimal intervention and respect of the aesthetic and physical integrity;
- reversibility and compatibility of conservation methods;
- training and qualification of skilled professionals and craftsmen through involvement of international experts;
- use of pilot conservation projects and sample prototypes;
- detailed project documentation and archiving during and after the project.

RECOMMENDED CONSERVATION TECHNIQUES

The conservation solutions outlined below provide a framework of technical procedures and protocols to be further developed, tested and adapted *in situ* during the implementation of restoration works in Lahore Fort. These solutions respond

to the recurring causes of deterioration discussed in the previous chapter, including water-induced dilapidation, structural failures and damage resulting from pigeons and vandalism.

RESPONSE TO MISSING OR DETERIORATING *CHAJJAS* (EAVES AND CORNICES) AND WALL COPINGS

The continuity of the damaged eaves and cornices, whose function is to redirect rainwater away from the building, is to be re-established by repositioning the existing *chajja* elements and replacing the missing pieces. Replacement elements will

Rainwater is penetrating and washing the masonry out of walls as a result of exposed wall tops and defective roofs.

be manufactured to match the originals. In the case of facades that have lost their upper parts and cornices, one or two protective coats of hydraulic lime mortar will be applied to avoid rainwater ingress.

RESPONSE TO DEFECTIVE INSULATION AND WATER PENETRATION INTO MASONRY STRUCTURES

Depending on whether the deterioration involves flat roofs or courtyards, first any added fill or later interventions are to be removed and possible repairs carried out. After a careful survey of the underlying hydraulic network (with archaeological supervision), a new lightweight screed is laid to level surfaces and shallow slopes for rainwater disposal are provided. Damp-proofing primer and layer are then applied with lapped joints and skirting at the edges. Finally, a protective screed made of compacted sandstone gravel is to be applied over the damp-proof membrane.

RESPONSE TO FAULTY DRAINAGE CAUSED BY INVERTED WATER FLOW

Reversing the flow of the drainage system, where faulty, calls for a reassessment of the current slopes. Rainwater coming from roofs and courtyards should be redirected to underground piping so as to connect to main sewers or soak pits. During the heavy monsoon rains, stagnating water infiltrates the lower parts of the walls and wall footings, causing serious damage. This needs to be addressed by creating French drains along the base of the buildings.

RESPONSE TO GROWTH OF VEGETATION AND MICROFLORA CAUSED BY TRAPPED MOISTURE

The mechanical cutting and removal of infestations of trees and vegetation near or on walls and rooftops may require the installation of scaffolding and the use of aerial lifts and work platforms. Elimination of microbial growth on wall surfaces will require a combination of non-invasive chemical and mechanical solutions based on best practices.

Above, deteriorated plaster, washed-out brick joints, disintegrated wall tops, dirt and formation of biofilm.

Right, consolidation of the Picture Wall's tiled decoration.

RESPONSE TO STRUCTURAL FAILURE OF COLUMNS, FLOORS AND/OR WALLS

Any intervention should be preceded by feasibility studies that include an analysis of structural stability in response to current and projected dead and dynamic loads, as well as to ensure compliance with international conservation standards in identifying appropriate solutions. In certain cases, structural interventions may call for the introduction of non-invasive modern technologies, together with traditional masonry repairs. Repairs of unstable masonry, such as the cantilevered/corbelled towers at the top of the Picture Wall, will be carried out by reinforcing the structure with lime grout injections combined with masonry repairs employing traditional construction techniques and materials.

RESPONSE TO PIGEON BEHAVIOUR AND DROPPINGS

Pigeons in Lahore Fort are a nuisance and a public health risk. Locally, the installation of static power cables and anti-pigeon netting and spikes placed on cornices and other resting places can be effective deterrents and prevent damage to built structures, thus leading to a gradual elimination of pigeon presence near the monuments. These measures could be supplemented by constructing modern pigeon houses in the vicinity of the Fort.

The Hathi Pol reception court. The wall at the south-east corner is missing, making it difficult to understand the formerly enclosed space.

Above, the dark stains covering this wall are visible proof that the Picture Wall is affected by dampness from within.

Right, pigeons peck lime from the mortar joints of the Picture Wall.

RESPONSE TO VANDALISM

In order to identify appropriate measures to address vandalism, a survey of all locations subject to the problem is to be carried out urgently. This survey will help to anticipate and plan mitigation measures. Possible solutions, in addition to a public education and awareness campaign, include reinforcing security personnel to discourage inappropriate behaviour on the part of visitors, as well as installing visible security cameras and strategic lighting along with physical and protective barriers.

PRIORITIES IN CONSERVATION AND FUTURE SITE PRESENTATION

Strategic conservation priorities are closely interconnected with the need to address the main causes of dilapidation. Given the large size of Lahore Fort and the extent of deterioration, it is expedient and more efficient to subdivide the Fort into subsections that constitute well-defined historic or architectural systems, and plan the recommended interventions accordingly. Once individual building envelopes are restored and their decorative elements stabilized and preserved, subsequent interventions can focus on the interpretation and presentation of the site. Priorities are organized at three levels, from those most urgent to the ones that can be implemented over the medium to long term.

FIRST PRIORITY ACTIVITIES

These consist of emergency stabilization measures. Unsafe or unstable buildings pose considerable risk to the security of visitors and the integrity of the structures, due to the possibility of collapse and irreversible loss of material. Therefore, before preparing work plans to address the general causes of decay, immediate interventions should focus on measures to stabilize building components at risk of collapse. These cases are observable in many locations on site. Recommended priority interventions, which are to be implemented in the first twelve months of activities, are as follows:

Above, pigeons pecking lime from mortar joints destabilizes the structural brickwork and seriously damages the glazed-tile decoration.

Left, vandalized *pietra dura* details at the base of columns in the Sheesh Mahal.

Both the Naulakha Pavilion and the Sheesh Mahal, inside and out, contain excellent examples of *pietra dura* **workmanship.**

‣ a check of all unstable *chajjas*, the cantilevered stone or masonry eaves. These should be repaired whenever possible. Alternatively, they should be numbered, dismantled and stored until full repairs can be carried out;

‣ a review of all broken marble and terracotta *jalis*, as well as broken or bulging sandstone panels;

‣ stabilization of brick masonry in the corbelled Mashriqui Burj tower, currently unstable;

‣ repairs to the Picture Wall masonry cavities carried out with compatible brick masonry techniques;

‣ removal of solid-waste deposit north of Akbari Gate and west of the employee's colony.

SECOND PRIORITY ACTIVITIES

These consist of interventions that are to be implemented on building envelopes. These constitute the bulk of conservation activities to be carried out throughout the site. The order of actions is to be determined by the availability of funding and synergies to be established with ongoing works on especially sensitive structures or areas. Rainwater management is the prevailing infrastructure problem. This must be resolved prior to subsequent rehabilitation actions on the exterior components of buildings and structures. Remedial interventions will focus first on re-establishing proper drainage and ensuring that buildings are properly waterproofed in order to reduce rainwater ingress into the buildings and exposed courtyards to the maximum extent possible. These interventions are made more complex by the need to prevent damage to subsurface archaeological remains when exposing pipes and concealed conduits. Similar attention should be paid to seal the flat roofs, water tanks above and rainwater conduits on top of walls against water penetration. Once all of these critical water-related issues have been resolved, subsequent interventions will focus on the stitching of cracks, consolidation of horizontal and vertical structures and substitution of faulty or missing bricks.

In the case of the Picture Wall, the consolidation of the decorative composite including glazed-tile panels, frescoes and 'brick-imitation' render is a priority, as it is exposed to active weather deterioration and closely interconnected with the under-lying structural masonry. This level of priority concerns all building areas subject to visible and ongoing deterioration. In particular, recommended interventions include:

‣ correct slopes, carry out waterproofing of rooftops and make good the connections to mains and soak wells;

‣ correct slopes in courtyards and improve connections to rainwater mains and soak wells;

‣ repair *chajja* cornices and carry out waterproofing of flat rooftops;

‣ remove vegetation and carry out biocide treatment of microflora;

‣ carry out structural repairs to columns, bearing walls, floor slabs and rooftops;

‣ install deterrents or protective devices to remove pigeons;

‣ reinforce presence of security personnel and install physical barriers to discourage vandalism.

THIRD PRIORITY CONSERVATION ACTIVITIES

These consist of long-term interventions on interior finishes. Once the drainage systems have been reinstated and the building envelopes restored, interior finishes and decorated surfaces can be addressed. Generally, the interiors are not in any immediate danger of collapse or material loss, with the exception of some decorated

Stone inlay work inside the Sheesh Mahal.

ceilings where water has infiltrated and the resulting damage is severe and requires urgent stabilization.

SITE PRESENTATION

In addition to implementing activities to preserve Lahore Fort, a series of other planned actions aim at re-establishing missing components and details that have been lost or modified over time in order to reinforce a presentation of the Fort more in line with its original configuration. The general aim is to recover as faithfully as possible the original intent and architectural layout of the rulers and builders who created the Fort, while avoiding false and unsubstantiated reconstructions.

Top left, detail of mirror and coloured-glass inlay decoration.

Top right, *naqqashi*, or fresco painting, is ubiquitous in Lahore Fort and is found in the Lal Burj, the Daulat Khana-e-Jahangiri and on the Picture Wall.

Bottom left, an outlet (possibly the remains of a fountain) at the foot of a large niche in the Picture Wall serves as a drainage outlet for the Shah Burj.

Bottom right, mirror decoration in the Sheesh Mahal covers an older layer of thinly carved decorative stucco.

A first observation is that the site, as it stands today, is the result of a succession of construction campaigns and transformations, initially to improve the fortified enclosure and strengthen its defensive system, and then aimed at expanding the Fort's residential function as the seat of the imperial court under successive Mughal emperors. This process culminated with Shah Jahan's construction campaigns, which gave the palaces and interconnected courtyards their very coherent and highly sophisticated appearance, which is today much compromised by the many layers of subsequent transformations. For the most part, the later additions and modifications contradicted or detracted from the site, thereby rendering it difficult to interpret and fully appreciate the special genius of Mughal architecture and decoration. A few actions can, however, be imagined to present the site in ways that enhance its fuller appreciation and recover some of its contextual qualities. These can be subdivided into the following actions:

1. Actions aimed at reinstating individual elements that are essential for an understanding of the underlying formal composition and visual perception of the Fort's design components, including re-establishment of axes, enclosures, screens, voids, solids and various architectural details. Even apparently minor aspects can offer the visitor interpretative clues. Although in some cases some measure of conjecture is inevitable, visual clues and archaeological remains can offer a reliable indication of what the original composition might have been.

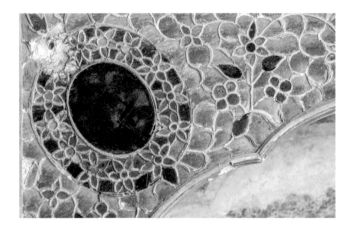

2. Actions aimed at reintroducing the all-important water element that today is fragmentary and no longer functioning. The role of water is essential in understanding and appreciating the character of Mughal landscaping and architecture. The formal arrangements of pools, channels, fountains and water cascades in Lahore Fort should be reinstated as an integral component of the general composition.

3. Actions aimed at introducing limited contemporary additions to re-establish the architectural integrity of specific zones of the site. Today, the south-west area of the Fort, for example, is cut off from the rest of the site, and its relationship with the adjacent formal quadrangles compromised as a result of the vehicular ramp inserted by the British garrison. While the ramp needs to be maintained for functional reasons, it is recommended that the timber bridge over the passage be repositioned and enlarged in order to re-establish the former alignment of the general architectural layout with the historic gate, located north of the Imperial Kitchens.

Left, interior decorative mirrors.

Above, an ad hoc current waterspout on the north-east corner of the Fort.

Below, wall erosion due to rising damp.

283

OVERHAULING THE DRAINAGE SYSTEM AND RE-ESTABLISHING THE HISTORIC LANDSCAPE

ANTHONY WAIN, FRANCOIS DU PLESSIS

OVERHAULING THE DRAINAGE SYSTEM

The present evaluation of Lahore Fort's drainage system focuses on what is arguably the most relevant systemic issue affecting the entire monumental area. Even though drainage is a fairly complex matter, not yet fully understood, the 2018 'Lahore Fort Precinct and Buffer Zone Master Plan' provides an engineering assessment of the present-day drainage and irrigation conditions on site and makes preliminary recommendations as to how the situation can be improved. There are, however, important technical details still to be checked in the field. The results of these further investigations will help formulate a fully fledged programme for the general improvement of drainage conditions in Lahore Fort.

It should be noted at the start that drainage is inextricably linked to the re-establishment of the historic landscape, which, in the case of Lahore Fort, is as important as restoring the buildings. The close complementarity between drainage, landscaped areas and built structures in Mughal architecture demands that all aspects be considered as part of a single undertaking and be resolved concurrently.

ANALYSIS OF EXISTING CONDITIONS

The existing systems for the operation and monitoring of drainage and irrigation are described under two categories: (a) surface drainage, which is the rainfall run-off on surfaces, such as roofs, paved or landscaped areas, channels and so on; and (b) subsurface drainage, which comprises pipes to dispose of water from the upper two metres of soil; drain pipes acting as subsurface conveyors of run-off water; and weep holes in retaining walls to release the pressure of built-up water inside the terrain.

Generally speaking, surface drainage is a critical issue. The original topography of the site upon which Lahore Fort was built was considerably different. Draining the elevated mound would probably have been fairly simple due to adequate slopes directed towards the surrounding valleys. Later interventions, especially during the British colonial period, changed this condition in several locations. There are today several zones where water is drained towards the north, that is, towards the Picture Wall. This drainage water is discharged towards the wall by way of spouts, old and new downpipes, as well as drainage channels embedded within the structure. Most of the spouts are at the top level of the Fort, and considerable energy is released when water hits the ground, causing damage to the wall and surrounding areas. Some of the spouts release water directly against the wall, causing serious damage to the decorated wall surfaces.

Opposite page, interior of the Diwan-e-Khaas, looking south onto Shah Jahan's Quadrangle and the Khwabgah.

Above, aerial view of Lahore Fort after rainfall.

Below, rainwater cascading down the Hathi Pol stairs during the monsoon season.

Subsurface drainage and weep holes

Subsurface drainage systems consist of buried slotted terracotta pipes that collect subsurface free water in the soil. Normally, these drains are buried at a depth of between 1.5 and 2 metres, spaced 30 to 40 metres apart, and discharge the flow into a collector pipe, which eventually releases collected surface water at a suitable location. At present there are no signs of any subsurface drainage infrastructure within Lahore Fort. In fact, there is evidence of high moisture content in the soil. This can be due to deep percolation of surface water into the ground, or else deep drain pipes that are leaking or blocked. It does not appear that there are any weep holes in the walls. The lack of weep holes may indicate that originally water build-up behind the fortification's walls was simply not foreseen or supposed to happen.

Irrigation and fountains

These constitute another issue to be considered. The water source for the irrigation of the green landscaped areas is a well located in Zone S. Water from the well is pumped to the overhead water tank in Zone K, from where a centrifugal pump distributes the water via underground pipes to hydrants positioned at strategic locations. At present, the irrigation is carried out using big rain guns in the larger areas, and hose pipes and sprinklers in the smaller areas, as well as water tankers. It appears that the system is adequately pressurised for the sprinkler systems to function satisfactorily. However, water-use efficiency is most probably low and operational costs quite high. None of the fountains and water features are in working condition, and very little is known about the adduction pipes and how they drained originally.

Existing drainage network in Lahore Fort.

- - - WASA City Drain
- - - Existing Drainage Cum Sewer
——— Existing Open Drain
- - - - Existing Underground Drain
■ Existing Manhole

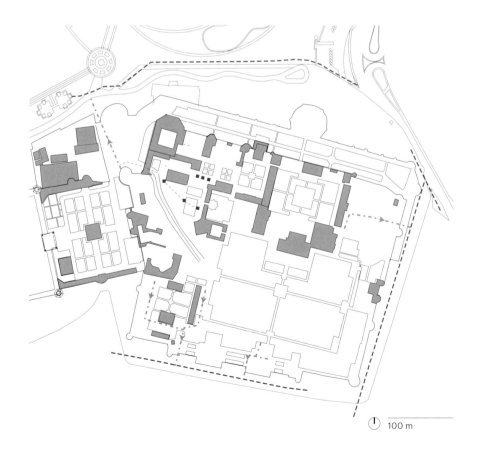

100 m

RECOMMENDED INTERVENTIONS

Based on the observations and the available information, the 2018 Master Plan for the Fort and its Buffer Zone proposes a series of water-related interventions. As more information becomes available through ongoing investigations these proposals can be tested and refined.

Surface drainage

Drainage releases towards the Picture Wall in Shah Burj and other structures via spouts need to be reversed as they cause considerable damage. Water must be channelled and then released at the base of the Picture Wall into a new drainage canal. The capacity of individual outlets needs to be established through field tests. The drainage catchment area should be restricted to the maximum allowable flow for each outlet, with the balance redirected away from the wall. The amount of time required for water discharge must be discussed before implementation, but ideally it should not exceed a period of two to three hours.

The map on p. 288 (below) shows in diagrammatic form the proposed surface drainage routes. A challenge will be the installation of subsurface piping without disturbing the hard surfaces and historic structures. Important in this respect will be the selection of the least sensitive route. Directional drilling may be employed in this case.

The catchment areas in the Fort.

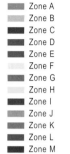

▨	Zone A
▨	Zone B
▨	Zone C
▨	Zone D
▨	Zone E
▨	Zone F
▨	Zone G
▨	Zone H
▨	Zone I
▨	Zone J
▨	Zone K
▨	Zone L
▨	Zone M
▨	Zone N
▨	Zone O
▨	Zone P
▨	Zone Q
▨	Zone R
▨	Zone S

100 m

Proposed drainage network of Lahore Fort.

—— Proposed Route of Sheesh
    Mahal Roof Water
—— Proposed Underground Drain
---- Proposed Undergound Connection
--▸ Proposed Surface Flow
● Proposed Soakage Well

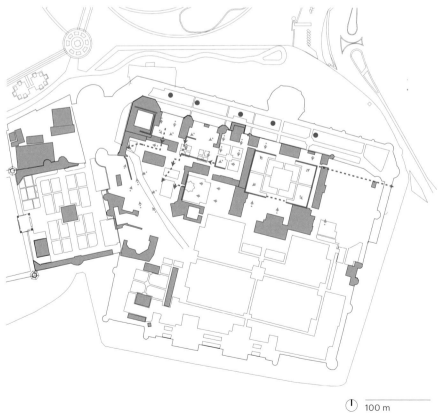

100 m

This is a procedure whereby underground pipelines are installed without disturbance to the ground surface and minimal disruption of subsurface structures.

Subsurface drainage

Subsurface drainage systems should be considered for the irrigated areas after careful investigations by soil scientists. The purpose of subsurface drains is to ensure a well-drained soil, suitable for healthy plant growth. It will collect free water in the soil due to over-irrigation and rainfall, so as to avoid free water accumulation into the ground and the occurrence of saturated conditions behind the walls and/or within subsurface structures. The application of weep holes and pipes in the lower levels of high retaining walls should be considered.

Irrigation and fountains

It is recommended that lawns be irrigated preferably with an automated pop-up sprinkler system. The spacing of these sprinklers will be approximately every 12 by 12 metres, and will be served by subsurface sub-mains connected to an automated hydraulic valve. The valves will be served by a branched main pipe network from the centrifugal pump at the overhead water reservoir. This main pipe is currently largely in place, although there are certain sections of it that will have to be replaced by larger size pipes. If fountains are made operational again, then the water for these will be drawn from the irrigation network, and preferably circulated in order to reduce water consumption. More in general, from a water-balancing perspective, the Fort appears to be self-sustaining.

THE WAY FORWARD

The 2018 Master Plan recommends the gathering of key data and information to advance, fine-tune and finalize the general and detailed drainage improvement design for each of the sub-zones under consideration. Of special relevance are:

- to ascertain the nature and condition of the existing drainage pipes and their functionality;
- to validate the status of other existing infrastructure networks and their efficiency, such as irrigation pipes;
- to commission soil investigations to determine the chemical characteristics of the terrain and its suitability for plant growth;
- to determine the condition of the existing pipework in and around fountains and other water features;
- to acquire detailed long-term time series weather predictions, preferably on a daily basis;
- to employ laser-scanning equipment as an alternative to more destructive forms of investigation.

RE-ESTABLISHING THE HISTORIC LANDSCAPE

APPROACH

The scale of Lahore Palace-Fort's landscape is monumental in its various components: the moat garden acting as a buffer, the Fort's elevated podium, the geometry of the intimate, interlocked courts, and the surrounding defensive spaces. Many elements of the Mughal gardens still exist, particularly the architectural and landscape compositions, but the primary vegetal components are largely missing. However, even if the existing horticultural components are missing or reflect later interventions and styles, the underlying historic structure of the landscape survives and can itself be

Above, detail of the northern aspect of the Picture Wall.

Below, present condition of the southern perimeter wall of the Sheesh Mahal.

Big rain guns are used for irrigation in the larger areas.

considered monumental in value. These issues are of fundamental importance in re-establishing the gardens as an authentically planted composition.

In any reconstruction or replanting of significance, the garden's evolution must be respected. When nothing remains of a particular period, one can refer to documentary evidence for precedents as well as look at similar or associated gardens in the region.

Lahore Fort's structures and gardens are a lesson in history and illustrate an extraordinary chapter in the cultural and artistic heritage of the Punjab plain. Its combination of rugged fortifications, refined Mughal palaces, garden forms, decorative pavilions, potential museum spaces and the magnificent Picture Wall constitutes a catalogue of the region's artistic and cultural history. The restoration of the gardens and greater landscape will also restore the intimate and sophisticated quality and character of this unique, fortified, historical mound. These gardens, once dedicated to the exclusive use of the emperor and his court, now belong to everyone, to serve education and to be enjoyed.

AIMS AND PROCESS

Defining strategies and priorities for re-landscaping Lahore Fort must proceed from the recognition that the successive reorganizations and transformations of the site, some carefully planned and intentional and some the result of casual adaptations or simple neglect, have built up a complex palimpsest that must be unravelled through the pragmatic re-establishment of what is likely or possible. The result will neither be a faithful restoration, impossible to achieve today, nor a gratuitous injection of contemporary ideas, but an adaptation of the current state of the gardens to conditions that take into account today's uses, reinstate some of the lost integrity of the place and offer an opportunity to visitors to better understand the history of the site as a whole.

Landscape restoration efforts should target the core areas of interconnected courtyards, garden courts, water pools and fountains, mostly concentrated in the northern sectors of the site. The combined effect of a sequential series of restored structures and architectural elements, together with the renovated paved courtyards, waterworks and plantings, would display to best effect the practices and extraordinary achievements of the Mughal tradition in garden design and horticulture.

Other areas, mostly on the south side of the gardens, will be respected and, in fact, given new life in keeping with later landscape tradition. This would certainly mean confirming the presence of the wide lawns and mature trees, which it would neither be appropriate nor wise to cut down today. The major shade trees and hospitable lawns would be factored in for the contribution and functional variety they bring to the Fort.

The following three-step process can be identified as necessary to move forward with the initiative, keeping in mind that many pre-construction activities can occur simultaneously. This is not only to gain time, but also to ensure a better integration between the different components of the design process as each of the elements to be considered affects the others and should not be treated in a piecemeal or rigidly sequential fashion.

Step one

The fundamental analytical phase; it is indispensable to get a better understanding of the complexity of the site and its historical layering. To this effect, prior to any form of planning, all archaeological, literary and visual records must be considered. At

the same time, the site must be properly inventoried in all its constituent elements, including existing planting or evidence of previous plants, in addition to all garden structures and forms of paving. The latter must be considered not only from an 'archaeological' point of view, but also with a view towards its vulnerability. Where restoration is possible, this must take into account the availability of replacements and the future management and carrying capacity of different paving solutions. Of special relevance is the revitalization of the waterworks as a key element of Mughal garden design and appeal.

Above, general view of the Fort, with the Badshahi Mosque in the background.

Below, aerial view of the Diwan-e-Aam Quadrangle and Jahangir's Quadrangle, seen from the west.

Above, aerial view of the Fort showing the relationship of the quadrangular spaces and the British-period road.

Below, the Diwan-e-Aam maidan.

Step two

This is the time to ensure that the operational conditions for the functioning and maintenance of the garden are in place before the inception of works. Imperative actions in this respect include an understanding of the current capabilities of the planting maintenance group to improve management processes and practical know-how through training, as well as carry out an assessment of the quality of the soil, the effectiveness of the supply and drainage of water, and the performance and reliability of the *in situ* irrigation system. Of fundamental importance are also preparations for the availability of plant materials on site. A strategy to source and grow semi-mature plants, especially trees and palm hedges, close to or even on site will need to be put in place. The establishment of a nursery on site, whether within the citadel's compound or in nearby Iqbal Park, appears necessary in order to acclimatize and toughen plants prior to planting.

Step three
Initiate implementation of landscaping works as soon as acceptable conditions for plant life are established and the restoration work on the architectural structures related to specific components of the site are completed. This is important because the complementary and integrated nature of architecture and garden in Mughal planning demands that both aspects be effectively completed if a site is to be considered fully restored. It is also important, especially at the beginning, to identify solutions through the implementation of samples, mock-ups and pilot project activities in order to ensure that specific outcomes are tested, confirmed and, if necessary, fine-tuned.

CONCLUSION

World heritage cultural landscapes have been customarily selected as extraordinary examples of the encounter between human civilization and exceptional natural landscapes, highlighting how evolving societies transformed a landscape in a remarkable and lasting way. Such a transformation begins with a systematic change of the landform, through agriculture and horticulture, and the application of human-built forms to the landscape. The evolution of a cultural landscape continues and changes through successive historical periods, creating a historical record, awaiting interpretation and explanation. In the past, many narratives focused on a single historic event, ruler, empire or monument. The result was a narrow, exclusionary narrative. But a cultural landscape can and should display parallel narratives. These must be broad and inclusive in order to recognize the contribution of ordinary people over time, their lives, craftmanship and labouring efforts. How did such efforts come to symbolize a walled paradise garden in Lahore? This is a story worth telling.

Stately trees in the Diwan-e-Aam maidan.

THE PICTURE WALL'S ICONOGRAPHY AND AESTHETIC ANALYSIS

NADHRA SHAHBAZ KHAN

The *Shahi Qal'a*, or imperial Fort, stands in the old part of Lahore as a testimony to the city's Mughal history. Built by Akbar and enlarged by both Jahangir and Shah Jahan, it has several elements that connect it to Agra and Delhi forts. One remarkable feature though – its Picture Wall – surpasses the other two. The superintendent of Punjab for the Archaeological Survey of India (1901–14) Jean Philippe Vogel, a Dutch Sanskritist and epigraphist, believed that: "The imperial palace of Lahore outshines all these buildings by the truly princely magnitude of its colour decoration. A wall nearly 500 yards [457 metres; in fact, 461 metres] in length and 16 yards [14.5 metres; in fact, 18 metres] in height – in other words a surface of about 8,000 square yards [6,689 square metres] – has been adorned with panels of tile-mosaics."[1] Like an open-air picture gallery, the entire breadth and height of Lahore Fort's northern and western walls are embellished with several decorative techniques, such as wall painting or *naqqashi*, glazed-tile mosaic or *kashikari*, carving or *munabbatkari* and terracotta filigree or *jali* work.[2] The surface of these walls is divided into panels of various shapes and dimensions by raised string courses, mouldings, arc-shaped window openings and arched blind niches while some are subdivided into smaller sections. Spandrels of most of these windows and arched niches, as well as sunken panels, carry figurative imagery that includes humans, animals, birds and imaginary creatures, as well as geometrical patterns and vegetal motifs in *kashikari*.

This decoration is datable to two Mughal eras. The area of the Picture Wall ascribable to Jahangir (r. 1605–27) spans between the first tower on the eastern end of the northern wall to the limits of Kala Burj, while Shah Jahan's (1628–58) segment starts at this point and culminates at the Hathi Pol towards the end of the western wall (see the plan on p. 296). While the epigraphic panels on the Hathi Pol attribute its completion to Shah Jahan, no written evidence found thus far offers precise evidence of Jahangir's involvement in it. It is only material and structural signs that corroborate this theory. Recent scholarship refers to Lahore Fort's northern and western ornamental walls as the Picture Wall, but Mughal chronicles make no mention of their embellishment nor of the message intended to be conveyed by their pictorial narrative. European travellers visiting the city in the seventeenth and eighteenth centuries are also almost silent on this. Only William Moorcroft, a veterinary surgeon working for the East India Company who visited Maharaja Ranjit Singh in May of 1620, mentioned the Picture Wall in passing:

"The palace within this inclosure [sic], called the Saman Burj, which is of many stories, is entirely faced with a kind of porcelain enamel, on which processions and combats of men and animals are depictured. Many of these are as perfect as when first placed in the wall."[3]

Opposite page, an arched panel in the western Picture Wall. The Picture Wall is embellished with several decorative techniques including fresco, glazed-tile mosaic and terracotta 'filigree' work.

Above, the imagery on the Picture Wall consists of humans, animals, birds and imaginary creatures, as well as geometric and floral motifs.

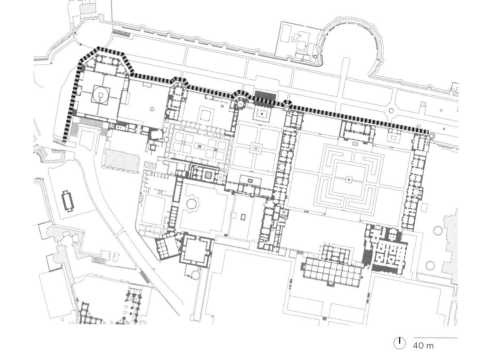

40 m

Above, location of the Picture Wall in the context of Lahore Fort.

Opposite page, above, aerial view of the western facade of the Picture Wall. Below, EDM documentation of the wall.

The first person to highlight the beauty and significance of these walls was T. H. Thornton, a British officer who served in various capacities in Lahore after Punjab's annexation in 1849. He brought it to public attention in his guidebook titled *Lahore*, published in 1860. Thornton discussed the two walls in some detail under three different headings: "Coloured Designs on the Palace Front", "Historical Interest of the Designs", and "Origin of the Art Called Kashi".[4]

The credit for the first monograph on this extremely important feature of Lahore Fort goes to Vogel. He first visited the Fort in April 1899 and decided to record the Picture Wall tile mosaic for reasons of "their far-advanced decay and their unique nature".[5] Vogel's monograph is remarkable as it not only includes a discussion of the Fort's buildings and descriptions of narrative panels but also presents drawings prepared from tracings of existing panels. What struck both Thornton and Vogel in this mosaic decoration were the representations of living beings that Thornton believed were "in defiance of Muhammadan orthodoxy".[6] Featured on 116 panels, Vogel, for his part, had his assistants make tracings of these panels in the beginning of 1902. Completed in almost four months, these were then used to prepare drawings on a reduced scale that took almost five years to finish.[7] The painted or *naqqashi* panels of the Picture Wall that are barely visible at present had already lost much of their brilliance when Vogel saw them.

Vogel's work is the only detailed study of this subject to date and provides invaluable information about several panels now lost due to decay and damage. After a gap of more than a century, the Aga Khan Cultural Service-Pakistan (AKCS-P) team, with funds provided by the Royal Norwegian Embassy, became involved in 2015 to document and conserve the Picture Wall, but also to take the process a step further and to explore the iconology of its extant panels in an attempt to understand the overall narrative. During these recent investigations, several panels covered with plaster

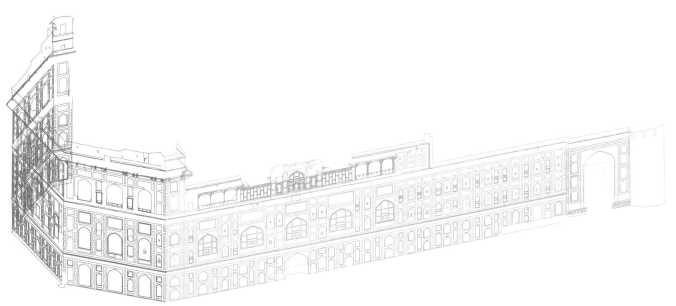

The conservation of the Picture Wall's north facade is scheduled for completion in 2021.

have been reclaimed where the intact biscuit makes the composition readable. Since access to the Fort is mostly through the Hathi Pol, it is the western section of the Picture Wall that garners attention and was therefore the first to receive conservation measures.

The *kashikari* narrative panels on these two walls are of particular interest. Iconography used here is reminiscent of not only Mughal but also Persian miniature paintings in which representations of royal processions, hunting scenes, animal fights, winged creatures hovering over imperial heads, and dragons and simurghs abound. While some panels offer glimpses of everyday events at the Mughal court – such as elephant fights, dromedaries brought to the emperor led by their masters, equestrian princes strolling at their ease or engaged in a fight – others carry images of various types of winged creatures that appear to represent esoteric meanings and messages. Seyyed Hossein Nasr explains that "birds, their flight, and their wings are universal symbols of the spirit and of spiritual journeying".[8] Ali Asani, expressing similar thoughts, states: "A whole range of birds [...] populate the 'alam-i mithal, the 'world of symbols', through which the Sufi poet accesses the hidden reality that underlies existence".[9] The winged creatures on the Picture Wall manifest the Mughal rulers' fantasy of flight as well as connections forged with the heavens. At present, the approach to the Picture Wall is from the western side and the most prominent feature of this section are spandrels of five large arches in what Vogel calls the curtain wall of the Summer Palace.[10] All five feature winged creatures.

Spandrels of the central large arch of this set of five carry images of an angel/fairy or *pari*,[11] with a lassoed *div* or *jinn* on each side (see partly in the top-right image below). With a rope tied around their waists, the *divs* appear to be floating in an unconscious state, lying on their backs against a bright yellow background. The head of the *div* in the left spandrel is turned downward while the other lies straight. Their claw-like feet are turned upward and there is no tension in the rope that softly curves between the hands of the winged figures and the *divs'* waists, indicating a lack of resistance on the captives' part. Spandrels of two smaller arches near this large arch carry a single *div* on each side caught in mid-flight holding a cudgel and a buckler (a small round shield) in their hands (see below, bottom right).

On the western part of the Picture Wall, spandrels of arches carry images of angels (top right), *divs* (bottom right) and winged figures.

Ebba Koch explains that "in the Persianate world, angels are designated as *paris* – fairies, or positive winged spirits – and the demons as *diws*".[12] The latter are comparable to the *jinn* mentioned in the Qur'an (literally hidden from sight, thus invisible to the human eye). Although their physical description in these texts is very limited, their visual representation shows them as composite creatures; a human body with an animal head, black or greyish blue in colour, fangs protruding from their mouths and claws instead of hands and feet. From the Qur'anic perspective, they have been created from smokeless fire and are different from angels made from light. Their leader was Iblis, who disobeyed God in prostrating himself before Adam and was thus condemned forever, and thereafter known as *shaitān* or Satan. The etymology of *div* is not straightforward as it presents Indo-Iranian origins with positive connotations and needs more investigation to trace the demonization of this expression over time. Unlike angels, *divs* or *jinns* are understood to have a free will similar to humans and are good or evil. They are also mentioned in connection with Solomon who had complete control over them and deployed them for many hard tasks, like metalwork and buildings projects. One instance of his domination is described in the Qur'an as follows:

Quite a few panels of the Picture Wall carry images of elephants, both wild and tame, horse-riders and camels.

"And before Solomon were marshalled his hosts – of jinn and men and birds, and they were all kept in order and ranks" (Qur'an 27:17).

A curious characteristic of these creatures circulating in fiction is that they tend to sleep during the day and roam about at night. Any effort to catch them, therefore, must be carried out while the sun shines. Once overcome by a king or a hero, they serve him for the rest of their lives or as long as the master lives. The bright yellow background of the large arch probably indicates their abduction taking place in the

Above, a portion of the northern Picture Wall where flora and fauna first appear, as well as human figures juxtaposed with animals, birds or flowers.

Below, dragons and lesser animals also make their first appearance on the north facade.

301

daytime while they are deeply asleep and therefore not offering any resistance to their captors. Instead, their individual images in the smaller spandrels depict them as loyal slaves serving their master, guarding the garden-like space of the interior. Allusion to this verdant space can be readily conjectured from the faded flowers painted in the slightly sunken arched niche of this panel, above which the *divs* are hovering. Other than mystical allusions, can these panels also be read as political statements – allegories or warnings denoting heavenly assistance extended to Shah Jahan to capture and subdue evil forces in his territory?

Flanking this central arch are exquisitely rendered images of fantastical simurghs (literally *si*: thirty, *murgh*: bird; "the king of the birds" *shah-i murghan*)[13] and dragons or the Persian *azdhá* (see p. 301, below).[14] While the simurgh pounces on the dragon in each spandrel, it turns its head backwards seeking to release itself from the bird's talons. The bright yellow background enhances the light green, turquoise and deep blue body of the dragon and some parts of the simurgh's feathers in the upper section. Following Chinese tradition, the dragons shown here are quadruped with prominent claws and flame-like wings on top of their legs. Their long scaly bodies have white dots on their vertebrae-like backs that end in sinuously curving tails.

References to these two fantastical creatures abound in fables, poetry and epics universally. Interesting for the purpose of discerning iconological content is Persian and Arabic literature and illustrated manuscripts, such as Ferdowsi's *Shahnameh* ("The Book of Kings"), Farid ud-Din Attar's *Mantiq Ut-Tair* ("The Conference of the Birds") and the *Kitāb Manāfi'al-Hayawān* ("The Book on the Usefulness of Animals"), which are known to have circulated in Mughal courts.[15] An emblem of good luck and

Ornate panels of floral motives juxtaposed with servants bearing gifts for the emperor.

a symbol fit to represent the emperor in Chinese art, the dragon takes on a demonic persona in Persian literature and art where it must be subdued by the hero. The simurgh, on the other hand, resonates as a protector and nurturer of heroes, as well as the search for self and the flight of the soul up to heaven. The position of these two creatures in each spandrel in which the simurgh appears to fly in from above and pounce on them is laden with symbolism. The dragons struggling to break free are shown moving backwards with their heads turned away from the predator and downwards as if wanting to slide back into the deep waters they emerged from. Where this battle alludes to the primordial tension between good and evil, it also signifies the simurgh's victorious and superior position as a representative of the heavens and skies over earthly beings: furthermore, it offers interpretations in terms of victory of the higher self over *nafs-e ammara* or baser instincts – Sufi concepts articulated in Persian and Arabic literature.

Panels depicting princes off on a hunt; a prince on horseback leading a maddened elephant away; a dromedary; and keepers controlling two fighting elephants.

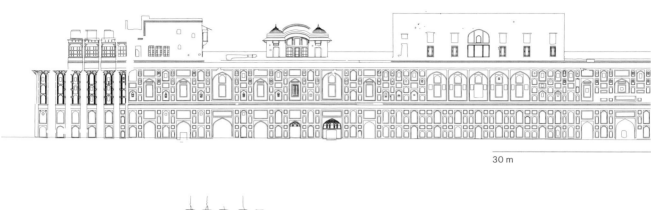

30 m

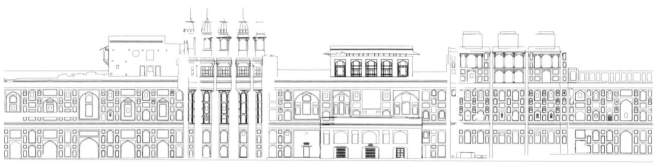

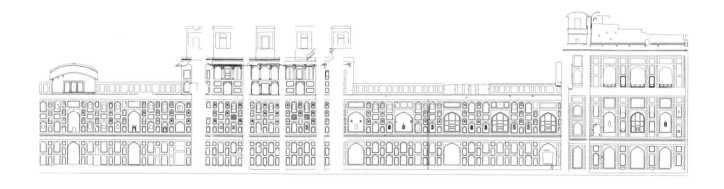

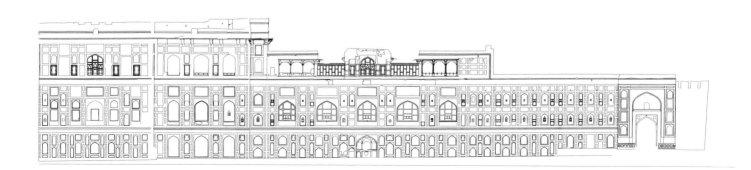

Opposite page, EDM documentation of the
Picture Wall's northern and western facades.

Above, a pair of riders on a decorative panel.

Considered to be a measure of the strength and pomp of the owner in early modern South Asia, quite a few panels of the Picture Wall carry images of elephants, both wild and tame, richly caparisoned with a mahout (elephant driver) holding a *mehmīz*, or goad, with an attendant in the rear. Annemarie Schimmel states that men were assigned as caretakers of elephants according to the animal's rank and value. A young and strong one of the highest class "had five and a half (!) servants, namely the driver (mahout) and another servant sitting behind him, and other men of both higher and lower ranks to feed, saddle and deck him out. Even the smallest imperial elephant had two servants, and the largest female elephant had four."[16] These panels speak volumes about the resourcefulness, majesty and magnificence of their owners. In Thomas T. Allsen's words:

"Since this measure was so widely accepted, rulers in India and South East Asia lost no opportunity to demonstrate their elephant power. They displayed their beasts in endless processions, diplomatic receptions, religious celebrations, entertainments, and rites of passage in the royal family – weddings, coronations, and funerals."[17]

The walking elephants appear to be led towards fighting arenas as none of these carry a howda, while others are rendered while being poked in the hind legs to charge against their opponents (see p. 303). This dangerous sport of elephant fighting was something over which the Mughal emperors claimed a monopoly and even princes had to seek royal permission if they wished to hold such an event. Abraham Eraly explains the spectacle:

Panels depicting a person of importance receiving a visitor; a camel caravan; and a sword fight.

"A pair of carefully matched elephants [...] set to fight against each other across a mud wall three or four feet [1.2 metres] wide and five or six feet [1.5 to 1.8 metres] high. The fight began with the elephants rushing on each other and butting, and it ended when the mud wall was demolished and one elephant chased away the other, or they got into a clinch, in which case they were separated by setting off fireworks." [18]

Camels and horse-riders are the next important theme depicted in the mosaic panels. Out of the extant panels on the western section of the Picture Wall, eight are dedicated to the first and six to the second. Schimmel explains that camels during Mughal times were used for transporting logs and other heavy goods but were also trained for riding. The best specimens, according to her, came from Sind, especially the Thatta region, but the two-humped Bactrian camels were also popular.[19] Referred to as *shutr bakhti*, Muhammad Salih Kamboh notes that a hundred of these were presented to Shah Jahan by Kabul's governor Saeed Khan in Lahore in 1634.[20] As with other riding animals, the girths and breast bands of these camels were heavily ornamented, "set with shells or metal bells, [...] their caparisons were made of fine, colourful material – no fabric or jewellery was too valuable for the best camels".[21] The Picture Wall depicts both single and double-humped camels, known as 'ships of the desert'. Bactrian camels were termed *shutur-i sahraī* and "were held to be a most fitting and formidable opponent for a prince" a reference perhaps related to the difficulty in taming them.[22] All the square and oblong panels show a single camel led by its driver or *shutr-bán*, who walks ahead of it holding the rope attached to its muzzle. For purposes of narrative complexity or emblematic variety, the camels are shown treading flat and uneven terrain (see left).

The Picture Wall features diverse supernatural creatures positioned in symbolic actions carrying equally meaningful objects, birds and animals of a variety of species, both predators and prey, and men of different races, occupations and statures captured in multiple activities. The ornamental programme thus relies heavily on symbols and parables that appear to be intended for informed viewers, as they were expected to be decoded and understood. When viewed in reference to the Picture Wall patrons – Jahangir and Shah Jahan – this careful selection of visual metaphors and their intended messages seems natural.

Reliance on symbols and metaphors to circulate ideas of power, glory and spirituality for both Jahangir and Shah Jahan was not limited to court chronicles and epigraphic inscriptions.[23] It was, rather, the entire literary, artistic and architectural vocabulary that was built on synecdoche meant to inflate ideas of hegemony and grandeur at the receiver's end. Drawn from Central Asian, Persian, ancient Indian and European artistic traditions, these symbols were adapted and assimilated into the local vocabulary for their own specific purposes. Allegorical paintings symbolizing temporal and divine powers were another genre used especially by Jahangir and Shah Jahan for the self-projection of being stronger and more prestigious than others. What leads us to investigate the Picture Wall's potential for being used as a means to broadcast carefully formulated royal statements through these representations is Shah Jahan's court chronicler Muhammad Waris's statement about images on the wall in Delhi Fort's Diwan-e-Aam behind the *jharoka,* or high balcony. Here, the wall is divided into panels in which each panel carries an image of a bird, except for one that features Orpheus placed at the top.[24] Waris writes that the wall carries "different kinds of designs having allegorical themes (*tamasīl*) [...] painted on them".[25] The Persian word *tamasīl* means "allegory, parable, proverb or exemplum" and unambiguously illustrates that Shah Jahan chose imperial public places to engage with his audience through carefully chosen messages. This historical annotation reinforces the possibility that the visual narrative of the Picture Wall may also carry a concrete connection between imperial thought and the public gaze. It also confirms its function as an active site for encoding imperial allegorical memoranda and poses interesting questions of how this space and its visuality were negotiated by both outsiders and palace dwellers. Moreover, it opens up several avenues of investigation for exploring the relationship between producers and consumers of these images and the social, cultural and aesthetic power of the signs and symbols employed.

The range of extant animate images on the Picture Wall is fascinating and extensive. The inflatable visual vocabulary and aesthetic appeal allows the Picture Wall to be seen as a *muraqqa'*, or an album showcasing novel ideas and images intended as *tamasīl* rather than an illustrated manuscript meant to communicate self-affirmative messages echoed in the court chronicles and epigraphs. In short, the overall impression the images impart may be of grandeur and majesty from a distance but a closer study softens these claims of supremacy as the Picture Wall offers something interesting to every onlooker who cares to 'stand and stare'.

Following pages, part of the recently restored western front of the Picture Wall of Lahore Fort.

Note: I would like to acknowledge the efforts of my research assistant Maleeha Hameed in collecting and compiling material for this project.

1   J. Ph. Vogel, *Tile-Mosaics of the Lahore Fort*, John Marshall (ed.), Superintendent Government Printing, Calcutta, 1920, p. 2. For a detailed history of the Fort, see "Historical Notes on the Lahore Fort and Its Buildings" (in the *Annual Report of the Archaeological Survey of India, 1902–03*, Calcutta, 1904) by Maulvi Nur Bakhsh, assistant to Vogel, who consolidated several scattered pieces of information and published a detailed article on the history of the Fort's site and structures.

2   For details of the *kashikari* technique see Syad Muhammad Latif, *Lahore: Its Historical, Architectural Remains and Antiquities*, New Imperial Press, Lahore, 1892, pp. 392–393.

3   Horace Hayman Wilson (ed.), *Travels in the Himalayan Provinces of Hindustan and the Panjab; in Ladakh and Kashmir; in Peshawar, Kabul, Kunduz, and Bokhara by Mr. William Moorcroft and Mr. George Trebeck from 1819–1825*, John Murray, London, 1841, vol. 1, p. 104.

4   Anis Nagi, "Preface", in *Ancient Lahore: A Brief Account of the History and Antiquities of Lahore*, Gautam, Lahore, 1994, pp. 71–75. Nagi reprinted Thornton's 1860 publication with the addition of his own preface and without the original author's name. For details of this see Nadhra Shahbaz Khan, *The Samadhi of Maharaja Ranjit Singh in Lahore: A Summation of Sikh Architectural and Decorative Practices*, EB Verlag, Berlin, 2018, pp. 18–20.

5   Vogel, *Tile-Mosaics of the Lahore Fort* op. cit., p. i.

6   T. H. Thornton and J. Lockwood Kipling, *Lahore*, Government Civil Secretariat Press, Lahore, 1876, p. 53.

7   Vogel explains in the preface that the drawings project took this long as it could only be done during parts of the summer months. See Vogel, *Tile-Mosaics of the Lahore Fort* op. cit., p. ii.

8   Seyyed Hossein Nasr, "Foreword", in Alexis York Lumbard and Demi, *The Conference of the Birds*, Wisdom Tales, Indiana, 2012.

9   Ali S. Asani, "Oh That I Could Be a Bird and Fly, I Would Rush to the Beloved", in Paul Waldau and Kimberley Patton (eds.), *A Communion of Subjects: Animals in Religion and Ethics*, Columbia University Press, New York, 2006, p. 172.

10   Vogel, *Tile-Mosaics of the Lahore Fort* op. cit., p. 27.

11   *Par* literally means feathers or wings. Ebba Koch offers a detailed description and discussion of such images in Mughal art in her essay "Solomonic Angels in a Mughal Sky: The Wall Paintings of the Kala Burj at the Lahore Fort Revisited and Their Reception in Later South Asian and Qajar Art", in Katharina Weiler and Niels Gutschow (eds.), *Spirits in Transcultural Skies: Auspicious and Protective Spirits in Artifacts and Architecture Between East and West*, Springer, New York, 2015.

12   Koch, "Solomonic Angels in a Mughal Sky" op. cit., p. 158.

13   Ibid., p. 158.

14   British plaster covering the spandrels of the right arch was recently removed by the AKCS-P team. Almost all glaze has been lost but the intact biscuit and mortar edges adequately yield the original image.

15   The *Kitāb Manāfi'al-Hayawān* is one of several similar illustrated manuscripts commissioned in Persian and Arabic (sometimes translated from one into the other) bestiaries that appear to have been inspired by Aristotle's *Historia Animalium*. For details, and the English translation of the title, see Anna Contadini,

"The Kitāb Manāfi'al-Hayawān in the Escorial Library", in *Islamic Art*, vol. 3 (1988–89), pp. 41–42.

16   Annemarie Schimmel, *The Empire of the Great Mughals: History, Art and Culture*, Reaktion Books, London, 2004, p. 216.

17   Thomas T. Allsen, *The Royal Hunt in Eurasian History*, University of Pennsylvania Press, Philadelphia, 2006, p. 72.

18   Abraham Eraly, *The Mughal World: Life in India's Last Golden Age*, Penguin Books, New Delhi, 2007, p. 74.

19   Schimmel, *The Empire of the Great Mughals* op. cit., p. 219.

20   Ghulam Yazdani (ed.), *'Amal-i-Ṣ̲āliḥ or Shāh Jahān Nāmah of Muḥammad Ṣāliḥ Kaṃbo*, Asiatic Society, Calcutta, 1923, vol. 2, p. 6.

21   Schimmel, *The Empire of the Great Mughals* op. cit., p. 219.

22   Allsen, *The Royal Hunt* op. cit., p. 132.

23   There are two buildings in Lahore Fort carrying epigraphic inscriptions in Persian by Jahangir and Shah Jahan. The Makateeb Khana (the Room of Letters/Petitions) for the former and the Hathi Pol for the latter.

24   See Ebba Koch, *Shah Jahan and Orpheus: The Pietre Dure Decoration and the Programme of the Throne in the Hall of Public Audiences at the Red Fort of Delhi*, Akademische Druck-u. Verlagsanstalt, Graz, 1988.

25   Translation of the *Padshahnama* by Muhammad Waris, Ms. Or. 1675, The British Library London, pp. 38–56, in Syed Ali Nadeem Rezavi, "'The Mighty Defensive Fort': Red Fort at Delhi Under Shah Jahan – Its Plan and Structures as Described by Muhammad Waris", in *Proceedings of the Indian History Congress*, vol. 71 (2010–11), p. 1118.

CONSERVATION OF THE PICTURE WALL

CHRISTOPHE BOULEAU, WERNER MATTHIAS SCHMID, ZEINA NASEER

In terms of its scale and grandeur, as well as its uniqueness as a work of art, the Picture Wall is an exceptional feature of Lahore Fort. It is one of the largest decorated architectural surfaces in the world (461 metres long with an average height of 18 metres) and is embellished in a variety of mediums, which span across architectural and painterly forms – tile mosaic and fresco panels, brick imitation, terracotta friezes and 'filigree' work. As a classic example of the craftsmanship of the Mughal period, the Picture Wall is partly responsible for the Fort's UNESCO World Heritage listing in 1981. However, conservation efforts made in the past were not comprehensive or thorough, and have left behind a host of problems and issues for the conservator.

The Picture Wall has suffered long periods of abandonment, improper use and neglect. It seems that after the death of Emperor Shah Jahan in 1666, the Fort remained largely unused for more than a hundred years until the Sikh period. The first large-scale restoration intervention did not come until the beginning of the twentieth century. At that time, low-rise structures built by the British army against the western Picture Wall were removed and waterspouts were inserted for rainwater drainage. On the Picture Wall, missing masonry was reconstructed and lost areas of decorated surfaces were repaired with a brownish plaster. Since then, only localized small-scale interventions have been carried out.

Beginning in 2017, the current conservation intervention on the Picture Wall stands as a pioneering intervention. Due to the heritage sensitivity of a World Heritage listed site and the level of deterioration of the structures and decoration, it became obvious that a set of criteria was necessary to support the proposed conservation methodology. Currently accepted conservation practice involves procedures necessary to understand the complexity of a structure and assess its level of dilapidation in order to design solutions for specific requirements. While each case is different due to its nature, immediate context and general environmental conditions, there are universally accepted principles, procedures and methods that regulate the implementation of conservation projects, whether heritage structures or larger sites. These principles, rooted in the international heritage conservation norms, cover the full range of pre-construction surveys and studies, good practice during implementation and post-construction archiving. These principles form the methodological framework applicable to all present and future conservation interventions in the Picture Wall:

Opposite page, a conservator at work cleaning a glazed-tile spandrel.

Above, consolidation of glazed-tile work.

Below, an expert transferring knowledge and methodology.

The Picture Wall of Lahore Fort, seen from the west.

1. *Documentation and technical studies.* The process of the collection, critical evaluation and interpretation of data from various multidisciplinary sources such as archives, archaeological remains, technical and material science studies, architectural and structural surveys, drawings and photographs. Different types of analyses in combination reach informed conclusions regarding the most appropriate and effective interventions.

2. *Historic evidence and authenticity.* Information, whether archival or collected in the field, is used in combination to provide a better sense of the original configuration and the subsequent transformations that have affected the various structures and components of a site. This is in order to avoid alteration or destruction of important features in the course of implementation. Interventions should rather aim at preserving the authenticity of significant spaces and structures.

3. *Traditional methods, materials and techniques versus work plans developed with contemporary technology and knowledge.* Conservation activities cannot be limited to the use of traditional technologies and methods. As a rule, conservation repair works must use traditional materials and construction techniques or use those that are similar and compatible with the traditional ones. However, problems affecting a structure can at times be best resolved with the introduction of compatible modern conservation methods that have proved effective to resolve specific

problems. Only when traditional solutions prove less efficient or effective should contemporary methods be introduced. The use of advanced scientific solutions is, in any case, to be preferred in carrying out material investigations and analyses as these provide more reliable and accurate results.

4. *Minimal intervention.* Any intervention must be calibrated to achieve the required results with the minimum possible amount of change, and should aim at respecting the aesthetic and physical integrity of the site or monument to be preserved. In this respect, there should be no attempt to reconstruct lost decoration.

5. *Reversibility and compatibility.* In the context of the Picture Wall, conservation reversibility may be understood as 're-treatability' – a concept that provides for intervention that does not damage the original material, and that would accept another cycle of conservation in the future.

6. *Training and qualifications* are increasingly important as conservation works are often designed and implemented by skilled professionals and craftsmen. The works therefore involve important training and educational components that are best transmitted via practical conservation workshops or through direct training on conservation building sites.

7. *Pilot conservation projects and sample prototypes* have proven beneficial in experimenting with different approaches and testing remedial solutions on

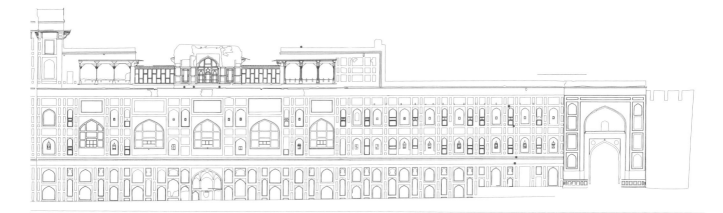

10 m

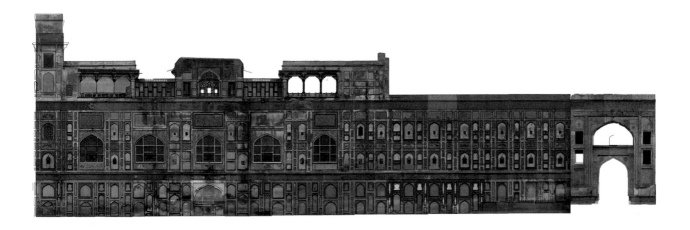

a medium scale. In order to develop successful conservation methods, the long-term effectiveness of certain techniques is tested through prototypes that have been subjected to accelerated or extreme weathering conditions. Presenting results of prototypes to local and international experts encourages feedback and, if needed, the adjustment of methodology.

8. *Supervision, involvement of international experts and capacity building* are key factors in developing and guaranteeing quality conservation work. It is critical to establish design and implementation teams made up of local professionals, crafts-men and conservators, trained by international experts and building specialists to achieve better expertise, supervision and quality control. Building the capacity of construction staff in the field is a key to achieving long-term sustainability and local self-reliance.

9. *Detailed project documentation and archiving* during and after a conservation project are essential. Survey and planning documents must be archived as these are indispensable to establishing reliable records on building conditions and the conservation process during implementation. Drawings and specifications describing the building in its restored status will, in fact, become part of a permanent record for future reference. Such documents will constitute a technical reference for any future work that may be carried out on the same structure or site, as well as in other, similar cases in the region and beyond.

Opposite page, top and middle, EDM documentation of the Picture Wall's west facade. Bottom, documentation of the as-found condition of the same facade using high-resolution orthorectified photographs.

Above, the Picture Wall: conservation of the western facade in progress.

1 m

Deterioration and damage analysis of glazed-tile panels.

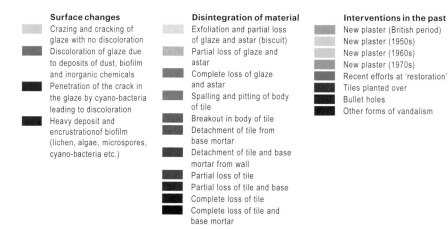

Surface changes

Crazing and cracking of glaze with no discoloration

Discoloration of glaze due to deposits of dust, biofilm and inorganic chemicals

Penetration of the crack in the glaze by cyano-bacteria leading to discoloration

Heavy deposit and encrustation of biofilm (lichen, algae, microspores, cyano-bacteria etc.)

Disintegration of material

Exfoliation and partial loss of glaze and astar (biscuit)

Partial loss of glaze and astar

Complete loss of glaze and astar

Spalling and pitting of body of tile

Breakout in body of tile

Detachment of tile from base mortar

Detachment of tile and base mortar from wall

Partial loss of tile

Partial loss of tile and base

Complete loss of tile

Complete loss of tile and base mortar

Interventions in the past

New plaster (British period)

New plaster (1950s)

New plaster (1960s)

New plaster (1970s)

Recent efforts at 'restoration'

Tiles planted over

Bullet holes

Other forms of vandalism

Conservation interventions and procedures for the Picture Wall were designed in alignment with the above criteria and in response to the priorities of the damage patterns as they were noted during condition mapping.

The conservation of the Picture Wall is one of the major elements of a larger programme for the conservation of Lahore Fort, as described in this section of this volume, which the Walled City of Lahore Authority and the Aga Khan Trust for Culture/ Aga Khan Cultural Service-Pakistan have embarked upon. In September 2015 the WCLA and AKTC/AKCS-P began the documentation of the Picture Wall with significant support from the Royal Norwegian Embassy. The completion of detailed documentation work led to condition mapping reflecting site conditions and deterioration, associated with a performance of detailed studies and material testing by local and international specialists. A conservation prototype presenting a typical combination of conservation issues to be addressed was carried out. A 10-metre-wide and 15-metre-high segment of the western section of the Picture Wall was selected to implement conservation treatments and test different presentation modes. This sample work was reviewed by national and international experts in a workshop held in January 2018 together with the various aspects of documentation, proposed conservation approaches and methodologies. The interaction with experts in this workshop allowed the team to arrive at a course of action for the conservation of the entire Picture Wall that adheres to modern conservation principles, respects authenticity and is in consonance with the context.

In addressing the problems faced by the Picture Wall, the most urgent priority was to mitigate sources of rainwater ingress infiltrating the brickwork structure and the decorative programme. Monsoon rain run-offs infiltrate the building fabric in depth, causing a vast array of problems that were proposed to be addressed by conservation activities, such as re-routing of waterspouts, repair of cornices, stabilization of fragile glazed tiling and frescoes, and the treatment of the microbial algae and cyanobacteria deposits, all consequences of constant moisture. Damp conditions also facilitate the growth of infestations of higher plants in masonry cavities, where roots aggravate the existing problems by weakening mortar joints and dislodging bricks.

An overall condition assessment concluded that water was the vehicle of most of the natural decay mechanisms affecting architectural surfaces. Most of the decay patterns found on the Picture Wall are related to progressive rainwater erosion and persistent structural moisture. As a probable consequence of modifications made during the early British period, the highly sophisticated original drainage system that once discharged the water collected by the terracing of the Fort ceased to function. During heavy rains, floods of water had to find their way through the substructures, contained on the northern and western side by the Picture Wall. Once absorbed, much of the water moved towards the outer walls where it could evaporate.

Large cavities that have formed in the brick masonry on the northern facade indicate that massive quantities of water reached the surface in these places. Over time, this caused the loss of the decorated surfaces and then the gradual disintegration of the masonry support itself. Improved protection against direct contact with rainwater and the control of excessive structural moisture are essential prerequisites for the long-term conservation of the Picture Wall, and a main objective of the architectural part of the project.

The evaluation of areas where the brick masonry is exposed shows that on the northern facade more than fifty per cent of the decorated surfaces have been lost. The losses amount to approximately forty per cent on the western facade where the situation is slightly better. The preserved parts show severe signs of decay characterized, firstly, on fresco panels and brick-imitation frames, by losses of the paint layer and erosion of the plaster support, and secondly, by losses of glazes on tile mosaics where in many parts only the ceramic bodies are preserved with a pronounced instability of all surfaces due to detachment at various levels. Moreover, a thick biofilm layer made of algae and cyanobacteria is present in areas where water has been retained by porous surfaces over a long time.

Before any practical work was begun, a measured survey combining high-resolution rectified photographs, topographic documentation and laser scanning was carried out, providing a detailed visual record of the as-found condition and establishing an important reference for study and planning activities. As part of the

Above, reconstructing the terracotta and glazed-tile 'filigree' frieze.

Below, consolidation of glazed-tile work.

condition assessment, several thematic maps were produced, which graphically describe issues such as former interventions, different decoration techniques and the condition of decorated surfaces. Historic research was also carried out, including the study of original manufacturing techniques and an iconographic study of the tile mosaics (see pp. 294–309).

In Pakistan, heritage artisans traditionally carried out the repair of wall paintings and other decorated architectural surfaces and there was no conservation practice intending to preserve original surfaces. The essential strategy of this Picture Wall conservation project is to introduce modern conservation practice and focus on preserving and protecting the remains of original surfaces in their material authenticity. This conservation approach, while internationally recognized, was innovative in Pakistan and called for training and capacity building by international specialists of a young team, the first generation of Pakistani conservators specializing in this field.

The intervention was carried out by two different teams: heritage crafts people dealing with the reintegration of part of the lost brick-imitation and filigree decoration, and conservators responsible for the stabilization, cleaning and presentation of the original surfaces. In order to warrant a smooth development of the intervention and to avoid negative interference between these two groups, it was important to establish a chronological sequence of the complex set of operations to be carried out.

The first conservation issue to be tackled was emergency stabilization in the most endangered areas. For the filling of large gaps that have formed in areas where the tile-mosaic panels have lifted from the wall, the use of an injection grout consisting of lime putty, brick dust and a small amount of acrylic resin emulsion proved to be effective. In order to reduce the width of these gaps and to improve adhesion, pressure supports were used. The re-adhesion of detaching lime plasters and tiles was achieved through injections of a special, chemically stable, hydraulic binding agent

Left, biofilm deterioration before conservation.

Right, interventions carried out in previous decades.

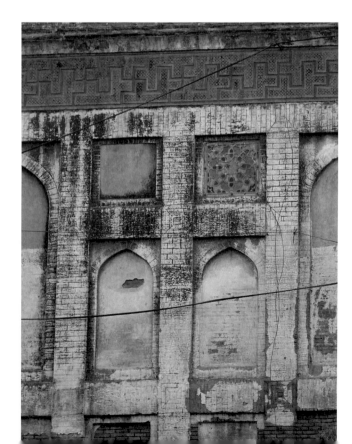

manufactured in Italy and used since the 1990s for the stabilization of lime-based wall paintings and other decorated surfaces. The same hydraulic grout was used to re-establish adhesion between ceramic tiles and bedding plaster and to locally fix fragments of detaching glaze. A final stabilization treatment followed the completion of cleaning operations.

The unusually hard plaster applied in the British period covered most of the larger losses but in many cases also portions of tile mosaic, where it had been applied on an already deteriorated and extremely fragile original surface. As a consequence, its removal was an extremely delicate operation. The plaster was cut in small portions that were then carefully chipped off with a small chisel.

The disinfection and removal of the blackish biofilm that covered most of the surfaces with varying intensity was necessary not only because it was aesthetically detracting but also because its presence hindered the smooth implementation of all other operations. An international microbiologist carried out tests to identify the type of bacteria and analyse the patterns of its occurrence. Upon completion of the pre-stabilization treatment, hydrogen peroxide was used as a disinfectant in order to destabilize the biological growth. This was followed by mechanical cleaning with brushes and water, which also functioned as a general cleaning for the entire wall.

Left, scaffolded western facade of the Picture Wall.

Above right, the "as-found" condition of a section of the same facade; below right, another part of the western facade after conservation.

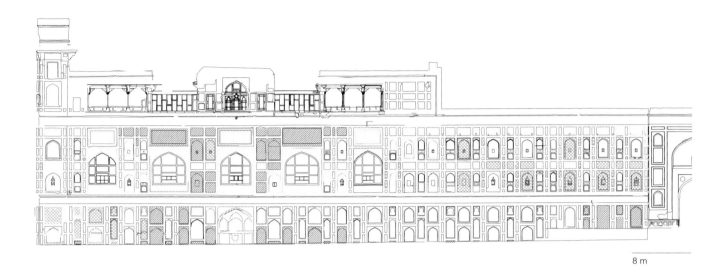

8 m

Above, condition analysis of glazed-tile work on the Picture Wall.

☐ Partial Loss
▨ Complete Loss
▧ Intact Tiles

Opposite page, the Hathi Pol entrance.

From the beginning it was clear that the most challenging part of the intervention would be the stabilization of the tile mosaics. This is because no ready-made treatment methodology nor references are available for this type of architectural ceramics in outdoor conditions. It was necessary to first study in detail the decay mechanisms of the ceramic material and to then develop specific conservation techniques. Extensive laboratory research and on-site experimentation was carried out by the AKTC/AKCS-P team in cooperation with international consultants. It was shown that the detachment of glazes is due to an excessive difference in hardness and porosity within the ceramic bodies, which absorb large quantities of water that cannot evaporate through the glassy, impermeable surface of the glaze. Once the protective function of the glaze is lost, the ceramic bodies become the subject of gradual erosion.

A special colloidal silica sol was experimented with for the re-adhesion of loose glazes and the strengthening of tile bodies. It is a water-based dispersion of nanoparticles of silica which, upon setting, forms an amorphous silica gel that is physically and chemically similar to glass and highly compatible with the silicic components of the original tiles. Since the initial trials on site and the first laboratory examinations, the product, used in sandstone conservation since the 1980s, appeared to be suitable.

The consolidation procedure took many additional trials and experimentation to be finalized since the even, in-depth, penetration of the consolidant through the surface of the tiles was difficult to achieve. Such an innovative procedure required scientific evidence to confirm the validity of the treatment. Measurements of drill resistance were made to evaluate the different techniques that were experimented with. Based on these results, the final treatment involved injecting the silica solution systematically around the edges of the remaining glazes and where necessary through fine drill holes. Furthermore, all exposed tile bodies were soaked with the consolidant using a special tissue paper that allowed a more even distribution and the prevention of surface deposits to be achieved. As a result of these treatments, the mechanical strength of the tile body improved, and the adhesion of glazes has notably increased.

The aesthetic presentation of the original decorated surfaces and the integration of lost parts were the final phases of the conservation treatment. The development of an agreed presentation concept involved extensive team discussions, as well as numerous on-site trials and computer simulations. The solution that was adopted had

the objective to safeguard the 'as-found condition' and to enhance what is left of the original decorations by creating a visual 'order' and by reducing visual interferences. This was achieved through the selected reintegration of lacuna, mainly in the brick-imitation frame.

Reconstruction with new filigree work was only considered in areas where the original decoration was totally lost and where there was a clear aesthetic benefit. The colour remains of fresco paintings and brick imitation were rendered more legible through a respectful pictorial reintegration.

New techniques for restoring weathered tiles were also experimented with and locally applied. Following the reconstruction of the tile body with a special silica-gel-bound mortar, the coloured glaze was reconstituted either by silicate paint or by attaching thin layers of specially fired glazes. These innovative interventions, still in an experimental stage, allowed intervention with small-scale reconstructions in weathered areas of the tile mosaics.

The conservation and presentation of the decorated architectural surfaces of the Picture Wall was an unprecedented project, not only because of the quality and the scale of the work, but also due to a multitude of challenging issues that required

Top left, a conservator carrying out material tests.

Top right, a master craftsman repairing the 'filigree' work.

Bottom left, reconstruction of glazed-tile work.

Bottom right, designing geometrical patterns of glazed tiling.

special research and the development of innovative solutions. In a project of this nature the focus on conservation and presentation of decorative surfaces of unprecedented quality and dimension was clearly challenging. The Picture Wall, being part of a UNESCO World Heritage Site, necessitated employing state-of-the-art technologies and work methods for its conservation and restoration while meeting international standards. Conservation professionals from many different disciplines were associated to advance the project according to international standards applying to World Heritage Sites. The focus of the project was to consolidate the original remains by introducing some pioneering methods in Pakistan. The synergy achieved between international and local conservation practice also helped develop a team of young conservators, which was also a first example in the Pakistani context. These young professionals worked on the scaffolding side by side with traditional craftsmen, taking advantage of the excellent learning opportunities made available in modern conservation practice.

As-found condition of prototype area (left) and prototype area after conservation (right).

ADAPTIVE REUSE
OF THE IMPERIAL KITCHENS

RASHID MAKHDUM, SHUKURULLAH BAIG

PROJECT BACKGROUND AND SIGNIFICANCE

There are twenty-one monuments remaining in the present-day complex of Lahore Fort. These monuments reflect the architectural characteristics of the historical periods they represent and the brilliance of the artistic excellence and workmanship of these eras. One of these buildings, known as the Imperial Kitchens, had lain in ruinous condition for a few decades. From 2016 to 2019 the Walled City of Lahore Authority (WCLA) took up the conservation of the historic Imperial Kitchens and their adaptive reuse under a five-year development scheme for the Fort approved by the government.

The British occupation of the Fort in 1849 and its use to station a British garrison until 1924 resulted in large-scale mutilation of the site. A new road was added to connect Shah Burj Gate with the quadrangle south of Moti Masjid which altered the layout of the Fort in its western quarter. To accommodate the garrison, numerous new buildings were built within the open areas. However, after vacation of the Fort by the military, concerted efforts were started to restore historic structures.

The Imperial Kitchens, located in the south-western quarter of the Fort, served the needs of the royal palace during the Mughal and the Sikh periods. Their spatial connection to the royal residences was truncated in the mid-nineteenth century when the British built accesses and the new road mentioned above, and used this part of the Fort in general to house their sepoy barracks. As a consequence, this area of Lahore Fort fell into increasing neglect. In the early days of British occupation they were used for storage of the garrison's liquor, and at one time an upper floor was added above the eastern wing.

Their use from that time onward is not certain. The British army vacated the Fort and handed it over to the Archaeological Survey of India in 1927. However, the south-western part of the Fort, including the Imperial Kitchens, remained in the custody of the Police Department, who continued to occupy this and other buildings in this zone of the Fort and even made large-scale additions for their use. When the Police Department vacated this area in 1986, the buildings had been used as a prison for political detainees for several decades.

After taking over possession of this part of the Fort, the Department of Archaeology set up a training institute and removed several British-period structures. The upper storey above the Imperial Kitchens building was also removed. New buildings were constructed in the vicinity, but in general the Imperial Kitchens building remained unattended until a partial collapse in the late 1990s. Temporary supports were then added to stabilize the remaining structure.

Opposite page, interior of the Imperial Kitchens after restoration. The ruined parts have been structurally stabilized and consolidated.

Above, work in progress.

Aerial view of the Imperial Kitchens (lower left) before restoration, with the Badshahi Mosque in the background.

The WCLA has now taken the initiative to save the building by conserving the historic structure and converting it into a quality restaurant that is expected to enhance the cultural environment of this part of the historical complex and to generate financial surpluses which could be utilized for continued conservation and maintenance of the Fort.

PRESENT CONDITION OF THE HISTORIC STRUCTURE

The extant structure of the historic Imperial Kitchens building sits in a square piece of land measuring about 3,000 square metres. It is a single-storey brick structure covering an area of about 1,200 square metres in a partial 'U' shaped configuration. The building faces north towards the major residential quarters of the royal palace. The large open space on the north of the building and foundation remains in its northeastern corner suggest that once there were structures surrounding an open courtyard that no longer exists.

The building plan consists of 4-metre-square arcuated bays with 1.5-metre-thick walls. These bays are spanned by brick domes rising from brick piers and brick pendentives. The domes are shallow and enable a flat-topped roof. The bays are two-deep in the southern wing, and two-deep in most of the western wing. The eastern wing appears to have been three-bay deep, but most of this section is ruined and only a few of these domes were intact at the commencement of the project. A British-period cladding wall in 1.5-metre-thick brickwork with slanting piers seemingly intended to act as buttresses has been added along the external periphery. This cladding also acts as an enclosure wall between the arches along the external wall, and is punctuated with wooden ventilators or other openings in each bay.

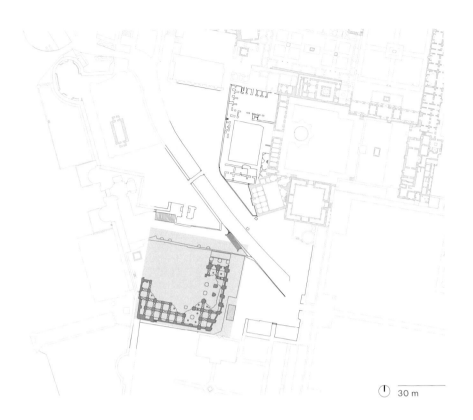

Location of the Imperial Kitchens in the context of Lahore Fort (left) and three sectional elevations of their structure (below).

30 m

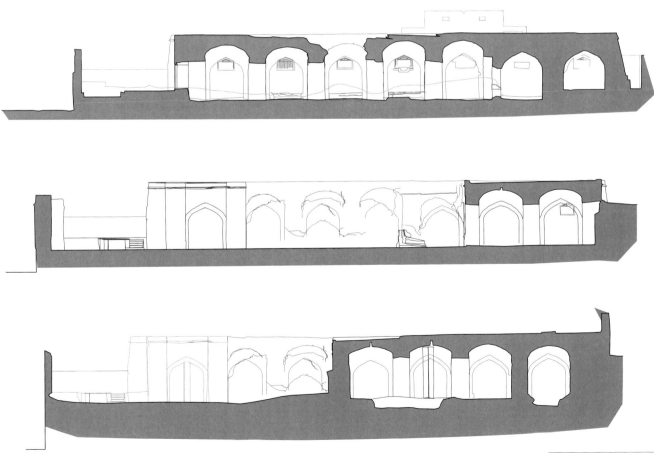

10 m

The state of the Imperial Kitchens at the beginning of the project was very poor. While some brickwork of the still existing arches had been recently cleaned and pointed, there were large sections that lay in ruins and that required reconstruction with only limited available information regarding their original state. As described earlier, some time in the recent past there had been wholesale demolition of the building. Piers supporting the roof had collapsed in several locations, resulting in the collapse of domes at those locations, with heavy chunks of brickwork precariously resting on the more stable parts of the structure. Debris of some of the collapsed areas was removed at the commencement of the project.

Some repairs using modern brick tiles appeared to have been carried out along the lower parts of certain piers, and temporary supports in the form of brick pillars had been erected supporting the arches and domes at various locations. At some places timber support had been erected, but these were completely inadequate and merely served as eyewash.

PROPOSED ADAPTIVE REUSE

The premises had been lying abandoned and neglected ever since it was transferred from the Police Department to the Directorate General of Archaeology, even though some measure of structural support to strengthen and consolidate the deteriorated

Opposite page, the interior of the Imperial Kitchens after restoration.

Below, the Imperial Kitchens courtyard after completion of the project.

Above, before and after views of the Imperial Kitchens courtyard.

Below, before and after views of a section of the facade.

and undermined lower portions of the brick piers had been carried out using modern bricks and cement mortar. However, after the collapse of the eastern portion, the area was totally abandoned.

Upon taking over the Lahore Fort precinct in 2014, the WCLA embarked upon an ambitious plan to preserve Lahore Fort and improve its tourist appeal by rehabilitating and improving visitor facilities, and by introducing arranged group tours. One of these initiatives is the "History by Night" tour of Lahore Fort on two weekend evenings of the week, which includes visits to selected areas of the Fort culminating in a small performance and refreshments for the participants.

The WCLA also took the initiative to save the Imperial Kitchens and their contiguous areas from further decay through conservation and reuse of the structure and the area around it. The conservation work was completed in the spring of 2019 and has resulted in the restoration of the historic structure including preserving the ruins *in situ*. To make the interventions sustainable, and to give this previously neglected "heritage a function in the life of the community" in line with the World Heritage Convention, the rehabilitated historic structure is being used to provide a night-time dining facility as part of the general policy to extend the visitor experience of the Fort during night-time.

The historic structure of the Imperial Kitchens has a robust construction, with no decorations or embellishment of any significance. It has a covered area of some 970 square metres and an enclosed courtyard big enough to accommodate large

gatherings without causing any negative impacts on other areas of the Fort. It lends itself well to being used independently for the purposes intended. Thus the previously neglected historic Imperial Kitchens structure has been conserved and rehabilitated.

When operational, the restaurant will be open to paying customers after the closing hours of the Fort and, in addition, will be coupled with the already operational night-time guided visits of the Fort.

Although the dining and restaurant function has not yet been inaugurated, along with the large open courtyard, the structure is already being used for evening performances and cultural shows that are sold out well in advance. A separate, reversible structure that provides kitchen and toilet facilities is located at the former site of a building constructed during the 1990s, and later demolished, to the south of the historic building. This facility has been erected below the ground level of the area to the south of the kitchens, and has been so designed to have the ability "...to be removed in the future without any damage to heritage significance; in particular, without damage to significant fabric," thus following the principles of reversibility.

The existing network of utility services, which has already been in place and in use due to establishment of offices of the Directorate General of Archaeology and a training institute, has been rehabilitated and state-of-the-art drainage arrangements have been installed to service this previously neglected section of Lahore Fort.

This part of the Fort is already proving itself to be a main generator of revenues as well as a backdrop for festive events and music and cultural shows.

Two before (left) and after (right) views of the same section of the facade of the Imperial Kitchens.

SITE VISITS AND MUSEUMS

FRANCESCO SIRAVO

LAHORE FORT'S CURRENT MUSEUM OFFER

The three museum buildings currently located in Lahore Fort have a total area of approximately 810 square metres apportioned between the Mughal Gallery in Jahangir's Khwabgah (222 square metres) and the Armoury and Sikh galleries on the ground and first floors of the Maharani Jindan *haveli* (respectively 200 and 180 square metres). The actual space devoted to exhibits in these three galleries is 460 square metres.

THE MUGHAL GALLERY

This gallery is located in the central pavilion built on the north side of Jahangir's Quadrangle. Since 1962 the interior spaces of the pavilion have displayed artefacts of the Mughal era, including manuscripts, coins, miniature paintings and examples of Persian and Arabic calligraphy, as well as an ivory miniature model of the Taj Mahal.

THE ARMOURY MUSEUM

The museum is located in the Dalaan-e-Sang-e-Surkh (red-stone antechamber). Originally built by Emperor Jahangir in 1617–18, the two-storey building was enlarged during the Sikh period to become the *haveli* of Maharani Jindan, the youngest wife of Maharaja Ranjit Singh. It now houses the Armoury Museum on the ground floor, showcasing a collection of eighteenth- and nineteenth-century arms and weapons used by the Sikh army. These are mostly displayed in the central hall. The two adjacent rooms display paintings of Sikh rulers and dignitaries, as well as lithographs depicting battles between the Sikhs and the British.

THE SIKH GALLERY

This gallery is housed above the Armoury Museum in the Maharani Jindan *haveli*. Most of the objects displayed are from the Sikh period and were originally on show in the ruler's apartment and in Lahore's Durbar Hall. The collection includes oils, watercolours, prints, paintings on ivory, photographs, statues, decorative pieces, crafts and models illustrating the lives and times of Maharaja Ranjit Singh, his son Maharaja Duleep Singh and the Sikh durbar in Lahore.

The three galleries are affected by water penetration through the roof and walls, as well as rising damp at the base of walls, which has led to the deterioration of the artefacts displayed. The latest improvements, never followed by regular maintenance

Opposite page, interior view of the Armoury.

Above, the Bari Khwabgah, Jahangir's former sleeping chamber, today converted into the Mughal Gallery.

Below, the *haveli* of Maharani Jindan, now housing the Armoury Musuem and Sikh Gallery.

The proposed Public Walkway.

‑ ‑ ‑ East-West Walkway
‑ ‑ ‑ Hazuri Bagh and Badshahi Mosque
Circuit
◼ Reserved for General Public
◼ Public Space
◼ PIATR, Pakistan Institute of
Archaeological Training and Research
◼ Imperial Kitchens Restaurant
◯ Gates
① Alamgiri Gate
② Akbari Gate
→ Ceremonial Steps Entry / Exit Point
→ Hazuri Bagh Entry / Exit Point

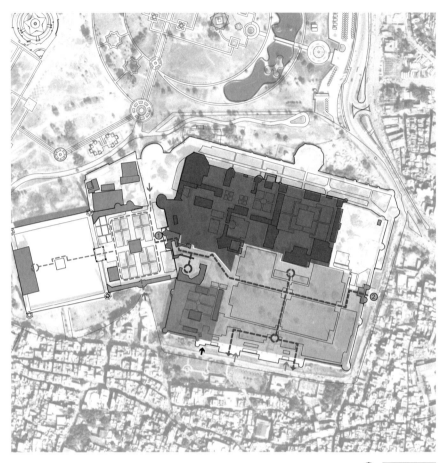

100 m

campaigns, were carried out as far back as 1986. But the principal criticism that can be made about the current museum set up is that visitors come to the end of their visit without having gained a comprehensive view of the site and its historical development, a situation that is only worsened thanks to a lack of coordinated signage, illustrative boards, leaflets, informative literature and multilingual guides.

The current challenge is to enable – through a comprehensive reassessment of the spaces – exhibition materials and available human resources, the formulation of presentation circuits and a display programme that takes into account current visiting patterns and that is capable of offering a more inclusive and stimulating appreciation of the entire site. This should not only respond to the need for more comprehensive displays, but also to the expectations of different audiences for flexible and diversified spaces that provide opportunities for education, social interaction and conviviality.

PROPOSED VISITOR ROUTES

Pending a further review of the site's capacity, and based on recommendations made by UNESCO in 2006, the proposals below foresee two distinct *Visitor Routes*: a "Public Walkway" open to the general public and a "Museological Itinerary" where guided tours would ensure control over access and use of the site. In order to provide

Above, ivory model of the Taj Mahal in the central hall of the Mughal Gallery.

Below, interior view of the Sikh Gallery.

visitors and residents with as much flexibility as possible, both visitor routes can be accessed from the west and the east, respectively via the Alamgiri and Akbari gates for the "Public Walkway", and via the Postern and Akbari gates for the "Guided Museological Itinerary".

The purpose of the new "Public Walkway", located in the southern half of the complex, is to allow the public to access and traverse the site. The proposed east-west walkway would connect Akbari Gate via the Diwan-e-Aam to Alamgiri Gate. Then, from Alamgiri Gate, visitors descend to the Hazuri Bagh below and proceed to the Badshahi Mosque. Conversely, moving from west to east, visitors would enter the complex from the Hazuri Bagh through Alamgiri Gate from where they would be able to walk to Akbari Gate across the Diwan-e-Aam and connect to other monumental sites in the

The lawns of the Diwan-e-Aam are enjoyed by the general public for picnics and family gatherings.

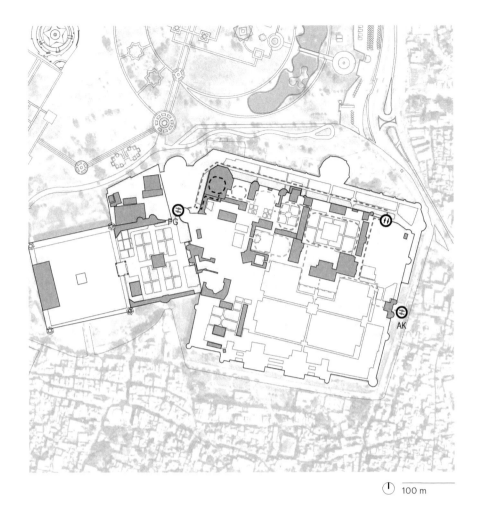

The Guided Museological Itinerary leads
visitors through the site's imperial palaces.

- - - Diwan-e-Aam Quadrangle
- - - Jahangir's Quadrangle
- - - Shah Jahan's Quadrangle
- - - Moti Masjid Quadrangle
- - - Paeen Bagh Quadrangle
--- Shah Burj Forecourt
- - - Sheesh Mahal
- - - Picture Wall
⑪ Vertical link between the upper and
   lower level
Ⓢ Gates
AK Akbari Darwaza
PG Postern Gate

Ⓘ 100 m

Walled City. This arrangement provides maximum flexibility and results in a public
flow that works in both directions depending on the point of entry. Additional access
to the public area would also be possible on special occasions via the two gates
located at the top of the Ceremonial Steps.

Those interested in a more in-depth visit to the restored gardens and private
emperors' quarters will be able to follow the "Guided Museological Itinerary". This
focuses on the northern half of the complex and includes a tour of Jahangir's and
Shah Jahan's quadrangles followed by a visit to the Paeen Bagh, Shah Burj and the
Picture Wall. Access is provided either from the east via Akbari Gate or from the west
via the Postern Gate. In both cases, the visitor flow would be from east to west, which
is in keeping with the historic sequence of the site's development. Visitors entering
the site from the west via the Postern Gate would see the Picture Wall first, before
accessing the upper level, touring the quadrangles and exiting the complex through
the same Postern Gate. Conversely, those who enter from Akbari Gate would visit
the Picture Wall last before accessing the upper level via an existing interior stair positioned in proximity of the Mashriqui East Burj in Jahangir's Quadrangle. They would
exit the complex through Akbari Gate.

MUSEUM DEVELOPMENT OPTIONS

Three possible levels of intervention can be considered in order to complement these
itineraries described with display spaces. These options are not mutually exclusive.
They could be seen as part of an incremental process by which the Fort complex
would gradually be equipped to offer fuller information and more complete displays,
and establish the conditions for a fuller appreciation of the site.

Following pages, the north-western sector
of Lahore Fort. Top left, the Shah Jahan-
period Sheesh Mahal, with the Khilwat Khana
and the Paeen Bagh to its right. Both these
quadrangles were established under Shah
Jahan by modifying Jahangir-period developments of which the Kala Burj and the Laal
Burj remain. The latter tower was modified
to make room for the Diwaan-e-Khaas of
Shah Jahan, of which a corner is showing on
the extreme right.

337

Proposed New Facilities
Summer Palace Museum
(1,720 sq. m)
Visitor Centre (940 sq. m.)
New Site Museum (2,276 sq. m.)

AK   Akbari Darwaza
PG   Postern Gate

100 m

Top left, the Level 3 alternative foresees
the establishment of a visitor centre,
a site museum and a cultural centre in the
Summer Palace.

Top right, location of the proposed visitor
centre outside Akbari Gate.

Right, plan and section of the visitor centre.

Ground Floor
1. Lobby
2. Ticket Sales (Visits to Lahore Fort)
3. Information Point
4. Garden
5. Display and Orientation
6. Restrooms
7. Storage and Technical Room
8. Lahore Fort Store
9. Lifts
10. Bookstore
11. Security

First Floor
12. Restaurant / Café
13. Kitchen
14. Storage
15. Staff Restrooms
16. Restrooms
17. Office
18. Lifts

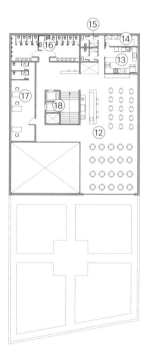

10 m

340

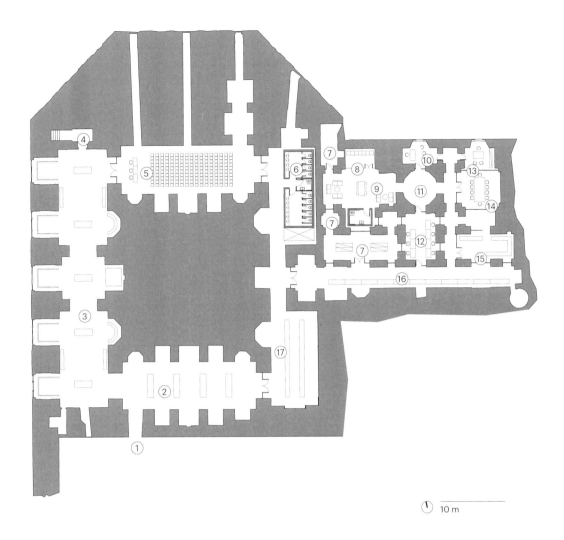

LEVEL 1 (MINIMUM)

This option is currently under consideration and consists in refurbishing the Mughal, Armoury and Sikh galleries, and introducing new exhibition spaces in the Summer Palace located in the basement chambers below the Sheesh Mahal Quadrangle (see plan above).

▸ *Pros* lie in the fact that these gallery spaces are available and already part of the site visitation circuit. These can be complemented by others to be established in the Summer Palace. In addition, restoration and reuse of the Summer Palace as exhibition space would be fairly inconspicuous as it would not require any visible addition within the site that might be considered volumetrically intrusive or visually inappropriate.

▸ *Cons* are that the present museum galleries are located in unsuitable spaces, in need of considerable conservation and adaptive reuse work. Moreover, the existing exhibits do not offer a comprehensive understanding of the complex. Converting the Summer Palace into a museum space and interpretation centre could in part address the lack of a general introduction to the site. Its spaces, however, present limitations as exhibition areas and for the provision of visitor services. In addition, they cannot be equipped to house the ancillary spaces that are today normally associated with important museums. Above all, this option would lead to further fragmentation of the museum experience, and to limiting a fuller understanding of the rich historic and cultural associations of this site.

The proposed reuse scheme for the Summer Palace as a cultural centre.

1. Entry
2. Reception and Events Room
3. Temporary Exhibits and Events Room
4. Stair to Upper Court
5. Conference Hall (190 seats)
6. Visitors' Restrooms
7. Storage
8. Kitchenette
9. Staff and Visitor Meeting Room
10. Director's Office
11. Secretary and Reception
12. Reading Room
13. Office
14. Meeting Room
15. Laboratory
16. Archive
17. Library

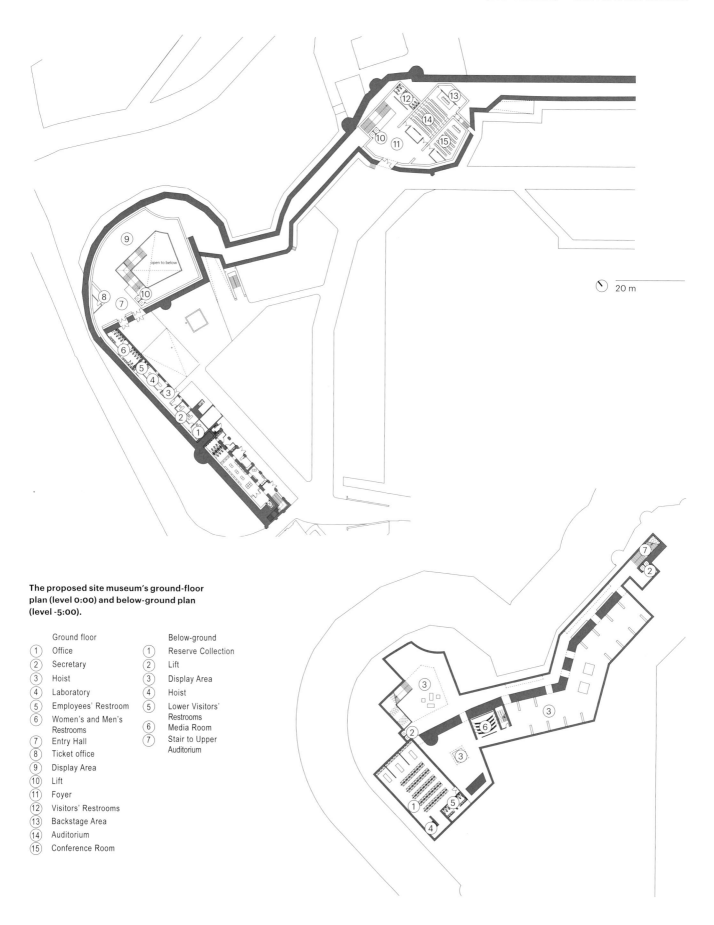

The proposed site museum's ground-floor plan (level 0:00) and below-ground plan (level -5:00).

Ground floor
1. Office
2. Secretary
3. Hoist
4. Laboratory
5. Employees' Restroom
6. Women's and Men's Restrooms
7. Entry Hall
8. Ticket office
9. Display Area
10. Lift
11. Foyer
12. Visitors' Restrooms
13. Backstage Area
14. Auditorium
15. Conference Room

Below-ground
1. Reserve Collection
2. Lift
3. Display Area
4. Hoist
5. Lower Visitors' Restrooms
6. Media Room
7. Stair to Upper Auditorium

LEVEL 2 (INTERMEDIATE)

This option would add to all of the above a visitor centre located outside Akbari Gate. This added facility is part of the redevelopment of the east flank of Lahore Fort, to be implemented after the planned reorganization of the area surrounding the Maryam Zamani (or Begum Shahi) Mosque (see plans on p. 340). The centre would be a very simple structure with a large orientation and display space, a shop, information point, ticket sales on the ground floor, and a café-restaurant in the mezzanine above. It would have a total area of 940 square metres.

- *Pros* include the establishment of a second alternative to the present, single visitor entry point from the western side. Visitors entering the Fort from Akbari Gate would have the opportunity to buy tickets in advance, be briefed on their visit to the Fort and learn more about the displays. Conversely, visitors exiting the site from the same gate can learn about the rest of the Walled City and the monuments to be found along the Shahi Guzargah.
- *Cons* lie in the fact that, while it is useful and expedient to provide an alternative entry and exit point and establish a centre to introduce the Lahore Fort site and other monuments in the Walled City, the proposed facility cannot take the place of a fully fledged site museum. From this point of view, Level 2 would not be substantially different from the Level 1 option.

LEVEL 3 (MAXIMUM)

This alternative foresees the inclusion of the visitor centre outside Akbari Gate, as well as the creation of a new, fully fledged site museum in proximity to the Postern Gate. It would include the reuse of the present British-period Curator's House, as well as the installation of new exhibition areas and a lecture theatre inside and adjacent to the two large bastions of the nearby Sikh fortification. This new facility would be partially underground, except for the parts resulting from the remodelling of the Curator's House and adjacent structures. The museum itself would contain an entry hall and exhibition area at ground level (below the larger bastion's terrace) and more exhibition spaces and storage for the reserve collection at the -5 metre level. The corridor below the upper rampart serves to distribute the exhibition areas and connect the museum spaces to an auditorium and conference hall located in the smaller bastion (see plans on p. 342). With this option, the galleries presently in Jahangir's Khwabgah and in Rani Jindan's *haveli* would no longer be useful as exhibition areas, and could be made available for other purposes.

- *Pros* include the establishment of adequate space for the establishment of a fully fledged site museum as well as putting important public and educational functions in the Summer Palace. The new site museum would be conceived as a thematic exploration of Mughal and later rulers and cultures that have left their mark in the Lahore Fort complex. The reuse of the existing building, interior remodelling of the nearby bastions and expanded display areas would not require the introduction of additional volumes as most of the new museum surfaces would be located below ground level. In addition, this option provides greater flexibility and diversification in the organization of spaces on site, and ensures the necessary concentration of exhibits in a single facility complemented by ancillary spaces near one of the principal entrances and the Picture Wall, arguably the Fort's greatest attraction.
- *Cons* are the extra costs in terms of staff and resources that would be entailed in creating and concurrently operating a new site museum and its ancillary spaces, as well as using the Summer Palace for public and educational functions.

Interior view of the site museum's display area.

RECOMMENDATIONS ON OPERATIONS AND MANAGEMENT

CAMERON RASHTI, JURJEN VAN DER TAS

In recognition of its complexity of scale and phases of development, there is a need to develop a comprehensive operations and management plan for Lahore Fort that is in alignment with a programme of carefully prioritized conservation projects, improvements to visitor amenities, an adequate site curatorial system and ongoing daily, monthly and seasonal maintenance activities. There is a need to distinguish between the implementation of a heritage site's 'conservation master plan' activities and its standard operations and management requirements. Each of these processes supplements but does not replace the other and the Fort's long-term operations and maintenance needs require formulation independently of the consideration of the additional complexities of conservation interventions or archaeological investigations, which will be governed by their own specific set of requirements. These are two different areas of technical responsibility, which will run parallel when periods of conservation work occur during the Fort's normal operations.

MANAGEMENT RESPONSIBILITIES FOR IMPLEMENTING THE 2018 CONSERVATION MASTER PLAN FOR LAHORE FORT PRECINCT

A fundamental assumption is that management of the Fort as a heritage site will need to continue with most areas open to the public even while significant campaigns of conservation and restoration take place as planned under the approved 2018 'Lahore Fort Precinct and Buffer Zone Master Plan'. Lahore Fort is simply too large a heritage site to be closed for the number of years that the various conservation projects may require. A secondary concern for site management will be the aesthetic screening of ongoing works and the safety of the public as well as workers.

The key public parties entrusted with the responsibility of the orderly implementation of the new 2018 Master Plan consist of the government of Punjab, represented by the Walled City of Lahore Authority (WCLA), the Archaeological Department and the Planning and Development Department, with day-to-day executive authority residing with the WCLA. External parties providing technical conservation and heritage management services such as the Aga Khan Trust for Culture/Aga Khan Cultural Service-Pakistan and other involved parties will need to develop protocols concerning their respective areas of contribution, governed by 'Memoranda of Understanding' or similar project agreements.

To maximize coordination of the requisite conservation projects, the 2018 Master Plan proposes that the public parties, under the WCLA's lead, consider establishment of a Lahore Fort Technical Coordination and Oversight Committee, which would allow

Opposite page, a school trip to visit the restored Shahi Hammam.

Above, sweeping the steps of the Hathi Pol stairs.

Below, the sprinkler being activated in Jahangir's Quadrangle.

Above, view of the Naulakha Pavilion in the foreground, with the Badshahi Mosque and the *samadh* of Ranjit Singh in the background.

Right, an overview of part of the Jahangir Quadrangle showing, on the right, what is left of the Daulat Khana-e-Khaas-o-Aam and the remains of its impressive foundations on its northern side.

Present site visitation and tourism in Lahore Fort.

⇅   Main Entrance and Exit
◉   Gate (Closed to the Public)
●   Gate (Staff Only)
○   Staff Entry (PIATR)
- - -   Main Visitor Circuit
- - -   Secondary Visitor Circuit
▨   Moti Masjid
🎫   Tickets
🅿   Electric Shuttle Parking
——   Electric Shuttle Circuit
▨   Exhibits
▨   PIATR (Pakistan Institute of
     Archaeological Training and Research)
▨   Visitor Facilities
▨   Visitor Toilets

Ⓣ 100 m

for joint public-private technical oversight of the programme of projects (project scope, schedules, quality standards and finance) and implications for general site management. This committee would include project communications as part of its general mandate and would be one of six entities that might ultimately be involved, notably:

1. Lahore World Heritage Sites Executive Board (a high-powered entity led by the Chief Minister);
2. Lahore Fort Technical Coordination and Oversight Committee (a public-private entity including groups like AKTC and others);
3. Site Commission (effectively the WCLA in conjunction with the legally mandated role of the Punjab Archaeology Department, and in collaboration with UNESCO and external funding and technical assistance agencies);
4. Technical Committee (the technical oversight arm of the Site Commission, managing operations, technical standards, flow of funds, oversight of project implementation and overseeing the presentation, museological and educational aspects of management);
5. Project Implementation Team (agency responsible for general programme implementation and implementation of specific target projects within the overall programme);
6. Local Support Organizations (civil society and public participation).

The proposed multi-tier framework allows ample forums for various parties to interact according to role and responsibility. It is assumed that the above governance structure would be created upon approval of the new 2018 Master Plan for Lahore Fort and

Painting on display in the existing Museum galleries.

its Buffer Zone and would be kept in function for the duration of its implementation or for such time as external technical parties are involved. Initially the Technical Coordination and Oversight Committee would be charged with development of its general mandate and rules of engagement. The operations of this committee (the term 'committee' below used to refer to the Technical Coordination and Oversight Committee) would be reflected in individual project agreements between private technical and financial donors and the public parties. Furthermore, it is recognized that individual project agreements will define separately more specific performance requirements and mutual responsibilities.

As with most World Heritage Sites, public relations will be a critical function of the committee. Donor entities that have or still are contributing to the rehabilitation of Lahore Fort would normally expect to be provided with periodic reports by the committee and could be invited to special sessions in accordance with their availability and interest. Long-term, local corporate and private sponsorship of ongoing site maintenance will be an important element of the site management plan and a special team should be appointed that could assist in the establishment of such a group as "Friends of Lahore Fort". Finally, the above committee would operate parallel to the general Lahore Fort Site Management Team under the direction of the Site Commission, responsible for ongoing site operations and management.

OPERATIONS AND MANAGEMENT OF THE GENERAL HERITAGE SITE

GENERAL FUNCTIONS OF THE SITE MANAGEMENT TEAM

The Site Management Team would report to the WCLA for direct governance but also to the committee to ensure that its operations are well reviewed and in line with recommendations and larger objectives. The management plan must take into account the climatic conditions of the site and Greater Lahore in terms of both visitation patterns and physical conditions (heat, humidity, rainfall and so on) that will impinge on the site, the historic structures and their fabric in a variable and cyclical manner.

GENERAL MANAGERIAL RESPONSIBILITIES

The Fort would be maintained and operated by the Site Commission in line with the following objectives:

▸ ensure that the built-up area within the Fort, its surrounding walls, its entry gates and any satellite buildings considered part of the Fort but located inside the Buffer Zone are maintained at the highest standards;

▸ maintain and, where necessary, strengthen the Fort's function as a centre of education;

▸ ensure that the operation of the Fort is carried out in a manner that is financially sustainable and transparent;

▸ create a reserve fund for contingencies from financial surpluses.

DAILY MANAGEMENT

The Site Commission's management responsibilities would include the following:

▸ ensure smooth visitor flows throughout the day;

▸ monitor wear and tear resulting from visitation and carry out timely repairs of minor damage;

▸ monitor major damage caused by weathering, earthquakes, flooding and so on, and initiate periodic activities aimed at full rehabilitation;

▸ prevent vandalism and other forms of wilful destruction;

▸ sustain a positive cash flow from the income of ticket sales and the lease of amenities within the Fort.

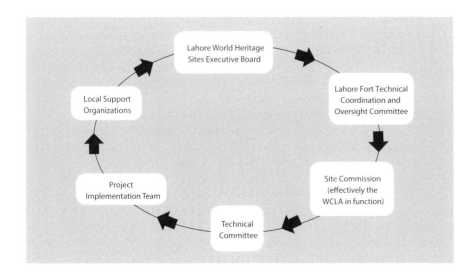

Above, Akbari Darwaza, the city entrance to Lahore Fort.

Below, Greater Iqbal Park.

Left, the proposed technical committee will ensure general oversight in coordination with the other entities recommended by the UNESCO Master Plan of 2006.

Ultimately, a 'Lahore Fort Site Management and Operations Plan' will need to be developed as a joint exercise and adopted by the Site Commission as well as the Lahore World Heritage Sites Executive Board, with all relevant topics treated.

EDUCATION AND COMMUNICATION

At an educational level, the Site Commission, under a dedicated team, would need to ensure that the museography of Lahore Fort established under the new 2018 Master Plan is kept in good order. Furthermore, that the objects on display and the quality of the information provided are relevant in relation to the Fort's history. As the mission of the Site Commission is to inform the public at large, the complexity and the volume of information should be taken into account and be made palatable for a wide audience.

As the Fort will in all likelihood be used frequently as a background for major events hosted by the government of Punjab or by the federal government, a protocol would have to be developed and approved that would allow governmental institutions to make use of the Fort without compromising its integrity. The same principle would apply to large private events.

OUTREACH TO THE LOCAL COMMUNITY OF THE WALLED CITY OF LAHORE

The resident population living within or near the Buffer Zone may expect to benefit from an increased influx of visitors entering and leaving the Fort, whether through Akbari Gate or any other gate that might be opened up in the near future. As a result, the Buffer Zone and adjacent areas further south and east can expect to see spontaneous development of commercial activities related to tourism. In order to preserve a level of authenticity of the area surrounding the Fort, it would be of interest to the Site Commission, in its capacity as manager of the Fort, to see the resident population of the Buffer Zone becoming actively engaged in such activities, rather than leaving the field open for commercially driven individuals from outside the Walled City.

Above, the inauguration in 2018 of the first Lahore Biennale event at Lahore Fort.

Below, costumed soldiers on guard during special events.

Right, a group of students visit the Wazir Khan Mosque.

STAFF TRAINING AND CAPACITY BUILDING

There is urgent need for initiating a well-supported programme of recruiting and training conservation-related staff to manage the ongoing conservation and maintenance
activities in the Fort. A hierarchical structure for such training needs to be established,
ranging from professional training in conservation to lower-level skills. The maintenance crew for the historic built environment would follow a different trajectory from
other staff. Not only would maintenance staff members be selected on proven abilities,
but this group would also receive regular training in the documentation and repair of
minor damage. This would allow such repairs to take place on an ongoing basis and
prevent the accumulation of a backlog of all sorts. Interventions of major dimensions
or requiring specific know-how would generally be carried out by external experts
upon evaluation of damage reports by the Site Commission, until such time as senior-
level local conservation skills are found to be sufficient and sustainable.

On average, the Fort has 950 to 1150 visitors within its walls at any given time. To
look after such large groups, some 200 permanent staff would be required for ticket-
ing and sales, maintenance, gardening and guiding, as well as security and prevention
of vandalism. Staff would be given initial training at the onset of the operational phase.
Such training would be followed up with periodic sessions every six months or so.

Left, consolidation of glazed-tile and fresco
paintings on the Picture Wall.

Above, architects and surveyors receive
training in using 3D laser scanners for architectural documentation.

Below, team members meet to discuss project
progress.

PROPOSED ACTION AREAS AND PLANS FOR THE BUFFER ZONE

FRANCESCO SIRAVO, RASHID MAKHDUM

The Buffer Zone proposed in the 2018 'Lahore Fort Precinct and Buffer Zone Master Plan' includes some fifty-seven hectares of land surrounding the monumental complex. The northern side is occupied entirely by the recently redeveloped Greater Iqbal Park, while the western side contains the Lady Willingdon Hospital and institutional zone located to the west of the Badshahi Mosque. Both of these two sides constitute a solid protective buffer for the heritage area and have therefore been excluded from the interventions proposed in the Buffer Zone. Interventions focus, instead, on the remaining two sides: the Rim Market area to the east (Action Area 1), and the two areas to the south, respectively Ali Park in the south-east sector (Action Area 2), and the "Triangle" and adjacent traditional neighbourhoods in the south-west sector (Action Area 3). These three Action Areas were planned in greater detail in view of their immediate relevance for the protection, access and contextual appreciation of Lahore Fort's monumental enclave. They are part of the Zone of Special Value 1 (ZSV 1) identified in the 2017 'Master Conservation and Redevelopment Plan' (MCRP) for the Walled City.

Even a cursory visit to the Rim Market and Ali Park areas shows critically unacceptable conditions that most directly affect full appreciation of the World Heritage Site. These two areas are at present severely undermined by disorderly commercial transformation on formerly unbuilt public land, unregulated vehicular traffic, pollution and environmental degradation. Today these conditions have reached unsustainable levels and their combined effects threaten not only the prospects for tourism development in one of Pakistan's greatest cultural attractions, but also the viability of these sectors as functioning parts of the city.

Conditions in these areas, and particularly in the vicinity of Rim Market and the shoe market developments along the eastern edge of Lahore Fort, have been under the consideration of the government of Punjab for many years. It is evident that, in order to relieve the excessive and unsustainable pressures presently affecting the old parts of Lahore, these businesses must eventually be moved to a different location, ideally outside the historic Walled City. To this effect, a 'Resettlement Action Plan' is being considered under the management of the Walled City of Lahore Authority (WCLA), which is the entity responsible for its preparation and future implementation.

Overall, the aim of the project, as defined by the WCLA, is the safeguarding and enhancement of Lahore Fort and its surroundings. These constitute a unique heritage asset capable of furthering the development of an economy centred on culture through the creation of jobs and the development of traditional skills in the economic

Opposite page, aerial view of Ali Park, the Ceremonial Steps, and nearby urban fabric, with the Badshahi Mosque in the background.

Above, Akbari Gate, the historic east entrance to Lahore Fort, is no longer open to the public.

Below, the polluting Rim Market, an informal commercial development next to Lahore Fort.

The Buffer Zone: proposed Action Areas.

- ▪▪▪ Buffer Zone Boundary
- East Sector (Rim Market Area)
- ① Fort Road including Akbari Gate
- ② Begum Shahi/Maryam Zamani Mosque
- ③ Rim Market
- ④ Gali Sher Pahlwan and Ghahya Pahlwan
- South-East Sector (Ali Park and its vicinity)
- ⑤ Fort Road
- ⑥ Lahore Fort's Ceremonial Steps
- ⑦ Ali Park
- ⑧ Immediate surroundings of Ali Park
- South-West Sector (Triangle and neighbourhoods)
- ⑨ Triangle
- ⑩ Access to Hazuri Bagh Pavilion/Ranjit Singh's Baradari
- ⑪ Access to Badshahi Mosque
- ⑫ Sheikhupurian Bazaar

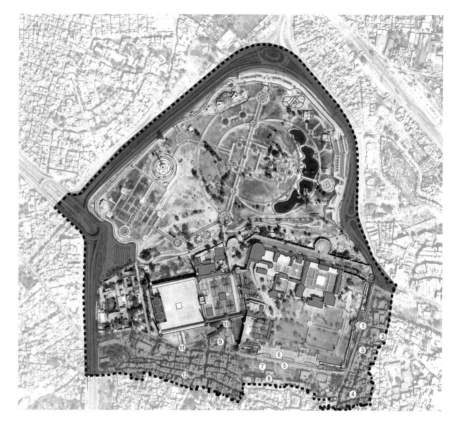

Land use in the Buffer Zone.

- Residential
- Mixed
- Commercial
- Industrial
- Storage
- Health-Related
- Religious
- Educational
- Cinema
- Wrestling Arena
- Park
- Tomb
- Utility Stations
- Other

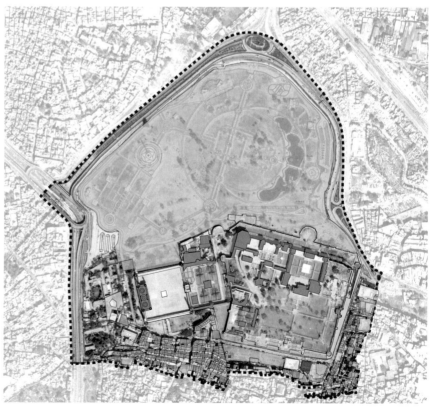

200 m

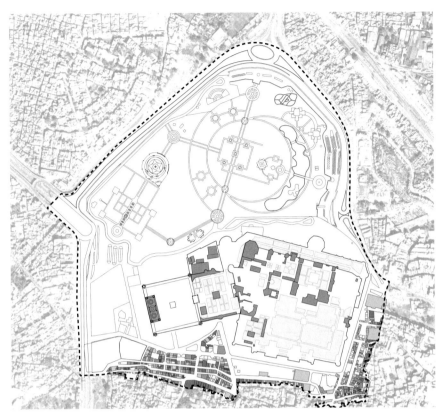

Condition of buildings in the Buffer Zone.

☐ Single Storey
▨ G+1
▨ G+2
▨ G+3
▨ G+4

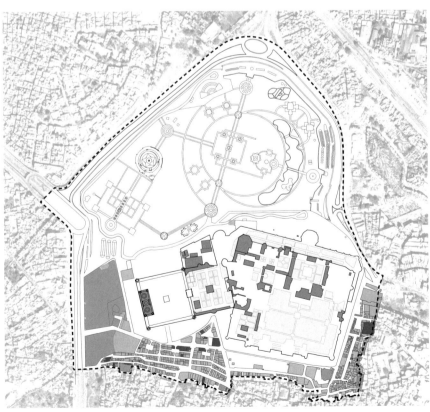

Identification of monuments and structures of historic significance in the Buffer Zone.

▨ High
▨ Medium
▨ None

Ⓘ 200 m

ecosystem of the Walled City. Specific initiatives, apart from the ongoing activities for Lahore Fort's conservation, focus on new infrastructure and urban regeneration in the surrounding Buffer Zone. These include the restoration of the Maryam Zamani (or Begum Shahi) Mosque, the reorganization of the access to the Fort from the east flank, improvements in mobility, landscaping of public and green spaces, particularly Ali Park in the south sector, and the general upgrading of the infrastructure network.

In advising the WCLA for the development of the project, AKTC/AKCS-P have included the integrated programme outlined above in their larger redevelopment plans for the east and south sectors of the Buffer Zone. This stems from the belief that a comprehensive, holistic vision of the entire zone is a necessity: there is a need to consider the entire infrastructure and mobility systems as interconnected issues to resolve coherently, together with, in ways that are mutually interdependent, access to the Fort from its south and east sides. At the same time, the reorganization of Rim Market and the upgrading of Ali Park must be seen as a single landscaped band adjacent to the Fort's walled enclosure, capable of bringing into the area a diversified

Aerial view of existing conditions in Ali Park and Rim Market (above) and the same view showing the proposed remodelling of the two areas (below).

○ 50 m

Master Plan for Lahore Fort's south-east and east Buffer Zones (Action Areas 2 and 3).

1   New Bus Station and Shuttle Parking
2   Visitor Centre
3   Akbari Gate
4   Begum Shahi/Maryam Zamani Mosque
5   Bazaar Stalls and Gardens
6   Proposed Hotel and Forecourt
7   British Ceremonial Steps
8   Ali Park Renovated
9   Government Middle School
    for Disabled (existing)
10 Electric Grid Station (existing)
11 South-East Bastion

range of public and private uses compatible with the character of the historic complex and the cultural potentialities of its immediate surroundings. Even though the plans for the two Action Areas are presented as independent schemes, they have been conceived in relation to one another, particularly the east and south-east sectors. These are, in fact, closely interrelated and come together as a single integrated system. Whether or not the relocation of the present undesirable activities will become possible in the short to medium term, the urban design solutions presented for the east and south sides of Lahore Fort are worth pursuing for the long-term regeneration of the entire zone and the appropriate redevelopment of the World Heritage Site's context.

Finally, it should be noted that the urban design proposals for Action Areas 1 and 2 are more characterized and developed than the proposals for the south-west sector (Action Area 3). Such an approach reflects the different nature of the areas in question. In the cases of Rim Market and Ali Park, the aims are the complete redevelopment of the zone vacated by the commercial enterprises and the reorganization of the existing Ali Park and adjacent streetscapes to form a coherent ensemble. The south-west sector (Action Area 3) is characterized, instead, by fine-grained interventions. Rather than imagining a complete redevelopment of the area, a course of action that would be unnecessarily disruptive, the interventions proposed consist in a plot-by-plot improvement of the existing fabric, reuse and extension of selected buildings, introduction of commercial activities in underused spaces, amelioration of the Food Street and access to the Hazuri Bagh from the south side.

All together, the combined plans for the redevelopment of the south and east sectors of the Buffer Zone can potentially offer an alternative to the disorderly and chaotic urban conditions currently prevailing throughout the area. By removing incompatible uses and initiating a gradual process of urban improvements, the Fort can be returned to its central role in the context of the Walled City of Lahore and its closely related Buffer Zone.

357

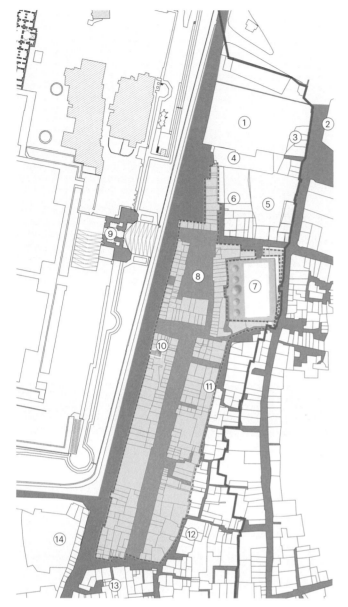

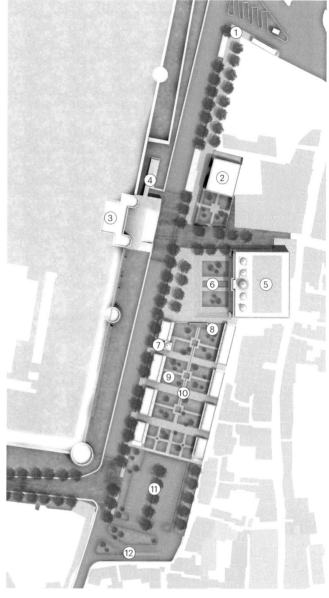

10 m

Left
1 Federal Government
  Girls Middle School
2 Masti Gate
3 Shrine
4 Plaza – Shoe Market
5 Masti Gate Police Station
6 Commercial
7 Begum Shahi/Maryam
  Zamani Mosque
8 Rim Market
9 Akbari Gate
10 Shrine of Syed Jaffer
  Hussain Shah
11 Plaza – Shoe Market
12 Khai Bohar Wali
13 Mohalla Barood Khana
14 Graveyard

Right
1 Bus Station and Electric
  Shuttle Parking
2 Visitor Centre
3 Akbari Gate
4 Access Ramp to
  Lahore Fort
5 Begum Shahi/Maryam
  Zamani Mosque
6 Begum Shahi/Maryam
  Zamani Mosque's
  Sunken Forecourt
7 Shrine of Syed Jaffer
  Hussain Shah
8 Linear Fountain
9 Garden Court and Bazaar
10 Pools and Channels
11 Surface Car Parking
  (48 bays)
12 Access Road to the Parking

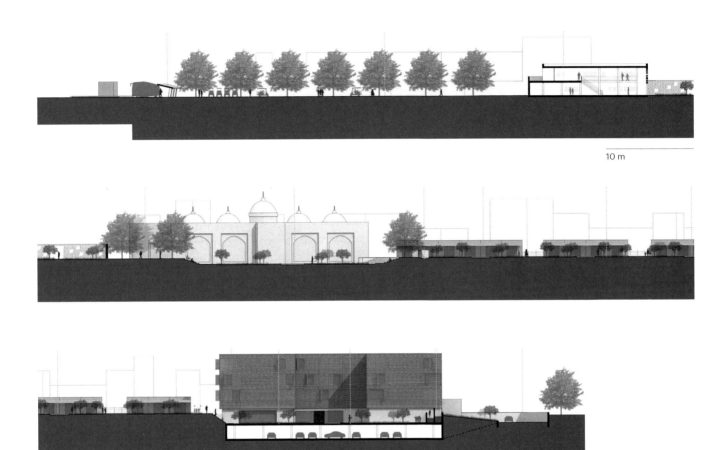

10 m

ACTION AREA 1: THE EAST SECTOR AND RIM MARKET

The relocation of Rim Market and the wholesale shoe manufacturers and vendors to a new development area will create a virtual *tabula rasa* along the east flank of Lahore Fort and its former access point through Akbari Gate. The only exceptions are the presence of the Maryam Zamani (or Begum Shahi) Mosque, an important listed structure directly opposite the gate, and the shrine of Syed Jaffer Hussain Shah, located south of the mosque. Of special significance is the proposed reopening of the access to the Fort via Akbari Gate and its link to the Walled City via the Shahi Guzargah, the principal historic pathway that connected Delhi Gate to the Fort.

The proposed plan for the reorganization of the unbuilt area resulting from the re-location of the market structures assumes the continued preservation of these heritage assets and takes into account the functional programme defined by the WCLA for the urban regeneration of the area. This includes a landscaped zone containing a visitor centre to the west of the Maryam Zamani Mosque, a small park incorporating

Opposite page, above left, present layout of the Rim Market commercial area with the boundary of the 'Resettlement Plan'. Above right, plan of the proposed remodelling of Rim Market with the car parking option at the south edge. Below, aerial view of the domed Maryam Zamani (or Begum Shahi) Mosque engulfed by the informal develop-ment of Rim Market.

Above, longitudinal section along the entire length of the Rim Market site after the proposed remodelling.

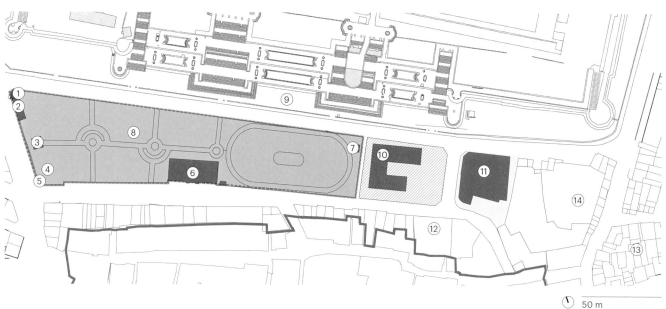

1 Health Club
2 Exercise Area Semi-Covered
3 Mosque
4 Tube Well
5 Service Centre and Shop

6 PTCL Customer Service Centre
7 Water Filtration Plant
8 Ali Park
9 Ceremonial Steps
10 Government Middle School for Disabled

11 Grid Station
12 Mutawalli Sufi Siraj Din Masjid Tomb
13 Mohalla Barood Khana
14 Graveyard

10 m

Above, plan of Ali Park showing present conditions in the area.

Below, cross section through the Ceremonial Steps and Ali Park.

a crafts bazaar for tourists and a hospitality/hotel facility at the southern end of the site. The new 2018 Master Plan also considers the possible extent of the setback rule contained in the 'Antiquities Act', whereby any new construction should maintain a zone of respect of almost sixty-one metres around listed monuments. Although this requirement has been totally ignored in the past, particularly in the immediate proximity of Lahore Fort's external walls and around the mosque, it was felt that any plans promoted by the public authority should be mindful of this constraint and seriously consider means and ways to mitigate the impact of any new developments in heritage-sensitive areas. Accordingly, the plan foresees the removal of the encroachments that over the years have progressively engulfed the Maryam Zamani (or Begum Shahi) Mosque, to the point where it is today entirely hidden from public view. The 2018 Master Plan aims to limit new construction and maximize the extent of public open space and walkability throughout the area. A substantial trunk infrastructure improvement programme is also envisaged, involving in the main the removal of high-tension transmission lines feeding the Lahore Fort grid station and associated pylons and the relocation of the cables underground.

ACTION AREA 2: THE SOUTH-EAST SECTOR AND THE ALI PARK AREA

The proposals for Ali Park and its surroundings hinge on the complete pedestrianization of Fort Road South. This single measure can by itself create the conditions for a completely different use of the area, which could then become a place of social concourse and community interaction, rather than the polluted and encumbered vehicular road it is at present. In particular, pedestrianization would make it possible to link Ali Park to the foot of the Ceremonial Steps and expand the potential of both to become public open areas to the full, and thus revitalize the entire south flank of the Mughal citadel.

In order to achieve this ambitious vision, the plan proposes the following actions:

▸ *Establish an alternative vehicular road* to replace Fort Road through the improvement of the existing road south of Ali Park in order to create a viable road to take on the increased volume of traffic with the minimum possible amount of demolition.

▸ *Reactivate the Ceremonial Steps* as an open-air garden with a set of imposing stairs descending towards the park. This flight of stairs was created after 1927, when the British cantonment moved out of the Fort, with the intent of demilitarizing the citadel and opening it to the city. The UNESCO 'Lahore Fort Master Plan' of 2006 recommended the full restoration of the Ceremonial Steps and the establishment of special activities to encourage the presence of residents and visitors.

▸ *Create small squares at the foot of the Ceremonial Steps*: the pedestrianization of Fort Road South allows for the virtual expansion of Ali Park to the north, considerably enlarging the perception of the park. As shown in the plan, the pedestrian use of the place would be further enhanced by the creation of a series of small squares below the existing steps. Rather than imagining a prosaic pedestrian boulevard flanking the park, the proposal explores the possibility of creating poles of attraction along the base of the Ceremonial Steps in the form of open, multi-purpose, small pedestrian squares. These could be used for different seasonal events, displays and market activities, accompanied by the installation of temporary tents, kiosks, vending stalls and raised stages for night events, fully enjoyable from the height of the Ceremonial Steps.

▸ *Enhance the green park's landscaping*: finally, the park itself is reconfigured in the proposal to establish a green linear expanse bisected by a line of pools connected by a central water channel fed by a fountain placed in proximity of the existing school. As shown in the plan, the rhythm of the pools could be extended in future if the school and electrical station were to be relocated. This appears as a remote prospect at the moment, but hints at the potential to enable the gradual, community oriented transformation of the entire area, where the current patterns of erosion and haphazard private development of public open areas are discontinued in favour of the enhancement of existing communal assets.

ACTION AREA 3: THE SOUTH-WEST SECTOR

The area to the south-west of the Fort comprises: (a) the Sheikhupurian Bazaar which has long been the specialized bazaar for traditional embroidered shoes and includes an early twentieth-century theatre building; (b) the block of urban fabric known as the "Triangle" north of Fort Road; and (c) on the other, southern, side of the road, an interesting housing development dating from the 1930s – a series of small urban squares formed by the period houses that surround them. Interventions in the zone will comprise infrastructure and road surface improvement, civic amenities, rehabilitation and upgrading of individual buildings, and general area conservation and rehabilitation, all carried out on a social extension and community development model already tried out in the Walled City under the Shahi Guzargah project.

Top, current view of Ali Park looking east.

Middle, view of Ali Park looking east after the proposed remodelling.

Bottom, view of the proposed remodelling of Ali Park from the top of the Ceremonial Steps.

PLANNING FOR SOCIO-ECONOMIC DEVELOPMENT IN THE ACTION AREAS

JURJEN VAN DER TAS, FATIMAH KHAN

The current social and economic living and working conditions in the Buffer Zone have undergone major changes over the past fifty years. The entertainment industry that once dominated the western part of the Buffer Zone with restaurants, cabarets and cinemas is no longer there. Over the course of the past decade, many of the occupants of Lahore's famous Heera Mandi Street moved out in successive stages. Still, this street and the adjacent area continue to be associated with Lahore's once famous red-light district.

The recently created Food Street attracts substantial numbers of visitors. However, few of these visitors venture east beyond the "Triangle" where Food Street is located and where buildings show obvious signs of deterioration and dilapidation. Many residents of this part of the Buffer Zone have moved out while small manufacturing establishments – in particular those related to shoe manufacturing and selling – have taken root.

A household and business survey of the Buffer Zone south of the Fort, carried out by the Aga Khan Cultural Service-Pakistan (AKCS-P) in June and July 2018, confirmed earlier assumptions regarding the conditions of houses and the state of well-being of local residents. This survey, which, on the one hand, provides a baseline against which future change may be measured, serves, on the other, as a means of needs assessment for possible initiatives that would benefit local residents and businesses. The survey covered eighty-three households and seventy-seven businesses, which represent respectively 38% of the total number of households and 30% of all the businesses in the area. As the planning for the relocation of Rim Market at the eastern edge of the Buffer Zone is in an advanced state, the survey did not collect data from this section of the Buffer Zone.

The findings of the two surveys reflect existing conditions in the neighbourhoods or mohallas of Neewa Chait Ram, Uncha Chait Ram, Shahi Mohalla, Sheikhupurian Bazaar, the new Food Street south of the Hazuri Bagh and the row of buildings that face the southern perimeter of Ali Park. Like many parts of the Walled City, these areas are considered underprivileged in terms of available municipal services. In general, however, services in the old city tend to be better where infrastructure has recently been upgraded, such as in the Delhi Gate and Wazir Khan area.

The buildings in the survey area date back to the 1920s to 1940s, with numerous additions and modifications made over the following years. The average size of land parcels found here is relatively large in comparison to building footprints elsewhere in the Walled City. The survey found a number of properties under dispute, owing to

Opposite page, view of Circular Garden.

Above, aerial view of the western part of the Buffer Zone, with the Food Street in the foreground.

Below, current view of the Ceremonial Steps looking west from the Fort's ramparts along Fort Road.

**Zone of Special Value 1 – Buffer Zone
(south and east sections).**

- Shoes
- Rim
- Eatery
- Music
- Service
- General Store / Dairy / Vegetable
- Mechanic / Metalwork
- Entertainment / Sports
- Plaza
- Parking
- Other

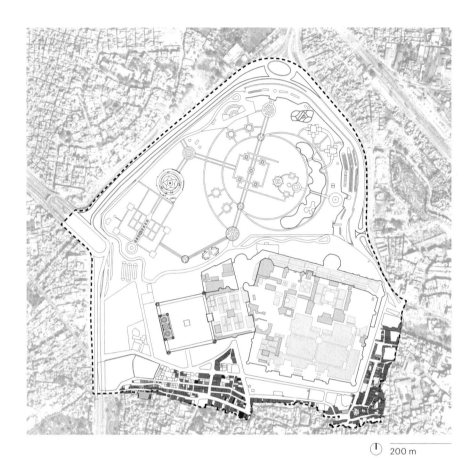

200 m

**Rim Market, seen from the eastern rampart
of the Fort.**

multiple claims to ownership. Conversations with residents hint at a general low level of social cohesion in comparison to other areas of the Walled City, such as the Bhatti Gate or Delhi Gate areas. The most likely cause for such low levels of social cohesion is the continuous commercial pressure felt from the eastern part of the Buffer Zone, where manufacturers of cheap footwear are situated.

RESIDENTS

The average number of households per land parcel stands at two with only a few exceptions. The highest number of households found by the survey on a single parcel of land exceeds ten families. The average household size in the survey area comprises six people, with around 55% of the population of the households classified as male, 44% as female and 1% as transgender. With 30% of the sample population below the age of fifteen, 67% between the ages of fifteen and sixty-four and 3% above the age of sixty-four, the population pyramid for this part of Lahore is quite similar to that of Pakistan as a whole.

Higher education is not necessarily correlated to higher incomes: a relatively high proportion of women have college or university education, but not many appear to have found permanent jobs. In terms of employment, just over a third of college or university-educated residents are engaged in income-generating activities. Of these, most are self-employed or daily wage earners while some work in the private or government sector.

Data on residency and housing show that, on average, the family as a unit has lived in the current premises for approximately forty-six years. Eighty per cent of households are also the owners of the house in which they live, while the rest are tenants. A small proportion of households occupy their dwelling on the basis of *"girwi"*, which implies that the owner of the property has received a lump sum in advance on condition that the lessee can occupy the premises for a given period of time. Living spaces are small. On average, the available space for a household is 63 square metres of living area, spread over four rooms. Fifty per cent of households, however, have just three rooms. A kitchen or separate space for cooking is generally available for about 54% of the households.

Regarding the physical conditions of the house: less than 20% of dwellings are considered to be in reasonably good condition, with the remaining 80% ranging from fair to poor. Regular maintenance is rare. Most housing repair is carried out if and when the need becomes apparent and ranges from small interventions, such as the fixing of leaking toilets, to major undertakings where structural issues may be addressed.

Most households have access to basic services such as piped water, electricity and gas. However, there are instances where households need to fetch water from external sources such as public taps, or where the household depends on water provided by neighbours. Most households have their own flush latrine. Slightly less than 10% use shared toilet facilities and only a few houses depend on the traditional pit latrine. Disposal of solid waste is a major issue in this part of the Walled City. People dispose of garbage just outside their dwellings and many households do not think twice about doing so.

In terms of financial well-being, the situation in the Buffer Zone is not much different from anywhere else in the Walled City. The average household has two male income earners. Fewer than 10% of the households include female income earners. Some households are compelled to sell domestic items to purchase food or to meet educational or medical expenses. The median daily income, at USD 1.36 per person, is just above the World Bank poverty line of USD 1.25 per person per day. However, expressed in Purchasing Power Parity the average daily income level is somewhat better at almost USD 5 per person per day.

Access to green open space for residents and shop operators in the Buffer Zone is relatively easy. Members of households mention Greater Iqbal Park, Ali Park or the Hazuri Bagh as the preferred destinations as they are close by. Still, a relatively high proportion of respondents are of the view that they do not have access to adequate open or green spaces. Furthermore, none of the nearby green open spaces appear to have proper playgrounds for children. Subsequently, children usually play at home or in their neighbourhood.

On the whole, local residents tend to feel safe in their neighbourhood during the day as well as the night. In some instances, *chowkidars* (watchmen) are hired to guard the streets at night. Respondents also feel that fellow residents can be trusted. There is little dependency on local institutions such as the Union Council representative for conflict resolution. In most cases when there is a conflict, the local police is called or the local *biradari* (kinship group) is consulted and asked to help reconcile differences. A major concern is the presence of drug users. Although most respondents rate the overall quality of life in their mohalla as good, there is a clear desire to bring about improvements in the local physical infrastructure. Likewise, residents would like the government to enforce a ban on drugs and toxic chemicals.

Above, Moti Bazaar, east of Rim Market – the outlet for shoes made in the Walled City.

Below, food vendors in the streets of the Buffer Zone.

Zone of Special Value 1 – Buffer Zone (south and east sections).

- Households
- Business
- Project Area East
- Project Area South
- Project Area West

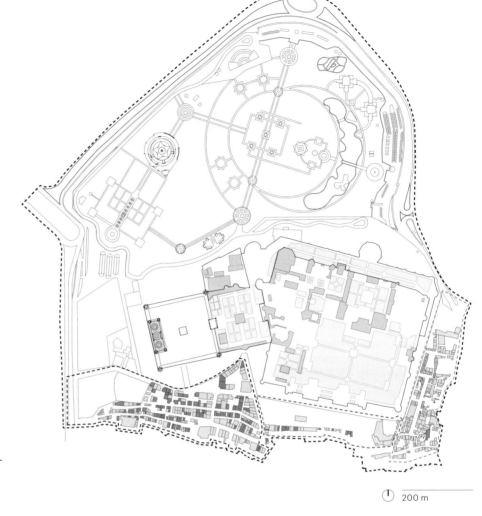

200 m

Greater Iqbal Park, from the northern fortifications of Lahore Fort.

BUSINESSES

Over the past decade, various activities related to the supply chain of footwear have moved into the Buffer Zone. Enterprises include manufacturing outlets, followed by retail and wholesale activities. Just over 10% of the local shops are made up of food and beverage outlets and restaurants, serving both the local clientele as well as external visitors. The latter tend to frequent the more expensive restaurants, such as those found in the recently created Food Street (2010). The number of shops catering for musicians has been on the decline after the phasing out of the entertainment industry around Heera Mandi Street. What currently remains are a few shops that repair musical instruments (see map on p. 364).

Around half of the shopkeepers and manufacturers that were interviewed stated that they live in the Walled City. A smaller group live up to eight kilometres away from the Walled City, but commute to the Buffer Zone on a daily basis. While two thirds of respondents claim to have completed either middle or high school, close to one fifth cannot read or write. Employees are generally more likely to be uneducated.

Businesses have been operating in their current location for an average period of about ten years and up to 50% have been present in the area for not more than five years. Only 30% of businesses are registered. In 42% of all cases the business operator also owns the premises. In all other cases the premises are rented. A majority of businesses operate on a single floor. Just over 25% of businesses have access to two floors.

Common issues in the buildings where businesses operate pertain to poor electric connections, leaking water and faulty sewerage pipes. Internal working spaces tend to be tight and poorly ventilated. Waste material from ongoing production activities is usually thrown just outside the shops. Fewer than a quarter of all businesses surveyed have arrangements for garbage collection on site. The presence of various toxic chemicals used in shoemaking is believed to be a key factor affecting safety in the workplace and surrounding buildings.

The average number of employees per shop is low, with a median of two. In almost all cases employees are hired through word-of-mouth. Almost three quarters do not have any contract, whether verbal or in writing. Employees work up to ten hours per day on average.

TRAFFIC CONDITIONS AND PRELIMINARY PROPOSITIONS

A Traffic Survey, carried out during the month of July 2018, identified ten measurement points within the Buffer Zone from which data pertaining to the movement of traffic, pedestrians and the status of parking were collected over a four-day period (Wednesday, Thursday, Friday and Saturday) in the latter part of the month. During these days traffic counts were held for sixteen hours a day, starting at 7 a.m. and ending at 11 p.m. The parking situation was assessed along the entire road network marked by points T1 to T10 as well as on Shahi Mohalla Street, which connects Fort Road with Heera Mandi Street (T4 to T5) (see maps on pp. 370 and 371).

Fort Road is, without any doubt, predominantly used for transit traffic. There is a high volume of traffic entering the Buffer Zone from Data Darbaar Road through the entrance adjacent to the Lady Willingdon Hospital, north of Taxali Gate, using Fort Road as a transit route to reach Circular Road near Masti Gate. Assuming that

In the Buffer Zone, less than 20% of dwellings is considered to be in good condition.

by eliminating access to Fort Road beyond the Food Street "Triangle", transit traffic would be discouraged from circumnavigating Lahore Fort along its southern and eastern edges, and so the inflow of traffic from the west through Taxali Gate could be reduced by half. What would remain would mainly consist of dedicated traffic to the Walled City heading for the area south and east of Heera Mandi Street. Traffic coming from the north, entering Fort Road from Circular Road, also consists of nearly half of transit traffic. As access routes to the centre of the Walled City are narrow (Kali Beri Bazaar in particular is very narrow), thought would have to be given to the introduction and enforcement of one-way traffic circulation in this part of the Walled City. Currently all streets in and around the Buffer Zone are open to two-way traffic – something that is considered a major impediment to the development of a smooth-flowing traffic system for local destinations.

The number of people moving on foot through this part of the Walled City is small in relative terms. Along Fort Road east of Lahore Fort, the average number recorded throughout the day was thirty pedestrians per fifteen minutes or one person every thirty seconds. For a city that until seventy years ago fully relied on pedestrian traffic and animal-pulled carts, the limited number of pedestrians that currently are part of

Various small-scale businesses. Clockwise from top left: traditional *dhol* and *tabla* drums; shoes; delivery; and *charpai* webbing.

Traffic conditions.

the streetscape is astonishing. It reflects the continuing expansion of the commercial sector coupled with the loss of local residents. On the other hand, it also signifies a major shift in attitudes whereby vehicular traffic always appears to have the upper hand over people moving on foot – as is evident from the lack of facilities for pedestrians. A partial return to 'pedestrian normalcy', that is, adhering to the norms for pedestrians in the Walled City that were in force until modern vehicular traffic made inroads, would greatly benefit the Buffer Zone and adjacent areas and make this part of the Walled City a much better place to live in and to visit for locals and for tourists alike.

A road inventory survey of parking possibilities along thirteen roads in the Buffer Zone and adjacent areas showed potential availability of 1,265 linear metres of parking space. At five metres per car, this would amount to roughly 250 parking spaces.

Traffic survey locations.

Ⓣ   Traffic Survey Locations
- - -   Study Area

Parking survey locations.

——   PS-1
——   PS-2
——   PS-3
——   PS-4
——   PS-5
——   PS-6
- - -   Study Area

200 m

In view of the findings from the analysis of the traffic survey data covering the Buffer Zone of Lahore Fort, anecdotal evidence collected and suggestions for the wider improvement of the Buffer Zone of Lahore Fort, the Walled City of Lahore would stand to benefit substantially from the closure of Fort Road to all vehicular traffic. Excepting emergency services and traffic destined for entities located on Fort Road itself, Fort Road would be closed from the northern entrance at Circular Road until the junction with Shahi Mohalla Street. Furthermore, the flow of traffic along the south side of Ali Park would have to be sharply reduced – making it accessible for local traffic only. In addition, the possibility of introducing and enforcing a one-way street plan for access to the Kalay Pipe Wala and Pani Wala Talab Road area, by improving access through Moti Bazaar and Kali Beri Bazaar, would have to be studied. Lastly, the creating and enforcing of 'pedestrian only' zones and creating better facilities for pedestrians, such as elevated pavements, shaded areas and so on, would have to be considered. It would appear to be important to engage with local residents to develop a Pedestrian Raj theme for the Walled City.

PLANNING FOR THE FUTURE

The gradual disappearance of Lahore's entertainment industry from the Buffer Zone, coupled with the expanding manufacturing and retail sector, continues to negatively affect the quality of life of local residents. In view of future changes to the Buffer Zone that would create an environment that is favourable to the development of tourism as the mainstay for the local population, development efforts would increasingly need to focus on:

▸ discouraging further expansion of the shoe market and addressing the most pressing discomfort that it creates in terms of rubbish, toxic waste and excessive noise levels;
▸ ensuring solid waste is collected on a regular basis;
▸ encouraging employment at the local level that is geared towards tourism;
▸ improving local infrastructure for the benefit of residents and visitors to the area;
▸ discouraging transit traffic through the Buffer Zone and the creation of a number of fully pedestrian streets.

Preliminary traffic proposal.

	Limited Access Two-way Road (Local Traffic Only)
	Improved Vehicular Road (One-way)
	Pedestrian-Only Zone
👤ııı	Shaded Pedestrian Walkway
▲	Pedestrian Access to Lahore Fort (Under Consideration) Ali Park
P	Car Parking

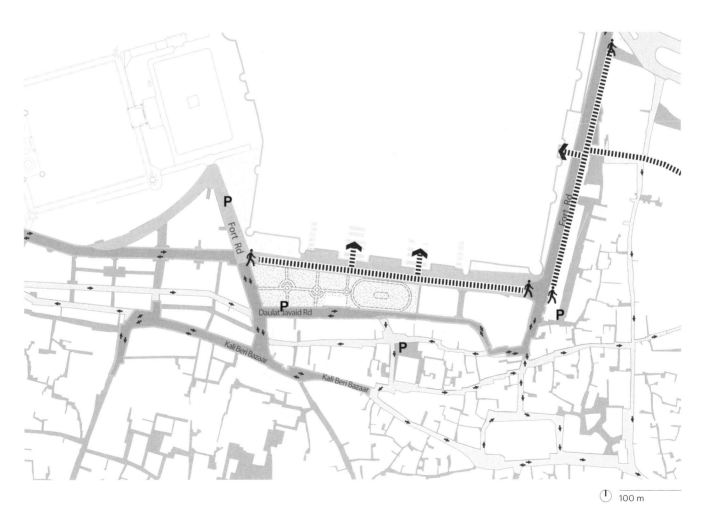

100 m

THE WAY FORWARD

RECOUNTING CHALLENGES
AND ASSESSING IMPACT

SALMAN BEG, JURJEN VAN DER TAS

THE STATUS QUO AT THE ONSET OF THE PROJECT

The wave of destruction that washed over the Walled City – following the 1947 partition of British colonial India into the Hindu majority nation of India and the Islamic Republic of Pakistan – caused irreparable damage to the physical and social urban fabric of the city in many instances. Part of the physical damage was repaired through the 1952 'Punjab Development of Damaged Areas Act'. However, at the time, few paid attention to the historic context in which the new development was carried out. Subsequent rebuilding was generally not carried out in line with the Walled City's historic land-use pattern. The best example of misguided development, perhaps, is that of Shah Alami Road. This broad entry road was created in the wake of destruction that took place during partition. Coming in from the south, it leads directly to the centre of the Walled City and has allowed commercial activities of considerable scale to become established all around it, thus creating a permanent scar to the cityscape.

The Walled City's resident population has been negatively affected over the years in various ways. Many of the arriving Muslim families from India moved into residences left vacant by the emigrating Hindu population. Lacking adequate and modern infrastructure, the Walled City had poor housing values and thus became attractive for groups with low-income levels. As these groups moved in, the wealthier families moved to the outskirts, where more living space and adequate infrastructure were available. This trend continued until recently: between the early 1970s and late 1980s an estimated twenty-nine per cent of the resident population of the Walled City had moved out. With replacements made up of low-income groups from outside, on the one hand, and commercial takeovers by non-residents, on the other, the Walled City saw its overall resident population drop from an estimated 200,000 in 1970 to fewer than 160,000 by 2008 when the Shahi Guzargah project was initiated.

Where the space left by emigrants was filled by commercial interests, significant changes occurred in land use. Properties along main bazaars nearly all became commercial outlets, while the backrooms, as well as the first and second storeys of these properties, found new usage as storage and manufacturing space, sometimes in combination with living space for residents. In a departure from the past, the new commercial sector was run in majority by non-residents. Meanwhile, the back alleys, which serve no commercial interest, became the domain of the resident population.

Surveys carried out by the Aga Khan Cultural Service-Pakistan (AKCS-P) in the Walled City in 2008 and 2017 found that newly established small-scale manufacturers and wholesalers do not serve the local community in terms of the goods and services

Preceding pages, the Hiran Minar, located in Sheikhupura.

Opposite page, both the interior and the exterior of the Wazir Khan Mosque are almost entirely decorated with frescoes and glazed-tile work.

Above, people leaving the Wazir Khan Mosque after Friday prayers.

Below, entry to the mosque is gained through a large *iwan* lined with fresco paintings.

on offer. As many of these entities rely on staff of their own family network, employment opportunities for the resident population of the Walled City in the commercial sector were found to be limited. The marked difference between a well-off commercial sector, on the one hand, and a dependent, impoverished resident population, on the other, had, until the start of the project, exacerbated the process of decline. It allowed shops to operate in relative anonymity, thus avoiding having to pay national and local taxes. Furthermore, in the absence of enforcement of building regulations, it had given space to speculative developers who would not feel inclined to pay attention to the historic built environment. The resulting commercial encroachment showed a pattern of abuse of building stock through inappropriate reuse of structures intended for small-scale industries and use of space for storage – this often in combination with older buildings being replaced with quickly erected structures of lower quality.

CHOICES THAT WERE MADE AND DEVELOPMENTS SINCE

In order to arrest the negative developments that had occurred in the Walled City over the preceding sixty years and in order, where possible, to safeguard and rehabilitate anything of value that had been left, both the SDWCLP (later the WCLA, the Walled City of Lahore Authority) and AKCS-P were faced with a number of critical questions that required clear answers at the onset of the Shahi Guzargah project. Most important, perhaps, was to determine who the planned interventions would be for. Would they only have to serve the needs of the resident population and future visitors? What then would be the role of the commercial sector? Another important dilemma was how to rehabilitate and protect the historic built environment without losing the dynamics of the living culture. In other words, how could one avoid creating a picture-perfect historic environment that lacks the vibrancy that was once associated with the Walled City of Lahore?

As data collection and planning for the Shahi Guzargah project got under way, it appeared that for this initiative the interests of both the resident population and the commercial sector could be served in a straightforward manner. Permanent removal of encroachment along the section of Shahi Guzargah between Delhi Gate and the Wazir Khan Mosque and upgrading of the streetscape and shopfronts, combined with the rehabilitation of major monuments such as the Shahi Hammam and the Wazir Khan Mosque, served as an important outreach to both the established commercial sector and to the future visitors of the Walled City. At the same time, some of the most pressing needs of the resident population were looked after by initiating a pilot project for two *galis* (Gali Surjan Singh and Mohammadi Mohalla). Under this scheme, a total of thirteen houses were fully rehabilitated and the essential infrastructure for both the streets and the adjacent houses was fully upgraded. The results have been so successful that the WCLA has continued the rehabilitation of *galis* in other parts of the Walled City since the completion of the pilot initiative, with the aim of eventually addressing all parts of the Walled City that are in urgent need of improvement.

The lessons learned from the first phase of the Shahi Guzargah project are now being applied by the WCLA and AKCS-P in various parts of the Walled City. It is clear, however, that what was accomplished will have to be adjusted to local circumstances as the project moves into other areas. The initial choices that were made, seeking to halt the decline in the number of residents of the Walled City, will need to be matched with facilities and conditions that give residents an incentive to stay. The redevelopment of the commercial sector would call for measures that discourage further expansion and eventually reduce the manufacturing sector and wholesale markets.

Above, a street vendor just outside Delhi Gate selling tobacco.

Below, historic building stock of architectural value at risk in the Walled City.

Traffic conditions just outside Delhi Gate.

At the same time, the development of commercial activities through services, food and beverage outlets and the retail sector would need to be encouraged, as these industries benefit both residents and visitors.

Both the provincial and federal governments have shown high levels of interest in the development and the well-being of the Walled City of Lahore, as a place of residency as well as a destination for visitors. As a result, the enforcement of building regulations and monitoring of land use has been stepped up over the years. With its greatly expanded authority and with the identification and enhanced regulation of Zones of Special Value, it appears that the WCLA now also has the proper tools to continue to steer the development of the Walled City in the desired direction.

The Wazir Khan Mosque's north facade after conservation.

THE NEED FOR PROGRESS MEASUREMENT

In order to sustain development activities in the Walled City over the coming years, including those inside and around Lahore Fort, there will be a need to continue data collection and data analysis concerning the well-being of residents on a regular basis. Such information would be key in advancing the purpose of the project, a question that was raised at the start of the first phase of the rehabilitation. The information would also assist the agencies involved to steer development during implementation and to make periodic adjustments where necessary. The success of the components that make up the project would be determined by positive feedback from residents and representatives of the business sector about their well-being. Positive feedback from visitors to the Walled City would also be considered an important part of the success of the project.

Assuming that socio-economic data collection and data analysis will become institutionalized in the near future and that findings will feature regularly in progress reports, it would be possible to show the contribution of the Walled City to the economy of Lahore at the aggregate level – thus providing justification for the funds that have been made available for its redevelopment over the years.

The 2008 and 2017 studies carried out by AKCS-P concerning the developmental status of residents, as well as the business sector, provide benchmarks against which future progress can be measured. It goes without saying that, since these studies were limited in geographic reach, additional baseline material for areas in the Walled City that were not covered by the earlier studies would need to be collected. Such material would not only help in establishing new benchmarks for future progress measurement, but would also highlight the most urgent needs of the resident population. Those needs would not be limited to the well-being of the resident population in terms of household economy and the levels of human development, but would also highlight the status of the physical environment, that is, housing conditions, infrastructure of the neighbourhood, street safety and cleanliness.

ATTRIBUTION

In a dynamic urban environment, such as that of the Walled City, it is difficult to assess whether notable changes that can be observed in daily life are directly attributable to actions taken at the project level. For most activities aimed at improving socio-economic well-being, direct attribution is generally not possible because the chain of events between a project activity and its outcome or its impact contains a number of unknown factors or consists of factors that cannot be controlled. At a level of results, however, it is easier to make a link with the original project activity –

Left, Gali Surjan Singh and Koocha Charkh Garan after completion of the Mohalla demonstration project.

Right, conservation of the fine-grained residential urban fabric of the pilot project area was itself a key component of the project.

particularly if the result is related to a physical intervention such as redirection of traffic, creation of essential infrastructure and so on.

In order to be able to predict the outcome of intended project activities that are likely to be influenced by external factors over which no control can be exercised, activities aimed at improving socio-economic conditions through increased income levels and through better education, health, water, sanitation and hygiene can be measured through the creation of an improved enabling environment that addresses these issues – rather than by measuring progress at the level of individual benefi-ciaries. Improving and maintaining this enabling environment would be the main objective for the project implementation.

FIRST INDICATIONS OF PROGRESS MADE

The most striking improvements in the enabling environment are the remarkable gains that have been made in hygiene and cleanliness. The meticulously planned and implemented sanitation and drainage systems have led to the disappearance of rats from the areas where the project has been completed. Rats can now only be found in the Akbari market where there is no shortage of grain. Also, the absence of foul odours, which were all pervasive, has been maximized. The removal of the

Below, the rehabilitated Shahi Guzargah at night.

Opposite page, looking into the Walled City through Delhi Gate.

Children playing in the field adjacent to the Badshahi Mosque.

encroachments by the WCLA, compounded with the facade restoration of the Shahi Guzargah and the conservation of several historic buildings, including the Wazir Khan Hammam, has improved the appearance of the site considerably and mitigated the unsightly mass of overhead cables and unsympathetic commercialization of the historic quarter. A corollary to the removal of encroachments is that air circulation has improved.

The first projects in terms of quality and standards but also insofar as economic and functional sustainability are concerned, the Shahi Hammam and the Wazir Khan Chowk have had a considerable impact on heritage conservation and tourism in the province with attendant socio-economic benefits:

- sixteen tourist guides are currently working for the WCLA, including two women. Their average earning is over PKR 25,000 (USD 178,50) per month;
- fifteen Rangeela Rickshaws provide transport in colourful open rickshaws playing local Punjabi music and are very popular;
- the WCLA-managed Shahi Hammam historic site employs fourteen staff. There was a 12% increase in visitor numbers for 2018 (29,744) over 2017 (26,468). Revenue increase over the same period was 17% as the numbers of international visitors also registered an increase;
- the Shahi Hammam provides a venue for holding meetings and exhibitions, and also for bridal shoots or other events that generate additional income. A privately run café caters to visitors.

In the eyes of local residents, the reclaimed *chowk* is treated with respect, with the WCLA holding public events, such as Sufi gatherings, every Saturday, while the occasions of national days are celebrated in this public space with enthusiasm.

Visitors to the Walled City, coming from different social, ethnic and religious backgrounds, now take home a renewed sense of the place and its inhabitants. Once visitors realize that local residents are welcoming and tolerant, a mutual sense of respect is created in which pluralism can be celebrated – making visits a pleasant experience not just for visitors but also for residents.

Top left, the WCLA's 'rangeela rickshaw' taking visitors on a tour of the Walled City – pictured here outside the Shahi Hammam.

Top right, Sufi music event at the Wazir Khan Chowk.

Bottom left, a play performed in the Imperial Kitchens courtyard, dedicated to the late 17th-century Sufi poet Bulleh Shah.

Bottom right, a music event in the Hazuri Bagh, Lahore Fort.

FUTURE VECTORS FOR CONSERVATION AND REDEVELOPMENT

CAMERON RASHTI, MASOOD KHAN

In this publication, connections have tenuously been made between the Walled City of Lahore and its constituent parts and its larger context – Greater Lahore. The former is a unique expression of a South Asian historic walled city and the latter is distinctive for its scale, diversity and pressures to serve an ever-increasing population in a metropolitan base – without walls. Lahore – the Walled City – and its present wider outer expanse encompass urbanity in different forms. Scale and urban texture, as well as streetscape dimensions and life, vary markedly between the two, as one would expect. However, as much as they may differ, the two must coexist in the twenty-first century.

THE COMPARATIVE ADVANTAGE OF HERITAGE DISTRICTS

The press of metropolitan-scale commerce, production and transportation in the immediate vicinity of the Walled City and its interior need not remain in contradiction. This opposition and the functional disadvantages accruing from it is the result of a history of planning inadequacy involving mutual disregard rather than accommodation between two opposed conditions. This accommodation has to be triggered in the next round of planning for Greater Lahore. As a departure from the current situation, the Walled City and the 2017 'Master Conservation and Redevelopment Plan' (MCRP) prepared for it (see pp. 152–175) must be comprehensively structured into several aspects of any future planning framework for Greater Lahore. These aspects would include land use, densities, infrastructure, circulation and transportation, and heritage and tourism.

In a parallel to the Riccardian principle of comparative advantage, in such a scenario Lahore's Walled City can exert its advantage as a heritage district and locus of important landmarks, including the World Heritage Site of Lahore Fort. Over the period of their engagement with the Walled City, this has been the primary thrust of the Walled City of Lahore Authority and the Aga Khan Trust for Culture's initiatives, while improving the quality of urban spaces and residential districts via urban action area projects. These projects have not been planned as isolated interventions; rather, they have sought to be integral aspects of systems involving the Walled City and what lies beyond. Early strategic master planning indicated how rationalization of the wider urban transport network, municipal services and land use would bring about benefits across a wider urban base. The 'Master Conservation and Redevelopment Plan' (MCRP) for the Walled City of Lahore addresses the issues of urban fabric, building morphology and heritage value across defined zones, anchored in vital districts.

Opposite page, the Wazir Khan Mosque's north facade after restoration.

Above, view of the encroachments along Wazir Khan Mosque's north facade before the restoration project was begun.

Central business areas in Lahore.

- ☐ The Walled City of Lahore
- ● Badami Bagh Bus Terminals
- ▬ Commercial (Warehousing, Retail, Production)
- ▬ Residential Areas
- ○ New Truck & Bus Parking/Depot: Options with Related Technical & Commercial Activities
- 1 Cloth
- 2 Machines/Metals
- 3 Chemicals
- 4 Freight Forwarding
- 5 Chicken
- 6 Paper & Stationery
- 7 Grain
- 8 Tires
- 9 Wheels & Rim
- 10 Kabadias/Foil/Paper
- 11 Opticians & Lenses
- 12 Fish
- 13 Printing
- 14 Automotive
- 15 Second-Hand Clothing
- 16 Fruit & Vegetables
- 17 Shoes
- 18 Timber
- 19 Leather & Hide
- A Truck Parking
- B Minivan Parking
- C Bus Parking

1 km

In order for the Walled City of Lahore to perform its heritage role with greater ease and efficiency, it will need to have better urban services provided on its edges and in its wider context, including new facilities for tourism and traditional crafts and places for the interpretation of its heritage. Some of these facilities can be located in re-purposed historic structures within the Walled City while others will be more conveniently located outside and accessible along heritage trails or routes, thus transferring inappropriate pressures away from the historic core.

CONNECTING THE HISTORIC CITY WITH THE MODERN

The increasingly shared goal of utilizing cities as vectors for balanced and sustainable growth has been espoused in recent years by public authorities and universities, professional institutions and development agencies. With regard to this wider context, the UN-Habitat's 2030 Agenda for Sustainable Development views cities as a "string that connects all other goals together; their density and economies of agglomeration link economy, energy, environment, science, technology and social and economic outputs".[1] The Agenda for Sustainable Development also stresses "the importance of the regional and sub-regional dimensions, regional economic integration and inter-connectivity in sustainable development".

The pressures of overdevelopment and inappropriate industrial land use within the Walled City have, until recently, prevented a proper review of more appropriate spatial distributions of the wide spectrum of functions that make Lahore a vital and living city. One important challenge in the case of Lahore would therefore be to combine the ongoing urban conservation agenda of the Walled City, now underway, with a renewed effort of strategic planning of critical functional zones within the outer city that are of mutual interest.

A recent editorial in the magazine *Domus* entitled "Everything Is Urbanism" remarks that "exponential population growth requires more products, more food, more oxygen, more energy, more water, better waste treatment. We need an agenda for change. Now!"[2] One might add that there is a common need for a method to mutualize many of these ambitious agendas for action within a broad-based and multidisciplinary planning process, one that would reflect the current convergence between disparate appeals and programmes calling for a new look and change in urban landscapes.

VECTORS FOR URBAN CONSERVATION AND REDEVELOPMENT

While the needs of historic and modern cities may be markedly different, the planning tools can be shared. In order to be sustainable, modern cities and urban centres that attract rather than repel residents require attention to detail at the small scale as well as for the wider whole. Successful examples in the nineteenth and twentieth centuries have provided legal and planning safeguards for urban spaces of quality. A wide group of practitioners and scholars have worked on this challenge from various

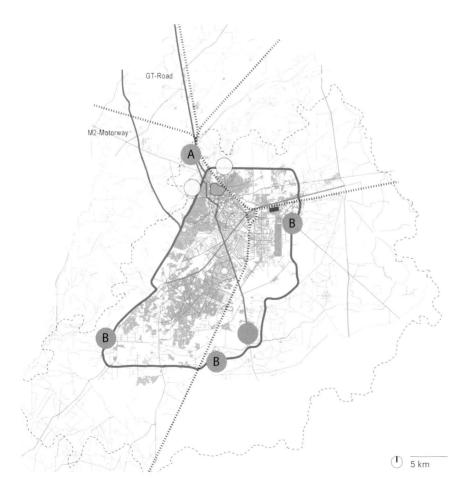

Traffic proposals at a metropolitan scale for Lahore.

▬ The Walled City of Lahore
○ New Truck & Bus Parking/Depot
Ⓐ Passenger Interchange
Pakistan Railway/Intercity Bus/LRMTS
Ⓑ Approximate Location of New
Transportation Interchange
— Proposed Rapid Mass Transit
▬ Allama Iqbal International Airport
▬ Lahore Dry Port
▬ Ring Road
⊞⊞⊞ Railway Track

5 km

Identification of varying densities of buildings with architectural merit per quarter hectare in the Walled City.

2-4
5-10
11-15
16-22

angles.[3] However, the present time is one of rapid change and traditional planning methods often lag behind, impacted by rather than impacting the urban agenda.

In the overview of AKTC's Lahore initiative, several key processes were highlighted and may be considered as representing some strategies for conservation and redevelopment at a wider scale:

▸ *Urban surveys* that document with precision the 4D richness of the urban fabric (three-dimensional plus time), capturing social-economic and physical data, and that allow the development of multiple and overlaid digital platforms for planning. What is surveyed and recorded allows for more experts and specialists to make meaningful contributions utilizing such base data, while making possible multiple regulatory frameworks to be coordinated.

▸ *Focus on carefully delineated 'urban clusters'*: while the spatial boundaries of a cluster can be modifiable, the notion is that each cluster should have a recognizable integrity and character that supports a series of enhancements with visible, tangible impact.

▸ *Use of incremental urban redevelopment* allows a modest intervention to grow via 'add-ons' and to eventually become a significant part of the whole. In the Walled City, the Shahi Guzargah initiative represented nine per cent of the total area of the Walled City, but this total consisted of numerous sub-parts. In turn, other modules, similar in size to the Shahi Guzargah, are being designed and await implementation.

▸ *Prototyping*: whether at a modest or ambitious scale, prototypes allow proposals to be tested in relatively short time frames and with reasonable levels of investment.

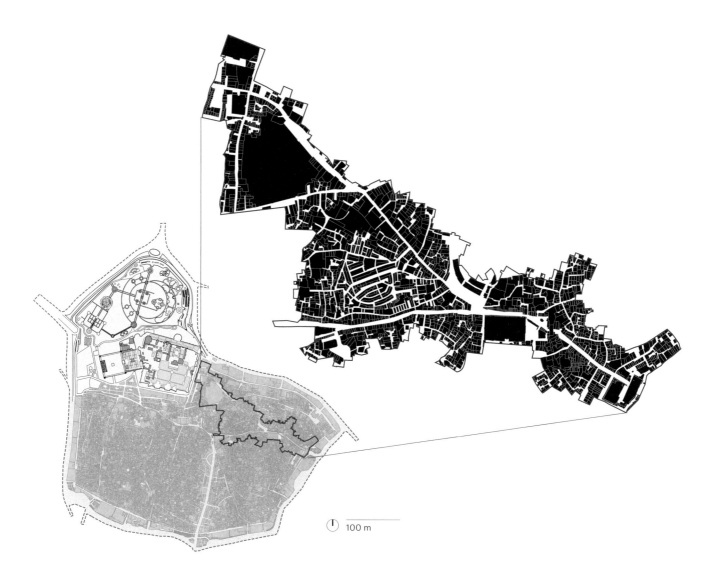

Complications are dealt with using iterative adjustments so that a solution can be found collectively and viewed by all.

▸ *Infrastructure investments*: as mentioned in the editorial in *Domus* cited above, infrastructure is a key, but sometimes invisible, aspect of the proper functioning of cities. Infrastructure is too important to be solely relegated to technical departments. Historic and modern cities have long neglected improvements to their municipal services for lack of funding or know-how. The Lahore initiative illustrates the benefits of reversing this trend.

▸ *Improved urban open spaces*: AKTC has long been an advocate of improved open urban spaces, whether small squares or large parks, connected to neighbourhoods or landmarks, cultural or natural. While making it possible to bring citizenry together in social, cultural and economic group-interaction, open spaces reveal the quality and character of cities as much as their inventory of architecture.

▸ *Urban conservation and redevelopment frameworks*: the mix of conservation and redevelopment needs careful balance if the goal is not to continuously condemn and tear down existing urban fabric of value. Modern cities are becoming 'historic' by the day and certain structures and districts that are just a few decades old are recognized as being endowed with heritage value. Thus, the heritage designation is not binary – on or off – but a spectrum.

▸ *Zones of Special Value*: while the Lahore Walled City's Zones of Special Value are three-dimensional in conceptualization and definition, an important element in guidelines for redevelopment are the controlling lines and proportions of building

Preceding pages, left, above, view of the Wazir Khan Chowk from the north-east *minar* of the mosque, showing encroachments on the diagonal street and in the *chowk*'s perimeter. Below, view of the *chowk* after reclamation of the public square and its restoration, with the Dina Nath Well and Syed Suf Shrine now clearly visible. Right, above, the Wazir Khan Mosque's east facade and the *chowk* before conservation. Below, during conservation, the floor of the *chowk* was lowered to its original level, which led to uncovering the previously buried lower part of the facade of the mosque.

Above, glazed-tile panels on Wazir Khan Mosque's north facade – before and after rehabilitation.

Opposite page, as-found and proposed street elevation of buildings in the pilot project area.

facades, especially along major streets and squares. Not wanting to promote 'facadism' as an isolated agenda, one cannot overemphasize the significance and influence of established historic street-front norms in urban character. The desire for urban design liberty and creativity in modern cities often needs to be balanced with a coherent reading of three-dimensional urban space.

▸ *Enabling frameworks*: mention was made of the importance of sufficient enabling frameworks for urban conservation and redevelopment initiatives, in the Lahore case involving a solid platform of 'Public-Private Partnerships' with multiple agencies bringing expertise and resources to bear on projects.

These project-specific strategies and tools have been seen to be highly effective under the right circumstances. To this set should be added a number of longer-term vectors that would require a wider base of support. These include, but are not necessarily limited to:

▸ *The establishment of new centres of urban design and research* that will attract the talent of motivated and qualified professionals who, through steady research and documentation of Lahore, can provide a growing knowledge base and publish

As-found street elevation

5 m

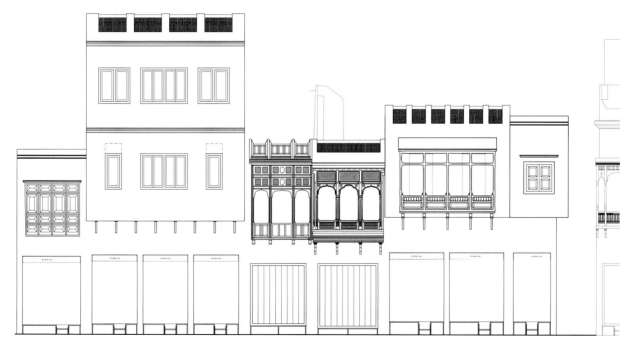

Proposed street elevation

393

much-needed information for the use of public authorities and practitioners. The number of publications on Lahore is already rising, reflecting its status as a World Heritage centre.

▸ *Training programmes for aspiring urban and architectural conservation professionals and archaeologists*: new programmes can be imagined that would connect formal studies with practical experience in the field. A consortium of universities could conceivably join with the WCLA in defining an incipient programme, which is in fact already envisioned in the 'Lahore Fort Precinct and Buffer Zone Master Plan' (2018).

▸ *Digital platforms for municipal networks and services*: in some cities, the municipal authorities have realized that public services can be made more accessible if these can be consulted and selected via smartphone applications. Such services include feedback, request for access to defined services and the more common needs, such as payments for utilities and so on.

The above have been shown via testing and real-world case studies to be valid approaches or methods and are replicable elsewhere in the Walled City or in the wider city that is present-day Lahore. In a city of the scale of Lahore, other proximate historic urban sites such as Shahdara, Ichhra, Mozang, Mughalpura, Baghbanpura, Begumpura, Nawankot and Mianmir could be drawn into the ambit of metropolitan planning with due deference to their historic footprint, should the protection of their tangible and intangible heritage, and issues of urban rehabilitation and access,

A detail of the walls of Jahangir's tomb complex, with marble inlay on sandstone.

be properly addressed. Small sub-area plans similar to the 2017 'Master Conservation and Redevelopment Plan' for the Walled City could be drawn up and 'nested' in the planning for Greater Lahore.

Replication at a wider scale across larger territories or regions remains a major challenge to be examined as urban centres and their peripheries become increasingly complex. Success in this effort will require more robust and complex planning systems which must also remain humane in dimension and goals. It is hoped that this publication not only illustrates the challenges but also inspires a wider participation in the process of urban revitalization that is now critical to increasingly urban societies.

The gateway to Jahangir's Mausoleum, detail of *muqarnas* in the entrance *iwan*.

1   See https://new.unhabitat.org/about-us/sustainable-development-goals, accessed on 3.9.2019.

2   Winy Maas, "Everything Is Urbanism", *Domus*, January 2019, editorial.

3   The urbanist, professor and writer Christopher Alexander approached the problem through the media of "pattern languages" and "timeless ways of building". More recently, university departments of planning have become incubators for research and innovation in addressing the demands of the 'new urban age', and a virtual sub-industry of interest groups, conferences and publications has emerged, feeding off and contributing further to this stream of research.

Acknowledgements

The Aga Khan Trust for Culture wishes to acknowledge the continuous support and collaboration extended by the Walled City of Lahore Authority (WCLA). Public sector support such as that extended by the Government of Punjab, its Planning and Development Department, the Department of Local Government and Community Development, the Directorate General of Archaeology, and other key departments, is essential to the urban regeneration of historic districts in any location. This initiative has illustrated how the public-private mechanism of collaboration can be a success.

PARTNERS AND DONORS
Over the period 2007 to the present, in addition to AKTC's own resources, the projects related to the initiative in Lahore benefited from important grant contributions from: the Government of Punjab, the World Bank, the Royal Norwegian Embassy, the United States Ambassadors Fund for Cultural Preservation, the Embassy of Germany, the J. M. Kaplan Fund, the Agence Française de Développement, Jubilee Insurance, and HBL. AKTC would like to thank its many partners and collaborators for their support of Pakistan's heritage and their financial assistance, which have been critical to an initiative of this scope.

GOVERNMENT OF PUNJAB
SUSTAINABLE DEVELOPMENT OF THE WALLED CITY OF LAHORE PROJECT (SDWCLP)
Director Generals: Humayun Farshori, Haseeb Athar, Orya Maqbool Jan Abassi, Saleem Chattha, Naheed Rizvi.
Directors: Nadir Aqeel Ansari, Amir Zamir, Abdul Ghafoor, Shahid Durrani, Talib Hussain.
Infrastructure Specialists: Khalid Javed, Hafiz Masood Ur Rasool.

WALLED CITY OF LAHORE AUTHORITY (WCLA)
Director Generals: Kamran Lashari, Jawad Rafiq Malik (former).
Directors: Shahid Nadeem, Najmussaqib Sheikh, Asif Zaheer, Shahid Durrani, Akbar Munir.

PLANNING AND DEVELOPMENT DEPARTMENT (P&D)
Board Chairpersons: Habib ur Rehman Gilani, Jahanzeb Khan, Javed Aslam, Suleman Ghani.

The Aga Khan Trust for Culture wishes to acknowledge the teams and individuals who have contributed to the planning and subsequent development of the AKTC initiative in the Walled City of Lahore since 2007 as well as the preparation of this publication.

AKTC MANAGEMENT GENEVA
Luis Monreal, General Manager; Shiraz Allibhai, Deputy Director; and Peter Trowbridge, Finance Director.

AKTC'S HISTORIC CITIES PROGRAMME, HCP
Cameron Rashti, Director HCP; Jurjen van der Tas, Director Partnerships and Development; Masood Ahmed Khan, Technical Director and Senior Architectural and Planning Consultant; Francesco Siravo, Senior Conservation Planning Consultant; and Christophe Bouleau, Senior Conservation Officer.

AGA KHAN CULTURAL SERVICE-PAKISTAN, AKCS-P
AKTC wishes to thank all members of the AKCS-P Board and the National Council President, Hafiz Sherali, who have supported and provided important guidance to the Lahore initiative. Present members of AKCS-P Board: Akbarali Pesnani (Chairperson), Mir Ghazanfar Ali Khan, Hafiz Sherali, Muhammad Yousuf Hussainabadi, Nazir Ahmad, Nishat Riaz, Yasmeen Merchant, and Ameen Lakhani.

AKCS-P MANAGEMENT
Salman Beg, Chief Executive Officer; Safiullah Baig, Senior Manager; Sher Ghazi, Technical Manager; Shukurullah Baig, Conservation Manager; Wajahat Ali, Conservation and Design Manager; Zilha Pari, HR Manager; Abdur Rehman Nasrali, Finance Manager – Lahore; and Karim Sakhi, Finance Manager – North.

Project Technical Teams and Main Consultants

INTERNATIONAL CONSULTANTS
Munir Albaz, Consulting Architect; Anura Krishantha Baragama Arachchi, Wall Paintings Conservation; Matt Benson, Statistical Analyses and Graphs; Ananda Colombage, Wall Paintings Conservation; Udaya Hewawasam, Wall Paintings Conservation; Robert Pilbeam, Consulting Architect; Francois du Plessis, MBB Consulting Engineers, Drainage and Irrigation; Deon Pretorius, Infrastructure Engineering, Aurecon Group; Didier Repellin, RL&A, Architectural Conservation; Werner Schmid, Surface Conservator; Anthony Wain, Planning Partners (Landscape Architecture); Thomas Warscheid, Microbiologist; Jagath Weerasinghe, Wall Paintings Conservation; Eberhard Wendler, Materials Scientist; and Dr Fritz Wenzel, BfB, Karlsruhe, Structural Engineer.

NATIONAL CONSULTANTS
Suhail Ahmad, Public Health; Ahmad Tariq Ashraf, Structural Engineering; Syed Murtaza Asghar Bukhari, Traffic Study; Anjum Dara, Archaeologist; Associated Consulting Engineers; Talib Hussain, Materials Specialist; Wajid Karim, Illustrator; Afzal Khan, Archaeologist; Fatimah Khan, Consultant Sociologist; Nadhra Shahbaz Naeem Khan, Historian; Rashid Makhdum, Consulting Architect; Maqsood Malik, Consultant Archaeology; Rizwan Mirza, Structural Consultant; Adnan Shuja, Mechanical Engineer; and Ahmed Ali Tariq, Electrical and Telecom.

AKCS-P CONTRACTORS
Gulzar Ahmed, Winner Marble; Sohail Ahmed, Laspa International; Suhail Ahmed, General Electric Services; Berkeley Associates, Geotechnical Services; Hameed Butt, Industrial Techno; Decon, Geotechnical Services; Allah Ditta, Mohammad Sadiq & Sons; Abdul Ghafoor, Wood Works; Muhammad Hanif, Historic Brick; Nazar Hussain, Nazar Glass & Aluminum; Zafar Hussain, Laspa International; Ali Khan, Ali Khan Wood Works; Hidayat Masih, Soakage Well Contractor; Sandal Engineering; and Mohammad Suhail Taqi, Electrical Works.

AKCS-P PROJECT STAFF
Nauman Abid, Khush Ahmad, Waqar Ahmad, Munir Ahmed, Muhammad Umair Ajmal, Ehsan Ali, Haider Ali, Jaffar Ali, Liaqat Ali, Maham Neha Ansari, Rabeeya Arif, Saboohi Arif, Mohammad Arslan, Meherunnisa Asad, Waqas Baig, Waseem Baig, Tahemina Baluch, Mehwish Bandealy, Ali Amin Chaudhry, Muhammad Ejaz Dinaly, Kashif Essa, Ashiq Faraz, Syed Ali Faraz, Usama Farooq, Asma Fayyaz, Mubashir Hassan, Salman Hunzai, Nazia Hussain, Naheed Iftikhar, Amna Jabeen, Muhammad Arbab Jahanzeb, Shahid Jan, Faiza Javed, Tanveer Johar, Ehsanul Karim, Hamid Karim, Adil Khan, Ameen Khan, Mohammad Khan, Suhail Alam Khan, Maryam Liaqat, Ali Madad, Khalid Mahmood, Mina Arham Makhdum, Arslan Malik, Hala Bashir Malik, Waqar Malik, Rabia Masood, Navera Mehboob, Shahid Mehmood, Ghulam Mohammad, Shoaib Mohammad, Zohra Muneer, Sumera Murtaza, Omar Mushtaq, Anita Nadeem, Waqas Nadeem, Rabia Naeem, Zeina Naseer, Sehrish Nizam, Mohammad Qasim, Maryam Rabi, Rozina Razzaq, Anees Ur Rehman, Tayabba Sabir, Noor Jehan Sadiq, Naeem Safi, Sumaira Saif, Mohammad Saleem, Farhan Sardar, Mohammad Sarfraz, Hira Seher, Basma Shafiq, Emaan Shaikh, Sehrish Shakeel, Kiran Shakoor, Rabia Shaukat, Hussein Ali Sheikh, Rashid Shoaib, Allah Rakha Sindhu, Abdullah Sultan, Durre Shahwar Syed, Maha Tariq, and Hassan Sarmad Toosy.

AKCS-P MASTER CRAFTSMEN
Abubakar, Muhammad Ajmal, Basharat Ali, Deedar Ali, Muhammad Ali, Muhammad Hashim Ali, Sharafat Ali, Taimur Ali, Muhammad Arif, Naheedullah Baig, Shaukat Habib, Taj Gul Hayat, Ashraf Hussain, Basharat Hussain, Muhammad Jameel, Mohammad Khalid, Baba Ramzan Ghulam Sarwar, Usman Shafiq, Waqar Shah, Ahmad Sher, and Alla Uddin.

AKCS-P SURVEYORS
Sarfraz Ahmed, Nek Ali, Shams ud Din, Javed Iqbal, Malik Kamran, Ali Kazim, Anwar Mehmood, and Ghulam Rasool.

AKCS-P INTERNS
Nouman Abid, Afnan Ahmad, Noor ul Ain, Aitizaz Ali, Mohammad Anwar, Ifrah Asif, Abdul Aziz, Syeda Sakina Batool, Mahvish Fazal, Waqar Hussain, Yumna Imtiaz, Maryam Shah Jehan, Shoaib Khan, Tehmash Khan, Navera Mehboob, Amber Shahid Mumtaz, Sobia Salman, and Saba Zahid.

AKCS-P ADMINISTRATIVE SUPPORT
Fakhir ud Din, Nizam ud Din, Afshan Imdad, Akbar Ali Khan, Shoaib Khan, Abdul Rehman Nasrali, Muhammad Nawaz, Karim Sakhi, and Hidayat Shah.

WCLA CONSULTANTS
Khurram Chughtai, Legal Consultant; Associated Consulting Engineers, Engineering and Project Management Consultants; Aslam Malik, Social Impact Assessment (SIA) and Resettlement Action Plan (RAP) Consultant; and Babar Khan Mumtaz, Consultant for Economic Enterprises Study.

WCLA CONTRACTORS
IKAN Engineering Services Pvt. Ltd., Main contractors, Package II; Qavi Engineers Pvt. Ltd., Infrastructure and Urban Upgrading.

WCLA STAFF
Mohammad Ahmed, Usman Akhter, Maria Ali, Yasir Arafat, Mohammad Arslan, Tayyaba Sadaf Ashraf, Zain Aslam, Noman Chaudhry, Kashif Dogar, Mohammad Farooq, Mehwish Ghaffar, Fasih Gilani, Ali Gill, Jamil Hussain Hayat, Asghar Hussain, Nadia Ikram, Yumna Imtiaz, Nadeem Jahangir, Waqas Kareem, Azeem

Dad Khan, Faisal Hayat Khan, Saleem Khan, Samina Fazil Khan, Sajid Mehmood, Nur Muhammad, Fatimah Munir, Abdur Rahman, Tayyab Riaz, Sadia Sajid, Asif Sajjad, Asim Sajjad, Waseem Sajjad, Syeda Faiza Shah, Ali Shahid, Sehar Amjad Sheikh, Ahmas bin Tariq, Sehrish Younas, Shehryar Zafar, Fatimah Zahra, and Nosheen Zaidi.

WCLA SURVEYORS
Asif Hameed, Ghulam Nabi.

Editing Credits

This publication benefited from a well-proven collaboration between Prestel's Editorial and Art Department and a number of individuals within the AKTC Editorial Group and its direction who interacted with project teams, photographers, the editor, and essay writers to achieve the fine balance required for a publication that combines cultural, socio-economic, urban and architectural concerns.

PUBLICATION EDITOR: The Trust would like to thank, in particular, Philip Jodidio, Editor; Markus Eisen, Prestel, Editor; Harriet Graham, Copy-Editor; and Torsten Köchlin, Graphic Designer.

AKTC EDITORIAL GROUP: Complementing and paralleling Philip Jodidio and the Prestel team, AKTC assembled an internal editorial group comprising Masood Khan and Maryam Rabi, complemented by Cameron Rashti, Francesco Siravo and Christophe Bouleau to oversee the balance and consistency of the various parts.

AKTC IMAGE COORDINATION/ DATA PROCESSING: Working closely and indefatigably with the Prestel team on AKTC's behalf, Maryam Rabi, Fatimah Khan, Muhammad Umair Ajmal, Doa Sarmad Khan, Ameera Zahid Malik, and Anusha Meenaz (Lahore), and Elisa Trapani, Consultant Conservation Architect (Rome), coordinated images, drawings and maps throughout the publication; Lobna Montasser, Archivist, provided photo-management services; Isabelle Griffiths organized central copies of all transferred final documents at AKTC.

Photo Credits

This publication could not succeed without a parallel set of high-resolution photography to illustrate the visual significance of these sites. The photographs displayed in this publication come from a wide array of sources, some more historic and some recent. In 2018, Adrien Buchet was commissioned to tour and photograph the major sites of our work and of related interest in Lahore, thus updating and making more comprehensive the photography of the project.

Aga Khan Cultural Service-Pakistan: 4, 11 (left), 12–13, 18, 19 (left, right), 23, 27 (left, middle, right), 51, 94, 95, 96 (below), 97 (left, middle, right), 101, 107 (above, below), 109, 112 (above, below), 114, 119, 123 (top, bottom), 124, 130, 131 (below), 133 (left, right above, right below), 135, 136, 137, 140 (above, below), 141 (left, right), 142 (above, below), 145 (left, right), 146, 147 (below), 152, 153, 154 (top, middle, bottom), 155, 156 (left, right), 158 (left, middle, right), 159, 160 (above, below), 172–173, 178 (left, right), 182 (right), 186–187, 190, 196, 197 (top, middle), 198–199, 200 (left, right), 201, 204, 206, 207 (left, above, below), 209, 216 (above, below), 217 (below), 225 (above), 236, 239, 253 (above), 272, 273, 285 (above), 291 (above, below), 292 (above, below), 295 (above, below), 297 (above), 299 (bottom left, bottom right), 300 (all four), 301 (below), 303 (top, middle, bottom right), 305, 306 (top), 308–309, 310, 311 (below), 312–313, 317 (above, below), 318 (left, right), 319 (right above, right below), 323 (left, right), 325 (above, below), 326, 330 (all four), 331 (all four), 338–339, 346 (above, below), 351 (left, right above, right below), 352, 363 (above), 365 (above), 367 (left, right), 376 (below), 377, 379 (left, right), 384, 385, 390 (above, below), 391 (above, below), 392 (left, right)

Aga Khan Trust for Culture: front cover flap, 254–255, 256 (above), 259, 263, 264 (above, below), 265, 266 (above, below), 267 (left, right), 268, 269 (above, below), 270, 271, 275, 276 (top, middle, bottom), 277, 278 (above, below), 279 (top, middle, bottom), 281, 282 (all four), 283 (left, above, below), 285 (below), 287, 289 (above, below), 290, 336, 345 (above, below), 350 (top, middle), 353 (above, below), 356 (above), 358 (below), 361 (top)

Aurecon: 125, 129 (above), 133 (right above), 134 (above, right)

British Library: Asia, Pacific & Africa Collections: 35, 38 (above, below), 46 (above, below)

Adrien Buchet: front cover, back cover (below), back cover flap, 2, 8, 9 (above, below), 10 (left, right), 11 (above, below), 14, 15, 16 (above, below, right), 17, 20 (above, below), 21, 22, 29 (above), 31, 34, 40, 41, 42, 43, 44–45, 47 (above, below), 48, 49, 50, 52, 54, 55, 56, 57 (above, below), 60, 61 (above, below), 62 (left, right), 63, 64, 65, 66 (left, right), 67, 68 (left above, left below, right), 69, 70 (above, right, far right), 72, 73 (above, below), 74 (left, right), 76, 77, 78 (above, right, far right), 79, 80, 81 (left, right above, right below), 84 (above, below), 85 (above, below), 86, 87, 88 (left, right), 89 (left, right), 90 (above, below), 92–93, 98, 102–103, 106, 116, 117, 138, 150–151, 176, 179, 182 (above, below), 183, 185, 188, 189 (bottom), 192, 193 (above, below), 202 (above), 203 (middle, right), 208 (above, below), 210–211, 212, 213, 215, 218 (above, below), 219 (above, below), 220–221, 222 (below left, below right), 223 (above), 224 (all four), 226 (below), 229, 230–231, 233 (above, below), 234, 235 (above, below), 240 (above, below), 243 (above, below), 244, 246, 247, 248, 249, 250, 260, 261, 262, 280, 284, 293, 294, 298, 299 (top left, top right), 301 (above), 302, 303 (bottom left), 306 (middle, bottom), 311 (above), 315, 319 (left), 321, 322 (all four), 324, 328, 329, 332, 333 (above, below), 335 (above, below), 346 (below), 348, 349 (right above, right below), 362, 363 (below), 364 (below), 366 (below), 372–373, 374, 375 (above, below), 378, 380, 381, 382, 394, 395

Directorate General of Archaeology, Government of Punjab: 32–33, 82–83

Masood Khan: 113, 228

Duncan Marshall, *Indian and Islamic Works of Art*, Simon Ray, London, 2018: 251

Sustainable Development of the Walled City of Lahore Project (SDW-CLP): back cover (above), 37

V&A Collections: 53

Walled City of Lahore Authority: 143, 147 (below), 344, 350 (bottom), 383 (all four)

Christopher Wilton-Steer: 25, 58 (left, right), 59, 105, 120–121, 122, 123 (middle), 203 (left), 365 (below), 368 (all four), 369, 376 (above)

Map and Drawing Credits

The architectural drawings and urban analytical maps throughout this publication derive from the years of professional work by in-house professionals and consultants working on the individual projects. In all known instances, these drawings represent original and field-based surveys and designs originating from AKTC's initiatives on the sites in question, and thus represent a major investment of time and care. They are an impressive set of assets that the Trust treasures and is pleased to add to the intellectual capital of the already impressive heritage of these sites. AKTC is grateful to Archnet for accepting to store and archive many of the drawings and images in this publication.

EXTERNAL CONTRIBUTORS TO ARCHITECTURAL DRAWINGS: Valerio Fonti and Pe Yang Teng, Architectural Renders; Simone Montozzi, Elisa Vendemini and Rossella Villani, Graphic Support.

Aga Khan Cultural Service-Pakistan: 24, 26 (above, below), 28 (above, below), 29 (below), 30, 36, 39, 75, 96 (above), 99 (above, below), 100 (above, below), 104 (above, below), 108 (above, below), 110 (top, middle, bottom), 111 (above, below), 112 (right), 115 (above, below), 118 (above, below), 139 (above, below), 144 (above, below), 147 (above), 148, 149 (all four), 157, 161, 162 (above, below), 163, 164 (above, below), 165 (above, below), 166 (all four), 167 (all four), 168 (left, right), 169, 170, 171, 172, 173, 174 (all seven), 177, 180, 181 (all four), 184 (above, below), 189 (top, middle), 191, 194, 195 (top, middle, bottom), 197 (bottom), 202 (below left, below right), 205 (above, below), 227, 296, 297 (below), 304, 314 (above, below), 316, 320, 327 (above, below), 386, 387, 388, 389, 393 (above, below)

Aga Khan Trust for Culture: 214, 217 (above), 218 (above), 222 (above), 223 (below), 225 (below), 226 (above), 232, 237, 238 (above, below), 241 (above, below), 242, 245, 252, 256 (below), 257, 258, 274, 286, 288 (above, below), 334, 337, 340 (above left, above right, below right), 341, 342 (above, below), 343, 347, 349 (above, below), 354 (above, below), 355 (above, below), 356 (below), 357, 358 (above left, above right), 359, 360 (above, below), 361 (middle, bottom), 364 (above), 366 (above), 370 (above, below), 371

Aurecon: 126 (above, below), 127, 128, 129 (below), 131 (above), 132

Directorate General of Archaeology, Government of Punjab: 253 (below)

Biographies

Editor

Philip Jodidio is the author of more than a hundred books on contemporary architecture and art, and has edited several books for the Aga Khan Trust for Culture Historic Cities Programme. He was Editor-in-Chief of the French art monthly *Connaissance des Arts* from 1980 to 2002.

Contributors

Luis Monreal is the General Manager of the Aga Khan Trust for Culture. He is a conservation specialist, art historian and archaeologist. He was previously Secretary General of the International Council of Museums at UNESCO (1974–85), Director of the Getty Conservation Institute (1985–90) and Director General of the "La Caixa" Foundation (1990–2001).

Cameron Rashti is the Director of the Historic Cities Programme, joining the Aga Khan Trust for Culture in 1994. A graduate of Dartmouth College, Pratt Institute and Columbia University, he is a registered architect in the US and the UK. Prior to joining the Trust, he held senior positions on major architectural/urban redevelopment projects with practices in New York (1979–89) and in London (1989–94), as Vice President of Perkins & Will International.

Masood Khan is a conservation architect and planner and has worked for the Aga Khan Trust for Culture in the Middle East, Central Asia, and South and South East Asia. A graduate of MIT and the National College of Arts, Lahore, he has led the AKTC collaboration in Lahore from its inception in 2007, and earlier worked on many other Trust projects. He has also taught at the Aga Khan Program for Islamic Architecture at Harvard and MIT.

Saifur Rahman Dar is a renowned archaeologist and museologist. He is the former Director General of Archaeology, Punjab (Pakistan), and a long-time Director of the Lahore Museum (1974–98). He is the author of thirty-two books and more than two hundred research papers on art, architecture, archaeology and museology, including the book: *Historical Gardens of Lahore* (1981).

Francesco Siravo is an architect specialized in historic preservation and town planning. He received

his degrees from the "La Sapienza" University of Rome, the College of Europe, Bruges, and Columbia University. Since 1991, he has worked for the Historic Cities Programme of AKTC with responsibilities for planning and building projects in various cities of the Muslim world.

Fatimah Khan is the Manager for Monitoring, Evaluation and Research at AKCS-P. She has an undergraduate degree in Economics (Lahore University of Management Sciences), a graduate degree in Political Sociology (London School of Economics), and a Certificate in Geographic Information Systems (Pennsylvania State University). Since 2007, she has worked on various projects in Pakistan, Kenya, Kyrgyzstan and Afghanistan.

Jurjen van der Tas is the Director of Partnerships and Development at the the Aga Khan Trust for Culture and oversees the Trust's engagement in socio-economic development initiatives. From 1991 to 2002, he worked for Oxfam Novib in the Netherlands, where he was responsible for Pakistan, Afghanistan, Bangladesh and the former Soviet Central Asian Republics. In the late 1980s, he was based in Pakistan, working for the Federal Bank of Cooperatives.

Deon Pretorius is a professional Engineer with Aurecon and manages the infrastructure master planning and design sections in the Middle East and Africa. In 2009, Aurecon was commissioned by AKTC to prepare a Conceptual Infrastructure Design for the Walled City of Lahore; these proposals were implemented over the subsequent decade. Deon is currently the Unit Leader for Africa Built Environment and is based in Cape Town, South Africa.

Maryam Rabi is a Consulting Architect at AKCS-P. She joined the organization in 2011 and has worked on the Shahi Guzargah, Shahi Hammam and Wazir Khan Chowk conservation projects in the Walled City of Lahore. In 2016, she received the Aga Khan Foundation International Scholarship for a graduate degree in Historic Preservation Planning at Cornell University. She is currently working on the conservation of the Wazir Khan Mosque.

Rashid Makhdum has been a Consulting Architect on urban and monument conservation at AKCS-P for the last twelve years. He has over thirty years' experience in the field of preserving and presenting cultural heritage in both Pakistan and the USA. Additionally, he has

co-authored publications on the conservation of the Walled City of Lahore and has been the recipient of both international as well as national awards for his work in Lahore.

Didier Repellin has worked as a Chief Architect in Historic Monuments since 1981, on the restoration and valorization of numerous historic buildings, such as the Palace of the Popes in Avignon, and the Villa Medici and the Colosseum in Rome. He has worked as an expert in heritage restoration in Asia, particularly on the Royal Palace in Phnom Penh, the Islamic museum in Penang and the Convent of the Holy Infant Jesus in Singapore.

Christophe Bouleau is the Senior Conservation Officer of the Aga Khan Trust for Culture Historic Cities Programme. He holds degrees from the Swiss Institute of Technology of Lausanne and the Centre des Hautes Etudes de Chaillot in Paris. He has over twenty years' experience in international projects related to monument conservation, archaeology and urban rehabilitation.

Anthony Wain is a Senior Director of Planning Partners, Cape Town, South Africa. A horticultural scientist and professional landscape architect, trained in the UK, he has thirty years' experience in twenty-one countries worldwide. He was the first Mellon Resident Practitioner in 2015 at Dumbarton Oaks, USA, and continues his studies in heritage landscapes at the University of Cape Town.

Francois du Plessis is a professional Civil Engineer and has forty years' experience in the field of agricultural and civil engineering. He is a graduate of the University of Stellenbosch, South Africa. His focus area is water-related projects, including irrigation and drainage. He has extensive project experience in many African countries, as well as countries in the Middle East, and Central and South Asia.

Nadhra Shahbaz Khan is an Associate Professor of Art History at Lahore University of Management Sciences (LUMS). A specialist in the history of art and architecture of Punjab from the sixteenth to the early twentieth century, her research covers the visual and material culture of this region during the Mughal, Sikh and colonial periods.

Werner Matthias Schmid graduated in painting conservation from the Istituto Centrale per il Restauro (Central Institute for Conservation),

Rome, and has an ICCROM certificate in stone conservation. In 1990 he joined ICCROM, where he managed projects in the conservation of mural paintings and related architectural surfaces. Since 2000 he has been working as a freelance conservator and consultant in Italy. Moreover, he cooperates frequently with ICCROM, UNESCO, the World Monuments Fund and other international agencies.

Zeina Naseer completed her Bachelor's in Chemistry from Columbia University. With an interest in history and culture, she chose conservation, where science, history and culture come together to preserve an identity. Zeina joined AKCS-P in 2017, where she established an on-site conservation lab. Currently she works as a conservation scientist, focusing on the conservation issues of the Picture Wall, as well as other components of the Lahore Fort project.

Shukurullah Baig is the Conservation Manager at AKCS-P. He has been with the organization since 1992 and was involved in a number of settlement rehabilitation and monument conservation projects in the Gilgit-Baltistan and Chitral region. In Lahore, he has worked on the Mohalla demonstration project, as well as the conservation of the Shahi Hammam, the Wazir Khan Chowk and the Imperial Kitchens. At present, he is in charge of the Wazir Khan Mosque conservation project.

Salman Beg is the CEO of AKCS-P since October 1998. He has a multifaceted background and a diverse education, which includes almost a quarter century in the army. He holds Master's degrees from Lahore University of Management Sciences (LUMS) and the United States Army Command and General Staff College, Fort Leavenworth.

Imprint

The Editor wishes to thank Luis Monreal, Cameron Rashti, and Masood Khan for their guidance and help putting this book together. Also thanks to Markus Eisen and the team at Prestel.

Front cover:
Evening commerce at the Delhi Gate entrance of the Walled City of Lahore.

Back cover:
Above, Lahore's Walled City from the south, with the Badshahi Masjid, the Minar-e-Pakistan and Lahore Fort in the background. Below, looking south out of the Diwaan-e-Khaas built by Emperor Shah Jahan.

Front cover flap:
The Wazir Khan Mosque's northern facade seen from the west. Shops that had been buried under the soil have been dug out and a special space created for them below the street level.

Back cover flap:
Cupolas and minarets with *kashikari* (glazed-tile work) – the Wazir Khan Mosque seen in the context of the city's roofline.

Page 2:
Alamgiri Gate, a principal element in the Hazuri Bagh Quadrangle, along with the Badshahi Mosque, Roshnai Gate and the *samadh* of Ranjit Singh.

Page 4:
A master craftsman working on the conservation of the *kashikari* (glazed-tile work) on the north facade of the Wazir Khan Mosque.

Prestel Verlag, Munich
A member of Verlagsgruppe Random House GmbH

Prestel Verlag
Neumarkter Strasse 28
81673 Munich
Germany
Tel. +49 (0)89 4136-0
Fax +49 (0)89 4136-2335

www.prestel.de

Prestel Publishing Ltd.
14–17 Wells Street
London W1T 3PD

Prestel Publishing
900 Broadway, Suite 603
New York, NY 10003

www.prestel.com

Library of Congress Control Number: 2019950750

British Library Cataloguing-in-Publication Data: a catalogue record for this book is available from the British Library; Deutsche Nationalbibliothek holds a record of this publication in the Deutsche Nationalbibliografie; detailed bibliographical data can be found under: http://www.dnb.de

Project management Prestel:
  Markus Eisen
Copy-editing:
  Harriet Graham, Turin
Design and layout:
  Torsten Köchlin, Leipzig
Production:
  Andrea Cobré
Photolithography:
  Schnieber Graphik, Munich
Printing and binding:
  Druckerei Uhl, Radolfzell
Typeface:
  Graphik, Ingeborg
Paper:
  150g/m² Profibulk

Verlagsgruppe Random House
FSC® N001967

Printed in Germany

ISBN 978-3-7913-5856-7
(trade edition)

ISBN 978-3-7913-6915-0
(Aga Khan Trust for Culture edition)